SELECTED VAUDEVILLE CRITICISM

edited by
Anthony Slide

The Scarecrow Press, Inc.
Metuchen, N.J., & London
1988

Also edited by Anthony Slide

Selected Film Criticism: 1896-1911
Selected Film Criticism: 1912-1920
Selected Film Criticism: 1921-1930
Selected Film Criticism: 1931-1940
Selected Film Criticism: 1941-1950
Selected Film Criticism: 1951-1960
Selected Film Criticism: Foreign Films 1930-1950

Selected Theatre Criticism: 1900-1919
Selected Theatre Criticism: 1920-1930
Selected Theatre Criticism: 1931-1950

Selected Radio and Television Criticism

Library of Congress Cataloging-in-Publication Data

Selected vaudeville criticism.

   Includes index.
   1. Vaudeville--United States--Reviews.
2. Entertainers--United States--Biography--Dictionaries.
I. Slide, Anthony.
PN1968.U5S35 1988   792.7'028'0922   87-28553
ISBN 0-8108-2052-8

In memory of the Duncan Sisters,
who represent vaudeville at both
its best and its worst

• CONTENTS •

Preface   ix

PART I: INDIVIDUALS

v

PART II: GENERAL COMMENTARY

● PREFACE ●

Selected Vaudeville Criticism collects together contemporary reviews, reprinted in their entirety, on some of the best known and most popular names in vaudeville history. Additionally, this volume includes a selection of general critical pieces on vaudeville, along with the autobiographical series of articles, "My Vaudeville Years," by Grace La Rue (1881-1956). The last is reprinted from various 1937 issues of Rob Wagner's Script and is included here for no other reason but that I felt it deserved reprinting and would be forgotten if I did not take the initiative.

Although vaudeville began in the last century, all of the items here date from the twentieth century and are primarily from the period when vaudeville was enjoying its "golden years" prior to the coming of sound to the motion picture in the late 1920s. Certainly the pieces included here are as eclectic as the best vaudeville bill, ranging from the intellectual to the popular. The majority of the reviews and articles are concerned with the vaudevillian's performance on stage, but I have included a few items discussing a specific film serving as a star vehicle for a former vaudevillian. Because of the overlap between vaudeville and other forms of entertainment, readers may find additional commentary on vaudevillians in the Selected Theatre Criticism and the Selected Radio and Television Criticism volumes (Scarecrow, 1985-1987). For general background information on vaudeville and its stars, readers are referred to this writer's The Vaudevillians (Arlington House, 1981).

Items included in this anthology were selected from the following periodicals: The American Legion Magazine, The American Magazine, The Billboard, Coronet, Cue, The Drama, Emmy, Esquire, The Film Spectator, The Green Book Album, The Green Book Magazine, Life, Los Angeles Times, The Moving Picture World, New Theatre, The New York Clipper, The New York Dramatic Mirror, (later Dramatic Mirror), New York Evening Sun, New York Star, New York World-Telegram and Sun, The New Yorker, Newsweek, Pageant, The Photo-Play Journal, Rob Wagner's Script, Scribner's Magazine, Shadowland, The Standard & Vanity Fair, Theatre Arts, and Variety, together with the book, Actorviews by Ashton Stevens.

For help in the preparation of this volume, I would like to thank the staffs of the Margaret Herrick Library of the Academy of

Anthony Slide

PART I: INDIVIDUALS

● FRED ALLEN

   Allen is a nut comedian who has been out for several seasons.
In the smaller houses he worked in the use of a phoney ventriloquist
bit with the aid of a stage hand, employed various gimcracks including wooden hands and mixed in juggling bits. All of the "junk" and
borrowed stuff has gone with the exception of a wabbly umbrella.

   With whitened face Allen is now more "legitimately" a comic of
the nut school, minus the trunkful of props. He could not resist the
use of a card placed before his entrance reading "Mr. Allen is deaf.
If you care to laugh or applaud, please do so loudly." With hand
placed in back of his ear he carried out the sign idea in part.

   Allen is not a monologist. His chatter is unrelated and aimed
for laughs, which he secured. Working up "illustrations" of a nut
number, "The Electric Chair," he worked in assorted nutty things
that sent him to the entrance in favor.

   Reappearing with a guitar, he said that he was a Hawaiian.
Once he was very dark, but someone left a pair of dice in the house
and he faded, faded, faded. Allen's number with the guitar, entirely
a comedy idea, was successful throughout and it brought him out for
more. He mentioned once that he might not be quality but he sure
gave quantity. His turn is overtime, but Allen's present act is big
time and it looks all his own.

                              --"Ibee" [Jack Pulaski] in Variety,
                                 June 10, 1921, page 17.

● FRED AND ADELE ASTAIRE

   The Astaire children are a nice looking pair of youngsters,

prettily dressed, and they work in an easy style, without the predominating "freshness" which usually stands out above everything
else with "prodigies." Dancing is the feature. It ranges from toe
to the more popular (in vaudeville) hard-shoe. The singing falls
almost entirely to the boy, who has a surprisingly powerful voice
for a lad of his years. The girl's voice is light. The boy sings
an Italian song as a solo, doing rather well with it, although at
times the value of the song-story is lost through an effort to squeeze
in a bright line the lyric writer had evidently overlooked until too
late. The toe-dance following the song could be replaced to advantage. It has a tendency to make the boy appear girlish, something
to be guarded against. His actions throughout are a trifle too polite, which is probably no fault of his own, as he appears to be a
manly little chap with the making of a good performer. The girl,
the larger of the two, does very well with the dancing. Her execution evidences careful training.

--"Dash" in Variety, October 17,
1908, page 13.

• AUNT JEMIMA

Aunt Jemima, whose burnt cork characterization employed for
atmosphere in the singing of southern songs, made her first Palace
appearance this week, although she has been in vaudeville and has
played around New York for several seasons. Her engagements were
with independent circuits, in production work and cabaret (formerly
in the cabaret field under another name).

That she was given the next to closing spot at the Palace
which held an especially weighty show indicated the booker's opinion
of her value and she went across for a real score. There is no
doubt about Jemima drawing a considerable number of friends and
none about her success, for she has something that none of the imitators could solve.

For accompaniment the Little Club orchestra is present with
Joe Raymond, the leader. The Little Club recently closed down,
which gave Jemima a chance to pick up a good band. The several
band numbers got over, but without Raymond having prepared any
particular stunts to detract from Jemima's work. The musicians were
dressed in white satin with bakers' caps that followed out Jemima's
former musical bunch and her own dressing, adapted from her mammy
picture formerly used in the advertising of a pancake flour.

Jemima's numbers though sticking to type are not of the restricted sort.

As for production there was none and the house setting might
just as well have been used. A back drop showed a river and levee

scene painted in plain white and black. Two wing strips meaning
little were also there. But Jemima has a place in big time vaudeville.
She proved it in the spot.

--"Ibee" [Jack Pulaski] in *Variety*,
October 20, 1922, page 18.

• BELLE BAKER

Singing "I'm a Baker," Belle Baker, one of the big favorites
of vaudeville aptly reintroduced herself to her audiences after an
absence of some time from the two-a-day. But she didn't knead to
do it, as the metaphor embodied in the song is a bit far-fetched.
Except that as a baker, she surely is some singer.

Miss Baker puts across a couple of new songs in the fore part
of her songologue, but it is when she repeats her past successes
in the concluding moments that she quadruples the audience's delight.
If she reckoned that in singing these old timers she was using a
graceful and gracious method of edging toward the wings for a getaway, she misjudged her audience. One old song from Belle and the
mischief was done. They wouldn't let her off at the Riverside at
her opening performance until she had given them "Nathan," "Put It
On, Take It Off, Wrap It Up, Take It Home," and others, after
springing such especially successful new ones as "Antonio, You Better Come Home," "Waiting Since Sweet Sixteen," and the Belle Baker
interpretation of "How I Wish I Could Sleep till My Daddy Comes
Home."

Really, the audience was so severe with Miss Baker that we
won't attempt to crush her with a weighty criticism. Every flaw in
her diction, every little catch in her voice, and everything-else
that character songs demand did not go unnoticed by her critical
clientele. They used their hands to let her know that they knew.

--*Dramatic Mirror*, November 16,
1918, page 727.

*   *   *

One of the big hits of the present Palace bill is scored by
Belle Baker, who is offering an almost wholly new repertoire of
songs, including special ones by Blanche Merrill. She starts with
a little melody about herself, "I'm a Baker," followed with "You've
Put It Off Since I Was Sweet 16," does a ballad, "Don't Cry, Frenchy,"
introduces a new Italian number, "I Gotta Da Proof," does "I Know
He's Only Teasing But I Love Him" and presents a combination of
her old melodies. Miss Baker received a thunderous welcome at the
Palace and the Monday matinee audience demanded her return. For
an encore she did "Put It On, Take It Off." It is hard to single

out any one of Miss Baker's new songs for special mention, unless
it's the wop number. This was a decided comedy smash.

> --Frederick James Smith in
> Dramatic Mirror, February 8,
> 1919, page 202.

● JOSEPHINE BAKER

A sinuous idol that enslaves and incites mankind. Thanks to
her carnal magnificence, her exhibition comes close to pathos. It
was she who led the spellbound drummer and the fascinated saxo-
phonist in the harsh rhythm of the blues. It was as though the
jazz, catching on the wing the vibrations of this mad body, were
interpreting, word by word, its fantastic monologue. The music is
born from the dance and what a dance! Certain of Miss Baker's
poses had the compelling potency of the finest examples of Negro
sculpture. It was no longer a grotesque dancing girl that stood
before the audience, but the Black Venus that haunted Baudelaire.

> --Andre Levinson quoted in Theatre
> Arts, Vol. 26, No. 8, August
> 1942, page 502.

● ERNEST R. BALL

Ernest Ball, formerly with Maude Lambert, is now doing a
single. He sings his own songs with the exception of one. As he
walked on he got quite a bit of applause and then announced his
new song "I'll Forget You," which got him off to a fine start. He
announced an Irish ballad "Laddie Buck of Mine" that almost stopped
the show in itself. He then sang "Saloon" using the words Gallagher
and Shean formerly used. This also pleased. At this he walked off,
coming back two more times. The first time he sang bits of his old
songs, the most popular being "Mother Machree," "Let the Rest of
the World Go By" and "Love Me and the World Is Mine." Although
most of these songs were Irish they got by here nicely. For his
last trip back to the piano he sang "another fellow's song" just to
show that he was not jealous. "Stand Up and Sing for Your Father
an Old Time Tune." This melody was placed with "Annie Rooney"
and done effectively. He will be a hit on any bill.

> --"Allen" in Dramatic Mirror,
> October 29, 1921, page 635.

● WILKIE BARD

After an unfortunate debut Monday afternoon of last week,
Wilkie Bard, England's premiere character singer and scena artist,

is now in his stride and working smoothly and most effectively and acceptably to New York audiences. He now offers but two numbers, "The Scrub Woman" and "The Night Watchman," at the conclusion of which, Monday night of the current week, he was called out and more demanded of him. He graciously complied with a little speech, explaining that an author-friend suggested to him before leaving London that he come fortified with some "rag" ditties and had written several for him. He offered two of them--parodies on "Sally in Our Alley" and "Alice, Where Art Thou," with the original melodies ragged. What immediately strikes those who have never seen Bard before is his wonderfully impressive personality, augmented by an especially clear enunciation. His first number, "The Scrub Woman," shows him as the cleaning woman in a theatre, doing a neat chorus song, a bit of monolog and a duolog with his wife, who enacts a theatre dresser. There is nothing very startling in this number, merely the characterization the artist brings to it that puts it over. Bard is a master at impersonating elderly women. It is to be hoped he will do his "Limericks" dame before leaving us. "The Night Watchman" is considered in London the most artistic thing he has ever done in a music hall. He portrays the role of an elderly watchman in charge of a street excavation, seated in his little wooden hut, with a charcoal fire burning just outside. First there passes an inebriate returning from a masked ball, which is relatively inconsequential. Then there comes along the leading lady (or is it the "principal boy?") of a pantomime show that is to open the following night. She has been rehearsing late and is on her way home, unable to secure a taxi. The old watchman engages her in conversation, explaining he is one of her admirers, had often seen her on the stage, and persuades her to sit with him in his hut. What passes between them makes for exquisite, most artistic, character comedy. Now that he is "onto" our ways, Bard can come here often and be sure of a hearty welcome. It is to be hoped he will.

--"Jolo" [Joshua Lowe] in Variety,
October 31, 1919, page 20.

• JAMES BARTON

The musical pieces of early summer are no more remarkable as to books or music, but one at least boasts an entertainer who could make even the telephone book interesting--if he were allowed to dance on it. I refer, of course, to James Barton, the greatest comic dancer in twenty-five years and two hemispheres, and a rollicking comedian even in blackface.

--Kenneth Macgowan in Shadowland,
Vol. 8, No. 6, August 1923,
page 49.

• NORA BAYES

After matrimony, Nora Bayes' principal occupation is sewing.
If one might borrow one of her own pet wheezes, she is a Singer
professionally, but a Domestic in her leisure hours.

The truth of the matter is that Nora Bayes isn't the least
little bit as you have imagined her. To be sure, she gets married
whenever opportunity and the law permit, but you can't fancy how
immensely happy she is between ceremonies. The popular estimate
of this pet of the varieties is that she is a roistering, rollicking,
devil-may-care sort of young person, to whom life is just a joyous
frolic of lights, laughter and tango parties. Shamefully I confess
that once upon a time I so regarded her. That was before she and
I in the course of a newspaper controversy signed an amnesty.

In fact, for a number of years Nora Bayes and the writer
hereof indulged in the pastime of making faces at each other. In a
misunderstanding that had arisen between her and one of her managers, which had resulted in an injunction restraining her from accepting other engagements, I editorially endorsed the manager's side
of the contention. Miss Bayes does not relish opposition. She is
particularly averse to it in print.

Also, it seemed to be the duty of an unbiased surveyor of
theatrical activities to poke fun at the style of billing adopted by
Miss Bayes, wherein she referred to herself as "Assisted and Admired by Jack Norworth," the latter being her husband of the moment.
Sarcastic telegrams and messages of rebuke delivered through a mu-
tual acquaintance assured me of Miss Bayes' honest conviction that
eventually I should be imprisoned for horse stealing or robbing an
orphan asylum.

Thus we sparred for several years. The first overture of
peace came at the time when Mr. Norworth ceased to "admire" and
"assist" Miss Bayes, professionally or otherwise, and gave way to
Harry Clarke, her current husband as this article goes to press.

Sarcastically, over the telephone one day, Miss Bayes asked why
I persistently persecuted her, and I refuted the charge of ungallant-
ry. The net result of the conversation was that Miss Bayes agreed
in the future to perform her contracts and to omit confessions of
love from her advertising matter, and I in turn promised, so far as
possible, to restrict my comments to her vocal and comic talents, for
which I had always possessed a profound reverence. The complete
truce was finally solemnized over a highball--the Peace Treaty of the
Haig and Haig, Miss Bayes called the incident--and thenceforth we
abstained from conflict.

Consequently it is only recently that I have been enabled to
study this preëminent singer of popular songs at close range. The

disclosures which a tranquil propinquity afforded were surprising.

I learned that, except when Miss Bayes was at the theatre, she spent most of her time at home. I learned also that she did not favor all-night sessions at the restaurants frequented by her colleagues, and that she would rather play with a book than a bottle of champagne. I learned, too, that her general outlook on her calling was serious.

Nora Bayes is able to "put over" a certain class of song a little better than any other woman on the American stage. If she has a rival, it is Blanche Ring. In her enunciation there is a precision, an attack and an emphasis that must make lyric-writers long to hug her. One of the saddest conditions of the stage to-day is that a very small proportion of singers give any heed to enunciation. Their ambition is to make their tones clear, no matter if the sense of the song becomes meaningless. Just in passing I should like to observe that this deficiency is the cause of as many failures of musical plays as are a faulty score or lame libretto.

Miss Bayes receives as much as $2,500 a week for singing twenty-five minutes twice a day. Few grand opera prima donnas are as fortunate. There are countless vocalists in vaudeville possessed of better voices than Miss Bayes', but there is none that makes it so easy for an audience to understand and feel the meaning of a song. And for this perfection in delivery Miss Bayes should receive a testimonial from the Song-writers' Union, if there be such an organization.

It was not always thus with Nora Bayes--that is, the salary. She was scarcely eighteen years of age, although already married, when she first felt a wild yearning to uplift the stage. As a child the neighbors had told her she was possessed of a wonderful contralto voice. In school and in choir she had established a parish reputation. She had noted Hopkins' Theatre in her walks through Chicago's State Street; and there she applied for a hearing.

At Hopkins' in those days, melodrama was the chief dramatic tid-bit. Shaft No. 6 happened to be the title of the particular thriller on the boards when Miss Bayes meekly rapped at the manager's door. She knew that the intermissions were enlivened by vaudeville offerings, and she hoped to find a niche in which to fit.

As a matter of fact, Miss Bayes was supposed to be at church when she was trying to get on the stage. Sunday was regular amateur day at Hopkins', and the novice was not especially encouraged, when she was conducted into the theatre for a trial, to observe a sign over the proscenium arch, reading "DON'T THROW ANYTHING." Charles Elliott, the manager, was impressed by Miss Bayes' voice, and told her she might report at the matinée performance for her début.

Foreseeing the need of a costume, Miss Bayes dashed home, and, unknown to the family, carried off her wedding dress. You will observe that she is forever mingling matrimony and art. Back at the theatre Joe O'Hara, a local favorite, took pity on her and showed her how to make up. Also he cautioned her not to leave the stage after her song, as she might not be requested by the audience to return. Miss Bayes, acting on this hint, courageously stood her ground until she had finished three ballads. One of them was a song, entitled "Always," which was a favorite at that time with the ribbon clerk and housemaid trade.

Kohl and Castle next engaged Miss Bayes at a salary of twenty-five dollars a week. At the old Chicago Opera House, under that contract, she was obliged to dress in an uninviting room with seven other girls. The next time that Miss Bayes appeared at the Chicago Opera House, she was in Little Miss Fix-It, and she occupied the star's room. The other room was no longer in use because of its unhealthful condition.

Little by little her salary grew, deriving sustenance along the way on the Orpheum Circuit at fifty dollars a week, at Percy G. Williams' theatres at one hundred dollars a week, and finally at the Palace Theatre, London, where her stipend was two hundred and fifty dollars. Broadway first knew her in The Rogers Brothers in Panama. A song in that piece called "Come to My Watermelon Party," was considered of too small merit for one of the principals to sing, and Miss Bayes accepted the place in the chorus at forty dollars a week in return for the chance to "put one over." She made the song the hit of the production, and, although her name was not on the program, she became known to managers and was soon on her way to fame and fortune.

When Miss Bayes returned from London, commanding a salary of three hundred and fifty dollars a week, it looked as if she had reached the limit of the pecuniary possibilities of her talents. Those who followed vaudeville closely were aware that she possessed extraordinary ability of a certain kind, but few guessed that it could be utilized outside of variety theatres. In those days Broadway managers were chary of invading vaudeville ranks to fill the complements of their more aristocratic and dignified organizations.

Several volunteer scouts made bold to recommend Miss Bayes to producing managers, but the latter ridiculed the suggestion of her value until F. Ziegfeld, Jr., always something of a pioneer, placed her prominently in Follies of 1907. He paid her four hundred dollars for her services, and she was largely responsible for the great success of that révue. About this time she first met Jack Norworth, and together they worked out the words and music of "When Mother Was a Girl" and "Harvest Moon," two songs that would go a long way toward bringing success to any musical entertainment.

Curiously enough, her legal contest with Mr. Ziegfeld brought
her salary to its topmost point. Miss Bayes and Norworth, by that
time her husband, had been engaged jointly for Follies of 1909 at
one thousand dollars a week. Probably Miss Bayes was taken ill.
Certainly she said she was, and both she and Norworth abruptly quit
their engagement. Vaudeville managers sought her services, and Lew
Fields tempted her into The Jolly Bachelors, but Ziegfeld and his
attorneys were hot on her trail. One injunction after another piled
up, each with its attendant newspaper notoriety, and finally Miss
Bayes abandoned the litigation in despair. For a period she was
idle, restrained by court mandate, and then at the conclusion of the
term of Ziegfeld's contract, she joyously learned that through publicity her value had been enhanced. She returned to vaudeville at
$2,500 a week.

That theatrical folk do not harbor business grievances long is
attested by the fact that Miss Bayes and Mr. Ziegfeld are now close
friends, and that the latter is at this writing seeking a play in
which to present her as star.

Miss Bayes' voice is not mediocre, and it is not great. Her
lower register is rich and her tones are powerful. But she sings
a lyric with as much artistry as a great actor might put into Shakespeare's most stirring lines. It is, of course, wholly as a singer
that her professional worth must be estimated. Her histrionic ability
is still to be demonstrated. In the title rôle of Little Miss Fix-It,
although she was equal to its demands, she found no opportunity
for serious or important work.

As in the case of most all the world's popular singers, a
happy choice of songs has been a tremendous factor in her success.
To desire good songs is one thing; to find them is another. And
therein Nora Bayes holds an advantage over many of her competitors,
because usually she is herself able to write the sort best suited to
her.

Lyrics and tunes are a kind of religion to most vaudeville
singers. They spend their lives in seeking numbers with a lilt and
a swing and a "punch" that will set an audience's feet a-tapping.
Such luminaries as Bert Williams, Harry Lauder, George M. Cohan,
the late Henry Fragson, Eva Tanguay and Irene Franklin either
write or inspire their own repertory. Miss Bayes also has the faculty
of evolving the sort of rhythm and lyrics she requires.

Her constant companion is the family piano player, who ac-
companies her on the stage and occupies a room in her house, in
order to respond to a call for help at any hour of the day or night.
Once Miss Bayes gets an idea for a number, she cannot rest until
it has taken shape. Inspiration may come to her after she has retired, in which case the household is aroused, and the entire staff,
equipped with pencil and paper, labors over the piano.

Recently when I chanced to drop in at her home I found her,
Mr. Clarke and the pianist deep in the throes of song-building.

Miss Bayes paused long enough to hum the melody.

"Like it?" she inquired.

"Rather," I replied. "It has a wonderful charm."

"It ought to have," retored Miss Bayes.   "It's a strain I've
stolen from Lohengrin."

And so she had, and so do countless other song-writers.
The formula seems to be first to get your tune, then disguise it by
change of tempo, add your lyric, and serve at the prevailing rates.

There are several songs which always will recall Nora Bayes,
because she was the first to make them familiar. Among them are
"Has Anybody Here Seen Kelly?" "Come Along, Mandy," "Straw-
berries," "The Lovin' Rag," "Turn Off Your Light, Mr. Moon Man,"
and "The Pinkerton Moon."

With Mr. Clarke, she is now presenting an elaborate number,
in which both dance and sing simultaneously for nearly ten minutes,
entitled "The Modern Craze." It tells in burlesque the story of a
jealous lover who discovers that his sweetheart actually has been
guilty of dancing the waltz. It forms the basis of Msis Bayes' present vaudeville act, and is both pretentious and comic. The idea
belongs to Ray Peck, and Miss Bayes worked out the details.

To meet Miss Bayes casually, one would get the impression that
life contained little that was serious to her. She is ready in repartee,
keen in satire and possessed of a gorgeous sense of humor.

A specimen of her retorts courteous was revealed for a few
evenings ago at one of the regular dancing parties in which social
Broadway is now indulging. There was present a young theatrical
man who from humble origin has attained prosperity and entry into
a favored coterie through his inherent brashness, and business
associations. His deportment is not quite up to Newport standard--
or even Shanby's, for that matter--and at one of the dances the
aroma of table d'hôte still clung to him.

On the occasion in question the young man burst uninvited
upon one of the little groups which contained Miss Bayes, and interrupted the conversation with an entirely irrelevant and tactless remark. Miss Bayes greeted the assertion with a smile of incredulity.

"You don't believe me, do you, Miss Bayes?" asked the young
man.

"No," she replied, "I always take everything you say with a grain of garlic."

Once on the stage Miss Bayes was appearing in a breakfast scene where eggs were being served, and a child sitting in a box made manifest his interest in the food. Stepping down to the footlights, she tendered the youngster an egg, but his mother drew back her child with a sign of annoyance.

"You should let the young man take it," said Miss Bayes quietly. "It is unique for eggs to be passed from this side of the footlights."

In her home, however, while Miss Bayes entertains resplendently,--for instance, promoting breakfast parties that begin at nine o'clock and last until evening,--she is in every sense the domesticated, industrious and dirt-chasing housewife. Her home is one of the handsome brick houses on West End Avenue, in the thick of New York's best residential section. It is a souvenir of the Bayes-Norworth nuptials, but Mr. Clarke, the present incumbent, seems to adapt himself snugly to the environment.

It is well and not garishly furnished, two grand pianos being the most conspicuous sign of extravagance. It is a homey sort of place, and in none of its decorations indicative of its mistress' profession. The absence of theatrical mementoes, such as photographs and framed programs, is a rather refreshing omission.

Miss Bayes spends most of her leisure in her own spacious bedroom on the second floor. She refers to herself as an "old maid," and in the ingenious provision for personal comfort and her devices for neatness, the appellation is apt. Each article of her wearing apparel, no matter how trivial, is neatly folded and wrapped in a covering before it is laid away.

At the head of Miss Bayes' bed is a button which, when pushed in the morning, unlocks the door of her room and lowers the window. The unlocking of the door is also the signal for the maid's entrance with coffee. This is served regularly at ten o'clock. Two hours later, Miss Bayes arises for what she terms breakfast.

Also hanging at the head of the bed is a pair of white woollen socks. They are Miss Bayes' remedy for insomnia. She is afflicted with cold feet--not the managerial brand, that most dreaded by player-folk of all blighting maladies--but the genuine physical variety. According to Miss Bayes' notion, cold feet make her sleepless. By drawing on the socks, she warms her feet, and slumber follows. By the side of the socks hangs a strip of black silk. Miss Bayes calls it her "blinders." In the morning when the daylight annoys her, she binds it over her eyes and resumes her beauty sleep.

One of the comedienne's weaknesses is dolls. Dolls of all
sizes and all styles repose on the pillows of her bed and divan.
One magnificent doll of wax, imported from Paris, cost fifty dollars.
Another old-fashioned China doll, dressed after the crinoline style
of fifty years ago, is equally treasured by its owner. Big dolls
and little dolls, flaxen-haired dolls and brunette dolls, are forever
tumbling over in one's lap when one sinks down in one of Miss
Bayes' sofas.

As mentioned at the outset, her leisure is devoted largely to
fancy work and sewing. Her hobby is what women call the cross-
stitch. Dozens of animals and figures, and even landscapes, worked
out in colors in this stitch, adorn the walls. Many of them are
framed in groups. Blushingly Mr. Clarke confessed to me that he
had learned the cross-stitch. He was induced to exhibit specimens
of his handiwork, done in a spirit of fun and presented to his wife.

Mr. Clarke's principal household duty seems to be to pare
apples for the apple of his eye. Apples are the favorite fruit of
the Bayes-Clarke ménage. Dutifully and solemnly Mr. Clarke
nightly perches himself on the edge of Miss Bayes' bed, pares
large red apples and passes them to his wife, who does the only
reasonable thing one may do with juicy apples. It is not uncommon
for the comedienne to devour six or eight of them before retiring.
She claims a record of twenty, but that is probably the press-
agent's miscalculation.

To all appearances and by their own testimony Miss Bayes
and Mr. Clarke are very happy. Mr. Clarke is a small man physically, a legitimate actor of good theatrical stock--the son of Creston
Clarke and Adelaide Prince--but he has cultivated a mustache and a
two-a-day atmosphere, and appears to get nicely into his new environment.

One of Miss Bayes' favorite topics is "Harry's gameness."
She refers proudly to the successful manner in which he has taken
his place by her side as a vaudeville partner, and she resents bit-
terly any suggestion that her husband is basking in the light of
her own greatness. Very, very confidentially she will tell you of
the sacrifices the young man has made in order to assist her. She
assured me, for instance, that when Mr. Clarke was convinced that
his voice was not up to her standard, he deliberately caused certain bones in his nose to be broken and removed, in order to improve his vocal plumbing.

On the subject of the possibility of happy marriage among
players Miss Bayes has definite ideas. She believes that separation
is fatal to connubial bliss, and, hence, holds fast to the rule that
a manager engaging her must also make Mr. Clarke a member of the
organization. It happens that the young man is a sufficiently good
actor to be welcome on his own merits.

At close range you will observe that Miss Bayes' hair is streaked heavily with gray. This touch of frost is attractive, and does not give a semblance of advanced age. At first she was sensitive about the gray hairs, and concealed them by wearing aigrettes. Now she pushes them to the fore and refers to them laughingly.

With three marriages to her credit, it is fair to concede to the comedienne expert knowledge of matrimony. Her views on it, therefore, may prove enlightening.

"Matrimony," she declares, "is the only state to be in. I believe that a woman should have as many love affairs as she likes, but only one at a time. Also I am sure that a woman may be really in love many times, but I do not understand how she can be on with the new before she is off with the old.

"A man or a woman may go direct from one love affair to another, and be quite happy. People always have said that it was impossible for a married couple on the stage to be happy. Once I proved the fallacy of this for five years, and now I am proving it again. Happiness is right up to the individual every time."

Perhaps I should let you into a little secret. Miss Bayes is shortly to adopt a baby and rear it as her own. By the time these words reach type she will in all probability have found and recruited the infant she is seeking.

Her love of children is pronounced, and she borrows her friends' babies for a day whenever she has the chance. In selecting a child for adoption she will not inquire into its parentage further than to ascertain the healthiness of the father and mother. She will not even ask their names, and will cherish the youngster as her own.

Above all else, Nora Bayes is democratic. Her reputation for outbursts of temperament is not altogether deserved. She and her managers have not always agreed on business matters, but it is not incongruous to conceive that the managers may occasionally have been in error.

Whatever her idiosyncrasies, they do not take the form of artifice and airs, as they do in many stage ladies of prominence. One may approach Nora Bayes comfortably. Also in any conversation with her lasting longer than a minute one may be confident of hearing a joke or a bright speech worth listening to.

Charles Dillingham, one of Broadway's acknowledged wags, is always eager for a bout of repartee with her, and whenever she chances to be in the jurisdiction he invites her to call at his office for an afternoon of gossip and persiflage. One of her closest friends is Ethel Barrymore, the possessor of a keen sense of humor, who finds in Miss Bayes a kindred spirit.

To this day Oscar Hammerstein, another of Broadway's wits, tells gleefully of his first meeting with Miss Bayes. The Victoria Theatre was then nearing completion, and Mr. Hammerstein had already moved into his tiny room in the loft. The decorators had not begun their work, and the walls were bare. Mr. Hammerstein's room was sparsely furnished, and utensils as necessary to his comfort as a cuspidor were lacking.

As he chatted with Miss Bayes on the occasion in question, he smoked vigorously a big black cigar, and at intervals wheeled in his chair and spat.

"Ah," remarked the comedienne, "I see that you do your own interior decorating."

At one of the Sixty Club's dances this winter, Miss Bayes appeared at Sherry's in a gown more décolleté than any she had worn on previous occasions. In fact, its daring depth made her nervous, and she confided to a group of friends that she was not sure it was intended for public exhibition.

"Why, darn it," she remarked, "when I tried it on at the modiste's shop the first time, I didn't know whether I was being dressed for the opera or an operation."

--Rennold Wolf in The Green Book Magazine, Vol. 11, No. 4, April 1914, pages 571-580.

*   *   *

Nora Bayes hasn't interested us so much in several years as she did upon her return to the Palace. She was distinctly better than in the past few seasons.

She started slowly, but finally achieved an emphatic hit. Opening with an old Irish dialect number, "I Work Eight Hours, I Sleep Eight Hours, That Leaves Eight Hours for Lovin'," Miss Bayes followed with a queer ballad which runs--

"When John McCormack sings a song, The angels seem to float along."

Then came a war lyric deploring the troubles of poor father while the family knits mufflers and mittens for the soldiers at the front. Indeed, papa, according to the song, "props his pants up with a pin."

Miss Bayes once more did "Since Mother Was a Girl," which reveals the difference between the minuet and present thé dansant days. Here the star struck her most artistic note.

She came back, and, as an encore, did a brand new Hawaiian melody with a catchy swing, of a brigantine bos'un named Billy, who encountered a Honolulu belle, with a new way of saying "I love you"--and other attractions.

Finally Miss Bayes brought Jean Schwartz upon the stage to act as pianist and presented his comic war song, "You'll Find Father around the Bulletin Board." Miss Bayes got some laughs out of the lyric, but even she couldn't make it sound like a good song.

> --Frederick James Smith in The
> New York Dramatic Mirror, April
> 7, 1915, page 16.

*   *   *

"Mr. Bayes! Mr. Bayes!"

It was the voice of a page in the Congress Hotel, where Miss Nora Bayes was lunching Mr. Irving Fisher, her handsome young singing mate in The Cohan Review, and the writer--meaning me.

"Mr. Bayes! Mr. Bayes!"

"Perhaps he means you," said Nora, who was meaning young Fisher.

He accepted the service. "I'll attend to it," he said--whatever it was--"and be back in a little while"; and he left us with one of those highly dental smiles through which he sometimes sings.

Nora's eyes followed him to the door. "Irving is a dear, sweet boy," she said. "And now--what shall we talk of?"

"Shall we talk of love?" I suggested.

"Nothing could be happier," said Nora; and did.

"There is no success in work or play without it," said Nora--meaning love.

"How old is the nice boy?" said I, meaning Fisher.

"Who? Irving? Oh--thirty-four. But he doesn't look within ten years of it, does he? His shyness makes him appear younger."

"Lucky youth!"

"He's a fine, clean nature all the way through. And you have no idea how bright. He has an elfin, Barrie-like spirit."

"I'm glad you're harmonious."

"I should say we are," said she. "Irving Fisher does some things that Jack Norworth couldn't do."

"Youth!" I apostrophized.

"When we are doing a song together, Irving resists answering my witticisms. He never spoils them by trying to get back at me."

"But when you are alone with him--?"

"Oh, then he's as funny as can be. He has a fairylike sense of humor."

"It's quite plain that you love him dearly."

"I should say I do! You know, sometimes I think that of all my mental lovers I love Irving best."

"Your what?"

"Mental lovers is what I said and meant."

"I'm afraid I don't follow."

"Why, bless your poor crude soul, I'm beginning to think you don't myself."

"You mean you aren't married to him, or going to be?"

"Now what did that dear, sweet boy ever do to me that I should make a husband of him!"

"But from what you said I thought--"

"Of course you did. You were listening with a low, earthly ear while I was talking on a higher plane."

"I thought you were talking of love."

"I was, you poor fish," she elegantly answered, "but not your kind of love. I meant universal love, mental love. That's the only kind I indulge in--now. I want no lovers but mental lovers."

"Your plurals are baffling--how many of these mental lovers have you?"

"Thirty-six in the trenches and two at home," said Nora Bayes without batting a lash.

And carefully, painfully she bored it into my heavy head that love to Nora Bayes of the nowadays is a flame of the spirit and a rapture of the soul.

"If I had found my religion sooner," she went on, "Jack and I could have been comfortably parted long before we were. Oh, not that we ever quarreled! We never did that. Every morning we woke up laughing.

"But now all my husbands and I are friendly. Two of them, my first and third, wrote to me last week and I got their letters in the same post. Jack, too, has nothing but the best wishes for me."

"I heard a story the other day--"

"I don't know what it is, but it isn't true," she laughed. "All the off-color stories are attributed to me. If you want to get an audience in the Lambs' Club all you have to do is say, 'Here is one that Nora Bayes told.'

"Why, one day an actor told an awful story in the Lambs'. Said it was one of mine. And who does he pick on to tell it to but my second husband, Harry Clarke."

"Did Harry kill the actor?"

"No; none of my husbands are violent men. But Harry convinced the actor that I couldn't have told him the story at the time specified--because I wasn't in town when the specified thing happened.

"Not that it worries me a little bit," she ran on. "My worrying days are over. Now not even an opening night rattles me. That's where my philosophy and religion come in. I ask myself: 'Is there any sane reason why God shouldn't love you on Monday night in Chicago when He permitted you to be a riot on Thursday night in Pittsburgh?' Not on your life!

"That's where the human family is prone to err--in trying to make God work according to a human time-table. I remember Florence Nash coming to me in fear and trembling at the Palace. They'd changed her time from four to three, and she was afraid the second week's opening audience would crucify her.

"'See here,' I says to Florence, 'you've got a hell of a nerve fixing it all up with yourself that God will make you good at four o'clock and rotten at three. Why, you're all trembling and sighing like a north wind--how do you expect the public to love you when you go out to them like that? That's what's the matter, Florence-- you aren't letting the public love you enough.'

"And while I talked to her the color came back to her face
and her eyes brightened--she had something to give. She wouldn't
accept my offer to trade places with her in the bill, but went on at
three and duplicated her four o'clock hit of the week before--and why
not?

"God," she summed, "has no union hours."

And then she was asking me what was humor--as though I
could answer that! And wasn't it something childlike?--which nobody
can deny? And don't you feel in your heart before you do in your
head?--which, of course, you do. And she named names to attest
the juvenescence of her favorite humorists of the stage.

"Laurette Taylor," she said, "is a gamine. Fred Stone is an
urchin. Warfield is a St. Bernard--in his best moments a romping
puppy of love and laughter. And who could be more childlike than
Eddie Foy? No! I did not say childrenlike. But I will--and laugh
at it. I always laugh at my own nuttyisms--it helps 'em along.

"Yet"--and she paused as though to say, "This is going to be
profound and way beyond your depth"--"yet Jake Shubert, who is
our greatest censor of the drama, once said to me:

"'Nora Bayes, who the devil ever told you that you are funny?'"

"And Mr. Shubert still lives?"

"Yes; and so does Sam Bernard. Sam, who is my friend, who
would do anything for me--Sam says to me with honesty in every
breath:

"'Nora, you are our greatest singer of songs, but why do you
think you must be funny?'

"'Sam,' I answered, 'you don't mean to say that I have so
badly hypnotized myself that I think the audience is laughing with
me when it's only laughing at me?'

"'Sure!' says Sam.

"Now, look here, Ashton Stevens," said Nora Bayes, "I want
to ask you--"

"No," I said, "let me ask you: Do you think Nora Bayes is
funny?"

"Yes," said Nora Bayes, "I think Nora Bayes is funny. I
think I am Irishly funny. I sit and laugh and laugh at some of the
things I say. And I wouldn't laugh if they weren't funny, would I?
Of course I wouldn't you poor fish!"

"Give me a specimen of your own kind of fun."

"All right.   I'll tell you something I wrote to one of my lovers.
I wrote to him:

"'I am so lonesome for you that I don't know what to do.
And I'm so glad that you are not here to see how lonesome I am--
because it would break your heart.'

"How do you like it?"

"Fine.   Sounds like poetry.   Is it?"

"No, you poor goat; it's an Irish bull, that's what it is.   I
think it's almost as funny as Shakespeare's joke--where Desdemona
says, 'Where's my handkerchief?'   And Othello says, 'Use your
sleeve and let the show go on.'   I think it is a very good Irish joke,
and that I am a very good Irish jokess."

"When do you go to France?"

"I'm not going.   President Wilson told me he thought I could
do better work for the soldiers over here, if I would.   So I'm giving
up this job with the Revue pretty soon and traveling around the
thirty-six Liberty theaters for about twelve weeks.

"And I'm not," she went on, "doing my bit--just because I'm
playing all these theaters and taking no pay for it and paying my
own expenses.

"I'm doing just a bit of my bit, that's all." she said with soft
star-spangledness.   "I want all the wives and sisters and sweethearts
to know that I feel that these audiences, before whom I shall have
the privilege of appearing, are getting ready to fight for us in
Europe.   They make it possible for America to have safe homes to
live in--and for me to have theaters open in which I can appear and
earn my living.   I'm not making any greater sacrifice than Irving
Fisher is."

"He tours the Liberty Theaters with you?"

"Yes, and so does another of my inseparable mental lovers--
Harry Akst, my pianist."

"Aren't you afraid?"

"Of marriage?"

"It's been known to happen!"

"Yes, especially to me. But I'm off the marriage stuff for

life, my boy. I can love a man now without giving up my name and
address. I can, so to speak, have a new husband for breakfast,
every morning--and without the horrible formality of living with them.
S-s-sh! Here comes Irving, and there are things he's too young to
hear."

> --Ashton Stevens in <u>Actorviews</u>,
> Chicago: Covici-McGee, 1923,
> pages 255-261.

● JACK BENNY

Mr. Benny is possessed of that most important attribute for
comedy--ease. He has an agreeable, but not <u>too</u> agreeable, manner.
His countenance expresses emotions in some mysterious manner without changing. He ambles on with a very good line of stuff, but
whether you like it or not seems a matter of indifference to him.
It is not that he is over-confident. Several of his remarks lie dis-
tressingly close to the footlights after delivery. Yet he takes it as
just a part of the day's work.

> --Robert Benchley in <u>Life</u>, June
> 23, 1926, page 23.

*   *   *

Employing his violin playing in the frugal manner characteristic
of his appearances in the local houses during the last decade. At
this show the wise-cracking fiddler revived the master-of-ceremonies
idea and did his own two-act in one of the feature spots. As a
master of ceremonies Benny is not so forte yet from the standpoint
of laugh scores. The same might be said of his act. He is the sort
of artiste who gives in entertainment more than expected, but he in-
jects his pleasure doses thru the back door as it were. It is hard
to conceive of one laughing heartily at any of Benny's wheezes or
verbal intimacies, yet it is just as difficult to discover one who would
confess that he didn't enjoy Benny's act. Benny works with a nice-
looking girl, who plays the role of a self-conscious "Dumb Dora."
He calls her out from the wings, presenting her quite frankly as a
dodo he picked up in Trenton. As the chatter proceeds, the girl
is really the comedian, since her lines draw the laughs, but Benny's
wise-guy feeding constitutes the strong point in the duel between
wit and the apparent lack of it. When the unbilled girl is whisked
off unceremoniously, Benny swings into the clowned violin playing
and, when reviewed, bowed out to a fair hand. The act--possibly
due to the insufficiency of material--would do better if Benny steered
clear of the m.-of-c. business.

> --Elias E. Sugerman in <u>The Bill-
> board</u>, November 5, 1927, page
> 18.

● EDGAR BERGEN

Edgar Bergen, ventriloquist, is the latest of the cult to figure
a production built up for his voice throwing demonstration. In fact
Bergen may be credited with having outdistanced many in weaving
a comedy of logical plot and plenty of entertainment in this two scene
episode which he has labelled "The Operation." Christine Caldwell,
as the charming nurse, comprises the support.

The mixed team are strolling through a parkway in opposite
directions at the opening. Their attention is arrested by moaning
sounds from a bench. Investigation reveals a boy dummy. He is
ill and says he's a newsboy and an orphan. The couple take him to
the man's office, who happens to be a physician.

The change shows the operating room and a three cornered
comedy conversation anent the impending operation is carried on with
the dummy allowed the usual laugh-getting wisecracks. The comedy
is brisk throughout with an essence of romance tossed in at the finish
with the couple becoming engaged and retaining the dummy for an
office boy.

Neatly set and well manipulated it clicked heavy here in the
trey. Set for either vaudeville or certain picture houses.

--"Edba" [Ed Barry] in Variety,
June 30, 1926, page 19.

● MILTON BERLE

The most improved comic in America today is a young man
named Milton Berle. He has developed into a dynamic personality
in cafes, in theatres and on the air. If he continues at his present
pace he will be America's ace comedian.

--Mark Hellinger quoted in a full-
page advertisement on the back
cover of Daily Variety, July 23,
1936.

*   *   *

One night this week in New York, 1,000 people were to sit
down to a black-tie dinner at the Waldorf-Astoria Hotel, having paid
$50 a plate for the privilege. For their money they could see a tall,
raucous comedian named Milton Berle receive Interfaith in Action's
fourth annual award for furthering the cause of racial understanding.
Specifically, the comedian was awarded this recognition for more than
150 benefit performances he has played in the past year, notably including the half-million dollars he raised during his celebrated 16-hour
marathon for the Damon Runyon Cancer Fund.

But the $50 guests, whose money went toward building an
Interfaith Center in New York, were on hand no less to see Berle
honored than to watch him perform. For a view of Milton Berle performing (and he rarely misses a chance to do his stuff) is a view of
a radio-stage-screen comic who has become not only the country's
top-salaried night-club entertainer, but the first and biggest star
in the newest and most difficult of all entertainment mediums-television.

In his doggedly chosen profession, one significant measure of
success is the relative bitterness of what your competitors say about
you. The best-known professional appraisal of Berle's present work
is that nobody likes it except his mother and the public. There is
therefore little doubt that he is magnificently in.

"Body and Face": It was not always so. Until less than a
year ago, the taste of rue was monotonously familiar to Berle's tongue.
All but the first five of his 40 years were spent in show business.
Nevertheless, he was a flop in radio and a poor bet in the movies.
He became a real vaudeville success--just as vaudeville died. His
night-club dates, for which he lately turned down offers of $20,000
a week, offered him only a limited audience.

Berle felt that he failed in pictures and was never a resounding Broadway hit because directors wouldn't let "Berle be Berle."
His trouble on radio, a lot of show people said, was that Berle was
a "body-and-face man." To be amusing he had to be seen. Whatever the difficulties were, they have now been resoundingly resolved
on the Texaco Star Theater (NBC-TV, Tuesday 8-9 p.m., EDT).

In New York City the Theater currently has an 80 Hooperating,
which means that of all the sets tuned at that period, 80 per cent
are turned to Berle. The estimate, based on 535,000 present sets,
is that more than 1,800,000 people see him in the nation's largest
city. In the 23 other cities where his program is viewed, his popularity, with very minor deviations, is proportionate. The total audience may reach 5,000,000. His sponsor and its advertising agency
claim that no other comedian has ever been simultaneously seen by so
many people.

Movie exhibitors and even Broadway producers have said that
Berle has made Tuesday night poisonous at the box office. Homes
that own both radio and TV sets almost black out on radio at that
period (although Berle's own Wednesday-evening Texaco radio show
undoubtedly gets a stimulant from his television operation).

The Show: There remain, of course, quite a few millions of
his fellow citizens who have never seen Milton Berle in action. If
and when they do, his offering may impress them as a combination
of medicine showmanship and the delivery of the text of a joke book
by an Anglicized whirling dervish.

Berle begins by warming up the audience of his variety show before it goes on the air with a few minutes of machine-gunner gags, some very old, some very bad, but all coming in such profusion as to wake up even the dullest customer. He then brings on the rest of the show. He has clowned with such eminent performers as Lauritz Melchoir, Gracie Fields, Basil Rathbone, and Walter Huston, and with an endless series of acrobats, unicyclists, dog acts--and even other comedians. His wealth of ad libs, his quick improvisation, and above all his seeming urge to work himself to death are qualities now regarded as the ultimate in good video.

The Show off: But the audience is the basic element. For almost as long as he has been alive, a crowd of people watching him has had about the same effect on Berle as catnip to a febrile tom. As a little boy he was so fond of mugging into a mirror that his father complained that the habit was ruining the child. Milton's mother, however, demurred, and Milton went right on mugging. Her espousal of Milton in this respect was the beginning of one of the American theater's firmest and most famous mother-son relationships.

Moses Berlinger was a paint salesman when he married Sarah Glantz (who then changed her name to Berlin, in honor of Irving Berlin, and then to Berle). She had been a successful department-store detective. Milton was their fourth son, brother to Philip, Francis, and Jack. Shortly after Milton's baby sister Rosalind was born, his father's health failed. The burden of keeping the family together in a railroad flat on West 118th Street in New York fell in the resolute wife. Mrs. Berlinger had to take part-time work, again as a store detective.

Psychiatrists probing into Milton's motivations might well find in these harsh early days explanation for the star's later behavior. Despite the fact that he is now a millionaire, a celebrity, an actor who has the profound, if sometimes grudging, respect of his colleagues, Berle is often loud, demands attention, yells to make his point, is easily hurt, and insists that things be done his way--all characteristics indicative of a basic insecurity, a sublimation of long-buried frustrations. For whatever he has gotten has been gotten the hard way.

Perhaps the test of a great comedian is whether or not the audience receives the impression that his personality is consciously superior to his material. Into the superiority group fall those great men of the classic mettle of W. C. Fields, Joe Frisco, Julius Tannen, Joe E. Lewis, Fred Allen, and Groucho Marx. This is not the group to which Milton Berle is usually nominated by his peers. By contrast, he is regarded by the profession as a sort of common man's common comedian, a gag artist, a feverish user of props and costumes, a mimic--but one of the first order. Humor being the rare commodity that it is, both types of comedians are forever welcome.

The Imitator: Berle's first job, to which his mother naturally accompanied him, was the performance of an imitation of Charles Chaplin. It was offered by him on an amateur show in White Plains, N.Y., and won him the $5 prize. To this day he is never happier than when he can put on an outlandish costume and corn up a role. The television audience has seen him as a French cancan dancer, Carmen Miranda's "sister," a Sherlock Holmes detective, an acrobat, a Mexican bandit.

His enormous versatility was learned the hard way too. After the victory at White Plains, Mrs. Berlinger took her young son to other amateur competitions and church socials, then into vaudeville. Milton loved it. Before he was 10, he was playing child roles in such movies as The Perils of Pauline with Pearl White. From early movies Milton picked up plenty of tricks from his elders and betters, but shows where he could see the audience and they could see him were more his meat.

The Know-It-All: In 1920, when Berle was 11, he was cast in a children's sextet in the Shuberts' revival of Florodora. Confidently, he suggested to Lee Shubert that he be allowed to execute a planned "ad lib." Shubert concurred. But, as Mrs. Berle recalls it: "I used to have to square him all the time with directors who didn't like to be told what to do."

The life the youngster led was a tough one. Home often was a cheap hotel room on the road. Dinner was cooked over a portable gas burner Mrs. Berle carried. The family was generally limited to his mother and sister Rosalind, who as the baby usually went along with Mom. The three of them trouped up and down the country. Their life left a lot to be desired. "I played toilets," Berle recalls in disgust.

And yet, wherever he could find an audience there was Milton. Benefits always appealed to him ("It was good experience," says Mom Berle) and by 16 he was an M.C. And all along the line he picked up other people's ideas and gags. This propensity for gag thievery is unparalleled and is now morosely taken for granted by the profession at large.

And Now TV: Until 1936 Mrs. Berle was her son's combination valet, manager, and stooge. For years her booming, infectious laugh cued audiences. But at 71 the boom is a little low, and while Mrs. Berle still attends as many of Milton's television performances as she can, her daughter Rosalind, now married to a physician and the mother of two children, stands by to give the loudest yocks.

Milton's (and the family's) big switch to television came about this way. Last year the Texas Co. decided to go into video and the Kudner ad agency sold it on a vaudeville show. The idea was to use a different M.C. every four weeks, with Berle as the starter.

By the time the comedian had completed three shows he had learned
the medium well enough to tell technicians how to work. After Texaco had used seven other M.C's including Georgie Price and William
Gaxton, it we evident that the job was a permanent one--and Berle's.
As the deal worked out, Texaco also bought his radio show. This
gave Berle an over-all net of between $5,000 and $6,000. In the
trade it is regarded as peanuts, considering all the work involved.
But Berle got a viewing audience and thereupon proceeded to make
himself the biggest talent news in the infant television industry.

In T-shirt and slacks, Berle runs the rehearsals of his show--
cast, band, and guests--with an iron hand, and indeed of so rough
a grade of iron that there are some performers who will not repeat
their visits on the program. How much of this pressure is caused
by his own personality and how much by the frantic demands of a
wild and unexplored new medium would be hard to say.

The Satisfactions: There are still those to whom television
itself, with its fledgling productions and unsure reception, is something like the Zeppelin: a great modern invention that doesn't quite
work. Nevertheless, some $9,000,000 was spent by advertisers on
time charges alone last year. That is not a great deal compared
with radio time charges of $398,000,000, but it is not the worst
quality of hay. Obviously, the great problem is to attract audiences
that will buy enough of the products of the advertiser to pay for
the shows. Milton Berle is the best audience getter the medium has
yet turned up.

Even so, Berle is not a particularly happy man. He has never
learned to relax. He "unwinds" by sitting in night clubs clowning
with anybody who will listen--but never touching whisky because he
doesn't like it. In 1941 he married a beautiful show girl named Joyce
Matthews, and they adopted Victoria Melanie Berle in 1945. When
the Berles were divorced in 1947, he asked and got joint custody of
the child and does his best to see her every day.

He is scourged by an urgent restlessness. In June he will
begin a daily newspaper column, full of Berlisms, for the McNaught
Syndicate. Next fall he intends to start Milton Berle Television Productions, Inc., to package video shows for other actors. During his
summer vacation he may try the movies again, this time as his own
producer.

And there will always be the benefits. No one can tell how
much Berle has raised for charity, any more than anyone can say
what the intoxication of people watching him work means to him.
But nobody gives more of his time to that particular kind of good
works than Berle. In the language of show business, can that be
wrong? In anybody's language, have his struggles been worth his
pains?

On the eve of the Interfaith affair this week his mother thought
back upon the rewards that have now come after so many bad years
and gave an answer. Just a bit grimly, she said: "It's those little
satisfactions that are so nice."

--Newsweek, May 16, 1949, pages
56-58.

*   *   *

"Where is Milton Berle when you need him?" came the plaintive
query from Charlotte Rae on a recent episode of The Facts of Life.
It seems an appropriate question to ask on one of the most popular
of current comedy shows on NBC, the network that holds an apparently permanent last position in the ratings struggle and the network
that for 30 years had Berle under exclusive contract. Berle had his
own show on NBC from 1948 through 1959. He should still have his
own show on NBC. Last December, when the network brought together all of its current stars to promote their upcoming fare, who
was it who stole the program, who was it whose ad-libbing actually
made the cast of Hill Street Blues display some human warmth and
laugh, who was the one person NBC could depend upon to brighten
the show? Why, Uncle Miltie, of course.

Berle's career does not need recapping here. It was one that
embraced vaudeville, revues, motion pictures and radio and that
turned, naturally, to television. Milton Berle was Mr. Television.
Tuesday evenings, from eight to nine o'clock, belonged to Milton
Berle. It has been claimed--and is probably true--that Berle deserves the credit for selling nearly all of the 353,000 television sets
in use in New York City by 1950. Eddie Cantor once remarked,
"When the rest of us knock Berle, we should remember he's selling
the TV set on which we'll be seen." Berle is the only entertainer
to have his face simultaneously--May 16, 1949--on the covers of both
Time and Newsweek.

Although Berle was the star of the very first Texaco Star
Theater, televised on June 8, 1948, he did not become the show's
permanent host until September of that year. He continued with
Texaco, its singing servicemen and its two spokesmen (pitchman Sid
Stone and ventriloquist Danny O'Day) until the summer of 1953, when
Texaco found sponsorship of a regular television series beyond its
means. Those five years with Texaco represent Berle and television
variety at its best. Was Berle really as entertaining and as funny
as television historians would have us believe? Yes, he was. His
shows had more vitality than any television series since has had.
He understood the need to blend comedy with music and the necessity
to mingle acrobats with opera stars. On a typical show--March 1,
1949--he presented an acrobatic act called the Gauchos, Billy Gilbert,
Robert Alda (plugging his latest film, April Showers) and Virginia
O'Brien from Hollywood and, for a touch of nostalgia, vaudeville's

great song-and-dance man Pat Rooney, Jr. Berle did everything
the audience expected of him. He told corny jokes ("I went to see
the doctor, but he wasn't in, so I took a turn for the nurse"), he
lambasted his brother Frank ("Frank is down in Florida; he made a
lot of money there, but he had some trouble passing it"), he demonstrated his ego ("Put the camera back on me--I'm the star"), and,
of course, he appeared in drag, as Pat Rooney's "Daughter of Rosie
O'Grady."

   With those early Milton Berle programs, one gets the impression
that to ad-lib is part of the art of entertaining. One leaves the show,
as one might leave a good performance of live theater, with a smile
and a warm feeling. Berle is a human being, and he never lets his
audience forget it. He breaks up after many of his own gags, and
his hilarity is catching. Here is a comedian who could teach today's
television performers much. (One can almost hear his retort: "Now
they want to steal from me!") Berle can make jokes about King Bag-
gott and Horace Heidt, who are hardly names to today's audiences--
or yesterday's for that matter--and audiences laugh. They laugh
because it's Milton Berle, because of his delivery and because he
understands television humor better than anyone who came before or
has come since.

   In 1952 Berle had started to change the format of his shows,
building them around a single theme, rather in the fashion of today's
situation comedies. He hired Goodman Ace to write the scripts and
forgot about the ad-libbing. The old Berle put-down humor was still
there--on the September 23, 1952, show he was introduced as "the
reason movies are better than ever"--but from today's viewpoint the
shows are simply not as entertaining. They lack freshness. They
are too close to what passes for comedy on modern television. To
confound his critics, Berle could still prove he was the comedian of
old, appearing, for example, in drag as Carmen Miranda when she
was his guest star. Berle tried to explain, "The old character clowning and getting a pie in the face was Milton Berle, laugh getter.
The new one is Milton Berle, human being. I felt I was giving the
audience too much--well, too much cake. And too much cake can
make you sick."

   Berle became still more regimented by his scripts when Buick
took over as sponsor in the fall of 1953. That first show, on September 29, 1953, featured a marvelous opening in which the Texaco
Star Theater logo was used and the singing mechanics appeared, only
to be fired by Berle because "this year I'm selling Buicks." Ruth
Gilbert was featured as Berle's secretary, Max, trying to cajole the
comedian into marriage with her catchphrase "It's bigger than both
of us," and Arnold Stang (one of the truly unsung heroes of television comedy) was introduced as Francis, the NBC stagehand,
denigrating Berle with cracks like "If anyone says you're funny, say
hello to your mother for me." The premise of that first Buick-Berle
show was that the comedian wanted to go legitimate and star opposite

Tallulah Bankhead on Broadway, but she had Frank Sinatra in mind
as her leading man. The three appeared together in a short dramatic
sketch, with Berle as a broken-down ex-comic meeting his former
wife, Bankhead, at a bus station coffee shop run by Sinatra--a device that today only a talent as willing to experiment with the feelings of her audience as is Lily Tomlin would dare attempt, forcing
a total change in tone from comedy to pathos. The three pull it off,
which raises the question of whether Berle might be as great a dramatic performer as he is a comedian. For an answer, take a look at
him in reruns of a 1964 Defenders episode ("Die Laughing"), a 1968
Ironsides ("I, the People") and a 1972 Bold Ones ("A Purge of Madness").

      Another angle that Berle handled well and that is unthinkable
today is to bring the sponsor into the comedic situation of the program. A Goodman Ace script for the January 12, 1954, show has
General Motors all set to unveil its new 1954 Buick when it is discovered that someone has stolen it. (Thankfully, the sponsor did
have film of the new car, so audiences were not totally deprived of
the commercials.) Berle has Basil Rathbone as Sherlock Holmes,
Mickey Spillane and others help in the search. In the end it tran-
spires that Max had taken the car and driven it to Flint, Michigan, to deliver a letter of complaint from Berle to the sponsor. "You drove all the
way to Flint, Michigan, and back in an hour?" asks an incredulous Berle.
Back comes the classic tag line: "The lights were with me."

      Reviewing the Milton Berle shows is not only reliving the Golden
Age of American Television; it is also seeing the gradual decline of
the medium's finest comedic talent. It is not Berle who gets smaller
(to borrow a cliché from the movies). It is television that submerges
him, that sculpts him to its mold. Berle needed freedom, but in
time television took that freedom away from him. It constricted and
restricted. Berle needed the talents of his peers, such as Ethel
Merman, Sammy Davis, Jr., or Gloria Swanson, but by 1956 he had
sunk to the level of introducing Elvis Presley and Debra Paget, both
of whom lack his professionalism. As Presley starts to sing off cue,
a look of anguish and contempt appears on the comedian's face--"I
could sing as well as he can if I was bowlegged"--and after two numbers from the King of Rock'n'Roll, Berle can only comment, "Give
me the good old Rudy Vallee days." Amen!

      Those later programs lack the infectious, informal atmosphere
of Berle's early days on television. His guests might have had personalities for one medium, but they could not make the transition to
the medium of television. Because they could not work acceptably
with the comedian in either comedy routines or song-and-dance numbers, Berle was restrained.

      We need the old Milton Berle back again on television. We
need a comedian willing to appear in outrageous make-up, quipping,
"What you've got to go through for a lousy $15,000 a week!" We
need a performer who can turn on an overenthusiastic member of the

studio audience and comment, "Lady, you've got all night to make a fool of yourself; I've got only an hour." We need an entertainer self-effacing enough to admit, "What has Bob Hope got that I won't do two years later?" It is not just NBC that needs Milton Berle. We all need him again.

> --Anthony Slide in Emmy, July-
> August 1982, pages 24 and 28.

● IRVING BERLIN

A quarter of a century ago a rabbi named Berlin immigrated from Russia to America. In his family was a baby boy named Irving, who was destined to become a writer of popular songs calculated to keep the neighbors of two continents awake.

Music hath charms to agitate as well as soothe the savage breast, especially when the music is "Alexander's Ragtime Band" played in the flat up-stairs or the house next door and the time is midnight. If Mr. Berlin had written that one song alone he might have to answer for having robbed the country's Tired Business Men of many hours of sleep and for having aggravated their restaurant dyspepsia. But he is the author of many other song successes, whose infectious rhythms and syncopations set first America and then England and the Continent to swaying. "Everybody's Doin' it," "That Mysterious Rag," "My Wife's Gone to the Country," "That Mesmeriz-ing Mendelssohn Springsong Tune," "I Want to be in Dixie," and "When that Midnight Choo-Choo Leaves for Alabam'," not to mention "Snookey Ookums"--all these hurdy-gurdy favorites, and more, are from Mr. Berlin's facile pen.

When Irving was a small boy growing up ad lib with other youngsters on New York's crowded East Side he gravitated to one of the cheap cafés of Chinatown. He had been taught to sing by his father, and at the café, for the edification of the many habitués of the resort, he would sing the songs that he picked up in the street.

As the lad grew up he became a regular attaché of the place, and was paid to serve in the dual role of waiter and entertainer. He had a fair voice, a quick, true ear for music, and early he dis-played a knack of parodying popular songs. The events of the world of sport were naturally the café's chief topic of conversation, and one day after Longboat, the Indian runner, had defeated Dorando, young Berlin wrote some verses telling how an Italian barber had bet his shop on his countryman, and lost. He thought so well of his effort that he tried to sell it to a vaudeville actor, without suc-cess. Finally he submitted it to a music publisher in the hope of selling it as a song lyric.

"Why don't you write music for it yourself?" asked the pub-

lisher, for whom as a partner Berlin subsequently made a fortune.
"If you do I'll buy the song."

Mr. Berlin wrote the song, and a few years later he was telling his chauffeur where to drive next. To-day he is known as the
man who (speaking in the language of a vaudeville ballad) made the
popular song what it is to-day. Incidentally the other composers
hope he's satisfied, for while he established the song hit as a money-
making institution, paradoxically, by the pace he set others of his
craft, he knocked the bottom out of the business. It is five years
since Mr. Berlin submitted his first song. Since that time his royalties are said to have aggregated two hundred and fifty thousand
dollars. One year they exceeded the one hundred thousand dollar
mark. Nearly two million copies of "Alexander's Band" have been
sold, while the sale of the ballad, "When I Lost You," written upon
the death of the composer's young wife and considered by him his
best effort, is in its second million.

In spite of his demonstrated ability to compose catchy melodies
Irving Berlin knows practically nothing about the technic of music.
He can play only chords on the piano and these only in the single
key of F sharp. His method is to sit at the piano humming and im-
provising, until he has evolved a melody that appeals to him, when
his secretary puts it down.

Success has left him a modest, unassuming young man. It
was George M. Cohan who said, in toasting Mr. Berlin at a dinner
given in his honor by the Friars, a New York theatrical club: "The
thing I like about Irvie is that, although he has made lots of money
and has moved up-town, it hasn't spoiled him. He hasn't forgotten
his old friends, he doesn't wear funny clothes, and you will find his
watch and his handkerchief in his pockets where they belong."

> --Ralph Brock Pemberton in The
> American Magazine, October
> 1914, page 58.

*   *   *

Irving Berlin has undertaken a vaudeville route that will serve
to increase the present popularity of his many songs. He is one of
the most facile of present day song writers, and every one is glad
to see this stalwart young composer in civies once more, after so
nobly springing to arms for the defense of his country. With Harry
Akst at the piano, his repertoire includes "Mandy," "Oh How I Hate
To Get Up in the Morning," and his latest, "You'd Be Surprised!"

> --"Randall" in Dramatic Mirror,
> October 23, 1919, page 1662.

- EUBIE BLAKE see NOBLE SISSLE AND EUBIE BLAKE

- BLOCK AND SULLY

This mixed team packs a carload of inherent talent, its clean
and sure-fire comedy being strong enough to fit in any big production. Its singing and dancing is on an equal plane of appeal with
its clever and hilariously funny crossfire. From the time it comes on
until it dances off it uncorks a refreshing routine that elicits a
laugh epidemic.

Tempo is its ace in the hole. It is good to look at and works
together with excellent showmanship. Two human bundles of animation and vivacity that are hard to beat in the vaude. field.

Petite damsel comes on asking partner if he believes in the
Jones (prohibition) Law. He answers in the affirmative, whereupon
he receives a Dempsey wallop on the jaw that resounds thruout the
house. This got a storm of laughter. They then launch into their
clowning concerning a diamond bracelet he has purchased for his
gal, about her family and her "wonderful" mentality. Her dumb retorts and braggadocio about herself and her kid brothers and sisters
are side splitting. This couple must sit up nights thinking up funny
gags. Each hits the bull's-eye.

Following their excruciating comedy talk they maneuver into
several song and dance numbers that click in a big way. The lolly-
pop and kissing bit wowed them. They finale by warbling in duo
"To Be in Love With You," and follow with an eccentric dance that
got a near show stop.

Their present vehicle is greatly superior to the fine work they
did when caught by The Billboard in December, 1928.

--Charles A. Siegferth in The Billboard, August 2, 1930, page 14.

- IRENE BORDONI AND LIEUT. GITZ RICE

What booking agent would deny that the combination of two
such prominent names would not be a drawing card in Eastern vaudeville theaters, and doubtlessly in the Western ones, too, where Sunday papers publish New York theatrical letters. They have registered
an enthusiastic hit because the effects of the war are still about us
and everybody knows of Lieut. Gitz Rice's wonderful service, and
everybody is in sympathy with the struggle which Miss Bordoni's
country has gone through. Upon these facts alone they would be
hits, but both are artists to their fingertips. Even on an almost
bare stage on the roof of Proctor's Newark theater they got over with

a bang. The reviewer followed them down into the main theater.
There with their own set and longer time, they demonstrated that
they can become the classiest song team in vaudeville. Immediately
with the lifting of the curtain, the continental atmosphere of the
act manifests itself. The Lieutenant's playing and singing needs no
further praise than it has already had. Each of his songs went
big, especially "The Marne" and "Fritzi Boy." Miss Bordoni singing
"Over There" in French received its usual ovation. For the first
time she sang Gitz Rice's "Dear Old Pal of Mine" in her own tongue.
It was encored repeatedly. But what comes only to a few actresses
and seldom in the careers of such fortunates, the audience springing
to their feet like a shot when she sang "La Marseillaise" in a French
soldier's coat and a ragged skirt holding a battered French flag.
She made a picture such as should be used as a poster for the current liberty loan. Her acting, too, was a splendid asset. If this
combination isn't a big success it will be the audience's fault and
the audience's approval has all been to the affirmative.

> --"Higgins" in Dramatic Mirror,
> May 6, 1919, page 672.

● IRENE BORDONI

The little word "bonehead" was not once spoken, up in Irene
Bordoni's room, when, without any formal funeral, we buried the
hatchet and sat down together like the lioness and the lamb. Some
reader with a twelve-month memory may recall that that little word,
descriptively applied by her to the intelligence of Chicago audiences,
got itself written into my last interview with this lovely creature,
causing her pungently to protest in print and me to reply politely
if not infirmly.

But neither of us uttered the fatal word now, and I am sure
that each secretly applauded the other for her and his tact. We
had met the night before at dinner--at a laughing, joyous dinner
where her words were brighter than her jewels--and she had said,
in answer to my request, which came with the coffee:

"Another interview? Sure. On one condition: that you write
what I say."

"Make it two conditions: that you say you say what I write."

She had laughed; and here we were--"together again," as
George Cohan and Willie Collier used to sing after a season's separation; and the bonehead of our contention was never mentioned.
You see, I had forgiven Bordoni for the loveliness of her performance in her new piece at Powers', The French Doll; and Bordoni had
forgiven me for the rapture of my review of it in The Herald and
Examiner.

"I should never have expected that review from the way you wear your face in the first row, so long, so blank, so dismal. I don't ask applause from a critic, I don't ask laughter," she went on, moving from her seat at the piano to a chair nearer to me and rhythmically rocking a gemmed slipper in the bar of late afternoon sunlight that fell across her living room in the Congress Hotel, "but I do ask for a smilling face. And you were so cold. Ugh! It was a face of hard snow."

"That must have been when you were in a love scene," I said, "and I was trying not to cry."

"But I did not know that then," she sighed. "I looked at you and I said to my companion on the stage, under my breath: 'Look in the front row there at my enemy, so cold, so cruel-faced!' And my companion, he say: 'Don't mind him. Look at the lady with him and be happy!'

"And I look at her with her beautiful smiles and her glad eyes and I was a little happy. 'Maybe,' I say to myself, 'she will reflect some of her happiness on my enemy.'

"I couldn't believe it when I read the paper next morning. I cry--almost. And when I tell my husband over the long-distance in New York--for he had been greatly worried because what you might say about our opening, with your great enmity for me--when I tell him he say, 'Ha! now I suppose he is your frrrriend!'"

She said "friend" as only a Frenchwoman can, and I welled visibly in the implication.

She was beautiful today in black crepe bordered with bronze. A single garment it seemed, and cut by a master sculptor. Her sky-slanted nose, tiny red-rose mouth, strong beautiful white teeth that could kill a careless critic in one bite, firm unsubdivided forward chin and big brown humid burning eyes, fairly trilled in the golden sunglare. Yet I felt it my duty to say, and I said, "Bordoni, why do they advertise you this season as a beauty?"

"My press agent, a very smart man, he say," she answered lucidly, "that the public they don't care a damn about a good play, but that they will come to see a beautiful woman."

"Do you think you're a beautiful woman?"

"Oooooooh! perhaps no. But maybe I have a personality. I don't think I am beautiful--no--but--well, they say you can't see yourself! Anyhow, I believe more in personality than in beauty. It is the same as in singing."

"Do you think you've got a voice?"

"Do you think I've got a voice?"

"No. But I'd rather hear you sing 'Do It Again' than Galli-Curci sing a whole opera."

"It is personality," said Bordini.

"Not to mention art," said I.

"That is for you to say," smiled Bordoni.

"I'll tell the--what is that immortal line in your play?" I asked Bordoni, just to hear her say it.

"I'll tell the cock-eyed world!" she laughed.

"Do you always wear your hair like that, in a Bordoni bang?"

"Always. And before me my mother. When I was so young I can hardly remember she cut it off in front--snip! You must see our picture." She fetched it out of an old book of Russia leather. "See my mother and me with the same bang. See me here in my communion dress, with all the hair hanging down my back." She looked like a black-headed Sutherland. "I had a funny grandfather, too. When he take me walking he sit me down on a bench first and let down my hair and tie it that way with a big ribbon, so all the world see his granddaughter's hair.

"But my mother tie it back when I go to school," she raced. "She tie it all back but the bang. And the teachers want to tie that back, too. Because they very clean in the French schools and do not want anything get into the pupils' heads but what they put there. But I say, 'No, you cannot tie back the bang. If you do I tell my mother, who will go to the department of public instruction and complain. The Bordoni family,' I tell the teachers, 'they always wear the hair this way, and we call it'--and I say it to the teachers in French--'the hair dressed like the dog.'

"Are you coming to my concert next Friday?"

"Wild horses couldn't keep me from it. But why do you give concerts?"

"To hear myself sing in all the languages I know, and in Spanish, which I don't know. And to make money. I hope to make enough money in concerts not to have to go into vaudeville between plays."

"What's the matter with vaudeville?"

"Nothing. It's me what's the matter. I am all right for the downstairs. But the upstairs--" She hestitated, but she positively

did not utter the word bonehead. "I am," she started all over, "too
French, too Parisian, too, what you say? subtle for the upstairs of
vaudeville. Is that the right word, subtle?"

"Yes, and the word was made for you," I told Bordoni, on
whom a solitaire diamond ring bearing a stone so huge it might have
had a name as well as an address, was the final note of subtlety.
This crown jewel was cut flat on top, like a historied ruby; and it
didn't flash, it burned; it was Bordonilike. "Why," I asked its
wearer, "are French women so much subtler in what they wear than
American women?"

She felt for the reason, found it, and phrased it perfectly.
"The Frenchwoman has color-modesty. She won't," Bordoni went on,
"wear a green hat with a red bag and an orange dress. Color is
as delicate as perfume to a Frenchwoman of taste."

"Yet all the violent perfumes seem to come from France."

"It's the way they're used that make them violent," she count-
ered. "I scent a handkerchief to-day for to-morrow's use--and then
with, oh, such a little drop. Myself I perfume only in the bath,
where most of it can be rubbed away--never sweet; never strong.
People on the stage that have to come close to me say, 'I never smell
anybody like that.!'"

It was like a song, that last phrase, "I nevaire smell anybody
like that!"--a French, jazzy companion-ditty to "Do It Again." But
I didn't suggest melodizing the sublety of scent. I thought of the
classic "and I smell like Mary Garden, my God, ain't that enough!"
and refrained, asking Bordoni only where and how she had got the
rights to "Do It Again."

"I'll tell you how I got that song, after heartbreak and anguish,"
and she showed me the revolving whites of her eyes. "My husband's
friend, George Gershwin, wrote it, and sang it to me, and said no,
I couldn't have it for a play because he and his partner wanted to
save it for a musical comedy and make a lot of money. I couldn't
beg him, I couldn't bribe him. And then one day came the benefit
matinee for the Jewish children, which Mr. Gershwin was handling.
All his big stars which he advertise they send him telegrams to say
they could not appear, and he telephone to me in tears to help him
out. 'I'll do anything in God's world for you if you'll come and sing
a song,' he said.

"' My dear friend,' I say, 'there's only one song I like to sing
at your benefit for the Jewish children, and that is your own "Do
It Again."'

"'All right, sing that--sing anything!'

"'But,' I say, 'if I sing that once I want to sing that always. I want to put it in my new play.'

"'But my partner--!'

"'No the song, no the Bordoni!' I say, and stick to it. And five minutes, ten minutes later, he telephone back that it is all right with his partner and I can have the song for The French Doll. So I sang it for the Jewish children's benefit and have been singing it ever since. But I don't sing it for the Victrola. They wouldn't let me--and you can't guess the reason why."

"Your voice?" I tried, timidly.

"Certainly not! It is a very good voice for the Victrola. But the good people who make the records they say the song is too naughty! What do you call people who say things like that--Vic, Vict--?"

"Victrolians," I helped out.

"I thought so," said Bordoni.

--Ashton Stevens in Actorviews,
Chicago: Covici-McGee, 1923,
pages 289-294.

• EL BRENDEL

There was one bright particular feature on the 5th Avenue bill the first half and that was the comedy work of the young Mr. Brendel of the vaudeville team of Brendel and Burt. He placed the old bill in the center of his comedy platter and walked off with it without any trouble.

When Bart McHugh--the busiest man in the staid old city of Philadelphia--paved the way for El Brendel and Flo Burt to offer their present hodge podge of song, patter and what not he put old sure-fire and laughing stock together for Brendel, and the result is an unqualified, uproariously funny act.

--Dramatic Mirror, December 18,
1919, page 1961.

• FANNIE/FANNY BRICE

Fannie Brice is really funny where most of our other come-diennes are just endeavoring to be amusing.

Miss Brice's songs at the Palace had a bit of bluish tinge, it must be confessed, but numbers of this type are always popular in the Summer time. Moreover, Miss Brice does them very brightly. First she gives a comic touch to the sentimentality of "When I Come Back," and next she puts over a rather spicy lyric of the bathing beach and an underwater hesitation, which sounds like "Down They'd Go." Miss Brice related once more "He's a Devil in His Home Town," the exciting story of a rakish agricultural gentleman who won first prize in checkers and "soaked up cider like a blotter."

Then the comedienne returned to her famous tight-fitting striped gown to do her classic of the Yiddish Romeo, "Fol-De-Rol-Dol." After giving a demonstration of how to act "ingenuish," she presented a little Southern rag, rather inconsequential for a finale.

Miss Brice has a genuine sense of humor. And there is no one quite like her.

--The New York Dramatic Mirror,
June 10, 1914, page 17.

*   *   *

There had been trouble in The Follies. Miss Ray Dooley, impersonating an infant in arms, had carried realism too far, some of the pundits and Puritans said. My colleague Mr. Hammond, although himself a parent, had frowned on that lifelike scene wherein a male comedian suddenly withdraws his supporting knee from an unrestrained babe of imperfect lap-manners; and last week Mr. Ziegfeld had come rushing from New York to reassure himself that more nature than art had not leaked into his show.

"I shall not mention the sad affair to Fanny Brice," I said to myself on the way up to her rooms; nor did I even when I discovered that Miss Brice has an infant of her own.

It mot me when I entered; it made straight for me. It made a gurgling sound.

"She's trying to treat you to a drink," the child's mother explained.

Hospitable just like mommuh, is Fanny Brice's sixteen-months-old daughter, Frances.

Big for her months and a mighty crawler on Hotel Sherman's carpet, the baby had made across the floor for me with her bottle. Now she deposited it on my lap, emitting an intoxicated "Blib-blib!"

So from the warm bottle I drank with and to Fanny's first-born.

"Frances," I said, "here's hoping your path to the stage is as
rosy as your mother's was."

"Don't!" cried Fanny, and grabbed her child from me. "Don't
wish what I got on her. It cost me thirty-five dollars cash and a
million dollars' self-confidence to become an actress. You know what
George M. Cohan said to me when I was rehearsing in the chorus
of The Talk of New York and he saw me dance? I was as tall as I
am now and a hundred pounds lighter--mostly shins--and clumsy!
Cohan takes one look at what I dance with, and says out of the corner
of his mouth:

"'Back to the kitchen for you.'"

"Don't be ungrateful, Fanny; wasn't that what drove you into
burlesque and got you discovered by Ziegfeld?"

"It was a boil back of the soubrette's ear that got me to Ziegfeld, and don't you ever forget that," Fanny corrected. "She was
the stage manager's wife and I was her understudy, and when she
grew this boil I said 'God is good to me,' and got ready to go on
in her place. And at the last minute she puts a big pink ribbon
around her neck and goes on herself--with me waiting to drop the
scenery on her. But it wouldn't stand the strain, the boil wouldn't.
It exploded and had to have a doctor, and I went on and got six
encores in a song where she'd been getting one; and Ziegfeld heard
about me and I was signed for the 1910 Follies."

"That," I told Fanny, "doesn't sound very hard, but rather
soft."

"Baby," wailed Fanny, cuddling her youngster, "that ain't
the half of what happened to your mommuh when she first went to
be an actress on the stage."

"Blib-blab-blub," answered Frances, sympathetically.

"She says, 'Go on with your story,'" Fanny translated, and
went:

"It was a newspaper advertisement that says the lady wanted
new beginners for the stage, and with my mommuh I answered it.
The lady was a Miss Rachel Lewis, little and Jewish and thirty; and
she has for partner an actor by the name James O'Neill, but not the
original. She says she will make me A Number One actress for two
hundred dollars paid now in advance. But my mommuh is Jewish,
too, and offers her thirty-five.

"For days and days," droned Fanny, "I go round to the bum
hotel where Rachel Lewis lives, and see no actors, no lessons, no
nothing. My mommuh is getting impatient, so one day I says, 'Why

don't you teach me?' and Rachel Lewis she shows me a Spanish dance,
and I take it home and show mommuh. She says, 'For thirty-five
dollars only a Spanish dance!' and wants to know where my costumes
are.

"So I went back and told Rachel Lewis and she said she'd
measure me, and showed me a tape measure. She shows me a tape
measure for two weeks, and that's all she shows me. She's busy
rehearsing a crowd of queer-looking creatures who say they're actors,
in a rented show which is called The Ballad Girl. Rachel Lewis is
the Girl, and I've got a part, too, but no costume yet.

"I get it," Fanny went on, warming, putting down the baby
and pacing the long living room in trailing Japanese negligee. "I
got the costume the night we open The Ballad Girl in Hazelton, Pa.
And it comes just to here." Fanny designated a place midway between
waist and knee.

"I was so thin those days it was a shame to show me the way
that dress did. And the longer the show stayed out the thinner I
got. They gave me a quarter a day for meals, but I had to split
the quarter with the dog. He was Rachel Lewis' dog and roomed with
me, the dog did--twenty-five cents a room for the two of us. It
cost a dime a day to feed the dog, and I was getting so thin, eating
on Fifteen cents, that my bones were coming through the skin at
my elbows.

"This isn't where you laugh! Lemme explain. I was working
on my elbows in the water scene--where stage hands hold strips of
cloth that were supposed to be waves. I played an alligator in that
scene. You couldn't see me, but I was the alligator just the same.
My right arm was one of his jaws and my left the other jaw, and I
lay on my elbows in the trough of this water scene and worked the
jaws of the alligator. And the joints of my elbows got so sore I
used to cry.

"When I got courage enough to tell Rachel Lewis my elbows
wouldn't stand the alligator part any longer, she patted me on the
back and said: 'But what shall I do? There ain't nobody else in
the whole company can play it so good as you.'

"I believed her. Poor fish! I kept on playing the alligator's
jaws, and business got worse and worse. We were so rotten the
little towns didn't want us even before they'd seen us. They'd heard
about The Ballad Girl.

"'There's only one thing left to do,' says James O'Neill--which
I tell you again, wasn't the original James O'Neill--'and that's to give
'em drama.' So they got The Royal Slave, which was sick with drama;
and because I said I could sew they let me make all the costumes.
But the only change I got for myself was a Spanish scarf out of

Rachel Lewis' suitcase, which made me look like a piano lamp. And
looking like a lamp, I'm supposed to get married in the last act of
The Royal Slave!

"'I've got to have some clothes to get married in,' I told Rachel
Lewis. 'I've got to have anyway a veil.'

"' I tell you what,' says she--'you take the curtains off the
window in your room at the hotel and you've got a swell wedding
veil.'

"So I took 'em off and put 'em on. But we had to ring down
quick on the last act. The hotel man was out in front and recognized his curtains.

"So I gave up," Fanny sighed. "Rachel Lewis and this number
four O'Neill had taken my chip diamond rings and pin and pawned
them. They were beginning to come slow with the quarter a day for
me and the dog. So I gave up and sat down to write to my mommuh
to send me a ticket for home. And as I started to write I happened
to look in a dingy mirror by the desk and I saw Lewis and O'Neill
with their suitcases beating it out the side door.

"I ran and told a girl in the company and her mommuh, and
the three of us followed 'em to the station. And when they got on
the midnight train by one platform we got on by the other. And when
the conductor says 'Tickets' we only pointed to Lewis and O'Neill
in a seat ahead--and they had to pay our fare back to New York....
Don't wish a life like that on my baby."

"But your troubles were over now, Fanny."

"For me--maybe; but my mommuh! That girl and her mommuh
I took to my home, and there they stayed for days and weeks, mostly
in bed. They wouldn't work, they wouldn't move; just slept and
ate. To this day my mommuh says: 'Don't bring me no actors!'"

"Are you going to raise this child to be an actress?" I asked,
taking little Frances on my knee.

"Why not? She's already got a talent.--Baby, show the man
what your mommuh does in the The Follies.

And I swear to you that the child actually did--shimmy. Right
there on my lap.

"Now, baby, show the man what Ray Dooley does in The
Follies."

I hastily transferred Frances Brice Arnstein from my knee to
the carpet.

"Coward! You'd think you were Percy Hammond!--Show him,
baby, what Ray Dooley does."

And I swear to you that the gifted infant opened a wide, wide
grin and covered it with its hand for all the world as Miss Dooley
does.

> --Ashton Stevens in Actorviews,
> Chicago: Covici-McGee, 1923,
> pages 221-226.

                              *   *   *

For the past few years Fannie Brice has had something on her
mind. Certain delusions of grandeur seemed to be creeping into her
acts in The Music Box and vaudeville, and there was a horrid suspicion that she was getting all crouched up to do serious acting.
As a consequence, she wasn't funny.

But now that she has been put into a serious play called Fanny*,
written for her by Willard Mack in August conference with Chevalier
Belasco, she is our Fannie once again. Into this bird's-eye maple
melodrama, of no use whatsoever as a play, she brings all the old
Follies gags which we were afraid that she had discarded, and, making a revue-sketch of the thing, is very funny indeed. All that was
needed, apparently, to cure our favorite of her desire to be serious
was to put her in a serious play. The old weight is off her mind,
and she leaps pigeon-toed into the air again in her new-found freedom. If you loved the old Fannie who used to work on Massa Zieg-
field's plantation, you will rejoice with us. The only drawback is
that you have to sit through the Belasco-Mack "Western" to get her.

> --Robert Benchley in Life, October
> 14, 1926, page 23.

● BOTHWELL BROWNE

Bothwell Browne has been trying for the past three or four
years to break into New York vaudeville. He has played often through
the west, finishing up each time with a try for a New York showing.
After this week's showing at the Fifth Avenue there should be no
further trouble for Mr. Browne, for he is putting over female impersonations second only to Julian Eltinge's. Browne works a great
deal like Eltinge, getting entirely away from the distasteful side and
making the impersonation a thing of wonderment. Opening with a
"show girl" number, Browne uncovers something of a marvel in the

---

*Opened at the Lyceum Theatre, New York on September 21, 1926,
and ran for 63 performances.

dressing line. A long clinging gown of soft black material trimmed
with gold, with a long cape hung from the shoulders and the whole
topped off with a big picture hat, makes a stunning costume, carried
as very few women would. The second number is a "Suffragette,"
introducing "The Pantaloon Girl," a divided skirt arrangement with
a long cutaway coat in which Browne reminds one strongly of Ray
Cox. It is a good novelty number that fits in nicely. The third
comes as "The Fencing Girl" in a short skirt above the knees with
a tight fitting sweater, in which the impersonator appears at his
best. It rivals the bathing costume of Julian Eltinge, and Browne
wears it capitally. The finale is a "Cleopatra" dance, with the stage
settings and light effects. Browne's dress is elaborate and the dance
nicely executed, making a very strong finish. In the matter of dressing and appearance Browne stands within striking distance of the
head of his class. In this department he concedes Eltinge very little
advantage. Voice is Browne's weakness. The lack of a good, strong
singing voice is missed. Well down on the bill at the Fifth Avenue
this week, Bothwell Browne was a good substantial hit. He can go
into any bill and make good, and with proper handling should become
a drawing power. It was talk along Broadway during the week that
the Fifth Avenue, after having released its headline attraction for
the week (Eva Tanguay) could have more safely taken a chance with
Mr. Browne to top the bill, than to have placed Rose Pitonof (in her
third week) as the advertised feature, as long as the management
decided to slip through short.

--"Dash" in Variety, October 1,
1910, page 14.

• GEORGE BURNS AND GRACIE ALLEN

George N. Burns and Gracie Allen have a new skit in "Lamb
Chops," by Al Boasberg; funny stuff, almost actor-proof, but further
enhanced by the team's individual contributions.

Miss Allen is an adorable "dizzy" with an ingratiating prattle.
Burns foils and wise-cracks in turn and the laugh returns are that
and many. They dance off before the routine encore, which brings
him back for a bit wherein he reclines on a prop mat on the stage,
"feeding" his partner.

A tip-top comedy interlude for the best vaudeville.

--Abel Green in Variety, August
25, 1926, page 26.

• MARIE CAHILL

The occasion of introducing Marie Cahill to New York vaudeville
was a theatrical function of importance. Not for a long time have so

many theater executives and professionals been present at a Palace
Monday matinee.   Such an audience made the ordeal all the more
difficult for her.   Miss Cahill no doubt realized this but her poise
and easy manners gave no indications of such knowledge.   The stage
hands nearly made a bad start for her.   As the curtain raised on
her setting they were still fumbling with the properties.   But when
once she was on, there was no hesitancy about her success.   Her
first number was a medley of her old song successes, which brought
an outburst of applause, when each one took its turn.   Next she
used a telephone monologue which resembles that in her recent play,
Just Around the Corner.   However, the new edition is much improved.   It could do credit to Harper's Magazine and still has no
high-brow taint of the classic.

Singing a Blue Song brought her repeated encores, as did
her acting a patriotic song by William Jerome.

Miss Cahill's dates in vaudeville are as assured as was from
the first the United States' and the Allies' victory against the Hun.
Hereafter she will be a distinctive vaudeville institution of a status
which will have the admiration of the whole family.   Each member of
the family, too, will attend her performances which fact will make
her one of the best drawing cards on the Big Time.

                          --"Higgins" in Dramatic Mirror,
                          March 25, 1919, page 457.

●   EDDIE CANTOR

Eddie Cantor, now in Ziegfeld Follies, opened his local tour of
the Keith houses at the Orpheum [Brooklyn] this week in an act
composed of popular comedy songs, broken up with several stories
and a bit of clowning with his leader, Louis Gree.   Edward Morgan,
programmed as the Cantor pianist, was not visible.

Cantor hasn't played vaudeville in a long time, except one
week at an independent vaudeville house.   He stepped right back
into the two-a-day with his ability to handle a vaudeville gathering
unimpaired by his elevation to musical comedy stardom.

Opening with "How Ya Gonna Keep Your Mind on Dancing,"
he followed with "Oh, Gee!   Oh, Gosh!" and "Yes, We Have No
Bananas," all sung in Cantor's machine gun style with the punch
lines punched across as only Cantor can.

Eddie sparred for breath with a few new stories, also neatly
intimated that he was not in vaudeville because he was money mad,
but because he thought he should keep his vaudeville following and
make yearly appearances.

After the laughs Cantor hopped into several more popular songs, all delivered in his own muchly imitated manner, while stepping all over the stage.

In a demand curtain-speech Cantor confessed that he hadn't any more act than a jack rabbit, and exited after praising and introducing the act following.

At the half empty house Cantor proved himself one of vaudeville's surest fire entertainers. Before a normal gathering his 19 minutes could have been stretched to any length desired.

Eddie Cantor is an entertainer with a capital "E." He is value received for vaudeville.

> --"Con" [Jack Conway] in Variety, June 27, 1923, page 28.

*   *   *

Broadway's week gave us Eddie Cantor in his own one-man show, and a rather wonderful show it is. I might even be inclined to vote for it as the best play of the season.

Cantor, performing before a huge audience at Carnegie Hall, with the overflow customers almost surrounding him on the stage, went all the way back to the days of his youth at Catherine and Henry streets and came on through the years as he offered his very special bill, Forty Years in Show Business. He brought forth laughter and applause, contented sighs and chuckles. He turned back the clock and sang the old songs and talked of the great moments and the great people of his theatrical career.

He pranced and he danced; he wiggled and squirmed; he jumped up and down, swung his arms, spread his fingers, rolled his eyes-- and delighted a multitude. He paid his tributes to some of the theatre's stars of today and yesterday--to Al Jolson and George Jessel, to Irving Berlin and Ted Lewis, and to Will Rogers, W. C. Fields, Marilyn Miller, Bert Williams, Gus Kahn and Walter Donaldson, George M. Cohan and the great Ziegfeld....

Eddie Cantor's show is expertly organized; he is in command all the way. I wish he would bring it into a Broadway playhouse for a limited engagement. He would sell out.

> --Ward Morehouse in the New York
> World-Telegram and Sun, March
> 25, 1950.

- EMMA CARUS

Emma Carus' act is a gem. Not that it is high brow. Heavens
be thankful for that. We need too much such hoydenish funsters as
she to have her wholesome comedy hide under an encyclopedia that
requires a magnifying glass to find out what it was all about. At
first on her entrance in a formal evening gown and grand dame stride
it was feared she would be a little stiff-necked. But quite the opposite, she has seen too much of life, as the humanness of her delivery
indicates, to hand out such a damp glove as that. She hustles right
in to make every one merry. Her "Howdye Do" song vanished any
particles of gloom. Then she brushed her accompanist out to make
hay before the fatal July 1st, and she spared not those who intend
to cheat her out of her stein full and destined milk and pop into the
suds pail. The audience approved of her grief. Her Irish Song and
emerald costume in her third number was a convincing census that
there were as many Blarneys as anti-prohibitionists in the audience.
In her exit lines, Miss Carus, almost left the comic for the pathetic
when she compared her life as an actress with those of the home
women out front. It demonstrated that nothing is so powerful as a
touch of human interest to endear one self to an audience. Her act
will be a long success because it reflects the feelings of real people.

--"Higgins" in Dramatic Mirror,
February 22, 1919, page 276.

- THE CHERRY SISTERS

When Walter Winchell, who, among other things, is a dramatic
critic, undergoes the misfortune of having to sit through a particularly pediculous performance on a stage, he consoles himself with
thoughts of the Cherry Sisters. Winchell, who is allergic to anything third-rate, knows that no matter how bad a theatrical performance is, it is far superior to a vaudeville act billed as "The Gypsy's
Warning" in which the Cherry Sisters appeared before and after the
turn of the century. By any standard of criticism, the Cherry Sisters were the worst actresses in the history of the American theatre--
but they made their singular lack of ability pay off handsomely.

There were, back in 1893, five Cherrys in all--Jessie, Ella,
Lizzie, Addie and Effie--daughters of a farmer who had for years
fought a losing battle with the good earth near a place called Marion,
not far from Cedar Rapids, Iowa. The girls, who ranged in age
from the late teens to the late twenties, found their sole escape from
the monotony of farm life in occasional visits to the peanut gallery
of Greene's Opera House in Cedar Rapids, which in those days was
a jump break for road shows en route from Chicago to Omaha.

The sisters--particularly Effie--a tall young lady of 20 with a
long face, a large nose and a belligerent stance--were deeply impressed
with the "corn" served up by the passing Thespians. Virtue was

usually melodramatically triumphant and retribution caught up with
the silk-hatted villain just before the last-act curtain.

The girls wanted to take in the Chicago World's Fair of 1893,
but didn't have the funds. It was Effie who conceived the idea of
giving a theatrical performance to raise money. She whipped up an
evening's entertainment that included dramatic cliches that had stirred
her in Greene's Opera House; in fact, just about everything except
the mortgage on her father's farm, and cast herself and her four
sisters in all of the roles.

The performance was given in the Marion Hall rented for five
dollars for the evening. Practically the whole town turned out. With
song and gesture and recitation, the local actresses wowed their
friends. It wasn't a case of their best friends not telling them;
their best friends simply didn't know a theatrical atrocity when they
saw it.

In the days that followed Marionites stopped the girls on the
street and told them that they should be on the stage. Thus the
Cherrys were flattered into hiring Greene's Opera House for a one-
night show.

Things were different at their second performance. Cedar
Rapids playgoers, while not exactly seasoned, at least had some
standards of comparison, and the five young actresses were hardly
into a dramatic skit in which a virtuous maiden, played by Lizzie,
was about to go wrong, when somebody in the gallery blew a horn.
There were many horns, left over from a recent election campaign,
in the audience that night and everybody started blowing. Soon the
demons were in possession of the playhouse. Those without horns
began to hoot, whistle and stomp their feet.

The farm girls, who couldn't be heard in the uproar, stepped
out of character long enough to group themselves awkwardly and
smilingly acknowledge what they sincerely believed was a thunderous
ovation. Then they stepped back into character again and the noise
suddenly subsided merely because the audience wanted to get a load
of what came next. During the remainder of the performance the
sisters were frequently interrupted by vociferous demonstrations
which they continued to mistake for clamorous approval.

While attending the World's Fair, Effie and Addie--the two
mentors of the quintet--visited a Chicago theatrical booking office.
An astute agent saw commercial value in an act that was so bad that
it was a novelty and the sisters were booked throughout the corn
belt in Effie's one-act dramatic thunderbolt, "The Gypsy's Warning."

The three principal characters were an innocent girl, a gypsy
woman and a wolf in the costume of a Spanish cavalier. The big
moment came when the heroine, heedless of the gypsy's warning,

succumbed to the blandishments of the wolf, presumably to suffer a fate worse than death.

Sister Addie always portrayed the Spaniard but the other girls took turns playing the maiden and the gypsy and two comparatively minor roles. Interspersed in "The Gypsy's Warning" were musical ditties such as "Don't You Remember Sweet Alice Ben Bolt?" and "She Was My Sister And Oh How I Miss Her," and recitations of the "Curfew-Must-Not-Ring-Tonight" school.

Effie's dramaturgical efforts, while they would probably have given George Jean Nathan apoplexy, were hardly as bad as the acting of her sisters. Old-timers who saw them in their prime are of the opinion that not one of them had a single saving grace. Their voices were twangy and irritating; they were personally ungainly and their choice of apparel--usually home-made calico creations--was a modiste's nightmare.

The girls--billed as The Charming Cherry Sisters--Something Glad, Something Sad--met with cries of derision wherever they played, but their fame--or notoriety--was like a snowball rolling downhill and they got to be quite a draft at the box office.

They were so naive, unsullied and completely devoted to their profession that, incredibly enough, they considered packed, demonstrative houses as nothing less than a tribute to their art. Booking agents and theatre managers refrained from telling them the truth for fear that a money-making attraction would break up in shame. Honest, critical opinions that reached the ears of the sisters were quickly pegged by them as sourgrapes stuff.

When The Charming Cherrys had been convulsing audiences for three years, Oscar Hammerstein, the great New York impresario, booked them into his renowned Olympia Theater on Broadway. On opening night, Effie, in full voice, was halfway through a touching ballad entitled "Three Cheers for the Railroad Boys" when a small head of cabbage flew through the auditorium and just missed her. Other patrons of the arts that evening had come well fortified with defunct fruit and vegetables and the Olympia stage was a mess by the time the Iowa actresses had retired to the wings.

Hammerstein, fearful of losing the best draw he had had in months, explained to the bewildered bucolics that fruit-and-vegetable throwing was a symbol of success in New York. "Other stage stars," he said to Effie, "are jealous of anybody who has outstanding talent and they hire people to throw things at girls like you." Hammerstein paused to note that the girls were falling for every word he said. "Your talent is so great," Hammerstein continued, "that you can expect fruit and vegetables to be thrown at every performance."

Tossing produce at the Cherrys became the thing to do in smart

New York circles. During the girls' six-weeks appearance at the
Olympia the amount of garden stuff that a given person had thrown
at them became something of a yardstick for measuring social standing.

On the strength of what they chose to regard as their New
York success, the Iowans received bookings in other cities, including
Chicago, at as high as 1,000 dollars a week. Effie kept up with her
playwriting. The only effort that rivaled "The Gypsy's Warning,"
however, was one called "Americy, Cuby and Spain."

Never for a moment did the girls lose their naive faith in themselves nor forget what Hammerstein had told them about professional
jealousy. Adverse newspaper notices, which began to appear about
this time, now that the joke had gone far enough, were similarly
laid to a conspiracy.

When, however, the Des Moines Leader gave the Cherrys both
barrels in 1900 there were repercussions that still have a bearing on
the laws of libel. The Leader merely reprinted a criticism of an obscure critic on an obscure paper which had described Effie as spavined,
Addie as a capering monstrosity, and the facial features of the entire
troupe as rancid. That, the Cherrys decided, was going too far, so
they sued the Leader for libel.

The Iowa Supreme Court threw out the case in 1901, finding
that newspapers have the right to criticise freely and even hold up to
ridicule public performers.

Undaunted, the sisters went on their incredible way. The
fruit and vegetables continued and there came the day when they
were obliged to perform behind fish netting and wire screens for
self-protection. The fact that they had to use protective devices
irked them, especially Effie, and the theatre began to lose some of
its enchantment.

Jessie, the oldest of the quintet, died in 1903, and the other
sisters, weary of trouping and financially well-fixed, settled down
on the farm near Marion. They lived in semi-retirement for two
decades, but kept abreast of theatrical doings by reading trade pub-
lications.

For a while, Effie operated a bakery in Cedar Rapids. The
sister who had been so closely identified with such a theatrical turkey
as "The Gypsy's Warning" found herself, ironically enough, roasting
turkeys in the bakery oven for the townfolk at Thanksgiving and
Christmas time.

None of the sisters ever married, or even came close to it.
It was one of their boasts that they had never been kissed. With
the theatre behind them, Ella, Lizzie and Addie seemed to be content
to sit on the farm, knitting and dreaming of the glories that were
gone.

Effie, however, had to have something to fill the void, so she chose reform. During Prohibition, she traveled the length and breadth of her native Linn County, smelling out stills and speakeasies and reporting them to Prohibition agents.

Then, in 1924, apparently still possessed of a streak of incurable ham, Effie went into politics. She ran for mayor of Cedar Rapids on a reform platform, although students of civics were agreed that there was virtually nothing in Cedar Rapids to reform.

Effie put on a fair-to-middling campaign, but was roundly trounced on election day. Then the stage bug bit her again, and she and Sister, Addie left the farm and tried a come-back at the Orpheum Theatre in Des Moines. They did songs and recitations, both glad and sad. The local reviewer for Variety said of their turn, "As terribleness, their skit is perfection."

Two years later, Effie ran for mayor again and was defeated again. Meanwhile, she and Addie made so many so-called farewell appearances in and around Cedar Rapids that they found themselves in a class with Sir Harry Lauder.

Ella died in 1934. The sisters, who had been living now for almost 30 years principally on money they had earned around the turn of the century, were in a hard way financially. The farm went, and they took up residence in a Cedar Rapids roominghouse.

In 1935, Bill Hardey, the proprietor of a New York night club called The Gay Nineties, which specializes in nostalgia, thought it would be a good idea to play the remaining Cherry Sisters. He sent an agent to Cedar Rapids where Addie and Effie jumped at the chance of another appearance.

Two old ladies, dressed in the long, sweeping attire of a by-gone day, presented an incongruous picture when they landed in Gotham's Grand Central Terminal. Many Broadway celebrities were on hand for the opening at The Gay Nineties and they laughed uproariously when the old girls came out and began their act with a song.

Then, as the act progressed, a strange hush fell over the night club. Even blase New Yorkers could not laugh at tragedy.

Hardey had sent money for Pullman transportation both ways for Addie and Effie. They had come by day coach to save the difference, and they went back to Iowa by bus. Although their meals were all paid for by Hardey, the two Cherrys ate little, the prices took their appetites away.

Elizabeth, the third sister, died less than a year after her sisters returned from New York. Addie died in 1942, leaving only Effie.

A reformer to the last, Effie Cherry was sure that the world was going to the dogs. She used to lie awake nights, in her cheap, lonely room, wondering what would happen if Sally Rand's bubble burst. She had dreams, too, had old Effie. She read in the papers about a pretty young woman named Clare Luce who had been elected to Congress. Effie wrote to the Cedar Rapids Gazette, announcing that she was going to run for the United States Senate on an anti-tobacco and anti-liquor platform. Then one day she fell and fractured her hip, and last August she made her final farewell appearance and went into the wings forever.

--Avery Hales in Coronet, December 1944, pages 92-96.

• ALBERT CHEVALIER

It is some years since Albert Chevalier, the English character singer, has been on this side. Upon his opening at the Colonial, Monday evening, the audience gave every evidence that the American public has a lasting regard for him. After four songs, and the announcement-card stand had been removed from the stage, they called for "Old Dutch." After that they insisted upon another encore. Chevalier has several new songs, the best being "The Workhouse Man," in which he tells the touching story of an aged pauper separated from his wife by the rules of the poorhouse. He opened with "A Fallen Star," sung over here not long since by Ralph Herz. "I've Got 'Er 'At" is a comic in the Cockney dialiect. "Wot vor De'er Love Oi" brings the singer forward in the role of a loutish Yorkshire farmer, a character which, with its accompanying dialect, is most unfamiliar to Americans. Chevalier is the same finished artist. His characters are made convincing without trickery or the slightest touch of exaggeration.

--"Rush" in Variety, October 2, 1909, page 16.

• PAUL CINQUEVALLI

After an absence of about four years, Paul Cinquevalli appeared for the first time Christmas afternoon at the above theater [Proctor's 23rd Street, New York]. Since he left these shores, a new era has developed in vaudeville, and it does not become necessary to speak of his "past performances." New faces will greet him, and while it will be remarked by many that this or that feat by Chinquevalli has been seen before, it will be acknowledged at the same time that it has never been executed with the same dexterity, grace and precision that Cinquevalli gives to it. He is the juggler par excellence. The juggling with the billiard balls has been used around the vaudeville houses by many since Cinquevalli introduced it, while Spadoni

and Conchas have ultilized the cannon balls to a greater extent, but
no one approaches Cinquevalli. His confidence is sublime, so much
so in fact that in dropping the billiard cue over the head of the
orchestra leader, catching it up with two other cues, and in allowing
a cannon ball to apparently slip towards the other players, he takes
a chance on over-confidence, with a possible accident resulting. The
comedy is well brought out by an assistant, with a face which be-
speaks humor in itself. The slips made are for the purpose of aiding the comedy only.

One of the best things Cinquevalli does is to hold up with his
teeth a chair with his assistant on it, together with a table. Previously this has been done on the chin.

Those who have seen Cinquevalli will see him again; those who
have not, don't miss him.

> --Sime Silverman in Variety, De-
> cember 30, 1905, page 5.

• CLARK AND McCULLOUGH

Bobby Clark is one of the funniest comedians we have seen for
a long time. We laughed at every expression; even the eyebrows
were funny. The Jean Bedini revue [Chuckles of 1921 at the 44th
Street Theatre, New York] is rather pretentious, and is, we understand, a recent burlesque show somewhat cut down for the present
revue, with most of the comedy retained. Opening with a country
fair scene, the comedy element starts when Bobby Clark is hired to
impersonate a lion tamer for a fake lion and is unaware that a real
lion has been substituted for the fake one.

The fight scene, which follows, is likewise very laughable.
Clark appears as Hamburger Kid, a would-be pugilist, who does most
of his walloping with his talk. Jim Corrigan and Joe Mazza put over
a couple of rounds as preliminaries.

A ludicrous scene taking place in a hotel room, with several
persons claiming the right to the bed, is typical burlesque stuff,
but went big. Again Clark and McCullough triumphed with their
comedy, and for once McCullough had more of an opportunity than
in the previous scene.

The "Syncopated Wedding" finale is elaborate.

> --Dramatic Mirror, November 26,
> 1921, page 779.

• BOBBY CLARK

From the moment that Bobby Clark walks out in a cloud of
flying cigars and walking sticks and begins opening up a pair of
beaming eyes in astonishment at and appreciation of the brilliance
of his own jokes, one finds it easy to forget what the dentist said
would have to be done to that second superior bicupsid and that the
income tax is due next month. Bobby Clark is just about my favorite
musical comedy comedian.

                                        --Robert Benchley in Life, Febru-
                                        ary 7, 1930, page 18.

• KATHLEEN CLIFFORD

If Kathleen Clifford were not headlining the Fifth Avenue program this week, she would go much better, and receive credit for
being a clever girl. In The Top o' the World, Miss Clifford was a
bright little satellite, doing well as a "kid" and showing considerable
promise. She was then "surrounded." In vaudeville she is alone,
depending upon herself and male impersonations, for in the two others
attempted (a "kid" and a young girl) Miss Clifford did not shine. She
failed on the "kid" because her conception of the one given is wrong.
It was of a bashful youngster instead of a lively kidlet, though the
song for this did all that possibly could have been done to hurt the
impersonation. Recently Miss Clifford led a "girl act" in the same
theatre. The "girl act" passed away, leaving her a "headliner."
Whoever got that impression, whether to save money on the choice
spot or because it was truly believed, has done this young woman
an injustice. As merely a feature on the program, she would have
attracted notice, and with experience might have blossomed forth
into some importance as a male impersonator in vaudeville. After
this "headline week," if the girl is satisfied to go on a bill in her
proper sphere, there is yet a chance. If not, she can remove to a
production and take care of herself very well, laying the blame for
any disappointment vaudeville has brought or will bring upon the
greed of some one wanting to pick up a "big act" before it was ripe.
And if Miss Clifford continues male impersonations, she had better
at once discard any imitation of Vesta Tilley, whether announced or
not. In "When the Right Girl Comes Along," with or without the
cigar, Miss Clifford is inviting a comparison that can not count any
way in her favor, despite her youth, for a long time yet. Some one
should also have had more sense than to allow a person so obviously
young as Kathleen is, to attempt smoking a cigar on the stage.
Some novelty is looked for in the changes made by the girl behind
a transparency. It simply covers waits. Done so often by other
impersonators, male and female, it is more than familiar. Finishing
in "one" with a neat dance, Miss Clifford responded to "bows,"
caused throughout for acts mostly by admiring friends in front.
There's something in Kathleen if she's handled properly. The girl

makes a dandy looking boy, though she doesn't carry herself over well, in bearing, or the wearing of her clothes, including hats.

> --Sime Silverman in Variety, May
> 21, 1910, page 16.

* * *

Kathleen Clifford, who is the most fetching of all stage chappies, came to the Colonial fresh from her hit in London. Miss Clifford returned with more poise and surety. The English stage is a splendid finishing school for the American variety artist.

The little masculine impersonator is still using her shadow curtain, making costume changes from feminine gowns to masculine garb and back again behind an illuminated screen--with accompanying silhouette revelations.

Miss Clifford has an almost entirely new repertoire. She's giving her impression of an English John--he's a nut over there--in "Gilbert the Filbert" (already done here by Donald Brian), and she is offering "I've Been Out With Johnny Walker," with just the suggestion of intoxication. For one of the feminine changes Miss Clifford does "I'm on My Way to Dublin Bay," which lacks the requisite smartness.

She does everything deftly and daintily, dancing with neat agility. Her numbers are slender--in fact, most of them lack any distinctive quality--but, after all, it's Miss Clifford.

She's still our favorite stage boy.

> --Frederick James Smith in The
> New York Dramatic Mirror, April
> 28, 1915, page 16.

• HERBERT CLIFTON

If an audience will applaud "Love Me and the World Is Mine" and "The Holy City," sung by a man in a soprano voice while dressed as a ragged urchin, managers are not to be blamed perhaps for the booking. Herbert Clifton is a male soprano. The Alhambra crowd like Clifton well enough. He appears as an urchin, in ragged attire. After singing "Love Me," he has "Stop Your Tickling, Jock" (in his natural voice) and then says he will give a dramatic recitation of "The Holy City." It is not dramatic, just a soprano song. The program and Mr. Clifton state his wife arranged the songs. What she could have arranged about them excepting the order in which they were sung no one can know. One other selection about a bonnet was also in his repertoire. Mr. Clifton had the next to last

position on the bill. This should have been given to The Three
Leightons instead, and Clifton have opened the second part, if he
were not to appear earlier. It may prove difficult for Clifton to put
over a ballad act on this side, with naught but his soprano and a
few tattered clothes for assistance. If he can, then new ballads
ought to be the thing. The "double voiced" idea in a man given as
Clifton does may be well enough, but there should be a better manner of presenting it.

--Sime Silverman in <u>Variety</u>, January 22, 1910, page 17.

●   GEORGE M. COHAN

It has long been my secret conviction that George M. Cohan
is our most intelligent contemporary American. There have been
moments when, moved by journalistic comment on our legislative and
judicial departments, I have been willing to give Elihu Root or Charles
Evans Hughes a break, but they were fleeting. The average states-
man or politician, however sound, is not picturesque, and the fine
flower of his oratory largely superinduced by the flag, compares un-
favorably with the nasal confidences of a troubadour who points his
remarks, to a stirring tempo of his own composition, with his feet.
When Mr. Cohan wrote "Over There," I was perfectly willing for him
to go right ahead with the Fourteen Points. We might have got somewhere.

The theatrical world, to which Mr. Cohan consigned his careless regards several seasons ago, now sees him again in a revival
of a former success, and Broadway, which is considered the world's
most hard-boiled and exacting theatrical playground, rises on its
hind legs and applauds as Mr. Cohan appears aboard that antiquated
and rickety vehicle, <u>The Song And Dance Man</u>, and makes the thing
run along with hardly a squeak in its venerable joints. It is a fitting
tribute to a grand trouper that he can enter the field equipped with
the obvious hokum and sentiment that gushes forth from this play
and make it more entertaining than nine out of ten of our modern
plays written around the more popular appeal of profanity and sex.

Nor does Mr. Cohan seek to change the original version of
<u>The Song And Dance Man</u> to suit the Broadway palate. As though
in defiance of the anti-emotionalists he gives you the same picture of
the small-time hoofer that he was dishing out way back when it was
considered proper for a man to sit next his own wife at a dinner
party--and making us like it.

It is a characterization that is impossible to resist, as was
proven by the dowager who was sitting in the fifth row of the theatre and had a large expensive diamond necklace which was sitting
in the second row of her neck. Before the curtain arose she made

loud and unequivocal statements relative to revivals of shows that
were only endurable in the days when women cried for fun and not
for money, and before the last act she had lost her amateur standing
and was frankly sniffling into a wisp of embroidered lace that reminded me of one of the motion picture animated cartoons I saw recently during which Mickey Mouse sought to comfort a distressed
hippopotamus.

Of considerable assistance to Mr. Cohan is Mary Phillips, whose
performance as Jane Rosemond, the barb-tongued boarding house
mistress, left nothing to be desired.

We left the theatre with an increasing antipathy for men who
go around striking little children and stepping on young birds, and
a love-your-neighbor spirit which would have probably held over for
another twenty-four hours if a certain gentleman had not been so
stupid as to place a label upside down on one of a sackful of bottles
which were left at our house during the evening.

> --Baird Leonard in Life, July 4,
> 1930, page 16.

• JOE COOK

Joe Cook, back in vaudeville after three years with productions,
has embellished his "one man vaudeville show" and increased its
comedy value.

Cook retains his opening, playing the accompaniment for the
raising of the asbestos curtain, followed by burlesque magic but
he has added a couple of new low comedy wows. One is a trunk
mystery. A "stooge" grotesquely made up enters from the audience
as a "committee." He is given a bottle of beer, his feet are placed
on a rail with a large cracker in his hand. He tried to drink the
beer through a blindfold which is misplaced across his mouth instead
of his eyes.

Another new bit is Cook's hoofing atop a toy piano while one
of his comedy assistants plays the box. Another is a bass drum
with a scene painted on it. In the scene an auto is seen sailing the
waves while a yacht is coming down a road. Another funny bit is
the Indian lecture. One of his assistants is a Chief. He illustrates
Cook's lectures by holding up different objects. A specimen of early
pottery was a beer mug. The Chief's bows and arrows were a collection of bowties and arrow collars.

The saxophone duet remains but the prop bludgeon which cues
the "stooge" to hit the bells by dropping on his head has been ela-
borated. The prop now resembles a derrick.

The comedy make up of one assistant ran to a speckled countenance. The other affected various types of mustaches. The third
is a bit of a musician.

Cook juggles clubs, does his comedy juggling on the wire,
explains why he can imitiate four Hawaiians and has a new nonsensi-
cal speech about "coincidences" that is as funny as the Hawaiians.

The act is as it always was, one of the greatest comedy novel-
ties in vaudeville. Cook is as versatile as he is clever and is blessed
with a gift for travesty and a whimsical personality that would bring
him laughs at an undertaker's convention.

--"Con" [Jack Conway] in Variety,
November 11, 1925, page 14.

● FRANK CRUMIT

From Main Street to Broadway is a long, broad jump--especially
if you land so high among the bright lights that you are never obliged to leave the glittering thorofare to "tour the tanks," which
are worse than "the sticks," or even "the tall timber." That is Frank
Crumit's record--or one of his many records; for, while he never
goes "on the road," he tours the country continuously, via the phonograph circuit. 'Way back in the days before he arrived on Broadway, he swore he would never leave Broadway again, excepting to
commute to his country home in Connecticut. This bold, but seldom
kept resolution was reinforced by a long-term contract from the Co-
lumbia Company, on whose list he is "second best seller" to Bert
Williams only.

All last season Frank Crumit cheered the Greenwich Village
Follies with his songs, and now he is putting the "tang" into Tangerine
at the Casino. Hence, the question arises: "How come, Frank Crumit?"

I am one of the few Broadwayites who can tell you. There are
four Jacksons in the U.S.A.--Jackson, Miss.; Jackson, Mich.; Jackson, Tenn., and last and least, Jackson, O. The cipher after it
indicates its desirability as a place of residence. Industrially, it
is of some convenience, because there are coal mines right under the
town, iron ore in every hill, and blast furnaces all around. When
these are all in full blast, letting loose sulphurous flares of fiercely
flaming gas, it looks like an inferior edition of the Inferno--a lower-
case hell!

Main Street is paved with cinders, over which barefoot boys
learn to glide gingerly, because the broken edges are sharper than
safety razors.

Frank Crumit was born on this Main Street, a thorofare cor-

rugated with cinders, rutted by heavy ore wagons and sowed inches
deep in coal dust--hotter than the hinges of an overheated Hereafter in summer--a slough of black muck in wet weather, dusty in
dry, and beautiful never. By way of compensation for this poor
choice of birthplace, a kindly Providence gifted Frank with a golden
voice, brought him golden rewards, and Broadway as a permanent
residence. Not only was his voice a natural light tenor, but it was
naturally developed. Fate kindly preserved young Frank Crumit
from any vocal impresario who might have fanned the flames of operatic aspirations in his youthful breast, and ruined his voice trying
to attain them. His first and only teacher was a tall, gaunt, red-
headed, serious-minded Welshman by the name of Jones, who taught
pitch and tempo with the pipe and baton above mentioned; incul-
cated correct phrasing by good example--and let Nature do the rest.
Such things as "breathing exercises" were unheard of! A would-be
singer was supposed to have enough sense to take sufficient breath
to carry him thru a phrase, and, if he failed, he was stimulated
with the baton afore-said to do better the next time. I am sure
the Rev. Mr. Jones would have considered even mention of the dia-
phragm and "control of the abdominal muscles" as highly indecent.
He confined his physical corrections to the cranium, apparently thinking that a few bumps, more or less, would not be noticeable on a
tenor's head--considering the general bumptiousness of the breed.
But apparently young Crumit was a very apt pupil, since his head
has always been normal, and even Broadway success has developed
no symptoms of megacephalosis. And it is quite possible that he
inherited a hard head from his ancestors.

For Frank Crumit was born of the best blood in Jackson County.
His paternal grandfather was a surgeon in the Civil War, and a fine,
upstanding gentleman of the old school, with white hair, military
mustache and imperial, which won him the sobriquet of "The Grey
Eagle." Frank Crumit, sr., the sire of our hero, was clerk of the
Court of Common Pleas. The death of our mother caused Frank to
inherit his Aunt Patsy as substitute mother. From her he acquired
his sense of humor. She had a lazy, nasal drawl, something like that
of Mark Twain, which heightened the humorous effect of any story
she told, and she knew how to tell a story as well as Uncle Remus.
She could chat darky songs in style to discount the darkies themselves, and imitate the camp-meeting "exhorters" in a manner that
the colored cook called "scandalous funny."

When I listen to Frank Crumit crooning a coon song to the
sketchy accompaniment of a guitar or ukulele, I can recall her very
intonations--so who knows how much of his unique vocal charm he
owes to Aunt Patsy?

"Ohio is cursed with colleges," as the saying goes. Naturally,
young Frank Crumit went to one of these colleges, where he distinguished himself principally by leading the glee and mandolin clubs,
and introducing the ukulele into the curriculum.

Moreover, here young Crumit learned that his talents were of
commercial value, when a progressive local vaudeville manager--they
really do exist in Ohio--offered him an engagement in place of an
act that failed to appear. Naturally, the college crowd rallied to his
support, and when the local manager, pleased with the extra patronage, not only paid young Frank in regular money, but offered to
book him a route, young Crumit saw a way to escape from both horns
of the dilemma--law or medicine--which confronted him in the choice
of his future profession.

Conservative Main Street did not at first approve of "the stage,"
which generations of orthodox preachers had proclaimed was "Satan's
own." But when reports came direct from the cashier of the First
National Bank that young Frank Crumit was "salting down" one hundred
dollars per week from his pernicious career over the unholy vaudeville
circuits, "a change came o'er the spirit of the dream." Suddenly,
from being a very doubtful character, classed in certain conservative
circles with wild youngsters who had "run away with the circus and
gone to the devil," Frank Crumit found himself a local celebrity, and
on the occasion of one of his infrequent visits to Main Street, the
Jackson Silver Cornet Band met him at the depot with the strains
of "See, the Conquering Hero Comes."

Can Fame do More? Not on Main Street! Hence, Broadway
for Frank!

> --Willard Holcomb in Shadowland,
> January 1922, pages 33 and 73.

• GABY DESLYS

Gaby Deslys, who made her reputation by losing it, is the
feature of the new Revue of the Revues at the Winter Garden [which
opened on September 27, 1911, and ran for 55 performances]. Personally, I doubt whether Mlle. Deslys would know the former King
of Portugal if she passed him in the street, but her supposed share
in the downfall of his dynasty has been advertised sufficiently to
give her much of the vogue once enjoyed in this country by the late
lamented Lola Montez. Mlle Deslys is pretty, in a blonde way, and
she sings and dances as well as do many obscure soubrettes in our
vaudeville houses. The rest of the performance at the Winter Garden,
a general hash mixed together under the title of "In the Limelight,"
is unutterably stupid, a triumph of quantity over quality.

> --Channing Pollock in The Green
> Book Album, December 1911,
> page 1209.

                    *   *   *

As this [Infatuation, released by Pathe in 1919] is the first

picture in which Gaby Deslys has appeared, more than usual interest
attaches to it.   Yet to judge it by entirely ordinary standards is
almost impossible, because, first of all, it is of foreign make, and
French-made pictures have characteristics that place them in a slightly
different class from the American production.

It was appropriate that the settings for Infatuation should be
extravagant. Mademoiselle Deslys is an extravagant person. Her
stage appearances have always been tinged with the color of the
royal romance that gave her her first fame as the intimate of a king--
even in days when kings are held chiefly in contempt--presupposes
a close acquaintanceship with luxury. And just as Gaby Deslys scintillated and shone through her stage performances, so she glows and
sparkles through the thousands of feet of film that unwind the heart-
touching little story of the poor French flower girl, who finds a rich
husband and becomes the victim of a plot on the part of a rejected
suitor to discredit her in the eyes of both the men she loves, and
so take away her hard-earned happiness. Flora's problems are the
usual problems of a woman who marries money and later makes a
name for herself. In this case her reputation comes through her
dancing, and through her stage career she meets the man who for
a time supersedes her husband in the place he holds in her heart.
But the illness and heart-brokenness of the husband, who really
loves her very truly, brings out the finer points in Flora's complex
nature, and she turns nurse in order to help restore him to health,
giving in addition the gift of herself to consummate his recovery.

The story was, of course, written for Mademoiselle Deslys.
The part of the dancer brings her into character as she is most
generally known. The part of nurse commemorates her service in
the hospitals of France, from which she was taken to make this picture.

Mademoiselle is not a strong emotional actress. She requires
the embellishments of handsome settings and wonderful gown creations. She needs a touch of the bizarre, the sensational--they belong
to her. There are twists in her nature that are belied by her pretty
face. And yet she is softer in her picture than she has been on
the stage--it is the softening borne of close contact with indescribable suffering. It was the psychological moment in which to put her
into a photplay; we doubt if she would have risen to this occasion
before the war.

--Chester A. Blythe in The Photo-
Play Journal, Vol. 2, No. 6,
February 1919, page 34.

• THE DOLLY SISTERS

The Dolly Sisters--Roszika and Yansci--united once more and

assisted by Carlos Sebastian, headlined at the Victoria (New York)
in a new non-tango offering.

The sisters first danced before the audience in modernized
Greek robes of golden yellow. But the great white way of Athens
never had anything quite like this terpsichorean duet--a creation of
bewildering high kicks.

Then Yansci returned with Mr. Sebastian--black sashed and
quite Castilian--for the Papalatsa, a sort of Spanish maxixe. Next,
Mr. Sebastian did the Havana Rumba with Roszika.

The Rumba was the last work in acrobatic dancing catches.
Indeed, Mr. Sebastian made his entrance carrying Miss Dolly, who
wore an ideal Summer costume--a fringed shawl dress, abbreviated
stockings, and a waist that revealed a Kitty Gordon lack of material
when the dancer turned around. The dance was a thing of gymnastic
whirls.

While the three were preparing for the High School Gallop,
the orchestra played "The Drummer's Nightmare," a successful study
in noise.

The Gallop, a rather monotonous dancing trot around and
around the stage, concluded the specialty. Here the sisters wore
quaint black masks with odd animal ears, and were driven by Mr.
Sebastian, who held the reins and wielded a perfectly harmless whip.

The offering shows imagination in working out the numbers.
Dancing, as personified by the Dolly Sisters and Sebastian, is very
acrobatic. But to be a gymnastic dancer, with the mercury hovering
in the 90s--we'd rather see than be one!

--The New York Dramatic Mirror,
June 3, 1914, page 17.

*   *   *

Heralded with much pomp and ceremony and billed as the International Wonder Girls who Ruled London's Stage for 130 Weeks, the
Dolly Sisters inaugurated their return to the States by appearing at
the Palace. After witnessing their entertainment we feel safe in saying that the well-known twins need have no fear of ruling American
vaudeville. That is not with their present offering. At the Palace
"names" mean something and outside of a lavish display of wardrobe
that is all the girls had to offer. After watching the Dollys go
through a very ordinary routine we could not help but think of their
well-known high kicking and all-around dancing ability for which they
are famous, but for some reason or other is entirely lacking from
their present vehicle. The act opened with the Dollys appearing in
gorgeous orange-colored costumes singing a double entitled "It Must

Be You," which was followed by Kay Kendall in a descriptive Indian
dance. The girls then offer a comedy eccentric number with a clog
dance which was by far their best bit, after which Kendall renders
"It Was Wonderful in Madrid" and then removes his shoes to execute
a difficult and novel dance which took him off to a substantial hand.
The sisters attired in riding habits offered another double dance
followed by a solo dance by Kendall which could be cut down as it
is too long and left him gasping for breath. Another double dance
by the girls brought on the curtain and also an avalanche of floral
offerings that literally covered the stage. An encore was offered
in the form of "Yoo-Hoo" with revised lyrics pertaining to the girls'
return to Europe which was followed by a speech. However the turn
is not there and the applause at the finish was far from being substantial, as it came from various parts of the house and was inclined
to be spasmodic. The Dollys are capable of much better work and we
hope they have not decided to rest on their reputation.

--"Gillespie" in Dramatic Mirror,
April 1922, page 117.

• RAY DOOLEY

     Two boys and four girls assist Ray Dooley with her minstrel
offering. Only the lads are blacked up. They are dressed in short
brown Norfolk outfits. The Boys are programmed as Gordon Dooley,
tambo, and George Loff, bones. While neither tambo nor bones are
introduced, the boys have jokes, and Dooley sings "When I Wake Up
This Morning." The girls dress alike, with Bee Dingas acting as
interlocutor. They look neat in white Buster Brown suits. After a
short minstrel program, solos are introduced by Anna Webb, May King
and Flo Bert, the last named doing the best work. After young
Dooley has sung in "one" and Ray Dooley and the boys had put on
"Gee, You Are Awfully Hard To Get Along With," the close comes
with the girls in pajamas and Miss Dooley singing "I'm Afraid of the
Moon," a bedroom interior being used. It's this number which is
the piece de resistance of the act. Miss Dooley works hard and is
ably assisted by the girls, the boys coming in at the finale. Miss
Dooley affects the mannerisms and tones of a little girl throughout
her act, which are best employed in the bedroom "bit." The Dooley
act whips up strong with the closing number. Miss Dooley claims
all the credit for staging and producing. She should have put at
least one good voice in the offering. There is a little dancing, but
not enough for an act of this nature. The turn is too long. Several
old "gags" are used. Some sort of special setting for the minstrels
would help considerably. It's a cute act more than anything else
with the last number holding it up.

--"Mark" [Mark Vance] in Variety,
August 30, 1912, page 19.

● MARIE DRESSLER

All things that have a suspicion of pose or pretense are fair
marks for Miss Dressler's keen satire. She doesn't announce her
bits of clowing as caricatures. She doesn't have to. But every
minute she is on the stage she is hitting at somebody's frailties.
Whether she does it consciously or not the essence of her humor is
its satire on insincerity and affectation. Her recitation was a howling
travesty of the chesty elocutionist just as one of her songs was an
exquisite lampoon on the "classy" prima donna. And the beauty of
her method is that there is just enough accuracy and truth in her
burlesques to make the picture ridiculously plain. She opens with
"A Great Big Girl," followed in turn by a recitation, an odd "coon"
song and the "prima donna" number. That was all except five or six
curtain calls and a speech. The Joe Weber amazon is a great big
vaudeville hit.

> --"Rush" [Alfred Greason] in
> Variety, April 25, 1908, page
> 14.

*   *   *

Marie Dressler's return to vaudeville, following a two-year
tour of the country, devoted to war work, can be classed among
the great triumphs of her 31 years of stage experience. Monday
night when Miss Dressler emerged from her "entrance," she was
greeted with a two-minute reception that not only pleased her, but
apparently surprised her. She opened with an introductory speech
and followed with several witty stories constructed around her campaign experiences. These were followed by a comedy poem, a coon
song, a recitation and Miss Dressler closed with a travesty number
built around the drama, grand opera and the Russian ballet. It
made a fitting finish to an extremely good comedy act. The "finesse"
of the "old school" has become a lost art with modern comics, male
or female, and it is rather a treat to occasionally see a woman who
knows the intricate science of turning the most minute twist of a
situation into a laugh. Miss Dressler's programming says she is
benefiting herself. She is also benefiting vaudeville with this specialty. Miss Dressler carried off the bill's honors without any visible competition Monday evening [at the Palace, New York].

> --"Wynn" in Variety, April 4,
> 1919, page 27.

*   *   *

Marie Dressler, one of the greatest institutions of burlesque
on the American stage--not of the ten-twenty-thirty standard, but
of the strata that demands talent and brains--has returned to vaudeville. This is an occasion to make Broadway sit up and take notice.

All the Forty-second street bunch were at the Palace Monday afternoon to welcome her. And they were not disappointed. She was
in all her cut-up glory, exactly like the old days of Weber and Fields.
She satisfied everyone. In doing so she made herself a matter of
importance to the Associated Press. Few actresses, even considering those who play Ibsen and other queer fellow's scribbling are
quoted by the transcontinental press as much as she for the reason
that she has always some to say that even college professors can
understand as well as servant girls. According to announcement
her engagement is only for one week. Wait until the Alan Dales and
Burns Mantles out in the midland learn that their column filling Marie
has taken again to the footlights and the power of the press will
see that she buys a mileage book--two, three, four of them right
away. Miss Dressler is a household name and she will be a big card
for the two-a-day from the Atlantic to the Pacific.

                              --"Higgins" in Dramatic Mirror,
                              April 8, 1919, page 531.

• THE DUNCAN SISTERS

      The world's greatest Sister Act is lunching with me--and now
I am glad it's at the Drake. Even if I have to subsist the next six
days on hash and sinkers, this palatial place is the only place today
for the Duncan darlings. They are fresh from London (not too fresh)
and the King of Spain and the Prince of Wales.

      Of course I knew them when--but they don't look it. Rosetta,
with her Bond street walking stick and Mayfair turban and a dash
of hunting pink in her waistcoat, and Vivian, a tailored trance by
Redfern, are just too smart for anything less than royalty. But I'm
not downcast; I'm glad the old spring suit has been recently asphyzi-
ated; and I'm glad the little blonde Duncan Sisters still treat me as
a friend and brother.

      Royalty is served with the fish--with, to be meticulous, the
trout. But first, of course, comes melon--honeydew tortured with
lemon; and with the melon the stage is, in a manner of speaking,
set. Which is to say that during melon we get away from Chicago's
Colonial Theater and their great hit there with Fred Stone in Tip-
Top, and over to dear old London, where a couple of months back
they landed for a vacation, and instead of getting it were seized by
Mr. De Courville, the Mr. Dillingham and Mr. Ziegfeld too of the
United Kingdom, and on two days' notice interjected into Mr. De
Courville's Pins and Needles revue, where their success was instant
and enormous.

      That's a story too; but so much of that sort of thing and so
few kings and sons of kings come to me in my narrow life, that I
fain would pass it by in favor of the fish--which is to say of royalty.

They've finished now the story of their electrical engagement
at the London Gaiety--we've gone right down to the yellow jacket
of the perfect melon. Theater; there's been nothing but theater when
the headwaiter himself bears us the silver dish whereon lie six game
fishes done to a noble, if not indeed a royal, bronze.

"A dish fit for a king!" says Rosetta--who is the comic one,
we'll now remember; who is the one that in Tip-Top bumps the
base of her spine to achieve a skinned knee. Rosetta's appraisal
of the fish explodes the pent Vivian and then herself.

"King!" says Vivian with the grand rising inflection--"we met
the King of Spain!"

"And," caps Rosetta (you should have heard her enrichment
of that simple word), "the Prince of Wales!"

"Both well, I hope," I try to say--but it chokes and I am
speechless while Rosetta runs on:

"Why, we danced with the Prince every night--and how he
can dance! Everywhere he'd be asked out he'd say to his hostess,
or get the word there, 'You must have the Duncan Sisters!'"

"But we must," cries Vivian, "tell Mr. Stevens how we met
the King of Spain!" And Rosetta tries to:

"Mrs. Cornelius Vanderbilt called up from her London house
that she was giving a reception to the King of Spain and that we
must come--and--and meet the Prince of Wales. You see--"

"You see Mrs. Vanderbilt didn't know," Vivian relays, "that
we'd met the Prince the night before, and that that was why she
was now asking us."

"It amounted to a royal command, our invitation did," Rosetta
takes up; "only of course you can't 'command' American girls; it isn't
done. But when the Prince of Wales lets any hostess know there's
anybody he'd like especially to see, it's a cinch that person will be
asked to the party. You see how it was?"

"Perfectly."

"Only Mrs. Vanderbilt didn't know that we'd met the Prince
the night before at Major Fitzgerald's," Vivian laughed.

"You really should have been there at the Major's," Rosetta
swettly says to me. "You should have seen the Prince sitting on
the floor while we sang our songs at the piano. He always sits on
the floor when we sing."

"He played the drums with the jazz band before the night was over," Vivian sighs. Her sister goes her one better:

"And he sang with us--sat on the floor and harmonized. He's a--he's a regular prince, that prince is."

"How'd he sing?"

"So well I told him he could join our act," says Rosetta.

"What did he say to that?"

"Asked how much we'd give him. When I said two hundred pounds the Prince said, 'Oh, that's more than I ever got!' Then he said, 'I say, Miss Rosetta, what was that third song you and your sister sang?' And when I told him it was 'Feather Your Nest,' he shook his handsome head and fingered his tie--he's always fingering his collar and tie--and said:

"'No, no, that's one of our old songs; that's 'Me and My Gal'--I've known that song two years; you can't fool me!'"

"And he was right; it's a swipe," nods Vivian. "The Prince is wise."

"Wise?--he's just like an actor. And he knows it!" glees Rosetta. "The Prince said to me, and these are his very words:

"'My life's a vaudeville show; I'm booked up for every day in the week.' And then he said:

"'They princed me so much in Americah that I wanted to bark.'"

"He's a Prince Charming," Vivian murmurs. "His favorite phrase is 'That's so sweet of you.' And he's witty. He ran to the band as we left the Major's and asked the band boys to play 'Me and My Gal.' And the Prince himself played the drums, exultingly, as much as to say, 'There's our tune from which you swiped your tune!' That's the way he drummed us out."

"And next night we met him all over again," thrills Rosetta. "You should have seen that scene of Mrs. Vanderbilt's reception to King Alfonso--diamonds even in the buckle straps of their shoes-- every man loaded with decorations except, of course, the American polo players. The Duncan Sisters' family gems didn't go very far in that gathering."

"I don't think you needed any diamonds--with the Prince running to meet you as he did," Vivian puts in sisterly.

"As Mrs. Vanderbilt stepped to greet us we saw the Prince

above, on a landing. You should have seen her amazement," says
Rosetta wickedly, "when he rushed off the landing like a shot and
came up to us and said, 'I'm so glad to see you're heah--so glad!'--
and grabbed me and danced right off."

"Does he talk while he dances?"

"I should say! The first thing he said to me was, 'Well, Miss
Rosetta, I think I'll accept that position you offered me.'"

"And you must tell Mr. Stevens," Vivian warns, "what that
man--what that strange man"--she is deeply mysterious--"said to you
after you'd danced with the Prince."

"I was sitting there," Rosetta obeys, "when a dark distinguished
foreign-looking man leaned over me and said:

"'I hear you make a hit at the Gaiety. I'm sorry I can't see
you, but I leave tomorrow.'

"'Oh, I know who you are,' I said, 'you're the King of Spain.'

"'You know me?' And he seemed delighted. 'I want to meet
your sister,' he said."

"Yes," Vivian lamented, "and the Duke of Manchester had told
me in a whisper that I must be sure and make a little bob, which
is a curtsy, when I was presented to the King. But I was so scared
when he said, 'Miss Duncan, I want to present you to the King of
Spain,' that I said, 'How'd do, King?' and forgot to make a bob.
Five minutes later I remembered it and was bobbing all over the
place."

"Did you sing--this night?"

"At the request of the Prince," says Rosetta. "And what do
you think he asked for? 'Feather Your Nest.' And right there, as
everywhere else, he sat on the floor by the piano while we harmonized.
He's the sweetest boy over there. And shimmy!--you ought to see
the Prince of Wales shimmy. Vivian taught him how to do the Chi-
cago--you know that one."

"I'd taught it to one of his friends"--and Vivian names a nobleman whose title escapes me. "So the Prince asked me, fixing his
tie--he's always fixing his tie, he wears down three collars at every
dance--'Won't you teach me to do the Chicago?' and of course I did.
... I was awfully sorry he couldn't go with us for ham and eggs."

"He said he'd used up all his collars," Vivian laughs. "You
see, Lord Delmaney, the polo player, had said, 'You must all come
up to my place and have ham and eggs!'--at three in the morning.

And the King of Spain and several of us went; and everybody but
the King cooked or helped--he just supervised. He said to me so
drolly:

 "'Little would your American friends believe that at three
o'clock in the morning you are eating ham and eggs with a King.
The Americans,' he laughed, 'think that royalty is stiff.   They
don't know us. We like a good time. We're human.'"

 "Human? I should say!" says Rosetta. "At four o'clock that
morning the King of Spain was out on the street with the rest of
us, hunting for a taxi. When he said good-by to the Duke, 'Manchester, when you come to Madrid you must look me up,' he said.
And then I said, in the hoarse baby voice I use in our act:

 "'Well, King, when you come to America, just look me up'--
and they loved it."

 "He got into the common taxi with us, the King did," says
Vivian.

 "Yes," says funny Rosetta, "and little did that driver dream
he was driving a couple of Duncan Sisters and a King!"

> --Ashton Stevens in Actorviews,
> Chicago: Covici-McGee, 1923,
> pages 69-74.

*   *   *

The famous stars of Topsy and Eva whose engagement by
West Coast Theatres, Inc., at a fabulous salary is the sensation of
the coast, experienced their first picture house audience in Oakland.
Incidentally they got a thorough baptism the first two days, with
five performances Saturday and Sunday each.

They use three grand pianos Vivian does a little fingering on
the center one. A male accompanist handles one of the others,
flanked by a female ditto. The set is just drapes.

A couple of pop songs started, followed by some special numbers, one with Rosetta clowning with a rube chin piece that they ad
libbed for a pile of laughs. When fixed, Rosetta will probably have
this number one long howl. Her knack for cute stuff gets a chance
there.

Also funny is Rosetta's pantomimic opinion of her sister's ukulele
playing. Apparently Vivian is one of those mortals who can never
tell whether a uke is in tune or not. But it was impossible to tell
what was in the act and what just happened. Anyhow, the ukulele
gagging is good.

The sisters have a way of kidding between themselves under their breath, which, with them, is funny to the audience, although commonly audiences have no great relish for inside stuff that they're not in on.

Dressed in rompers as of yore, the girls made themselves right at home and found picture audiences enormously appreciative. The Duncans have class. Everything they do is surefire. The customers, figuratively hanging from the rafters, went for them hook, line and sinker.

The girls are going to be worth the money for West Coast. Bringing them into the picture house field was a smart move. They fit in the film houses like ketchup fits in a bottle.

The Duncans deserve the limit of topnotch rating.

--Variety, December 1, 1926, page 14.

*   *   *

A good time will be had by all if everybody agrees with me about the Duncan Sisters and their revived, rewritten, and vastly improved T. 'n' E. [Topsy and Eva, playing at the El Capitan Theatre, Los Angeles]. In case anybody wants to argue, let him be prepared to defend his position with assorted missiles at ten paces.

The score, by the Duncans of course, is almost entirely new, only the endeared "Rememb'ring," "Do-Re-Mi," and "I Never Had a Mammy" having been salvaged for the delectation of us old-timers. There are many tuneful new medlodies you'll be trying on your vocal chords. There are spirited dances and ingenious ensemble effects, devised and directed by Busby Berkeley. There's a stunning hoop skirt chorus, agile and engaging wenches in black face, an excellent orchestra under Harry James, the Rangers Sextette--and do those boys sing!

The Duncans themselves were never in better voice. Vivian is as pretty as ever and as appealing in her old-fashioned soubrette costumes, and Topsy has lost none of her infectious comedy and diablerie.

We saw it Sunday afternoon. The house was filled and the audience knew what hands are for in a theatre--and I don't mean groping. With nothing more potent under our belts than Pig 'n' Whistle cokes, we had the pleasantly exciting sensations, from the curtain's initial hist, of a metropolitan first night after a reasonable number of side cars.

The Duncans should be good for a record holiday run. Do your Christmas shopping early.

Simple justice demands the mention of everybody in the production, but since that hardly seems practical, I'll name those who
pleased our party especially: Vivian, Rosetta, and Vivian's baby,
who took a curtain call after the second act--a dollink who will doubtless take many more, with her inheritance of beauty, talent, and
fascination; Virgil Johansen, a first-rate singer of plantation melodies
and spirituals; Lucille De Wolfe; John Meehan, Jr.; Mary Frances
Taylor, première danseuse; Charles Bruins, Helen Wright, and the
Six Rangers who are Harry Furney, J. D. Jewkes, Lew Tetley, Em-
mett Casey, Rex Ricketts, and Jim Forstner.

The opening medley of negro melodies, "Moon Am Shining"
and "Just Give the Southland to Me," are the musical numbers we
list next to the Duncan girls' songs.

We suggest a change of title for "Two Little Arms," which
sounds too infantile, but the song itself is a hit, delightfully done
by Miss Wright, Mr. Bruins, and ensemble.

Anyway, we are quite mad about the whole thing and, contrary
to popular opinion, reviewers are never so happy as when they are
yessing.

> --Florence Hayden in Rob Wagner's
> Script, Vol. 6, No. 146, Novem-
> ber 28, 1931, page 12.

*   *   *

Some twenty years ago the Duncan Sisters, two local Los Angeles
gals, got up a little singing act called Topsy and Eva. They had
good voices and bright wit. Vivian was blonde and very Little Eva-
ish, and while Rosetta was prettier, she made a wonderful Topsy.
Up and up they went, climbing the Orpheum ladder of fame until
they became a theatrical institution. But always playing Topsy and
Eva. True, they wrote new songs and got up fresh gags, but the
act was the same.

Indeed, after making a million dollars (which the foolish kids
spent like new-rich movie stars, ultimately landing in bankruptcy)
they were afraid to change. But the skids ahead were plainly visible.

Ben Frank, sentimental as a schoolgirl when old friends are
involved, felt that the girls were too good to lose, so he decided to
haul them aboard the good ship Hotel Ambassador. But they'd have
to give up their black-face act and appear appropriately in soup
and fish! They were scared to death, but agreed to try.

Came their "preemeer" last week and you can imagine their
nervousness and embarrassment when in high heels and evening
gowns they stepped forth in the Cocoanut Grove. Not only were

they to make good in society, but they were to appear before the
Crowned Heads of Movieland. It was one of those moments--the End
of the Trail or the Beginning of a New Life.

To the delight of everybody, they went over with a bang!
The applause was tremendous and spontaneous. Ben Frank cried;
Johnny Brown, publicity, and another old L.A. boy who knew the
Duncan sisters when they were just starting out, grinningly burbled,
"I told you so." As for the sisters themselves, they were dissolved
in happy tears. "Our one ambition in life was to go over in the
Cocoanut Grove."

The reviewers have told about their new songs--gently naughty
but terribly funny. As far as this reporter is concerned, Topsy and
Eva are dead; long live Vivian and Rosetta! My only criticism of
their act is a rather too unctuous "See how I love my sister" cuddling.
A tie that can hold them together for twenty years is stronger than
syrup. The highest personal compliment I can pay these witty and
talented young ladies is that they kept me up--me with my peasant
habits!--until 12:30. Fortunately Ben Frank--also knowing my habits--
had asked us to spend the night, so we bogged down in luxurious
beds, pulled the blinds and to the surprise of the dicky birds, slept
until 8:00 A.M.

The new orchestra under the leadership of Al Lyons is delightfully soothing. No Jazz-mad crashings, but gentle harmony and the
most rhythmic dance music I've heard in years. Orchestras used to
be made up of dear old long-haired symphonic artists who knew the
classics and could play through the accepted grooves. But not in
these modern Cocoanut Groves. The present orchestras are made
up of alert young men, each of whom has mastered several instruments, many of them even singing.

Was also glad to see a fine acrobatic act. Having been something of a tumbler and hand-balancer myself, I know the difficulties
of such acts. And the long abstemious training. These boys are
wonderful.

With all the fun and carnival of the Cocoanut Grove, it is the
most charmingly restful dance hall in America. Ben Frank certainly
knows how to run a hotel.

                              --Rob Wagner in Rob Wagner's
                                Script, Vol. 14, No. 337, October
                                19, 1935, page 19.

                    *   *   *

Nostalgia, moist and enstrangling as the vapours of a steam-
bath, suffused the Music Box Theater [Los Angeles] the opening
night of the "renewal" of Topsy and Eva. Folk who had applauded

the mature Duncan Sisters when they originally essayed the roles
of children some decades ago at the debut of the musical, were present to exult in the return of the ladies to bum-freezer frocks, and
such of their contemporary confreres as Mae Murray and Clara Kim-
ball Young lent august, ante-bellum glitter to the come-back. From
the moment the sparse orchestra overturned a pastische of Duncan
tunes to the fall of the final curtain, applause, "bravos!" and similar
expressions of approval punctuated the proceedings; the repeated
hysterical ovations which greeted the slightest contribution of the
soeurs might well have convinced a casual stroller outside the edifice
that Madame Modjeska, Mrs. Siddons, Ellen Terry and the Divine
Sarah had all somehow miraculously managed to return to the local
boards.

The song and dance adaptation of the Stowe standard lacks
the wit and scintillance of Forman Brown's Uncle Tom's Hebb'n, and
this dramaturgical corpse only stirs into some semblance of life when
the Duncans, and such members of their company as Anne O'Neal,
Myrtle Ferguson, and the dancing feet of Cas Twid, are spotlighted.

The Duncans work valorously to turn back the entertainment
clock. It is quite possible that the show is only to be relished by
those who witnessed it in the long-ago, a titillation not vouchsafed
this reporter who was probably exploring the edifications of Hazel
Kirke and May Blossom at that period. For one viewing the curiosity for the first time, it is a bit difficult to reconcile the fourth-
rate production, incoherent book, and general aroma of dated stage-
craft, with the dogged enthusiasm the combination evoked.

The Duncans are survivors of vaudeville, a medium in which
vivacity was lauded over talent, and sheer exuberance replaced skill.
Like Eva Tanguay, who could neither sing, dance, act nor actively
participate in any of the acknowledged accomplishments of public
entertainment, Vivian and Rosetta, through protracted footlight experience, have cultivated stage presence. Despite fly-blown material,
they manage to make such moments as the music lesson an exercise
in personality, and Vivian's talents as a straight-woman cannot be
too highly lauded. Any damsel who can simulate the spontaneous and
convincing relish for the same dubious comedic devices over a period
approaching twenty years, possesses, in the opinion of this department, a faculty closely related to genius.

--Herb Sterne in Rob Wagner's
Script, Vol. 27, No. 641, November 7, 1942, pages 24-25.

• JIMMY DURANTE

The year was 1898. The nineteenth century was plucking at
the coverlet, preparing to leave us its legacy of horsehair sofas,

wax fruit under glass bells, anti-macassars, bronze statues of negro
boys strumming banjos, and gold-framed oleos. It was a noble time.
Even normal young men wore Hooverian collars, handlebar moustaches,
and peg-top trousers, and it was considered pretty snide to puff
on a Zira outside the livery-stable and swap drummers' yarns. Young
ladies' hats were marvels of fruit and bird life, and their owners
were esteemed only if they bulged in the strategic places. There
were only two kinds of girls--good girls and fly girls, but both had
to have sizeable balconies or the livery-stable contingent went right
on whittling.

It was in this golden age, among the voluptuous calendars of
his father's barber-shop on Catherine Street, New York City, that
Jimmy Durante was growing up. His experience in handling mugs,
porcelain and otherwise, came early. In between lathering customers
and plucking at his father's mandolin, Jimmy's nose was always buried
in a copy of the Police Gazette--no mean accomplishment even at
that date, for the famous schnozzle was already the pride of the lower
East Side. Having conquered (or rather subdued) the mandolin,
Jimmy's eye now fell on the family piano. His father suggested
casually that he take a few lessons from a teacher in the neighborhood.

"I don't want no middleman between me an' the piano," declaimed
James haughtily. From that day on there was no rest for the weary
in Catherine Street. Jimmy made up in energy what he lacked in
knowledge, and it wasn't long before his fame percolated to the ears
of the local alderman, Al Smith. Smith was in the habit of holding
informal Sunday afternoons at his flat, and soon Jimmy was massag-
ing the music-box for the approval of the fancy.

On Saturday nights Jimmy sprinkled his person with Florida
water, donned a striped gooseneck sweater, and journeyed down to
Coney Island, a far-flung amusement park in the Brooklyn sand-
dunes. A cubeb between his teeth, he patrolled what there was of
the Boardwalk and hung around the honky-tonks studying the technique of their pianists. His appealing nose attracted the attention
of one Diamond Tony, who gave him twenty-five dollars a week to
play at his establishment. Two dollars and a half of his first pay-
check bought him a gray derby with two ventilation holes on either
side, a badge of office and an emblem of maturity. With this on
his head and a schooner of light beer at his right hand, Jimmy was
ready for any and all requests. They ran from sentimental waltzes
like "After the Ball" to more red-blooded tunes like "Ace in the
Hole," "Stacker Lee," "Erie Canal," and "The Hop Song" with its
notable refrain "The key-rag was twisted and the pill was green."
In the café right next door to Diamond Tony's a ferverish youth
with a sallow complexion and popping black eyes was carving a niche
for himself with his pocket carver. Eddie Cantor was just another
entertainer, somebody who could sing loud enough to distract your
attention while your waiter shortchanged you.

The summer was over and sharp winds were beginning to whistle through the deserted pleasure pavilions. Jimmy returned to New York and the smoky warmth of the Chatham Club in Chinatown. The Chatham Club was pretty far downtown even for those days and its clientele was tough and sassy. You came there informally, in whatever clothes you had been paroled in. The management was lenient; it didn't care whether you were shaved as long as you didn't get yourself stilettoed on the premises. A platoon of singing waiters saw to it that the fun stayed clean, and there were numerous ways to quiet the objectionable client, among them the "hot seat" and the Mickey Finn. The former was a glass of boiling hot water thrown deftly upwards through the cane seat on which the client's derrière rested; the Mickey Finn, a mysterious potion of castor oil, jalap, and dynamite, is still in general use wherever people stay up late. As recently as the Parody Club, in which Clayton, Jackson and Durante gained their greatest Broadway fame, I have heard the mysterious commant "Ickeymay innfay" start the machinery which would quiet some high-spirited Dartmouth or Yale sophomore.

Coney Island's siren call sounded again the following summer and Jimmy resumed banging the box in the Auto Cafe, a cabaret on Oceanic Walk owned by a Mr. Kerry Walsh. This enterprising regisseur also hired Eddie Cantor to warble, hoof, and impersonate for the season. The tempo of this room is embalmed forever in one of Clayton, Jackson and Durante's best routines, the Cabaret bit which they used to do with the Greek washroom boy at the Parody and the Rendezvous. It was based on the principle that the customer was always right--but only as long as he could afford the seidlitz-powdered cider which passed for champagne.

It was in Harlem that fall that Jimmy Durante burgeoned into a band-leader. The tide of ragtime which had rolled out of the Barbary Coast swept Jimmy and his Collegians into the Alamo Club in 125th Street. It was an eight-year engagement for them. The Collegians were three; a banjo, cornet, and drum--mere froufrou to surround Jimmy's pulsating piano. For some time the proceedings were orderly, but finally Jimmy began to offer small ditties of his own. They were ancestors of the songs which were to make him famous-- "I'm Jimmy, The Well-Dressed Man", "I Can Do Without Broadway, But Can Broadway Do Without Me?", "Daniel", "So I Ups To Him," and thirty-four others. No matter what their reception from the patrons of the Alamo, there was one waiter who never failed to applaud till his palms were raw. This was Eddie Jackson, one-time singing waiter from Canarsie. Devotedly he followed Jimmy to Coney Island again during the summers and there, at the College Inn, the nucleus of a notable partnership was formed.

But it was not till one night the following winter when Lou Clayton walked into the Everglades Club on Forty-ninth Street that the team really flowered. Clayton and White had been big-time dancers for years; they had separated and Clayton had joined with Cliff Edwards for a time. Now, seeing Jimmy Durante and his Society Orchestra,

he was charmed. He watched Durante, Jackson, and still another
partner, Harry Harrin, sell their totally novel brand of insanity and
decided that this was his racket. He bought out Harrin for three
thousand dollars and Clayton, Jackson, and Durante (how they ever
figured out that billing is still a mystery) began to operate as a
unit.

The Club Durante was, in some respects, their peak. The
customers never asked for quarter and the trio gave none. With
Mademoiselle Fifi, the Shapely Hungarian, as their chief stooge, a
whirlwind melange of satire, burlesque, and parody rocked the club
from eleven till closing. The comedy was low and high, wide and
handsome. The bright aegis of the triumvirate was Jimmy's nose,
a nose which put to shame even Clayton's formidable beak. They
were doing turnaway business when a prohibition padlock appeared
suddenly on the door one night. The trade followed them to the
Dover Club. Business was even better there. One night Jimmy
Gleason wandered in; a few days later the boys received a large
gray wardrobe trunk outfitted with fifty-two unbelievable hats and
an armory of malacca canes with his compliments. Everything went
into the act except Gleason and he seemed to be on the verge of
buying out Clayton and Jackson for a time. But again the government padlock intervened, and this time they bobbed up at the Parody
Club, a bankrupt cafe on Forty-eighth Street just off Broadway.
The Parody owed its creditors seventy thousand dollars; eleven
months after the trio opened there it was showing a handsome profit.
They stayed there two years. The genuine admiration of their fellow-
comics on Broadway soon proved itself. People like Joe Cook and
Frisco could be seen there nightly limp with laughter. Durante's
admirers came from both Park Avenue and Tenth Avenue, from De-
lancy Street and Sutton Place. It was the finest roomful of bankers,
safeblowers, social tigers, columnists and petty pickpockets on Manhattan Island. New routines were born weekly; "The Shipwreck,"
"Perhaps," "Climbin' the Ladder," "The Book-Agent," "Annie Bohm,"
and countless others sprang to life in this crowded cellar.

In the next two years they appeared at the Silver Slipper, the
Rendezvous, Chez Les Ambassadeurs (Durante's pronunciation of
the club's name was alone worth the cover charge), and the Palace
Theatre. Vaudeville audiences took them to their hearts, and Ziegfeld gave them his accolade by installing them in Show Girl.

Two years ago Metro-Goldwyn-Mayer teamed Buster Keaton and
Jimmy Durante into an instantaneous success. His increasing fan mail
has left no doubt about Durante's value in pictures. His one concession to Hollywood is a lavish polo coat whose belt he knots instead
of buckling. "I tried to get a nosegay for the buttonhole but the
florist eyed me askrance," he confides sadly. But polo coat or no,
there is the same unruly straw-colored tuft on his forehead, the
same imperious look in the deepset eyes which flank that magnificent
nose. He is the same Jimmy Durante who, as Variety has lovingly

observed, "looks as though he came up out of the Bowery and forgot to remove the soup-stains from his vest." It is precisely that
soup-stained vest and that nose which have made Jimmy one of our
best comedians. Let the plastic surgeons go hang; one schnozzola
like that is worth fifty Barrymore profiles.

> --S. J. Perelman in Life, April
> 1933, pages 20-23.

• CLIFF EDWARDS

Cliff Edwards, who used to be the comedy end of the team,
Clayton and Edwards, is now appearing as a single with the assistance of Melville Morris at the piano. Edwards opens in blackface,
with his restless ukelele, and sings "Saturday" with all the motions.
He jumps quickly into his next number, "St. Louis Blues." This
has all the glorious jazz possible, and went over with a bang, in
spite of its being old. "Granny" is a good number, and Edwards
got the most out of it. His voice imitations of a clarinet is clever,
and he uses it in every number. Maybe it's personality, but, anyway, we didn't have half enough of Cliff, and when he jazzes we
just can't make out feet behave. A special word of praise is due
Melville Morris at the piano. He played the quietest but most effective jazz! It's a good act and sets 'em teasing for more.

> --"Conn" in Dramatic Mirror, No-
> vember 26, 1921, page 779.

• JULIAN ELTINGE

Eltinge is back in vaudeville with a new act for the twice daily,
but three-quarters of that shown by the wonderful impersonator of
girls in the Cohan & Harris Minstrels during the past season. The
other one-fourth is "The Incense Dance." It closes his act. In a
splendid setting, yellow predominating as the color, Eltinge executes
a dance while in feminine Oriental dress, that runs along the line of
the present (or passed) dancing craze. Eltinge does not employ a
"snake" or suggest a "Salome." It is the setting and himself as an
impersonator which place the effect above the others. As an impersonator of girls, or "the" impersonator of "the" girl, Eltinge excels.
He doesn't excel over anyone else for there is no one who can commence to approach him. His "girl" is an artistic study, from the
slippers to the coiffure. Eltinge is a good-looking fellow on the
street; well built and perhaps a little beyond the ordinary attractive
man to an impressionable young woman. As a girl on the stage any
man would rave over the genuine reproduction of Eltinge's impersonation. His "Brinkley Girl" is a dream; his "Bathing Girl" a gasp.
To those who know him, how he accomplishes these impersonations is
marvellous. Eltinge is as great an artist in his line as any artist is

or has been in any other. At the Plaza the audience liked him so
well he returned a neat impromptu speech appropriate to the occasion
(opening of the theatre with vaudeville). As to whether Eltinge
has improved in his technical finesse during the three of four years
since his first appearance in New York, that is merely a matter of
dresses or characters. As an impersonator of the girl he was great
then; he is great now.

> --Sime Silverman in Variety, April
> 24, 1909, page 12.

*   *   *

In presenting a new act or new characters in his creations of
female types, or more properly, perhaps, the presentation of female
types, Julian Eltinge has but to equal or excel the standards set by
himself in the past. This artist in female drawings, who has no
peer, is presenting two new characterizations at the American this
week, with four new songs, composing for vaudeville a "New Act."
In the first number, entitled "The Lady of Mystery," Eltinge wears
a magnificent black gown. It is draped from his right shoulder.
No woman could have worn the dress to more perfect advantage.
The song is one of Eltinge's soft melodies, up to any of his best.
In "Honeymoon in June Time" Eltinge is the simple girl in a blue
frock with black wig, thought a blonde one would have been more
becoming for the color. It is a pretty "Moon" song with a neat lyric
about the "Honeymoon." "The Days of Long Ago," in which Eltinge
wears again the colonial style becoming him so well, is a song in
melody and words closely resembling the gem in The Yankee Consul
("It Was Not Like That in the Olden Days"). For a finale "That
Spanish-American Rag" gave Eltinge scope for something entirely
new in the way of a dance following the song. He whirled around
the stage gracefully, swinging his arms in perfect rhythm and using
his hands to make one forget they are there. There is no one, man
or woman, who can as skilfully and gracefully employ hands and arms
as Mr. Eltinge. His popularity is at a point that whatever he attempts
is accepted without the littlest sign of disapproval in quantity of applause, and his artistic qualities are such that the artist in him does
not admit of the commencement of the word failure. From the strictly
commercial or the managers' standpoint, Eltinge is a "drawing card"
of the purest water--for Eltinge draws them all--from the gallery to
the boxes. His value is unknown to himself, but it is the common
talk that on the Morris Circuit this season there has been no "card"
(not excepting Harry Lauder) who drew the "class" into the theatres
that Mr. Eltinge has. When vaudeville possesses an artist of this
young man's calibre, he is entitled to receive all the credit due him.
That he was one riot at the American Monday evening, and that he
walked away with the hit of the show are both substantial facts.
That he closed the first half, holding the house intact from the intermission applause, they not ceasing to applaud until a speech was

forthcoming, are two more facts, both attesting to as great a performer as there stands on the stage today.

--Sime Silverman in Variety, April
23, 1910, page 12.

* * *

The first noticeable thing about Julian Eltinge is his appearance. For years he has stood out in the vaudeville "Who's Who"
as the peer of female impersonators principally because of his stunning appearance in feminine clothes and secondly because of his ability,
his voice and all the other essentials that make up the perfect man-
woman. Eltinge has been lost to vaudeville for some years, but his
return to the Palace as headliner this week showed that his following
is still intact and its enthusiasm still as strong as ever. His number
"I'm a Siren" was apparently the best liked number in his repertoire.
It tells of the woman who has learned by experience rather than that
of the youthful entrancer. His characterization of an Irish colleen
who is in the throes of a love affair brings out one of the best efforts of Eltinge's long vaudeville career. His dance, following an
Oriental number, earned him an encore and a speech. Eltinge stands
out in the vaudeville field as the peer of his class, the manliest man
off-stage and the girliest girl on-stage, an artist who can never
even be imitated. It's to be hoped that Eltinge will remain in vaudeville for a long, long time.

--Johnny O'Connor in Dramatic
Mirror, August 16, 1921, page
663.

● LEON ERROL

Leon Errol, of many musical shows, revealed at once with
settings at the Palace [Chicago] last week that he proposed to do
substantially the bedroom scene in which he worked in Hitchy Koo,
the one in which he smashed the three plaster of Paris statues and
rolled himself into bed after much comedy manipulation of the covers
and pillow. Jed Prouty, as a butler, worked the straight, and did
it with dignity and poise. Errol rolled in as "drunk" as ever, dressed
in an overfitting brown afternoon suit, a hat too big and huge comedy
shoes. He clowned through his accustomed backward walks, tipsy
bends and amusing falls, and in three minutes had the house wiping
its eyes with laughter. The act sagged a little after that, when he
attempted too much dialog, though the quips were good and at no
time was there less than corking entertainment. When he got to
ruining the crockery and pulverizing the statues the laughs were
so loud that the crashes could hardly be heard. He then went to
the pillow-and-blanket business amidst howls and landed in bed for

the curtain. Errol is easily a headliner anywhere, and, should he
desire to devote himself to vaudeville, need seek no further for a
full career in recognition or cash. There is no stronger comedy act
to be found.

> --[Jack] "Lait" in Variety, Octo-
> ber 11, 1918, page 16.

*   *   *

Mr. Errol is appearing in a sketch, "The Guest," in which
Jed Prouty is his only assistant. The author of the skit isn't mentioned but his name is really quite unnecessary because it it Errol's
laughable semblance of comic intoxication that puts the turn over.
The lines and idea are nothing. Errol merely is shown into a guest
room, has some amusing repartee and byplay with the butler and
smashes up some valuable statuary despite his blundering efforts to
save it. There is no one quite as amusing as Errol in this limited
type of comedy. "The Guest" needs trimming to prevent it becoming tiresome, for the laughs grow scattered towards the end.

> --Frederick James Smith in Dra-
> matic Mirror, January 11, 1919,
> page 58.

● FRANK FAY

Frank Fay who has been sojourning in musical comedy has given
that three-hour marathon the cold shoulder for a little prance in
twenty minute briefs of the two-a-day. His variety work has struck
a truer note. Fortunately, too, the padding of musical comedy has
not destroyed his artistic use of the blue pencil. Hardly a line or
gesture is not full of applause or laugh vitality. Hence every second
being so utilized his act is packed like sardines with meaty entertainment. His songs "Oh Bring Back Those Wonderful Days" and "The
Musical Comedy Ball" spoke success in abundant applause.

Fay is headed straight toward a headline position. And when
he gets there he'll be a drawing card too.

> --"Higgins" in Dramatic Mirror,
> March 8, 1919, page 346.

● W. C. FIELDS

Fresh from his American, Australian, and South African triumphs, W. C. Fields, the juggler and billiardist, is now back at the
London Hippodrome. When in 1902 he appeared at Mr. Moss's Palace
of amusing and interesting sights, he was pronounced not merely

the quintessence of originality, but a fellow with an infinite zest--
one who could make and see a joke when others were searching for
it, and its solution. Now the Philadelphia comique has come again
among us, and the good opinion he then won is not only maintained
but strengthened, for his new billiard absurdity, in which he pockets
no less than fifteen balls in one stroke, is one of those extremely
clever things which would alone make the reputation of any juggler.
His three chief moves on the green cloth are a trio of triumphs, and
those interested in the art made famous by Roberts, Peall, and others,
must make a point of seeing Fields "play the game." The fantastic
way he handles his cue, the smart manner in which he pockets the
balls, and his little bits of humour intervening all the while, make
his turn the most lively and interesting juggling entertainment before
the public.

The spirit of comedy lurks behind Mr. Fields, and by sheer
force of wit the mischievous imp causes us to laugh when perhaps
otherwise we should be serious, but mind you, the introduction of
the lighter element does not by any means detract the mind from the
juggler's more legitimate work, for the hand of skill is always there
to remind us that balancing is still the finest of fine arts. Since
he last visit to this country, the mirth-chasing juggler has been to
Boston, and from thence straight across to 'Frisco, playing the big
vaudeville houses under the government of the Keith and the Orpheum
Trusts.

After a delightful pleasure trip, Mr. Fields and his pretty
young wife, passing through some of Nature's most wonderful scenery,
arrived in Australia, where for six months he was a star feature at
the Harry Rickard's amusement establishments in Melbourne, Sydney,
and Adelaide, and he proved one of the biggest star features the
Australian importer had taken over, pleasing, because he, as he always does, thoroughly entertained them.

He spent three consecutive months under the Hyman banner
in Johannesburg and Capetown, making good artistically and financially.
The American juggler appeared before Lord Milner, who much enjoyed
the quaint billiard match. Traveling from South Africa to London
Mr. Fields immediately upon arriving opened at the Hippodrome,
where for some weeks past he has been achieving the success only
associated with those who instruct and amuse, for audiences visiting
Mr. Moss's circus and vaudeville house expect something more than
the every day juggling exhibition, and in the turn of Fields they
find the very latest ideas brought into prominent action.

Throughout his travels, from 'Frisco to Africa, Mr. Fields says
he has never encountered such a truly regal establishment as London's
Hippodrome. The Paris Opera House, declares Mr. Fields, is its
only rival, but then, he adds, one does not juggle in an Opera house.
On the conclusion of his run in London, W. C. Fields is to traverse
the Moss provincial Empires, and altogether hopes to spend quite a

year, if not more, with us, and forsooth, the freshness of his humour
will hold us for every extra month he cares to put in with John Bull.
Concerning the billiard table, upon which he plays his "matchless
match," it may be said that it is of American manufacture, being
built in Chicago by the eminent firm of Messrs. Brunswick, Balke,
Callender and Company, Mr. Fields personally superintending its
making from designs he prepared.

He is a twentieth century man, devotes himself entirely to his
work, and is satisfied to live on the earth without wanting to own
it.

--London Hippodrome program,
April 1904, page 10.

*   *   *

W. C. Fields, who recently returned from a successful tour
of the English and Continental music halls, is again making vaudeville audiences laugh in this country.

Mr. Fields does all kinds of things with all kinds of articles.
What he can't do with billiard balls and billiard cues; with hats and
cigars and other articles is scarcely worth doing. He is the only
man in the world to-day who plays billiards on an indiarubber table
with indiarubber billiard balls (we hope that's right, although Mr.
Fields refuses to say whether it is or not); and the way he makes
the balls carom around the table and land in his capacious hip pocket
is an amazing revelation in the gentle art of billiards.

Mr. Fields' comedy is quaint, unforced and quite unique. No
wonder managers pay him a big salary for making their patrons laugh.
He does that all right, and some more besides.

--New York Star, Vol. I, No. 12,
December 19, 1908, page 8.

*   *   *

W. C. Fields is devoting what amounts to a sabbatical leave
from revues and films in vaudeville, bringing with him two of the
better-known skits from the repertory with which he has long been
identified. No matter what else the literary highbrows might eventually discover (or probably have already perceived) in the burly
comedian with a wisp of a mustache, Fields is a low comedian. But
years and years of estrangement from vaudeville, where he might
have been if vaudeville encouraged talent as it should, have rendered
him rather ill at ease in technic for the field to which he now returns.
But surely not to remain for long when bidding for low funsters is
far too swift for the elephantine pace of slothful vaude-film circuits.

Because he does two and not one skit, Fields has to be distributed over two spots. The Palace booker solved this problem
neatly by causing the Stolen Bonds piece to close the first half and
Golfing to open intermission. At the Palace this week Fieldsian comedy
is the meat between two slices of fairly good entertainment in a sand-
wich of big-time vaudeville.

Low as the Fields brand of comedy is, it is not intended so
far as we can see for the consumption of cheap audiences. Fields
is almost a sure bet for a high-priced revue, yet it is not inconceiv-
able that he would flop badly in an outlying family house. To appreciate his mechanized humor one must think along with him; not
too much, but with more intellectual effort and a finer sense of the
ludicrous than is required of the average vaudeville patron. Maybe
that's why Fields made the grade all right but never threatened to
knock them dead at the Palace.

In Stolen Bonds Fields uses his recurring punch line, "'Tain't
no fit night for man nor beast," only as a Fields can use it. This,
whether the average audience views it as such or not, is a study in
calloused emotions. There is better character portrayal here than in
some acts of a Shakespearean play. But its entertainment value is
an unknown quantity. One thing we can state definitely; it'll either
hit home or fall before going over the foots. There's no middle course
for an act like this in the families.

The Golfing item is more slapstick and carries considerably
less of the quaint and sometimes subtle humor of Stolen Bonds. He
works here with a pair of fems and a caddie. His efforts to make
a drive are frustrated by countless obstacles, human and mechanical.
There's the caddie with his chirping birdie, something that might
well be fly paper and other distractions that are as impossible as
they are laughable. He got laughs galore with this one, and he was
looking for nothing else but. For the Palace Fields is okeh for a
briefly timed repeat; in other houses they'd be taking chances. Maybe he won't play in them on his own volition anyway.

--Elias E. Sugerman in The Billboard, April 5, 1930, page 14.

• FINK'S MULES

An animal act with an unridable mule, several plants (including
a negro), trained ponies, dogs, and for an added comedy attraction,
a couple of monkeys. Monkeys have not been employed in previous
acts of this description, of which there have been several, with
Cliff Berzac's the first. Fink's resembles Berzac's even more closely
through a revolving table and a colored boy "riding" it. In a circus
setting the Fink turn runs swiftly for 10 minutes, the comedy causes
laughs and the monkeys are of new and novel assistance in the laughing

department. Opening the Palace show at 8:05, with a light house
at that hour, the turn got over strongly. The trainer is middle
aged, the setting and apparatus are bright looking, also clean, with
the animals the same, and the act may be counted upon as a comedy
number in any program.

--Sime [Silverman] in Variety,
April 19, 1918, page 17.

• HARRY FOX

    As a light comedy entertainer Harry Fox has few, if any,
equals. His present vehicle, wholly constructed of light comedy,
is by far the best he has ever given vaudeville, consequently one
must practically consider Harry Fox of today one of vaudeville's
best light comedy acts. He is all that--and then some. Fox shouldered
a heavy burden at the Riverside Monday evening, following a string
of singing specialties which really read and played as one of the
best singing bills ever staged around here. Coming on in next to
closing position for a 25-minute period it looked a bit dubious at
first, but the distinctive personality which has always predominated
in the work of Fox soon thawed the chill and once in his stride, the
result was never in doubt. In this turn he has some rather unique
and original comedy "bits," one introducing five stage hands who
continually interrupt proceedings to wish him success. And Fox
carries in Lew Pollock a capable foil for his cross-fire patter and,
incidentally, an accomplished accompanist. Pollock soloed successfully and in musically aiding the rendition of Fox's vocal repertoire,
he was excellent throughout. The routine begins with the usual
introductory talk wherein the stage hands have their fling. Then
follows a number probably titled "My Dear Old Dad Wanted Me To
Learn a Trade." It's a typical Fox style of lyric and gave him a
bounding start. Then a rather quaint ditty called "An Old Horse
That Knows His Way Home" with "Mason-Dixon Line," "Meet Me at
the Station" and "We're going To Take the Sword Away from William." A piano solo interrupts the song routine, well timed and equally well arranged. It's a medley. After hearing "Mason-Dixon Line"
innumerable times it sounded like a new song as Fox handled it.
This alone cinched the hit he scored. During the action he also
eked a score of healthy laughs from a comedy recitation in which
Pollock aided nicely. Mr. Fox wears a brown business suit throughout, looks natty and carries himself as well as ever. He had little
trouble in gathering the program hit at the up-town house, earning
several genuine bows at the finale. It's a corking act for any bill
and a great vehicle for the headlining honors which Fox now owns
and deserves.

--"Wynn" in Variety, November
9, 1917, page 20.

- EDDIE FOY

In his annual spring trip to the vaudevilles Eddie Foy, lately of <u>The Earl and the Girl</u>, has chosen an idea which in its simplicity causes loud and prolonged laughter. It is unlikely that another comedian could have succeeded with it. It may best be described as a travesty upon the quick change act of Henry Lee. Mr. Foy has a similar stage setting, and gives burlesque impersonations of the Japanese Mikado, Admiral Togo, Russian Czar, President Roosevelt, John D. Rockefeller, and also of Elsie Janis' imitation of himself singing "I'm Unlucky." The character of President Roosevelt is far from being a burlesque, however, in the truthful representation Foy gives. A topical verse is devoted to each change, and for the final encore caused by the Elsie Janis number Foy does a song and dance. The applause following this finally obliged a speech of regret on Monday night. A musical conductor is carried bearing a striking resemblance to the theatre's [the Colonial] regular leader. Foy scored an unqualified hit. He has one of the funniest acts in vaudeville at the present time.

--Sime Silverman in <u>Variety</u>, May
19, 1906, page 6.

- IRENE FRANKLIN

"Original and Exclusive Character Songs" is the billing for original and distinctive Irene Franklin. Miss Franklin is presenting practically a new act this season, returning for her first New York appearance in it to Hammerstein's, where she is the hit of the bill this week without a shadow of a doubt. The singer proves two things conclusively by her reappearance. That her success last season, the first to bring her into the headline limelight, was not accidental or temporary, and that for singing character songs of comic texture, she stands second to none, with all due respect to any and all American or English comediennes. There may be English singers who are more popular in their native land than Miss Franklin can become, but it is asserted that no Englishwoman has been better liked in her songs in America than Irene Franklin would be in England with "Red Head, Red Head, Gingerbread Head" and "Expression." Could the English understand the lyrics of "The Talkative Waitress" that would be included. The "Red Head" number is new, a unique conception in theme and make-up, Miss Franklin appearing as a rough and ready little red-headed girl who tells the names other children call her. It is a work of art in character study, and Miss Franklin's delivery of the selection could not be improved upon. "Expression" is from last year's repertoire, a part of Miss Franklin's stage entertainment now. "The Talkative Waitress," while not entirely strange to New York, is a fine bit of slangy composition given in a "patter" fashion. In the costume for this, a waitress dress, the singer travesties the present lace collar craze; also the extravagent coiffures

women now wear. "Somebody Ought To Put the Old Man Wise" opened
the act, the title explaining the lyric, which was liked. "Grandmother's
Lullaby," with a "Umpty and Dumpty" song, also in the list, might
be dropped. Neither is strong enough for the others. "Expression" should be the second song, with "Red Head" and "Waitress"
further down and closer together. Burt Green filled in the time for
Miss Franklin's costume changes very agreeably upon the piano, taking for his serious effort Liszt's "Second Hungarian Rhapsody," the
execution of which brought a strong round of applause. The other
piano movements were of the lighter nature, Miss Franklin not re-
quiring an extraordinary time for changing, the first being made in
24 seconds. Among the pretty dresses worn by her is a handsome
Directoire cloth of silver gown. Irene Franklin won in competition
the title of "The Queen of Vaudeville." She writes the words of
most of her songs; sings them even better than they are written.
The title will remain with her in view of these circumstances for some
time yet.

> --Sime Silverman in Variety, Oc-
> tober 10, 1908, page 12.

                    *   *   *

Irene Franklin was the timely headliner for the opening of
the New Brighton Theater. Miss Franklin, be it noted, is quite as
invigorating as a breeze from the sea.

And she brought some new songs. One, "At thé Dansant,"
depicts the domestic complications engulfed in the maelstrom of thé
dansant. There's the slender debutante, who comes with a youth
of patent leather hair, in quest of her giddy dance-mad mother,
and the tired business man who discusses the furnace and the ice-
man with his wife between dips. It has plenty of comic possibilities,
which will work out as the number mellows.

The other new number--brisk and humorous--is, "If I Don't
Lock My Family Up, It's the Old Maids' Home for Mine," the plaint
of the long suffering Angeline, whose best efforts to acquire a husband are frustrated by bad family team work.

Miss Franklin is still doing her quaint little kiddie song, "I'm
Nobody's Baby Now," and the delicious feminist satire, "The Woman
Policeman." And Mr. Green contributes sympathetic accompaniment
and an excellent piano interlude.

We went all the way to Brighton to watch Miss Franklin--and
we'd go a good deal further to enjoy her splendid art. She's the sincer-
est artiste--in methods and actual personality--in all the stage world.

> --Frederick James Smith in The
> New York Dramatic Mirror, May
> 26, 1915, page 17.

I'll lay a wager of a Scotch-laden Mauretania to a thimbleful
of Chocker-Chola that when Irene Franklin was born there was a
buzz-saw, an electric fan, a thousand horse-power dynamo and a
block of radium working overtime in the room.

Wow! I interviewed the dynamic, electric, never-sleeping,
charming, creative, brilliant, nimble, effervescent, elastic, humorous,
unmuzzled and logocratic Irene, doing a shimmy on her heels from
stage to smoking-room, to dressing-room, to auditorium, to manager's
office--finally getting her last words while standing on the running
board of her highpower machine as it shot away from the Greenwich
Village Theater toward Mount Vernon, where Irene, known in private
life (fancy Irene Franklin having a private life, Hedda!) as Mrs.
Burton Green, lives en famille with hubby and two little female song-
birds.

I lost my hat and cane and aplomb in the adventure, all of
which I have charged up to Barney Gallant, maestro de ballet of
the Greenwich Village Inn, part owner and composer of The Beggar's
opera, the Burbank who makes two theaters grow where only one
saloon grew before, investigator and historian of the Great European
Beer Routes and American press agent for the Boul' Mich'.

The scene (there must be a locale in every interview) was
the Greenwich Village Theater on a blistery autumn afternoon between lunch-time and the hip-pocket aperitif hour. Wading thru
trunks, lingerie, Oliver Herford and a bevy of double-exposures,
I floundered onto the stage as a Follies girl leaped over my head
with one hand, as we boys used to do over fire-plugs in Philadelphia and Wilmington.

I could not see the little reddish blonde singer, Irene Franklin,
who has amused millions (always say millions) of Americans with her
songs and fun.

"Where is Miss Franklin?" I shouted from the stage to Oliver
Herford, who sat in the auditorium superintending the enunciation
and prosody of his verses that a young man was rolling off to the
sweetest chicken that ever caused a riot in the barnyards around
Forty-second Street.

Glacial stare from the Herfordian monocle. A la capella smash
of notes from the piano player. Blantant crash of cymbals.

Seized by the Arrow collar by Barney (newly shaved) I was
trunked to the lobby of the theater, where a quiet little woman sat
on an empty box of near-beer singing a song.

It was Irene the Iridescent.

"I talk, but I am never interviewed," said the comedienne.
"Did you ever hear of Lorna the Bootlegger? She's the only woman

bootlegger in the country on which the moonshine never sets. I'm
just back from California, which is a suburb of Hollywood, and I
discovered Lorna in--no, I won't tell you the town; we women must
hang together. But it was somewhere between Albuquerque and
Yonkers, so you've got a long-shot guess.

"Well, I blew into that certain town one night about two weeks
ago. Tired, frazzled, dry. Went to my room in the Ritz of the
town--Ritz without the hotel. I was reading, by the light of a half-
burner, Weininger's book on Sex and Character, having exhausted
all the automobile ads in The Saturday Evening Post, when someone
came lightly tapping on the busted panel of my chamber-door. I
picked up a gun and a Bible and opened.

"I was confronted by the bluest-eyed, sweetest looking young
thing that I have ever seen outside of a cradle in a Chautauqua home.

"'Miss Franklin, you are an actress, and I am Lorna the Bootlegger. Here is my price-list. Delivery in half an hour,' pratted
the darling.

"After recovering my sang-froid at such an apparition with
such a name, I ordered a Hollywood Shandygaff (if you don't know
what it is, you do not know the bright particular jewel in the head
of the prohibition toad) and fell into a ten o'clock reverie on what's-
the country-coming-to. Lorna the Bootlegger, to me, was a portent.

"Thruout the country wherever I have traveled in the last
two years I have noticed the terrible effects of prohibition and blue
laws on the conduct of young girls. They are not immoral; they
have simply become unmoral. The young woman of today has no
moral sense. I am bringing up my own two daughters in fear and
trembling. Will they have a moral sense?--you know that's entirely
different from being immoral. To be immoral is a delightful experience, but to be unmoral means that we can never experience the
pleasure that comes from being immoral."

As Miss Franklin let fly, this little bit of Nietzschean (or Eva
Tanguay) philosophy, a scrubwoman emptied a bucket of water on
our toes, and we fled to the smoking-room underneath the theater,
where Miss Franklin curled herself up on a lounge, and in the glim-
mer of a soft incarnadine light proceeded with her verbal callisthenics.

"Now I know you are going to ask me whether the pleasure of
being a mother interferes with the business of acting, or whether
the business of being a mother affects adversely the pleasure of
being an actress.

"I play at everything. Life is a form of sport. I lead a double
life. If you saw me at home rehearsing, teaching my girls how to
grow up in the funniest of all funny worlds, making home-brew,

superintending the cooking, and studying Freud and Flaubert, and
could hear me at night lining out my famous (please say famous)
songs, you'd say, 'That's the most extraordinary little woman since
Semiramis--no, I mean Joan of Arc.'"

"I'll say so!" I butted in breathlessly. "I think--"

"Of course, I know what you think," whizzed away Miss Irene,
with a merry gurgle in her eye. "Every woman knows what every
man thinks. I've got a husband--you're all alike."

My ego cuddled up in my pineal gland.

"You were thinking," she sizzled, "'When in the Name of Nox
does she sleep?' Well, I haven't had four hours' sleep a night since
Morpheus knows when. I have a great big reading-table next to
my bed, and after putting the old man and the babies to bed (that's
when I'm not on the road, of course), I read bits of all kinds of
books and magazines 'till I fall asleep. Up with the birds. Women
sleep too much. So do men. I believe in the strenous life--it is
perpetual youth. I utilize every moment of my time. I study and
write my songs in automobiles, Pullmans, street cars, and between
performances.

"I was born working, you know. At the goo-goo age of six
months I was carried in the arms of my nurse thru a paper snow-
storm in James A. Herne's Hearts of Oak. I was a redtop then,
much redder than I am now. Maybe I'm going blue-y with the rest
of the country. I can recall the uproarious applause at my debut.
I sat up in my cradle the next morning and read what the Percy
Hammonds and Alex Woolcotts said about my wonderful bawling.

"At the age of four I went over to the legitimate after two
years in vaudeville. I played in The Celebrated Case, The Banker's
Daughter, and Bobby Crockett in Davy Crockett. The mashers--
from six to eight years of age--impeded my way to the old hack after
each performance. It was at that age that I first used the classic
expletive, 'My Gawd!'"

"And Miss Franklin--" I interlarded.

"Then you know my career with Tony Pastor, of course. That's
where I met Mr. Green, who writes the music for my songs and is
incidentally my husband.

"'Kid,' says he, 'let me see to it that our graves will be kept
Green.'

"'You're on, Burt,' says I. And we've lived happily ever
after, both having a joint income tax.

"Why don't you write an article some time about the ravages
of temperament among managers? Some of them go on as tho they
had real brains, altho John Murray Anderson is a perfect delight.

"If you are collecting mottoes, here is one of my own, 'Dont
have a wishbone where your backbone ought to be.' Maybe you've
heard me sing that?"

I had. I was then on the running-board of the automobile,
as chronicled erst.

Anyhow, here was a personality off the stage as breezy, as
alive and as witty as you all know she is on the stage.

> --Benjamin de Casseres in Shadow-
> land, Vol. 5, No. 4, December
> 1921, pages 33 and 77.

• TRIXIE FRIGANZA

Miss Friganza calls her new act "At a Block Party." Jean
Havez is the author. The repartee and songs hinge upon the amusing events at a typical city block party. The material went strongly,
the Palace Monday matinee audience particularly liking Miss Friganza's
recitation about a crippled war dog, her clever comedy song about
the final farewell meeting of all the old war songs, and her "Garbage
Man's Romance." Miss Friganza defines her new automobile as a 1919
cootie and finds time to sing of the shimmy dance, as well. We doubt
if we ever saw Miss Friganza go better than at her opening Palace
showing this week. It's a vigorous comedy act.

> --Frederick James Smith in Dra-
> matic Mirror, February 8, 1919,
> page 202.

• LOIE FULLER

The long heralded dance production by Loie Fuller, in which
she is supported by eight young girls, had its first metropolitan
vaudeville showings at the Fifth Avenue last week. Except for the
fact that it gives the noted dancer an opportunity to stand in the
centre of a group of others who do most of the work, there is little
difference between this latest "classical dance" and those which have
won Miss Fuller so much fame in the past. And we do not say this
disparagingly to her or her supporters. The offering is artistic,
the girls dance nimbly, gracefully, and as if they loved their art.
The light effects could have been improved upon, but a Monday matinee is not a fair performance to judge by. The music is praise-
worthy and the conceptions of each dance number reflect credit upon

their originator. The act is divided into three parts, with sub-
divisions in the dances of each. The girls include Dickie Fuller,
Dorothy Harkis, Leoni Bruno, Donna Durne, Shelagh Courtney,
Sybil Maitland, May Woodward and Edythe Carl. The offering ran a
bit too long--twenty-eight minutes. There is one criticism that might
be taken seriously or not, according to viewpoint. Is it necessary,
for art's sake, to make young girls appear without fleshings and in
bare feet, with naught to shield their forms save a few folds of
filmy gauze?

--The New York Dramatic Mirror,
March 5, 1910, page 21.

• GROCK

Grock, the musical clown, is at the Palace this week. He's
also at the Riverside. For the double engagement he is reported
receiving $3,000. Grock must be more than a clown to receive that
much money from American theaters; he's a business man beyond all
doubt, and when he goes back to the other side with the biggest
part of his earnings here he will no doubt laugh longer and harder
than any one did at the Palace Monday afternoon. Grock is funny,
but he is not the "funniest clown in the world." In fact, he's a
much overrated entertainer, but by being new and having prestige
that clowns do not get here overnight, no matter how hard they try
or how they are billed by the biggest circuses in the world, Grock
bravely and gamely faces a test that benefits him more financially
than anything else.

Grock is a hard worker, but some of his "bits," gestures and
tricks in trade are motheaten and ancient when one starts comparison
with other entertainers. There are sections of his turn that stood
the acid test, but others will make some of our poorly paid burlesque
comedians groan inwardly every time they think of that $3,000 kitty.
Grock owes much to Walter J. Kingsley and we hope when the boat
carries Mr. Grock, Mr. Reece (Grock's manager) and the well stocked
money chest back to the Bank of England, that Walter is handsomely
remembered.

Grock is a busy individual, with loose-fitting baggy clothes,
a bald wig of grotesque cut and a pair of shoes of tugboat size,
who mugs and clowns one minute and plays musical instruments the
next. First a tiny fiddle--probably the smallest violin in captivity--
is used. Then comes a piano with "bits" employed here and there
to help along his style. The closing period is devoted to the concertina. Grock apparently follows a routine that he has followed
for years, doing some of it mechanically and making sure there is
no deviation from the line of stage work. At times he is painfully
and provokingly slow in working up his "bits." The first quick
laughing intake Monday afternoon came from his slide down the piano

board-cover that he had removed and had tilted against the side of
the instrument. Another instantaneous response was with the facial
contortion of the mouth and jaw. Not since the days of Billy Ker-
sands (colored), who used to place a glass tumbler inside his mouth
have we seen such an elastichinged jaw. Grock has some funny "bits,"
but he is not the greatest, nor the funniest, nor the cleverest clown
in the world by a long shot. At $3,000 per he may become the
richest, but shades of George Adams, we wonder what the chalk-
faced circus comics must think who work all summer for less than
one hundred simoleons. P. T. Barnum was right.

> --"Mark" in Dramatic Mirror, Jan-
> uary 8, 1920, page 21.

● YVETTE GUILBERT

Mme. Guilbert, by easy stages, has reached vaudeville again,
making her appearance at the Twenty-third street house. On Monday
her songs roused the ire of the gallery, being in French. After
that she sang alternately in French and English, distributing translations of the former, and on Tuesday afternoon the only complaint
was that she would not respond to an encore with a fifth song.
There was genuine applause and a genuine hit. Mme. Guilbert is
vastly different from the black gloved motionless woman whose up-
lifted eyebrow was an extravagance of gesture and whose songs were
for the better (or worse) part surcharged with suggestion. In her
present work she employs to advantage a wonderfully mobile face
and her every gesture is pregnant with meaning. She selected old
time songs of French and English ancestry and those who were unable to follow the French songs were at least able to appreciate the
wealth of expression, the flexibility of her voice and the vivacity of
her manner. She gains greatly in personal charm in her present work
and while still the artist she was when she first came to us, her
simpler selections are far better appreciated. Her rendition of "Mary
Was a Housemaid" was a revelation, and it was this in large measure
that was responsible for the generous applause. All four of her
selections had rollicking airs that made the modern day machine made
music seem stale and profitless. It is to be hoped that her stay in
vaudeville will be an extended one. It is also to be hoped that she
will enlarge her English repertoire.

> --"Chicot" [Epes W. Sargent] in
> Variety, April 28, 1906, page 6.

                    *   *   *

Yvette Guilbert made her first American reappearance at the
Colonial last week, after an absence of some years. The charming
artist was warmly greeted on Thursday night, although on her opening performance it was reported that many of those who graced the

occasion with their presence did not apparently have enough of gray
matter beneath their hirsutical roofs to convolute in accord with the
working of the artist herself, or those who could appreciate her.
Madame Guilbert is the same delightful, quaintly artistic singing actress that she was so few--we won't say many--years ago when she
first began to delight American theatregoers. There is a demureness,
a certain delicate and underlying humor, and a power of facial expression that makes Madame Guilbert's work most delightful. And
then her power of suggestion by the lifting of an eyebrow, the shrug
of a shoulder or the wave of a hand; it is the art of the pantomimist
combined with the art of the singer. The oddly voluminous hoop
skirt of the period when our mothers were maids lends an added
charm to Guilbert, while her beautiful shoulders and neck, with the
ringlets of hair which makes a sort of frame to her face, gives an
appearance never to be forgotten. "The Key to Heaven" was the
first song, it being a number that hardly another singer could render
and please therewith. Then came a French song, an old English
song, following "Mary Was a House Maid," which was encored and
responded to with another old English song. The Mirror takes this
opportunity to thank Percy G. Williams for again bringing Madame
Guilbert to American shores.

--The New York Dramatic Mirror,
October 23, 1909, page 19.

• TEXAS GUINAN

At the Fifth Avenue Theatre last week Texas Guinan presented
her latest vaudeville offering and scored a genuine success. Her
presentation is novel in many ways and, although it might be improved
upon scenically, it pleased the audience on Tuesday afternoon. She
makes her first appearance in a suspended basket, which is slowly
drawn across the stage in one. Her song during this part was "To
the End of the World with You." Following this she appears in a
sort of conservatory and warbles "Pansies." This is followed by her
reappearance in one, when "Shine on Harvest Moon" is rendered, with
a small negro boy joining in the chorus from an opening made by
the stage moon in the sky drop. Miss Guinan has a sweet voice,
which she used well, with the exception of not articulating distinctly.
Her gown, of a Directoire cut and of golden hue, is exquisite and
calls for pleasurable mention. The airship referred to looks artifical
and the lighting effects in the second part could be improved upon,
otherwise Miss Guinan's offering will always be welcome in the best
houses. Jack Mason staged the act.

--The New York Dramatic Mirror,
June 5, 1909, page 13.

● NAN HALPERIN

Miss Halperin's new song cycle presents the epochal periods in
a girl's life, from pinafores to beaux. In her opening number, in
which she is adorned with pigtails and a calico dress, with a nursery
environment, she deplores the arrival of another baby in the family,
as this deposes her from the position of special favor accorded the
youngest one. A recitative as a normal school girl follows, whereupon we see her in a debutante's reverie after the ball, the theme
of which is "why must I have so many clothes to capture just one
man." This is a dramatic satire effectively done, and presents Miss
Halperin at her best.

A "goodnight" number on the eve of her wedding day follows,
in which she disposes of photographic and epistolary reminders of her
romances and is wooed by dreams among the lace-and-lavender pillows
of her bed. A bad dream awakes her--she imagined her hero returning from the front with an empty sleeve. But she will hide her pain
and greet him with joy at the altar.

Then follows the concluding number, in which, as a military
bride, she awaits her aviator-groom as he descends from the clouds,
with the whirring of the motor as an undercurrent to the song.

--Dramatic Mirror, December 21,
1918, page 906.

● POODLES HANNEFORD

Back again and funnier than ever. This Poodles Hanneford
comes pretty near being a wonder in the ring, whether as a clown
comic or a bareback rider. An audience will give Poodles the percentage as a funny man and he is all that, but his funniments take
away from the layman that he's a remarkable rider of a ring horse.
Even the audience finally gets that angle toward the finish, despite
Poodles' funmaking and his burlesque dressing.

Doing most of his former fun-tricks, Poodles has stuck in a
couple of new ones, besides changing the billing from The Hanneford
Family to Poodles Hanneford and Co. It's better the present way if
a name is to be built up which means a card attraction as well as
money, something proven by Poodles this fair season. He has been
playing in front of the grand stand in some of the biggest of the mid-
western annual events, reported as sensational before the ruralites.
But Poodles isn't crazy about the fairs from reports--there are too
many winds from too many directions sweeping over fair grounds.
And even as funny a fellow as Poodles can catch cold now and then.

The principal new comedy business with Poodles is with sus-
penders. They loosen on him, flap into his face and hat and meanwhile he is in danger of losing his trousers. It's a yell for the house.

The other bit holds a laugh and also danger. Poodles falls
off of the horse's back and winds himself on the ground right beneath the animal. As though dazed, he tries to climb through the
back legs of the horse, prying them apart with his head in between
the legs just above the horse's knees. After considerable business
he escapes by that path.

Poodles may think he knows his horse, perhaps as well as
Freddie Schader thought he knew police dogs, but an animal is an
animal and there is not enough of a laugh in that, Poodles, for the
chances you are taking.

The "Company," otherwise the family, look charming with the
neat looking boys in tuxes also doing some corking riding along with
the girls, and the two girls look sweet in their Grecian-like gowns.

As the ring-master (or mistress), the matron was a picture
of dignity, handsomely gowned with a sweeping aigrette above her
head. It was she who received the elegant bouquet over the footlights at the finale.

An act for vaudeville, just built for the Hip [Hippodrome The-
ter, New York] and just the smash there it could not help but be.

These great riding acts don't come in crops--they are not so
easy to copy as a fall or a gag, which may be why the Hannefords
and the Wirths have been with us so long, without competition.

> --Sime Silverman in Variety, Oc-
> tober 29, 1924, page 41.

● MARION HARRIS

Marion Harris has personality plus. She is ingratiating. Miss
Harris bills herself euphoniously as Syncopation's Scintillating Star,
which we feel is no exaggeration. Her offering consists solely of
singing syncopated songs, and you cannot resist her appeal. She
has a manner of putting over her songs which wins her audience
from the start, and she does her work as though it was a great
pleasure in her life and not a condescension in giving the audience
just so much time. And while she sings she sways a mean shoulder,
as the curbstone describers would casually remark. Among the songs
Miss Harris introduces that were liked the best were "I'm a Lonesome
Southern Girl in a Great Big Northern Town," "Jazz Baby" and "I
Ain't Got Nobody."

> --"Tidden" in Dramatic Mirror,
> July 1, 1919, page 1022.

● TED HEALEY

     Ted Healey was the black-faced comic with <u>Cuddle Up</u> last
season. The girl [Betty Healey] looks like a newcomer--and a welcome one. Healey jumped the burlesque outfit early last spring and
has been playing the large Middle Western picture houses during
the summer. Caught here [Buffalo, New York] in June, he un-
covered a snappy single, somewhat dubious in material, but, although
uncertain of his destination, giving unmistakable signs of being on
his way.

     The present, vehicle, billed as "Dr. Jekyl and Mrs. Hyde,"
is Healey's first excursion into big time. On the strength of his
showing, it establishes him as having arrived. Spotted fourth on
one of the strongest bills seen here in months, he proved himself
a clever youngster with a fine sense of taste and discrimination in
his material and one who, given a reasonable amount of seasoning,
should more than hold up with the best of them.

     The girl knows what to do with clothes and does it. She
dresses the act down to the ground and makes a pretty foil for
Healey's gentle kidding style. In his routine he shows himself possessed of a nimble wit and carries himself with the confidence and
poise of a veteran. His material is new and proved sure-fire. The
act has two songs by Healey, done as an imitation of Cantor and
Jolson--probably carried over from the black-face days. The impersonations look like a mistake. Healey has a style he should develop.
His personality on its own will probably carry him farther than re-
liance on impersonations.

     On his showing and reception here, Healey established himself
as a juvenile. It is not too much to say that the act can easily hold
its own on any bill.

                              --"Burton" in <u>Variety</u>, September
                              1, 1922, page 20.

● ANNA HELD

     Anna Held returned to the American stage on Monday via the
Palace. A trifle slimmer, if anything, she looks just as pretty as
ever, and there doesn't appear to be any difference in her singing
voice. To be sure the red "foots" predominated during her stay
upon the rostrum, but it is the result that matters, irrespective
of the methods employed. She is still utilizing her talents in pro-
jecting rolling eyes, rhapsodic warbling and exaggerated Frenchy
hip-strolling back and fourth. After three brief numbers and the
passing of flowers across the footlights, Miss Held obliged with one
verse of "I Just Can't Make My Eyes Behave." It was all very well
received.

--"Jolo" [Joshua Lowe] in Variety,
October 29, 1915, page 16.

• RAYMOND HITCHCOCK

We drove sixty-five miles with Mr. Hitchcock at the wheel.
It didn't seem that long. He talked most of the way, but it didn't
seem that long.

There were times when I thought it was going to be much
shorter. There were times when North Shore policemen challenged
Mr. Hitchcock's interpretation of a lawful speed; there were times
when danger posts, curbstones, light poles and other habitually sta-
tionary objects forsook their sites and dodged menacingly in front of
Mr. Hitchcock's front wheels.

Raymond Hitchcok is a great musicomedian, a magnificent
manager--so magnificent that he is $80,000 to the bad and can't make
a cent out of a Hitchy-Koo that is nightly straining the capacity of
the Colonial Theater--and indubitably he is the best long-distance
talker that ever tooled a touring car.

But he is the world's worst driver. And I think he knows
it.

We had just dodged the jigging Edgewater Beach Hotel and
were skidding from under the prow of Northwestern University, which
had floated into Mr. Hitchcock's right of way, when he slowed up to
sixty miles to permit the safe crossing of a beautiful flaxen woman
wearing a beautiful black crépe hat. The tail of his artistic eye
lingered on her hat.

"The Widow Stevens would look well in one of those for Easter,"
said he.

Hatless, his straw-colored hair inviting the fragrant breezes,
he sniffed Nature welcomingly. Spring was good to "Hitchy," and he
knew his Nature. He knew the budding trees and piping birds by
name.

I don't think the center of his system is Broadway and Forty-
second street. His apparel--morning coat, white waistcoat, saffron
gloves, varnished boots with buttoned buff uppers, not to mention
a gold watch the size of a swan's egg with melodramatic diamonds on
both sides--does not proclaim the man within.

He was telling me now that you never can judge a man's
pleasures by his poses.

"There was 'Diamond Jim' Brady, who left me this watch. In

such jeweled junk he sewed up a million-and-a-half dollars. Most
folks thought he was diamond-mad and chorus-girl-mad. He wanted
'em to think so. That was his pose. Diamonds and chorus girls
were 'Diamond Jim's bait for the railroad men he did business with.
I know; I knew Brady as well as any man could. That stuff was
his pose."

"What was his pleasure?"

"Business--selling goods--making money. He was the most
consistent business man I ever met--and nobody knew it."

"What's your pose?"

"Being funny."

"What's your pleasure?"

"Being a manager."

Then he posed.

"There are four things for a man driving a car to beware of,"
he said, drawlingly: "A woman driving a car, a boy on a bike, a
hen, and a Ford."

"Have a cigar?"

"No thanks; don't smoke, don't drink. I swear" (I've never
heard him), "Flirt with the women and wear fancy vests, but I don't
drink.

"Flirting, at our time of life, Ashton, in homeopathic flirts, is
good for us. A mild flirtation keeps alive the sensation that, by
gosh! you're not on the shelf yet."

"How's Hitchy-Koo doing?"

"Fine! bully! about twenty thousand this week. The show's
doing so well in Chicago I think I'll close it out in about two weeks
more and go to London."

"!   !   !"

"I'll close it out because it is the most expensive show in the
world. It could make money in New York, but not here; the percentage is against me."

"And you added two thousand a week to the expense by adding Lillian Russell!"

"Well, I didn't want to slight Chicago," he apologized. "Grace La Rue and Rock and White were out of the cast and I thought I'd try to keep faith with a town that always has been pretty decent to me. Oh, I'm a far-seeing manager! Perhaps Chicago will let me come back. I always look ahead. I remember when I was a boy and--"

"You've told me before of your first job--selling shoes."

"That wasn't my first job," he corrected reproachfully. "My first job was cleaning bathtubs in a barber shop. If I had been a bright boy I might have been the head barber by this time."

"You've had some wonderful pasts," I said lightly.

"Yes," he answered with sudden seriousness, "I've had some wonderful pasts. And I'm not ashamed of any of them.

"I was fresh from jail," he went on, for the first time in our long acquaintanceship referring to those dark days in which he had an opportunity to check his list of friends. "Oh, I was fresh from jail. (What a boob I was--then!) And my lawyer advised me not to hang my head, but to go out among men.

"I went with him one night to a public banquet in New York. As I was about to seat myself, a man who had known me well said with a sneer:

"'I'm afraid you've made a mistake--this table is reserved for celebrities.'

"'I qualify for it perfectly,' I said to him--'I am both famous and notorious!'

"And sometime later, when this gentleman, cruel with wine, said, 'Mr. Hitchcock, didn't you use to clean bathtubs in a barber shop?' I answered:

"'Yes; but I don't recall ever preparing a bath for you.'"

We got out at a pharmacy and ate ice-cream soda and talked showmen.

"Billy Sunday and George Cohan are the greatest showmen in the world, and one of them is on the level," quoth Hitchy.

"Where'd you get the idea of hand-shaking your audience?"

"From Georgie Cohan. I sent him an emergency call to Atlantic City, and he came with his small selfesteem and large genius and knocked Hitchy-Koo into shape. He told me to get right down in

the aisle and talk to the audience by the hand. 'They'd hang anybody else, but you can get by with it,' says Georgie.

"And the first big mark to come sailing down the aisle was
Ambassador Gerald.

"'Hello, Jim. How's your excellency?' I sang out, and gripped
him; and the little old show was on and 'over'--thanks to Georgie."

"Did you make him a partner for that?"

"No! George isn't my partner--he's my friend. I couldn't
do anything for him for that. I couldn't even pay his board bill
at the hotel."

"Have you ever been broke?"

"What do you call this--being eighty thousand in the hole!"

"I mean actually broke."

"Yes. A month ago in New York I got up without a nickel in
my pockets--without a nickel in the world. And I'd had a pretty
good return from my Fulton Theater that week, too. Words and
Music had lost only twenty-three dollars. It was the best week the
Fulton had had under my management.

"Well, as I say, not a nickel to my name that day. And there
I was in my Packard limousine, with two men up--a driver and a
whatyoumaycallem. And two honest sons of toil with lunch pails see
me in my limousine and say right out so I can hear it:

"'Pretty soft for that guy!'

"That got me. I called 'em. 'Hey, you!' says I. 'Come here!'
And I told 'em I didn't have a nickel, and had to feed those strong
men on the front seat and keep them from worrying about anything
in the world.

"'I envy you,' I says to the working fellows--'I envy you
your wages, and your paid-for lunch in the pails, and the way you
can look your wife in the eye when you go home--not to mention
the corner grocer.'

"'It must be awful,' said I, 'when you are feeling particularly
bright and spontaneous, to have some major creditor shown down
the aisle right into your handshake.'

"Get back in the car and I'll tell you about it," said Hitchy.

"But first I want to tell you about the nickelless morning.

I was ashamed to touch anybody for ten or a hundred. So I drove
to the bank and borrowed ten thousand. And when that was due,
I borrowed fifteen thousand from a friend and paid off the bank and
have five thousand to pay housekeeping accounts.

"As long as you've got your health and a job, you can borrow.
That's the secret of my finances. I'm always healthy, and always
working. And another secret is, always pay the little fellows. Now--"

"Was this a little fellow that walked down the aisle?"

"It was not. It was none less, nor other, than New York's
distinguished money master, Jacob Wertheimer. I grabbed him warmly
by the hand and said:

"'How are you, Jake?--this is a pleasure. Ladies and gentlemen, I want to introduce you to my partner, Mr. Jacob Wertheimer.
I owe him forty thousand dollars, and he's never going to get it,
and that gives me the right to call him my partner.'

"And Jake beamed, bless him! beamed all over himself--positively
liked it. And during the intermission he came back to my dressing
room and said:

"'Say, Hitchy, how'd you like to make that eighty thousand?'"

"And you--"

"Not then--not then, Ashton! That would have been inartistic.
I told him I'd consider it. I told him I'd hold it open for him."

"Put him in suspense, as it were?"

"Yes suspense, as it were. You have a happy gift for words.
But I think I'll end Jake's suspense pretty soon and take his other
forty thousand with me to London.

"With a little sense of humor," said Manager Hitchcock, dropping me at my door, "you can get away with murder."

--Ashton Stevens in Actorviews,
Chicago: Covici-McGee, 1923,
pages 201-207.

• LIBBY HOLMAN

    Libby Holman needs material and plenty of work. She has
about every other requisite necessary to a big time single woman,
a position Miss Holman should find well worth striving for. Big time
women are gradually becoming as rare as good booze.

Among her present possessions, in their probable order of importance, are looks, voice, and a distinct personality. Looks should come first, because Miss Holman first impresses as a looker. After that she is a vocalist.

The current rep of three numbers was not happily chosen. Encore and fourth song best suited to her type of voice; should be pattern for the girl's future selection. She is a low-down songstress and, perhaps, awful mean under the proper conditions.

A future should be gained with the right coaching.

Miss Holman's only previous role of repute was in Ned Wayburn's recent amateur Gambols, she shows it.

> --"Bige" [Joe Bigelow] in Variety,
> February 20, 1929, page 50.

• BOB HOPE

Bob Hope has been one of RKO's young hopefuls for more than a year, but this is his first setting in the 47th street showcase [The Palace, New York]. He has youth, ability and natural cleverness. He went over big despite his material, which bears the Al Boasberg hallmark. Hope has a little bit of Ted Healy, and a lot of Ken Murray, but not enough of these to lose his identity. Assisting him in the cycle of box-planting, clowning and stoogerei are two capable girls and three boys. Of the latter, one croons appealingly.

> --Elias E. Sugerman in The Billboard, February 28, 1931, page 18.

*   *   *

What is disturbing about Mr. Hope is not the etiolation of his humor, which has been going on for years, but a sinister quality in his presentation. He has developed a gliding, swooping Dracula-like walk and his expression, as he waits for the audience to respond to his tired gags, also reminded me of the Count: a self-congratulatory smirk that often became a positive sneer--hello suckers!

> --Dwight Macdonald in Esquire,
> July 1962, page 126.

• HOUDINI

Houdini always tickles our senses of the theatrical. We like to hear the deadly serious way he addresses the audience: "Lay-

dees and gentle-men, in introducing my or-riginal invention--" and
so on. And, upon being imprisoned, head downward, in what he
graphically terms a "water torture cell," he reveals his Barnum sense
of the theatric by having an assistant stand close by, axe in hand.
"I honestly don't expect an accident to happen, but you never can
tell," Houdini has pleasantly warned.

Houdini is a showman of the old school. He does baffling
things, and he gets every ounce of value out of them.

> --Frederick James Smith in The
> New York Dramatic Mirror, April
> 8, 1916, page 17.

                              *   *   *

Of the late Harry Houdini, dead in Detroit as we write, a
hundred memories come back to us. Memories of countless parties
about town, with the little dark man always in the background but
always with a fascinated group about him, now wrenching his thumb
from its socket and returning it, now disgorging a pack of threaded
needles, now dazing the reverent circle by swallowing a sword.
Quiet, modest, unassuming and startlingly gifted by nature, he was
always obliging, always likable--and always daring beyond belief.

A million columns have been written of him as a showman. A
thousand times he had faced death. Padlocked and nailed in packing-
boxes and dropped into the sea, riveted into water-boilers, nailed
into hermetically sealed coffins, manacled to stakes at which roaring
fires burned, suspended head down from dizzy skyscrapers, the
broad Slavonic visage of Houdini had met death in rendezvous which
grew monotonous. Recently he had turned his inquisitive mind and
penetrating showman's eyes upon a subject which had haunted him
all his life--life beyond the grave. Seven times he had made compacts
in all seriousness with persons who agreed to communicate from the
grave if it were possible after their death. None of the seven came
back.

Now he is gone, and in a small brownstone house at No. 278
West 113th Street, the dust gathers on much unfinished work.

The many rooms of that house are lined and piled ceiling-high
with stacks of books, paper wrappings and crumbling envelopes in
which are held the records, experiences and secrets of fifty-two
years of the life of the boy Eric Weiss, son of a rabbi of Appleton,
Wisconsin, who developed into the mystic who branded himself with
the title trickster, a magician who gave the principal credit for his
art to the fact that he was a contortionist thewed like a wrestler,
a showman who combined in his personality the ego of Barnum, the
pose of Belasco, and a talent for publicity that was unique.

How many of the secrets of his work will come from those
archives waits the future; at present it is a lonely castle without
the spirit of the master.

--"Talk of the Town" in The New
Yorker, November 6, 1926, page
20.

• JOSEPH E. HOWARD AND ETHELYN CLARK COMPANY*

We take our hat off to Joe Howard. Just when the boys in
knicks are putting in their youthful licks slamming the merry old
jazz and shimmy acts and musical revues on the stage, that perennial
stager, Josephus Howard, steps up to the bat and whales out a homer.
It's at the Colonial this week. While its newness needs polishing and
a judicious cutting here and there will shorten it noticeably, the new
Howard and Clark act is there a city mile. And Joe isn't a bit stingy
with the stage, turning it over in full area at times to Jack King
(formerly of Stepp, Mehlinger and King), who does the "female prima
donna bit" from the old act; Maurice Diamond, who set the Colonial
crowd wild with that Russian legmania which always put him in big
favor in his own acts; Ruth Reed, who shows decided dancing ability
and works hard to please, and Gee Sum Ki, a real Chink, who works
in the closing scene with Howard dressed up as an Oriental, who sits
down to a dream as an upstage ensemble, is shown by the drawing
of a crutain hiding a little boxlike space which has the company in
the finale costumed to fill out the visionary picture. Howard has
four boys in the company that look like part of the imitators that
Frisco had at the Colonial recently. They work in for a "bit" and
do it so well that it helps the act materially in scoring. Joe has
picked up a brace of show girls that wear a layout of new stage
clothes advantageously. They appear first in a number entitled "The
World Is Mine," which serves as Howard's introduction. Miss Clark
makes her bow in an old-fashioned raiment of wealth, with the girls
on in olden day outfits, Miss Clark doing exceptionally well with a
number, "The Old Fashioned Girl." A pretty duet was "Take Me Now
and Make Me Understand," which Joe and Miss Clark put over in
typical musical comedy style. After Diamond had sung "I'm Lonesome
for Old Broadway" and then went into that clever dance of his, the
act closed with the Ching-a-Ling number, which Miss Clark sang and
danced. Miss Clark never appeared to better advantage and she
seems much more at home in the new act. Making all allowances for
shortcomings, the act ran smoothly, but has a lot of entertainment.
Looks like Joe has finally put it over. He sure has worked hard on
the new act.

--"Mark" in Dramatic Mirror, January 22, 1920, page 103.

---

*This act was billed as "Chin Toy," a 33-minute musical revue.

• WILLIE AND EUGENE HOWARD

   Eugene and Willie Howard repeated their new act at the Winter
Garden Sunday night. It's a little dandy. The boys put it on for
the first time up there two weeks ago. The first part has all new
talk, with both the brothers in evening dress. Willie has thrown
away the messenger boy suit. The Howards are going to the Coast
with The Passing Show of 1913. They are entitled to protection on
the new material while away. Willie has one "gag" about a pair of
opera glasses that is a scream. The talk runs to an evening at the
opera, concluding with an operatic selection both boys sing so well.
It's unusual for such a versatile performer as Willie Howard to
possess a voice, but he has one, and it could have earned his way
through life if he had not combined funmaking with it. Eugene becomes a Columbine for the final number, but Willie remains in his
dress suit until the finish. He makes a comedy twist out of that
even, and simply, by buttoning his vest one button short. Willie
explains it through illustration, pointing out to his brother that the
tailor put on one buttonhole and one button too many.

   Willie sang a parody on "Sooky Ookums," with a line "All night
long he's smoking opum." Among the imitations were Jack Norworth
(singing "Mandy"), Bernhardt, Thomashefsky and Harry Fox. Someone called for Harry Pilcer. Willie threw his hands up in the air,
ran around the stage and started to climb the proscenium arch.
Were Pilcer there he would have had a perfect idea of how he strikes
any number of people. The audience just howled. The Howards never
fail to become a riot at the Garden. They were that in vaudeville
before entering musical comedy, and can go back to vaudeville with
this act, duplicating their former successes there. If there is a Hebrew comedian in the world who can touch Willie Howard, trot him
out. And Willie can give his challenger all those things a Hebrew
comedian is supposed to have, including crepe hair, for Willie has
none of these, nor does he need them.

                                        --Sime Silverman in Variety, May
                                            23, 1913, page 15.

• MAY IRWIN

   Four songs of two verses each and a short recitation in which
she feelingly described the pathos of becoming fat, made up Miss
Irwin's offering. She is growing fat--no, "stout" won't do--and at
her entrance looks like a sister team. She might bill the act as "Me
and My Adipose," because her lack of visible waistline furnished the
subject of the recitation. There was no other talk. Time was when
May Irwin was "coon shouter-in-chief to the American public," but
since then she has lost a good deal of her unction, and others have
usurped her place. She employed but one "coon" number, opening
with "Much Obliged." Her closing song went the best. It is a newly

published novelty number called "I Couldn't Come Home in The Dark," with a good comic story and a "snapper" of a finish. This won Miss Irwin a recall, and came close to saving her from what threatened to be a decidedly indifferent reception at the Orpheum on Monday evening. Miss Irwin's first appearance in vaudeville in New York.

--"Rush" [Alfred Greason] in
Variety, December 7, 1907,
page 10.

*   *   *

A crash of welcome greeted the flashing of the old favorite's name [at the Palace], and a reception that held up the action for a full minute of her entrance testified that May Irwin is not forgotten, though she has been for years in professional retirement.

Appearing in a timely sketch by George Ade, with a role perfectly fitted to her as she is today, Miss Irwin wafted through a laughing hit, as well as a sentimental triumph that was heart-warming. She has lost none of her individual faculties, which made her a star for so long, in fact she has mellowed with the autumn years and her personality is irresistibly charming.

The skit plays in a split set, showing two rooms of an office, with several complications around a forty-year-old bottle of Kentucky rye and a jealous wife. Miss Irwin as a prohibition fanatic is accused of being in a compromising position with the jealous one's hubby, faints, is given two stiff shots of the liquor, and goes into a delicious stew bit to a wise-crack finale and a cinch success.

Insistent calls brought the star forth in "one," though the lights were up for intermission, and she did two of her old coon songs and a burlesque dramatic recitation, then made a speech holding the audience solid. The act had broken in only for two performances at the Hamilton Sunday, but Miss Irwin is a veteran and played as though she were rounding out a season with it.

By every standard of vaudeville, a great headline act.

--[Jack] "Lait" in Variety, February 4, 1925, page 8.

• JOE JACKSON

The Hippodrome has taken on a new glamor for us. Joe Jackson is back. Along about three in the afternoon and nine in the evening we feel the old call stealing over us, for we know that then the great stage is being made empty for the timid, gazelle-like entrance of our favorite hero. The back-drop is a different one this

season, and the Kum-apart bicycle is in a stylish rack instead of
leaning against the delicatessen store as of yore. But Joe Jackson
is the same. In the midst of world upheaval it is a comforting
thought.

> --Robert Benchley in Life, March
> 30, 1922, page 18.

• ELSIE JANIS

On the way to the Janis suite in the Congress--G 22-24-26-
38, and, for all I know, 30-32-34-36--I met a wise old theatrical
producer, who told me there were just two subjects of unfailing interest to theatergoers of today--Love and Liquor.

I was on the way to talk Love to, or at least with, Elsie, the
official sweetheart of the A. E. F. (not to mention the I. O. O. F.,
the B. P. O. E. and the A. F. L.), and nevertheless and notwithstanding still an unwedded bachelor girl. Which is to say that, Miss
Elsie willing, I was going to commit to memory her answer to the impertinent question, Why don't you marry?

And--well--the first dear thing that was said was said by Mrs.
Janis when she said: "It takes three-quarters of an hour to get
tea up--won't you have a tiny drop of old brandy?"

Never mind my scintillant reply, with which our story is not
concerned. I only wanted to show that there must have been something in what the manager said, for in a jiffy we were neck-deep in
the second of his "just two subjects"--and with the first ever ready
to spring.

"It used to be, when a man admired a girl and wanted to show
it," said Elsie--"it used to be flowers. But now it's a bottle of
Gordon gin."

"As a matter of fact," she went on, "I was notoriously the
drinkless wonder of my age. I didn't like the stuff. And it was
my pride to be the only one at a party who didn't. Just as it would
now be my pride to be the only one at a party to sit up with a
schooner of Scotch. Prohibition makes you perverse."

"What under the sun did we have to talk about before Prohibition?" Mrs. Janis helpfully asked.

"Well, we didn't talk about drink, for one thing," said Elsie.
"But now! Go to a luncheon and it starts with one of two sentences:
'I'm sorry I can't give you cocktails'; or, 'These are made from a
little bottle my grandfather left.'"

"The rich don't really suffer for it," I put in.

"Yes, and that," said Elsie, "is one of the reasons I'm ag'in' Prohibition.   There are fellows in our Gang at the Illinois who'd fondly love to park their shoes against a rail after the show and throw down a couple of long red ones with very low white collars. I got to feeling for and with the fellows 'over there.' They used to say, 'Those pussyfooters'll never be able to put it over; they can't get away with our beer and wine.' Wise guys they were, and I was a wise guy with 'em!"

"It breaks Elsie's heart," said her mamma, "when she thinks what our Prohibition has done to poor France."

"Think of it yourself," Elsie said.   "There was France, hard up, bled, wounded and all ready to step on her glorious grapes and crush them into wine for us, her ally.   There were her treasured champagnes all ready to be shipped.   When--bing! blah! Prohibition!"

This was no moment to talk marriage.   But we could always talk Gang, and we did.

"Irving Berlin advised me one day: 'Take my tip, Elsie, and don't put your Gang in uniforms.'

"I was just back--from you know what.   I'd stepped over dead bodies, to sing and prance for the fellows who were still going. And here at home I'd been in the hospital and seen some of the permanent wrecks--our fellows, once so tough and straight.   'Irv,' I said, 'if America don't want to see uniforms now, I don't want to see America again ever.'   I was that serious!   I felt that if America could face those fellows with their chevrons and not feel something--well, then I'd leave America flat.   Horrible threat!"

"But she's never told you," Mrs. Janis supplied, "the offers she had for big non-soldier shows."

"And isn't going to tell him," Elsie said.   "Only this--when Mr. Dillingham made his magnificent proposal I said, 'No, I can't. Charlie,' I said, 'I can't go out on the stage with a lot of nude women shaking their shimmies; I'd cry all over the place.   There's something--call it "spiritual" if you want to--that I've got to get out of my system.'   And I told him about this show, which I'd written-- written in bed, like Mark Twain (I mean the bed)--and how little it would cost, because that was the way we wanted it.   And he said I was crazy anyway and crazier since the war.   But to go ahead, which I did; and he never came to rehearsals--and when it was all done he said it was the only show he'd ever seen he didn't want to cut somewhere."

"Why didn't you show him the pay roll?" I brightly suggested.

"Oh, that was proof. I'd promised the boys, every one,
fifty bucks a week, rain or shine, and warned them all that I didn't
want to make a bad actor out of any man who had a good job. We've
done some grading and paving since then, since the show made good.
Now nobody gets less than sixty-five."

"The one who says 'It's all wrong!' is worth seventy at least."

"Don't worry about him; he's all right," said Elsie proudly.
"He was chauffing a car for Owen Moore when he came to me. Said
his brother had danced on a table with me in France. I told him to
send his brother around. And that night the stage manager wanted
to know how many Ryans I'd ordered. I told him one. He said
two'd shown up for jobs. 'I can sing a little tenor, and, anyway,
I'd like to stick with the Gang," said this Mr. Ryan, the chauffeur,
your 'It's-all-wrong' man; and he stuck. Sometimes," Elsie added,
"they dropped from heaven and sometimes I picked them up.

"For instance--I wanted a blonde, a female woman blonde with
looks and style and--Well, you know the regular chorus or show girl
type wouldn't do for the Gang; might stir civil war; imagine turning
loose half-a-dozen seasoned chorus girls among those thirty-six he
men! Chorus girls, of course, never look at anything less than the
regular leading man in the regular theatrical company--and usually
he's grabbed quick by the leading lady. But three dozen Heroes!
It would have been much too much. The flizzies would have raised
a riot.

"But, as I was or wasn't telling you--I was talking to Eva Le
Gallienne in a hotel when along passed a stunning blonde, just what
my heart had ordered. 'Who's that?' I asked Eve, who had bowed
to her.

"'That,' said Eve, 'is Miss Overhault--one of the Long Island
Overhaults.'

"'Ask her if she wants to go on the stage.'

"'What!'

"'_Ask_ her.'

"And Eve did. And she did. Said she'd love it.

"'When can you join?' I asked her.

"'In an hour--I've got a tea. But I can break the tea if an
hour's too long.'

"'What about your folks?'

"'There's only a sister. I'll telephone.'

"And she came to rehearsal that night, and stuck, and became and is, like the rest of us, a bum!"

Elsie was in great spirits. And Elsie's mamma had gone into 24 or 32.

"I don't want to be a pest," I told Elsie, "but when are you, or why aren't you, going to marry!"

"Never!" she said, with more to come--I could feel it, and I held my peace. "I've gone this way so long, so far, that I've grown a pretty healthy sense of humor. Thanks to that, it doesn't require marriage to make me laugh or cry at this weird old world. I've got a sense of humor, let's say, but, what's more, I've got the most marvelous companion in the world in my mother."

"That then's the answer to your bachelorhood--Mother?"

"Yes; but it must not be unfairly stated. Mother--at least I-- have a reputation of being the most carefully chaperoned girl on any stage. You'd think, from what you hear, that mother camps on a stool in the back parlor and asks every youth who tries to hold my hand what his intentions are! Why, do you know who the fellows ask for when the party is a foursome and we need another girl?"

"That exquisite 'bum,' Miss Overhault?"

"No; that exquisite 'bum,' Mrs. Janis. And when we get out, do you know who it is that has to be quieted down and said to: 'This is supposed to be a quiet party'?--do you know who?"

"Elsie Janis' mamma," I answered.

"And right you are!" said mamma's Elsie.

"Lemme tell you," she raced. "There's never a wild place in Paris or New York or Chicago that I wanted to see that my mother wouldn't go along with me to see it. There never was a dump so tough my mother wouldn't go to it with me, if I wanted to go. If my tastes don't happen to be chronically dumpish, that's not mother's fault. But lemme tell you that she's there for any time or place. If I wanted to sip a jazzbo cocktail or a shimmy fizz, mother'll go with me to the awful cave where they're brewed and we'll sip 'em together. She'll do anything I ever wanted to do--and more.

"And that's only a tiny side of her companionship. She's there for anything that happens to me. If I stub my toe and start to fall-- well, I don't land on a tack, but on mother. Show me a man like mother and I'll be willing to hear people say, 'Yes, he belongs to

Janis and Janis belongs to him.' But they aren't made. And I've
looked. And I--like Henry George--I'm for men, God love 'em! But
when I gaze around a luncheon at my girl friends that used to be
girls, and see most of them divorced or getting divorces, and hear
them say with the salad--it always comes with the salad--'Well, Elsie,
here's another luncheon and you're still a spinster!'--I can't help
but notice that their note, which was one time one of pity, is now
the note of envy. I tell you I'm glad of the privilege, the beauty,
the hell-roaring fine companionship that comes of batching it along
with mother."

> --Ashton Stevens in Actorviews,
> Chicago: Covici-McGee, 1923,
> pages 81-86.

*   *   *

Elsie Janis, the one-woman U.S.O. of World War I, is gone.

But Elsie will never be forgotten. Not so long as there is a
man left who heard her challenging shout "Are We Downhearted?"
and answered her with a resounding "No!" somewhere in France in
in that critical and decisive year of 1918.

She was almost 67 when she died in her Beverly Hills, Calif.,
home on February 26, nine days before her birthday, but she'll al-
way be young to the men who are getting on themselves. These
onetime doughboys of the AEF remember her as a slim, dark-haired,
bright-eyed girl in a steel helmet, the dancing, singing symbol at
the bloody, muddy frontlines of their own wives and sweethearts at
home. She was not called "the sweetheart of the AEF" for nothing;
the nickname was well deserved.

The most vivid picture of Elsie Janis a Legionnaire carries in
his memory was etched on a day in late March 1918, when spring was
greening the scarred fields of France. A whistle blew, a bell clanged,
and 4,000 men in khaki scrambled to get out of the way of a locomotive chugging down the tracks into the roundhouse at Nevers. On
the cowcatcher was a slender dark-haired girl, hanging on with one
hand, and waving an American flag with the other. Her smile was
incandescent. The men yelled and stamped and cheered and looked
and yelled some more. This was an American girl from home, the
first one they'd seen in a long time. She was young and full of pep;
and, as she jumped lightly off her precarious perch on the cowcatcher
onto the hastily built speaker's platform that had been erected there,
she threw her arms up and shouted her famous trade-mark "Are We
Downhearted?" Four thousand voices answered her with a thunderous
"No!" That's how the AEF remembers Elsie Janis best, a memory
golden bright over the dimming stretch of 38 years.

Elsie Janis was in her twenties when she sang and danced her

way through the American and British sectors of France. She was
the first entertainer to perform for the AEF, and the only woman
entertainer permitted to go to the frontlines. She was indefatigable,
and she thought nothing of giving nine shows a day for the soldiers.
Every show was 45 minutes long, nearly seven hours of solid, continuous work a day, and a mad rush in a staff car from one show
to another, over shell-pocked roads to the next hospital or base or
improvised stage on a rickety platform on the edge of the woods just
on the threshold of safety. The booming guns of the enemy and answering artillery were often an accompaniment to Elsie's songs and
imitations, her lively, highkicking dancing, and the sensational cart-
wheels at the finish.

She was in France for a year and three months, and she gave
a total of 610 performances. She was without any supporting company at all, sometimes even without the band the soldiers organized
when they had time to prepare for her. The doughboys worshipped
her; dozens of men would have married her. But her life, before
and after the war, was dedicated to the stage and her mother, Jennie,
who had been her constant companion, chaperone, and manager since
Elsie was a child. Not until years later, and after her mother had
died, did Elsie Janis marry Gilbert Wilson, a handsome, appealing
man 17 years her junior. Although cynics predicted the marriage
wouldn't last, it did--for 15 years. When they separated, without
scandal or recrimination, all Elsie would say with the kind of gallantry which so became her, was "We separated for no reason except
that he is still young enough to have another life, and I just want
to finish in peace the one I've enjoyed so much." They were never
divorced; and, with characteristic generosity, she willed a good part
of her estate to her estranged husband.

Perhaps the reason Elsie Janis enjoyed life so much was because she lived it so fully, got such a kick out of everything she
did. She was a great lady who could be a hoyden when the occasion
called for it. She had depth and quality, an effervescence like champagne, and a plain wholesomeness like good, homebaked bread.

She was born on March 6, 1889, in Columbus, Ohio, a descend-
ant of patriots. Janis was a stage name. The family name was Bierbower, and her father, John Bierbower, used to tell her stories of
his great- great- great-grandfather who helped build the stockade
around York, Pa. It was not suprising that with this heritage Elsie,
a proud member of the DAR, should feel so strong an urge to be a
part of World War I. She couldn't fight to "make the world safe for
democracy," but she could use her talents to cheer the fighting men.
And she did.

She was young when she went to war but she was also at the
height of her fame, a veteran of the stage from the age of ten, a
star at 17. As a matter of fact, she was launched on her career
from the White House. Her mother led the choir in the church which

William McKinley, then Governor of Ohio, regularly attended. When
McKinley became President, Elsie and her mother were White House
guests, and the talented little girl did her act with tremendous success before the diplomatic corps. That she was a natural-born mimic
was discovered when she appeared briefly with James O'Neil's company. And it was her amazingly accurate and entertaining imitations
of Mae Irwin, Edna Mae, Della Fox, and other dazzling stars of the
period which enchanted sophisticated Washingtonians. It might seem
incongruous for a child to evoke mental portraits of buxom, beautiful
women for an audience. But Elsie's inflections, gestures, and pos-
tures, her duplication of the stars' mannerisms, created a perfect
illusion every time; and the child's spectacular talents did full justice
to the grownup subjects. Washington loved the little girl with the
dark curls from President McKinley's home State. Elsie Bierbower
was soon in general demand as a society entertainer in the Capital,
and her local fame soon brought about her first professional engagement at Chase's Theatre in Washington. Soon her mother was invited
to bring her to New York. She was engaged to appear on the famous
old New York Roof Garden, and she stopped the show the first night.
The Gerry Society for the Prevention of Cruelty to Children stopped
it the second night.

Mrs. Bierbower was not stopped however. She was determined
now to see her daughter a great stage star. Elsie went to school
like other children; but, unlike most other youngsters, she spent
long hours studying music, dancing, and elocution, perfecting her
imitations, adding to her repertoire. A canny theatrical agent urged
her mother to change the cumbersome name of Bierbower to one which
would fit more neatly into lights, and "Janis" was contrived out of
the girl's middle name. And just in time, too, for her first real hit
was at the New York Roof in the summer of 1905, in a travesty called
When We Were 41. Her sleek, smooth imitations did the trick.

The following year brought her stardom. She was only 17,
the youngest star to shine on Broadway. The vehicle was The Vanderbilt Cup, and it ran two years. Elsie Janis was established. After
that she captivated audiences in one hit after another, The Hoyden,
The Fair Co-Ed, The Slim Princess, and A Star For a Night, which
she wrote herself when she was barely 22. Now other talents were
burgeoning, and her creativeness was asserting itself in song-writing
dramatic sketches, and comedy skits.

And all the time her solid achievement as a singing, dancing,
all-round performer was being duly noted by critics who were no less
enthusiastic than her audiences. In 1913 her greatest triumph to
date was her appearance as costar with the great team of Montgomery
and Stone in The Lady of the Slipper, at the Globe Theatre on Broadway, which had housed an earlier Montgomery-Stone hit of eternal
memory, The Wizard of Oz.

The story was the same happy saga of success in London where

she went the following year, 1914. In her first appearance there
she scored one of the greatest successes ever achieved by an American. But this was the year the war began, and the marching men
entraining for France at Waterloo Station, the stories of heroism and
gallantry sifting back from across the Channel fired her young, eager
heart and pity and a desire to do something, anything, to be a part
of the struggle.

There was nothing she could do beyond sweetening their last
days at home, and brightening the brief leaves of the British Tom-
mies with the magic of the theater and the illusion that, for a time
at least, everything was just as it always had been. She did that,
and she did it well.

She was in London again when the United States entered the
war, and she came home to recruit on street corners, to sell Liberty
Bonds, play benefits, and give camp shows. She also began her
campaign for permission to entertain our own soldiers overseas.

When that was finally forthcoming, she lost no time getting to
France. Her mother went along with her, a strong ally in the second
stage of Elsie's campaign. For she was not satisfied to be in Paris,
in comparative comfort and safety, or in any of the other safe "be-
hind-the-lines" places suggested to her as suitable for a Broadway
star and a woman. She argued and reasoned with colonels and gener-
als. The men in Paris didn't need her for diversion and entertainment the way the dirty, cootie-cluttered doughboys in the trenches
did. It got so that every time she saw a YMCA hut in some quiet,
safe place, she wondered why she had come to France at all. But
when the sign billboarding her show went up, and the word got
around that "Elsie Janis Tonight" was Elsie in person and not a moving picture, every man who could run, walk, or crawl to the hut
was there. Then Elsie didn't wonder what she was there for. She
knew. She sang and danced and turned cartwheels, and the whistles
and stomping and yells were all the musical accompaniment she needed.

Eventually, of course, she cut her way through the redtape
and began her tour of the front. She sang from a captured boche
truck; the fellows presented her with helmets and Iron Crosses until
she was so weighted down and encumbered by metal she could hardly
walk.

For 35 years Elsie Janis kept a diary. She wrote every night
she was in France on what she'd seen and done that day, where
she'd been, what it was like. Her vivid, illuminating style, so like
her, is one of the best personal records of the war. Take the entry
for Friday, March 29, 1918, for instance, after an unforgettable week
in Paris in which the gunfire of the advancing Germans could be
seen in distant flashes along the horizon, and heard in a booming
that seemed to grow louder each day:

"Everyone was confident the Germans were stopped. That day
'Big Bertha' hit a church, killing 76 and wounding 90. We started
out on our second tour. Our first stop was Nevers, the largest
railroad center in France. There, with an American flag in my hand,
I got aboard the cowcatcher of a Baldwin locomotive...."

That was the time 4,000 men converged on the yard to hear
her. They carried away a memory of gallant Elsie Janis so vivid
that it remains with them to this day.

Others remember her in other places, for she went on from
Nevers to Issoudun, where the aviation school was; to Tours, Angers,
St. Nazaire, Base Hospital 101; then to Saveney where 1,800 patients
were quartered in the biggest American hospital yet set up. It was
here, she records, that she found Alexander Woollcott making himself
useful.

At Rangeval she put on her show in an old brickyard. At
Moliens-le-Bois "the men were mostly from Chicago. They had built
a platform in the heart of the woods. They had a band that played
'Darktown Strutters' Ball.'" At the end of her show there she really
went wild, leading the band, dancing, turning one cartwheel after
the other. It was too much for the platform. It gave way and she
went through it and had to be hauled out, still laughing.

She began to sing again as if nothing had happened, and just
then a whistle blew and the men were off, on the double. That's
the way it went all the time. A whistle blew, she kept singing, and
the men kept looking back as they went away.

The whole war was like that. And one day it was over and
Elsie Janis came back home, to Tarrytown, N.Y., a town full of history and legend of the American Revolution. She had lived there
for years in the old Philipse Manor House, now preserved as a his-
torical shrine, open to the public. For weeks and months the newspapers had been full of stories about her, long accounts of her un-
remitting labors, those nine shows a day sometimes, always four or
five. The entire community turned out to greet her, for she could
not have been more affectionately or enthusiastically regarded if she
had won the war singlehandedly. The 27th Division honored her with
the title of Captain and gave her a medal. The 94th Aero Squadron
gave her the title of General.

She was soon off again, touring with "Elsie Janis and Her
Gang," up and down the country for months on end. When 1921
rolled around, she felt a great yearning to be in France once again
for the coming of spring. In May that year she was there, and almost her first stop was in the American cemetery in Romaigne. This
is what she wrote in her diary that day:

"As we stood there, beneath the flagpole, an aged Frenchman

laboriously pulled Old Glory from her place on high and in the distance 'Taps' sounded. It seemed to me that those 25,000 white crosses,
supposedly symbolic of death, slowly but surely changed into khaki-
clad smiling men, and I found myself wanting to cry out 'Are We
Downhearted?' Unconsciously, I was holding out my arms, just as I
used to do when I yelled the question to perhaps these same men.
The Old Frenchman thought I was mad, but I imagine he was used
to madness by that time. Mother, who was feeling as one is supposed
to feel in a cemetery, said gently, 'Come on, dear, let's go.' I
followed her in a sort of daze. I can assure you that I heard voices
calling 'So long, Elsie! Come again!'"

     She answered their call on February 26, 1956. Elsie Janis and
her gang are together again.

> --Irene Corbally Kuhn in The Amer-
> ican Legion Magazine, July 1956,
> pages 22-23 and 58-59.

•   GEORGE JESSEL

     It's George Jessel--the little Georgie Jessel of other days when
Gus Edwards put on acts and revues and dug up the juvenile talent--
with his own revue. The act is a good one. Too long however for
vaudeville comfort. There's considerable fun in it. Considerable
pathos too. Play for the serious comes at the opening when Georgie
makes a touch of his mother for $1,400 that she had saved to buy
a bungalow in Arverne and at the close when the costumer and scenic
artist strip Georgie of his costumes and scenery and destroy his
chances of being a second George M. Cohan with his mamma coming
in to find the $1,400 gone but not forgotten. There is an idea with
the turn. Away from other revue stuff but not bad at all for vaudeville which is always ready to accept something away from the stereo-
typed. Georgie slams a revue together right in the face of the audience. He shows that it's easy. He picks up a team from vaudeville
and calls for choristers from the audience. The girls are planted out
front and they skip to the stage when George calls. There is a
comedy "bit" here and there in the placement of the act and the
costuming and the equipping with scenic investiture. Georgie establishes credit. The act moves swiftly. Jessel does parts of his
former "single" specialty. Sings some of his own songs including
"Oh How I Laughed When I Think How I Cried About You," with a
new one entitled "I'm Satisfied To Be My Mother's Baby." Speaking
of songs there are special numbers with the best of the lot being
"Peach Pickin' Time," sung by Holmes and Wells. This variety pair
has one pleasing specialty and obtained direct results upon their
dancing. At the Palace they accepted the offering as of production
calibre but running heck-bent for election into the never ending.
Jessel, Louis Silvers and Roy Turk supplied the music, Jessel and
Andy Lewis taking care of the book. Allen K. Foster did the staging.

Perhaps the crowd responsible for the entire turn figured upon a full-sized show; it has the possibilities but would take much elaboration and attention to the dialogue. There are sections that amble along with others picking it in the tempo necessary to send a big act over. Jessel has tried hard. He works hard. Lopping over the time hangover the act will set right anywhere "big time" vaudeville is played.

--"Mark" in Dramatic Mirror, September 18, 1920, page 506.

• AL JOLSON

Al Jolson would be welcome to vaudeville in the specialty which he is using as a feature of Lew Dockstader's Minstrels. Dressing neatly in evening clothes of faultless cut and of the new color called "taupe," Jolson offers a quiet quarter of an hour of smooth entertainment. As a singer of "coon" songs Jolson has a method of his own by which lyrics and melody are given their full value. His talk moves along nicely and is kept within proper proportion to the rest of the act. Throughout the talk Jolson introduces little tricks of speech and for a finish has an odd, eccentric vocal performance in which he sings with a peculiar buzzing note. Of course, it's flagrant trick work, but it brings him back for a sure fire encore. For this purpose he has a whistling solo that brings another recall. Jolson makes an announcement for his second encore. He could well spare this. The comic ballad he sings can stand alone. The comedy announcement thing has been worked to death, and it brings him nothing. As it stands now Jolson's offering is capable of holding down a place in any vaudeville show. He is now in the next to closing position in the olio of Dockstader's Minstrels, following Lew Dickstader and Neil O'Brien among others, and Jolson is making good a mile.

--"Dash" in Variety, March 6, 1909, page 14.

*   *   *

A while ago we intimated that some one (we forget who just now) might take Al Jolson's place. We were just crazy, that's all. We doubt whether any one could ever take his place. Certainly no human being. We can't imagine what we were thinking of to have said such a thing.

To sit at Big Boy* and feel the lift of Jolson's personality is

---

*Opened at the Winter Garden Theatre, New York, on January 7, 1925; subsequently revived at the 44th Street Theatre, New York, on August 24, 1925.

to know what the coiners of the word "personality" meant. The
word isn't quite strong enough for the thing that Jolson has. Un-
impressive as the comparison may be to Mr. Jolson, we should say
that John the Baptist was the last man to possess such a power.
There is something supernatural back of it, or we miss our guess.

When Jolson enters, it is as if an electric current had been
run along the wires under the seats where the hats are stuck. The
house comes to tumultuous attention. He speaks, rolls his eyes, com-
presses his lips, and it is all over. You are a life member of the Al
Jolson Association. He trembles his under lip, and your heart breaks
with a loud snap. He sings a banal song, and you totter out to send
a night letter to your mother. Such a giving-off of vitality, personality, charm, and whatever all those other words are, results from
a Jolson performance that it is small wonder that on the day after
his opening in New York he broke down and had to close the show
until the following week. We got enough vitamines out of being present to enable us to ride our bicycle at top speed all the way out to
Scarsdale that night, and at that had enough left over to shingle
the roof before we went to bed.

It may be that we were hypnotized by Mr. Jolson's eyes but
it seemed to us that, in addition to everything else, he had the funniest material that we have ever heard him work with. It was so
funny that we lost track of all the good ones we were going to quote,
and can remember none of them now. That gives us an excuse to
go to Big Boy again--if we can get in.

> --Robert Benchley in Life, January
> 29, 1925, page 18.

• BUSTER KEATON

The tiny comedian is perfectly at ease in his work, natural,
finished and artistic, and his specialties have proved a fetching addition to the favorite act of the Keatons, that is known all over the
land by its title, "The Man with the Table."

> --The New York Clipper, July
> 20, 1901, page 438.

*   *   *

Returning to New York after an absence of several years, the
Three Keatons, including Joe, Myra and Buster, were received with
undoubted signs of cordiality by the Victoria Theatre audience last
week, on Thursday afternoon the trio being welcomed with a generous
round of applause upon their first appearance. Although the act is
along the same broad comedy lines as when it served to amuse audiences at Keith's Union Square Theatre and Tony Pastor's some years

ago, it has been brought more up-to-date and the way it was received
showed that it is an act that should again be in demand about the
metropolis from now on. They came on third, opening with the comedy
tumbling done by Joe and the now quite manly Buster, who attained
his sixteenth year on October fourth. The throws, falls and tumbles
done by him are on a par with the best work of this sort that has
been seen on any stage, and the laughter caused by the comedy
business, facial make-up, eccentric costumes and the clever clowning
of both father and son, was incessant during the entire act. Mrs.
Keaton played a selection upon the saxaphone as pleasingly as ever,
the number winning a genuine encore, while her natty appearance in
blue uniform, trimmed with gold braid, caused much favorable comment "out front." The big hit of the act was made by Buster's singing "Father Brings Home Something Every Day," and it is to be
regretted that he did not have more songs. He showed ability out
of the ordinary and by working along this line he should develop
into an excellent comedian, singer and possibly a monologist. That
he has a future upon the stage goes without saying. There is one
criticism that might be made regarding the act and that is that in
the middle it tends to drag a bit. If Buster were to render a song
here, or a short monologue and then have Joe break in with some
of his fast acrobatic, comedy tumbling and throwing of Buster, it
might tend to make the act move more rapidly than it does at present, which would be an improvement. As it is, however, the Keatons are a welcome feature for any bill and it is to be hoped that
the act will now be seen in town with much frequency every season.

--The New York Dramatic Mirror,
October 30, 1909, page 19.

• ANNETTE KELLERMANN

Who cares whether Annette Kellermann is "The Perfect Woman,"
as the program states! Who cares, anyway, for "perfect women"
such as have exhibited themselves on the stage oft and anon? The
title of "perfect woman" has been employed time and again to describe
any females. It doesn't commence to bring to the imagination the
wholesome beauty of form belonging to Miss Kellermann. She is a
rare jewel among women who expose their "figure" to an audience's
gaze. There could be no more perfect picture than Miss Kellermann
presents as she appears in her diving costume of black silk tights,
a one-piece suit enveloping her from the neck to the feet. It fits
snugly to the skin. After first entering the water, Miss Kellermann
from her head down reminds one of a handsome seal in the elegant
physique of a woman trained to physical perfection as far as that is
attainable through athletics and acrobatics. That has caused Miss
Kellermann to look wholesome in tights. There is nothing suggestive
or in the least mite objectionable; just a perfect figure in her build,
gained through out-door exercise. Even in the first section, before
the young woman's exhibition of fancy diving, one may notice her

suppleness, which no hothouse beauty could develop in an atmosphere
of cigarette smoke and press agents. Miss Kellermann is an Australian.
She has been in this country about six months, making her vaudeville
debut at Keith's, Boston, three weeks ago. Miss Kellermann's act
is in two sections, an unnecessary proceeding. The "Mirror dance"
in the first part of her program could easily be eliminated, when the
diving could be preceded only by her dextrous manipulation of the
"Diablo" spool. She is less dancer than athlete. Her diving is fancy,
pretty and expert. Miss Kellermann's "standing, sitting dive" (so
called by her) is a dandy piece of clean work. In the "neck dive,"
as the girl lies prostrate on the board preparatory to taking the
plunge, she leaves an image which will require a marvelous form to
surpass. For a finale after numerous dives have been illustrated,
Miss Kellermann does an "Australian splash." This finish indicates
the liveliness of her disposition. It is just a squatting jump, but
as she likes this, so does she evidence the fondness she has for the
water by her exhuberant spirits while performing off the board.
One is situated on either side of the stage, about seven or eight feet
from the ground. A tank below is reflected by an inclined mirror
at the back. Miss Kellermann is a great big vaudeville card. Her
fame will spread, not only through her exquisite form, but as well
because that is backed up by good looks--and a good, clean act.

> --Sime Silverman in Variety, No-
> vember 28, 1908, page 12.

                    *   *   *

Miss Kellermann is a beautifully-formed young woman, but, unlike others similarly endowed, she does not rely on perfection of
form or feature for her popularity. She does the most daring and
graceful dives ever performed by a woman. She is a veritable diving
Venus in action as well as name. With all the abandon of a sprite
and the grace of a mermaid--if there are mermaids, they must be
graceful!--Miss Kellermann performs so many different and difficult
"stunts" from a spring-board into a tank that it were almost impossible to keep track of the variations. She is a decided novelty and
drawing card wherever she appears; and, good to know and good
to tell, there is nothing even remotely suggesting vulgarity about
her act from its beginning to its ending.

> --New York Star, Vol. I, No. 18,
> January 30, 1909, page 8.

●   WALTER C. KELLY

Mr. Kelly returns after an absence of three years, with a budget of new stories. He received as warm a welcome as could possibly
be wished for. Preceding his routine of "Virginia Judge" stories,
he relates a couple of incidents alleged to have occurred during his

tour of the world. The first is about an Irishman in Dublin who
applied for a room at the Hotel Metropole, Dublin, and insisted on
getting room 37. When the clerk informs him that Room 37 is occupied
by a "Mr. O'Reilly," he replies that he's "Mr. O'Reilly" and that he
has just fallen out of the window. Told in Kelly's inimitable style,
it brought down the house. The other departure from his routine
is equally good. Kelly is in a class by himself in vaudeville--or out
of it. He is as unique and refreshing as was his namesake, the
late J.W. Kelly--but in an entirely different way.

--"Jolo" [Joshua Lowe] in Variety,
October 7, 1911, page 14.

* * *

Walter C. Kelly, "The Virginia Judge," appears in New York
all too seldom. This week he is at the 44th Street Music Hall, after
a long absence from America. It is two years since Mr. Kelly started
a trip around the world. His humor is the brand that anyone who
understands English must laugh at. Its wit, and the telling, whether
the dialect is of the Irish, English or colored race, never has a flaw.
Tuesday evening Mr. Kelly's stories were all new, with two exceptions. One is the "Corned Beef" tale which Mr. Kelly could not have
known without information was related here before he arrived in town.
The other was good enough to be revived. The Virginia Judge tales
are more laughable than ever. One is when a colored man, pleading
against a charge of stealing chickens, says, "Judge the Lord may
strike me dead if I stole." "Stand over there for five minutes,"
replies the Judge, "and if you are still living I'll give you 90 days."
Walter Kelly is the kind of an entertainer who should be held in one
theatre for a run. You never tire of Kelly. As a single-handed
character story teller he is without peer.

--Sime Silverman in Variety, November 14, 1913, page 18.

* * *

For years Walter Kelly played the Virginia Judge and the old
Orpheum Circuit with great success. A Southern accent and human
humor were part of his stage routine and, wisely enough, he's retained both for his first picture venture [Virginia Judge, released
by Paramount].

Against the background of a sub-Mason-Dixon hamlet, authors
Kelly and Octavus Roy Cohen (adaptation, Frank R. Adams) have
etched a father-stepson theme. It has moments of poignance for
which the Judge is responsible, and some brisk comedy furnished
by Stepin Fetchit and J. H. Allen.

Marsha Hunt plays a strictly program role in a strictly program

picture with a charm and quaintness that attracts attention. She'll
remind you of the Lillian Gish of the early Biograph days.

The older generation who have laughed at Walter Kelly's stories
for thirty years will thank Edward Sedgwick, director, for presenting
him so faithfully on the screen.

--Herb Sterne in Rob Wagner's
Script, November 23, 1935, page
10.

•   HETTY KING

Following the appearance of Vesta Tilley last season, Hetty
King's appearance here this year is given an added interest, although
the latter may be said to work at a slight disadvantage owing to
the undoubted popularity of Miss Tilley with American audiences.
And though they are both male impersonators, each has a different
method, and each assumes characters that are somewhat unlike those
used by the other, hence comparisons are hardly fair. Miss King
dresses her parts in quite as dapper a manner as does Miss Tilley
and her appearances as the typical London Beau Brummel are most
becoming to her and she wears her clothes remarkably well. Her
first character impersonation was that of a seaside youth who appeared in a natty blue sack suit, single breasted coat, straw hat
with black band, patent leather shoes with white tops and black buttons, black four-in-hand tie and high collar. The accompanying song,
"Beside the Seaside," was quite tuneful, and on the whole the number
was pleasing. This was followed by Miss King's appearance as a
young naval officer, for which character she wore a dark blue naval
officer's uniform. Next she was seen as a young chap in morning
walking suit consisting of a black cutaway one buttoned coat, top
hat, drab waistcoat with white facings, gray four-in-hand tie, patent
leather shoes with drab tops, gray suede gloves, violet boutinierre,
monocle, and walking stick. "In the Park" was the song rendered,
it also being quite tuneful and typically English. The closing number
was a semidramatic rendition, consisting of a recitative sort of song
entitled "My Birthday." Conventional evening clothes of faultless
cut and fit were worn, while a half stage C.D.F. set was utilized.
The song was about the twenty-first birthday of a society lad who
joyously anticipates his coming liberties as a full grown man as well
as the happiness of spending his own fortune. He picks up a letter
left for him by his father and to his horror learns that the latter
has lost his money through speculation. A telephone bell rings and
the boy is told that his parent had "accidentally" shot himself and is
dead. The story ends here with the youth bowed down by his disappointment and sorrow. Miss King not only held the interest of
her auditors, but showed that she has the ability to do serious work
quite as well as she can the lighter and amusing characterizations
and she is deserving of praise for her restraint in the latter part

of the impersonation and for not reverting to melodramatic methods.
An encore was called for on Wednesday night and the artist responded
with an old favorite of her's, "Going Away," in which song she im-
personates the character of a British sailor who is about to start
forth on a sea voyage. The dance, though not typical of the sea,
was dainty and pretty to watch and the audience seemed to forget
that it might as well have been done with skirts as in sailor's trousers. The act ran thirty-two minutes, including the encore number,
a long time for the usual vaudeville offering, but not for Miss King.

--The New York Dramatic Mirror,
December 25, 1909, page 20.

* * *

Hetty King, England's foremost Male Impersonator. This is
the billing on the program. Even though she were not billed as
such, Miss King can rest assured that she IS supreme in her line.
Making her initial New York appearance [at the Winter Garden, New
York], Miss King brought over with her a batch of new songs that
are corkers. Opening in evening clothes she sang "Fill 'Em Up,"
a fast number. Miss King has the honor of being the first woman
to smoke a cigar and pipe, in vaudeville. This she does in her first
song and in her sailor number. Her second number the "Poppy Show"
song, describing an old farmer coming to gay London for a fast time,
went over with a bang. Her description of the old man was cleverly
put over. She then sang a Sailor Song, "All Hands on Deck." For
her finale she delivered a corking Scotch soldier number, "Till I
Come Back Again." In delivering this number Miss King certainly
gave the audience an original idea of the Scotch soldier's walk and
other mannerisms. It was a great finale for her Monday night. Not
only receiving armful of bouquets, and a wonderful ovation, Miss
King also had the honor of having the British consulate there to
see her, besides other foreign representatives in both lower boxes.
A speech had to be made on her exit, and the entire house sent her
off to the strongest and most rousing reception that any English
artist has ever received in a vaudeville house in this country in many
moons.

--"Rose" in Dramatic Mirror, October 29, 1921, page 635.

● GRACE LA RUE

Returning to America after a season of triumph at the Parisian
capital, Grace La Rue opened an engagement at the American Music
Hall and Roof Garden last week under the most auspicious circumstances. Her coming had been loudly and broadly acclaimed and
added to the opening of the new roof-garden and an exceptional bill
of contemporaneous headliners, she was welcomed by capacity houses.

The first portion of Miss La Rue's act is particularly pleasing, and had she stopped there and not attempted the quite pretentious pantomime which followed, the impression would have been much better. Her first part consisted of three song renditions, including "I'm Related by Marriage to Melba," a fairly cleverly written comic song with an air that was tuneful, though not catching; "Highland Mary," sung by others previously, but rendered with exceptional unction and ability by Miss La Rue, and lastly "Love Thy Neighbor as Thyself, But Leave His Wife Alone," which was not only the best of her repertoire, but one of the funniest songs of the season. It is along a theme that might make it a "blue" song, but fortunately the author has kept from the shady side of melody lane and has been satisfied to let it stand as an amusing satire on modern everyday life. The tune is very good and in all likelihood it will become a popular ballad, undoubtedly so if it is sung by others as well as Miss La Rue sings it. During the first part the singer wore one costume, quite indescribable, but very Parisian and wonderful. The second part consisted of a pantomime showing a scene in a cafe of the French metropolis, utilizing fifteen supporting pantomimists, mostly women, who sat around and tried to look "bewitching." One or two succeeded in a mild way, while the men (roues of the rogueish, devilishly daring type) stood and sat about in a sufficiently fascinated way, sipping wine and keeping the cigarettes of the ladies lighted in a most decorous fashion. The pantomime had to do with a girl who had but recently married a real man (by make-up and general bearing, a true Hero with a capital H!), who had taken her away from a life of abandoned and gladsome unhappiness. The lure of the cafes called her back to her former life and habits, however, and hence the title--The Call of the Past. In the cafe she meets a former sweetheart, who endeavors to tempt her to return to him. Strife of the strenuous sort is suffered until the crucial moment when the fond and loving husband appears in the background and beckons to her in truly melodramatic fashion, finally clasping the almost weepingly relentful woman to his manly chest! It was all very dramatic and Laura Jean Libby like and will appeal most strongly to the lover of life as it is painted on the canvas of originality. Miss La Rue has a dance that is supposed to portray varying emotions and, aided by a costume that had been advertised as having "created the greatest dress sensation the Parisian capital has ever witnessed," she made an impression not soon to be forgotten. The gown was "sensational," to say the least, and as inartistic and garish as the modern fashioner of women's garb could make it. Enough! The supporting company were dressed appropriately and at the finish the star was awarded a sufficient number of bows and curtains to have satisfied her. Had she closed her act with the first songs she might possibly have been accorded an ovation. At least she showed her real talent and abilities, and of these she is abundantly supplied, for Miss La Rue is a true artist and it is to be regretted that she has fallen heir to the present day pining for pantomime in dance form.

--The New York Dramatic Mirror,
June 31, 1909, page 18.

• GEORGE LASHWOOD

We have had English, French, German and Scotch comedians
galore--some of exceptional merit, some that were passable and some
that simply "walked right in and turned around and walked right
out again." And now we are greeting the latest of such "importa-
tions" in the person of George Lashwood, who likes to call himself
"The Beau Brummel of Vaudeville." And it is a greeting both warm
and hearty, for if ever an artist stood in two shoes this Lashwood
is such. At the Plaza Music Hall last week, where he made his
American debut under the sheltering wing of William Morris, he won
instant recognition, just as Alice Lloyd did three years ago, only
in her case she came over unheralded and almost "on rubbers," and
awoke the next morning to find herself becoming famous. But Lashwood had been announced, and so loudly and widely that one began
to sort of anticipate a deep disappointment, such is so often the
case. Three big causes enter into the successful make-up of Mr.
Lashwood. In the first place, he has a remarkably exuberant and
appealing personality, to say nothing of stage confidence, real ability
and good looks; in the second, he dresses and stages his act in a
most admirable fashion, and in the third (which might well come first),
he sings a number of songs that are tuneful, witty and appealing,
some a bit risque, but not vulgar. Seldom--even recognizing the
songs hits of Miss Lloyd and Harry Lauder--has a European come to
our shores with such rattling good material, and on Thursday night
the audience commenced humming the choruses of most of his songs
after a first rendition. Mr. Lashwood opened in one with a comic
song, mildly risque in one verse, entitled "It's Another Fellow Looks
Like Me," appearing in evening garb of the latest London mode.
Then a special set in four, showing the deck of a Channel steamer
with a sea drop in the background, was used. The comedian appeared
in white flannels and straw hat and sang a most amusing song probably entitled "Sea, Sea, Sea, Why Are You Angry with Me?" calling
for much of the business relative to certain well defined consequences
of ocean travel. Returning to one, he next offered a London "bobby"
song, now appearing in the correct garb of the police officer of the
British metropolis. The song used here, though not as tuneful as
the others, was quite as amusing and won favor from the start.
"In the Twi-twi-light" caught the fancy of the audience from the
start, and, barring a few lines which might be taken suggestively,
it is a song that should become exceedingly popular. He wore an
immaculate brown frock suit, with high silk hat, which helped him
to prove his "Beau Brummel" title. A Scotch number came after this,
green plaid kilties, white military jacket and bare calves and knees,
showing the entertainer off to particular advantage. The song was
called "That's Why Sandy Tickled the Ladies So," and though it is
of the usual Scotch variety and not very remarkable in any way,
the audience began calling for more until Mr. Lashwood obliged with
what proved to be his best number, "My Latch Key." He worked
in a spot during this rendition and again wore evening clothes. The
number was partly recitative and had to do with the days of bachelor-
hood, which the singer was about to cast aside in favor of matrimony,

and hence his friendly latchkey and he are forced to part. At its
close Mr. Lashwood was called out for many bows, and the applause
did not begin to subside until the cards for the next act were placed
and the act had fairly gotten under way. A word regarding the
costume changes of the artist are due here, for seldom, if ever, has
a player been seen who makes such rapid changes and who appears
each time in such faultless attire. Both Americans and Europeans
can learn a big lesson by watching him. Not for this alone, but for
the other reasons that make him a vaudeville "star" worthy of the
name.

--The New York Dramatic Mirror,
December 18, 1909, page 19.

•   HARRY LAUDER

     The warmth with which the Lincoln Square audience greeted
Harry Lauder upon his return visit to America is indicated by the
fact that he held the stage alone for an hour and fifteen minutes
Monday night. But that statement gives no impression of the enthusiasm which swept over the huge audience when the little Scot
came upon the stage, or the din that held him speechless for minutes
at several points during his turn, unable to make himself heard.
Probably no actor has enjoyed such a welcome on the American stage
within the last decade. After singing five songs, making at least
three speeches and finally singing "Rocked in the Cradle of the
Deep" for want of something else the audience stormed for two minutes to an empty stage before the final act could go on. It is impossible to catch and analyze the peculiarly elusive charm of this
great artist. It is a thing so subtle and indefinable it has not a
name, and yet it exerts a force that cannot be escaped. Enough to
say the Scotchman in his field of character drawing is the perfect
artist, if such there be. His every word and gesture gives a line
or faithful touch of color to the picture he seeks to draw, and the
whole is a vivid, forceful characterization. Although Mr. Lauder
has brought over a budget of new songs, the old ones hold their
established place with "The Saftest of the Family" by long odds the
best of the lot. In it he reaches his greatest refinement of humor--
the humor that is touched with pathos. No one can watch his silly
youngster with unmixed laughter. "The Wedding Bells Were Ringing"
is the most enjoyable of the new numbers. In it the singer describes
a wedding feast wherein the toastmaster is overcome with feeling and
excess of spirits and addresses a speech to the bridegroom. As a
"souse" Lauder is utterly irrestible with his uncertain movements
and labored speech. On Monday night he sang "When I Get Back
to Bonnie Scotland" first, a light little descriptive ballad that is good
only because Lauder sings it. The silly boy second and in the order
named "Wedding Bells," "I Love a Lassie" and finally "We Parted on
the Shore." In the "Lassie" he is assisted by a pretty little girl,
who looks the part, a sweet girlish figure that adds a good deal to

the picture. Toward the end of the act members of the audience
became a bit unruly in their demands for more.   There were shouts
of "Give us another song, Harry," from all over the house and loud
cries for "She's Ma Daisy." Lauder's reappearance is a greater success than was his visit last year.

> --"Rush" [Alfred Greason] in
> Variety, October 17, 1908, page
> 12.

● JOE LAURIE

Joe Jaurie, known on the bills as of pint size, appears as a
single. His sketch has the title "Whatika?," which is of the same
language as "Attaboy," being a Gotham version of the phrase, "What
do I care?" It is a good act, as Laurie puts it out, and, in fact,
it could hardly be done by any one else. In the first place, Laurie
is one of the most likable chaps on the vaudeville stage, and he invites the entire audience to visit him at his home, and then introduces them to his father and mother, and makes everyone feel comfortable and top hole by his sheer good spirits.

> --"Mark" in Dramatic Mirror, Oc-
> tober 23, 1919, page 1662.

● EDDIE LEONARD

Eddie Leonard, who for many years has been the standard
bearer of burntcork entertainment, is still the minstrel of the hour.
The genial black-face singer and dancer was never in better form
than now, and his present routine, while similar in some respects
to previous offerings, has a crispness and glitter that make it different from its predecessors. His stage attire--lavender and scarlet
satin--is still one of the features of the act; his characteristic dancing is still magnetic and his personality oozes over the footlights
like a freshening breeze. His support numbers 16 men and a woman
and embraces vocalists, expert dancers, banjoists and pianist. Eddie
sings "Sam, the Alabama Man;" "I Lost My Gal" and "Mandy Jane,"
accompanying each ditty with some of his graceful stepping. He
introduces a character bit of a darky who had seen and had everything to the lilting melody of "I'm On My Way." This is an innovation to the Leonard routine and another departure is his singing of
a spiritual number, "Follow Me," in which the minstrel shows excellent
vocal improvement from other years. Between Eddie's numbers the
black-face choristers give several catchy numbers; a pair of hoofers
captivate the house with their fast and intricate footwork and a third
dancer goes thru his taps like a streak of greased lightning and with
precision and nimbleness. A mixed team offers some good hock steps
and the male part of this team indulges in some clever floor tumbling

and acrobatics. Medleys and croonings are given at opportune intervals and the entire act is resonant with old-time minstrelsy, but
in the spirit of the moment. Eddie Leonard ingeniously entwines the
strains of the popular "Ida" and "Roly Boly Eyes," that bring the
house to its feet whenever sung by their inimitable sponsor.

Eddie Leonard is a great showman; he knows minstrelsy to
the last lilt; his graceful stepping equals any of the former masters
of this art, and he deserves every favor extended to him by his audience. He is indeed the minstrel of the hour.

--"J.W.R." in The Billboard, November 5, 1927, page 18.

• ETHEL LEVEY

That Ethel Levey is a big drawing card in vaudeville was
demonstrated at the Harlem Opera House Monday night, when every
seat in the house was occupied and the overflow was standing four
deep behind the orchestra rail. In a handsome gray gown Miss Levey
sang three songs and would have stopped there but the audience
insisted upon one more. The opening number was the one she made
popular in George Washington Jr. This was followed by two songs
on the "coon" order which gave the singer an opportunity to show
that she is at her best when dancing. With her reappearance in
vaudeville as a single entertainer Ethel Levey scored a great big
solid hit.

--Variety, January 19, 1907, page
8.

• TED LEWIS

Ted Lewis, who has confined his activities of late to the neighborhood of Sheridan Square, is once more in the midst of what was
until the strike the well-known Gay White Way. He made his entry
at the Palace with a bang and kept on hanging clear through his
exit to a curtain speech. There are few who would dare dispute
his title of "Jazz King." His middle name is rhythm and he fingers
a wicked clarinet not to mention a mean shimmy. His four abettors,
togged out like the clown dog in an animal act, give valuable assistance. The laughing trombone is a wonder. Altogether, Ted and
the boys make a prize bunch of jazz banditti.

--"Martin" in Dramatic Mirror,
September 4, 1919, page 1406.

● WINNIE LIGHTNER

Just by way of putting it in a new light, the advance billing
read that the Lightner Girls just had to have their own revue. Well
the Lightner Sisters and Newton Alexander have that same revue on
tap at the Palace this week and it has a sure-enough revue kick.
But bright, shining star is little Winnie Lightner. She is a whole
show in herself. She is peppery, vivacious, clowning one minute
and singing a straight ballad the next. She has always appeared
as a comedienne heretofore yet she has a few minutes in the revue
where she displays a serious side. The act has girls, special stage
setting, special songs and a wardrobe that would do credit to a
production. There are some corking numbers, perhaps the best
remembered being "Since That Jazz Has Gone to China Town" (sung
by the sisters and Alexander), "Tric-Tric-Tricoline," (a fast snappy
number by Miss Winnie and the Chorus), "Wonderful Eyes" (solo by
Winnie), "The Ragtime Drummer Boy," with a fast dancing specialty
by an unprogrammed team. This dancing pair is a "find" for the
Lightner-Alexander revue and fits in like a glove. The woman is a
little chic, a pert dresser, but unusually agile and graceful. All
told the entire revue is just right for vaudeville and at the Palace
Monday was the biggest kind of a hit.

> --"Mark" in Dramatic Mirror, Oc-
> tober 16, 1920, page 686.

● BEATRICE LILLIE

Miss Beatrice Lillie must be rather tired by now of reading in
the newspapers that she does wonders with the libretto of any show
she happens to be in but that when she is not on-stage things are
pretty dreary. Certainly we newspaper boys are tired of writing it.

Being a still-born librettist ourself, we have great sympathy
for the authors of She's My Baby,* for there are plenty of cracks in
in the book which ought to be funny but which suddenly, on being
uttered, undergo a horrid metamorphosis, like cream during a thunder-
storm, and become duds. Then, too, there are many cracks which
were sour to start with. At any rate, as in her last year's show,
Miss Lillie has to fight an uphill fight all the way against the book.

But Miss Lillie is one of the best little uphill fighters on the
stage. Simply to watch her simulating polite and aristocratic interest
in the conversation of her dinner-companion, or to hear her sing "A
Baby's Best Pal Is Its Mother," is enough to salve the wounds caused

---

*Opened at the Globe Theatre, New York, on January 3, 1928, and
ran for 71 performances.

by fifty previous rusty gags. In her single-handed combat against
the authors she is forced to return to many of her old tricks, but
to complain of Beatrice Lillie's old tricks would be like complaining
of the same old pay-envelope coming around every Saturday.

The fortunately indefatigable team of Rodgers and Hart have
written their customary satisfactory music and lyrics, and Messrs.
Clifton Webb, Jack Whiting and Nick Long, Jr. , and Miss Ula Sharon
supply the show with enough graceful dancing for three productions.
There is also an octet of Tiller Girls who conduct a brave and at
least temporarily successful charge to regain the old Tiller machine-
gun position recently captured by Albertina Rasch and Chester Hale.

And, in case you have been skipping around on this page,
just reading the short paragraphs, there is Beatrice Lillie.

> --Robert Benchley in Life, Janu-
> ary 19, 1928, page 21.

• ALICE LLOYD

Alice Lloyd has the Lloyd dental laugh, the broad cockney
sense of humor, and the zest of twisting a line into an innuendo,
although she is a bit more "Americanized" and less amusing than her
sister, Marie.

First Miss Lloyd appears in a pink minaret gown, topped by
a black hat, to sing "How Shocking"--or something that might have
had that title. At least shocking rhymes with stocking and we heard
the effect a slashed crinoline gown had on a mere masculine passerby.
Then she returned in a demure nurse costume and cap to tell of the
courtship of Mary and how "Mary Told the Story to a Soldier." "All
the Nice Girls Love a Sailor," so popular in the English halls, is
done in a nautical suit, and Miss Lloyd follows in a recitation song,
"The Four Ages of Women." To show her versatility the comedienne
presents a typical Lloyd cockney number, relating her adventures
with interested spectators, while climbing the steps of a street 'bus
and on the bathing beach. "Who y' Lookin' at, Eh?" is the refrain.

Finally she told in "Mother, Mother, Mother," of Lucy, who
didn't return from the party at eleven, because she was afraid to
come home in the dark--and waited for the break of day.

Most of Miss Lloyd's numbers come under the category of "blue"
--but the broad English humor somehow strikes home. We can't help
laughing at Marie Lloyd's melodic innuendos or smiling at Alice Lloyd's
touch of risque suggestion.

It was interesting to watch Miss Lloyd's reception at the Colonial. Now the Lloyds--like all English variety stars--are

favorites of the masses. By her third number she had the Colonial
gallery--the gallery which had caused a good many shudders to per-
formers--whistling and humming along with her. They were hers
to a man.

Downstairs she even interested the blase tango-tired Monday afternoon gathering. And the Colonial orchestra patrons are--
well--Central Park West. The girls are the debutante slouch-Venus
half veil-tilted hat-shrinking glide idols and the masculine followers
are the kind that have tiny moustaches and plenty of time on their
hands.

Outside of the musical director, Julius Lenzberg--who is an
institution as well as a joy forever--they don't enthuse particularly
over anyone.

But Miss Lloyd's cockney humor reaches them. Just at present
she is giving too many songs--six in all--and taking a bit too long
to make her costume changes. Still, she's worth waiting for.

> --Frederick James Smith in The
> New York Dramatic Mirror, April
> 29, 1914, page 19.

• MARIE LLOYD

Marie Lloyd is a wonder. More than that, she is a consummate
artist. No one who knows her work and songs in other days can
fail to realize that fact after hearing her specialty at the Palace this
week.

To be strictly frank, Miss Lloyd's songs this year are not quite
as clever as usual. But that does not hurt her performance as a
whole. Her songs with scarcely an exception, are clever--immeasur-
ably superior to most of the ditties of the same class which are written over here, and superior, too, to most of the songs which other
vaudeville stars have recently brought from the other side; but no
matter what they are, Miss Lloyd sings them with so much subtlety,
so much expression and such an infinite and adroit indelicacy and
yet so wholesomely that they become in their rendering works of art.

No one can have climbed to and won and held the position which
she holds in the vaudeville world without having won her spurs legitimately. And that is what Miss Lloyd's work shows and demon-
strates at every turn. It isn't the way she says the things she
sings, it's just simply the way she does it. This woman with a few
notes of music to help her out could make the City Directory sound
like the bluest of Blue Books, and she would achieve her purpose
not with her voice, which may be regarded as a strictly limited asset,
but by a mere glance of the eye.

Last winter, when Mme. Sarah Bernhardt in the course of conversation said that she considered Marie Lloyd to be the most artistic comedienne on the English stage today she was neither talking
through her aigrettes nor throwing sweet nothings in the way of
encomiums to the desert air.

Being more or less of a vaudevillianess herself--as Mme. Bernhardt appears in England almost exclusively now on a vaudeville
circuit--the great French actress when she made this remark went
on to explain exactly all her songs, no matter whether they were
either black or blue, always gave you a type which was invariably
true to life, and that while most of the English actresses on the so-
called legitimate stage were so busy sipping tea and the upper crusts
and incidentally forcing their way into society, Miss Lloyd and a
few of her followers were the only artists who were really doing
justice to a certain class of London types which most of the other
actresses were too snobby to even attempt to depict. The most remarkable feature of Miss Lloyd's present appearance is the way in
which she wins her audience song by song. Last night it took at
least three songs to make the audience thoroughly appreciate her,
and from that time, as they realized her cleverness and versatility,
they were her friends for life. As some cockney wit in a moment of
enthusiasm, and possibly alcohol, remarked of her in London years
ago: "Marie Lloyd is more than a dissipation; she's a beloved 'abit,
which grows on you just like your mustache."

--Acton Davies in New York Evening Sun, October 16, 1913.

● CISSIE/CECELIA LOFTUS

Indefatigable, ever youthful, and now intrepid enough to return to Los Angeles with a whole evening of items old and new,
"Cissie" Loftus showed plenty of spunk and flashes of her rare
mimic wit when she presented "Impressions and Impersonations" at
the Biltmore. A friendly audience applauded each offering, and there
is probably no woman alive who could try what Miss Loftus attempted
and come as near to complete success. But the fact remains that
her show clamors for intimacy and informality, for musical backgrounds
and interpolations that would give the artist a breathing spell and
the audience some contrasts. With these elements lacking (when the
chubby pianist played Palmgren's "May Night" to first-nighters I
was positively chagrined) Miss Loftus worked against handicaps, and
her offerings were uneven. Possibly she was indisposed, too proud
a veteran of the theater to ask any concessions or sympathy. When
she was good, like the little girl, she was very, very good. When
she was bad, she wasn't Cissie Loftus.

Her virtuosity is chiefly vocal, requires gestures and mannerisms only to enhance the general effect, dispenses with costumes, and

hand props almost entirely. While jolly fun, impersonations of Bea
Lillie, Lynn Fontanne, and Florence Reed offer no real test of a
mimic's skill. Ethel Barrymore is easy too, but by choosing a scene
from The Kingdom of God Miss Loftus surpassed all competitors and
crept up on Ethel too. Noel Coward and Gertrude Lawrence deserved
better than they got, but Fanny Brice and Walter Huston should be
well satisfied. Miss Loftus is at her best when she is gently savage,
so that "Mrs. Pat Campbell in Hollywood" was a gem--and I think
Cissie meant it! She recreated stars of the past with uncanny fi-
delity, notably Mrs. Fiske and Jeanne Eagels; scorched Libby Holman and the torch singers; paid tribute to Bernhardt in a fluent and
inspired impersonation that was unerring down to the last detail.

> --Richard Sheridan Ames in Rob
> Wagner's Script, Vol. 21, No.
> 495, February 11, 1939, page
> 19.

● LYDIA LOPOKOVA

Lydia Lopokova is a charming little dancer, trained in the
thorough Russian school of Pavlova, Mordkin and Volinine. She came
to vaudeville assisted by the Morgan dancers--six young women,
who interpret an Egyptian ballet of angular arm gestures, a Greek
bacchanal and a number--the best of their repertoire--descriptive
of the Roman games.

Mlle. Lopokova herself appears in three divertisements--the
first a pizzicato ballet danced to the music of Delibes, the second
the Xylophone (Ivanoff), and finally the Russian National Dance.
This is invested with a compelling Tartar fire and Slav artistry.
Mlle. Lopokova is an able and pretty dancer. She lacks the drama
and passion of Pavlova, but she possesses a delightful grace, an
excellent skill of pantomime and a splendid technique. There is a
fresh girlishness in Lopokova's dancing where there is an infinite
drama in Pavlova's art.

The specialty is well arranged. The Morgan dancers are the
most spontaneous of the classic interpreters yet observed in vaudeville. There is pagan joy of nature in their dancing. They give
thoroughly interesting assistance to Mlle. Lopokova.

> --Frederick James Smith in The
> New York Dramatic Mirror, April
> 28, 1915, page 16.

● WILL MAHONEY

We caught Mahoney under conditions that would be a great

handicap to most performers, and that was at just the one performance where he had been called in from another house to lengthen the
bill at the Coliseum. Despite that, Mahoney succeeded in stopping
the show cold here.

Mahoney does a "nut" routine of talk, verses, and songs, in
a style that is decidedly different from the average and with material
that is great. In addition he does a routine of tap-dancing in a
comedy manner that can't miss for applause, for it's a great dance.
There is only one weak part in the routine which can be built up or
replaced to be worthy of the rest of the material in the act. That
is in the "I Used To Love You" bit. Which reminds us to state that
Mahoney is also unusual as a nut comedian, inasmuch as he really
does possess a very good singing voice. He'll please on most any
bill.

> --"Hoffman" in Dramatic Mirror,
> October 22, 1921, page 598.

• FAY MARBE

Smart dresser. Pert looker. Displays a world of vivacity,
dynamic energy and ability. Is young and has personality plus.
Has both a musical comedy and screen experience to boom her vaudeville percentage. All this pertains to Fay Marbe who made her Broadway "big time" debut at the Palace last week. Miss Marbe proved
quite a feminine asset to the bill. She got along swimmingly with
the vocal numbers assigned and then cavorted in the style of pep
and animation that established her in big favor. Her numbers included "The Kiss" (special), "Tra Tra La," also written especially
for her, "The Jazz Vampire," "Sweet Daddies" and "Mexico," the
last named bringing Miss Marbe out in becoming Spanish attire and
giving the pretty young woman a chance to display unusual agility.
She wears some stunning clothes--all designed by Miss Marbe and her
talented mother. Miss Marbe was voted a genuine success. Miss
Marbe has triumphed most satisfactorily and successfully upon her
initial vaudeville conquest.

> --"Mark" in Dramatic Mirror, Sep-
> tember 18, 1920, page 506.

• MARX BROTHERS

When Gus Edwards' "School Boys and Girls" recently appeared
at Hammerstein's, it was mentioned in a criticism in this paper that
there were "school acts" on the "small time" much better than Mr.
Edwards' played out turn. The act arrived sooner than expected.
It is the Marx Brothers, from the west, with seven people. They
make the Edwards number look foolish. A lively set of youngsters,

with four comedians. One is the school teacher doing "Dutch."
The other three are a "Patsy Bolivar," Hebrew and "Cissy." The
Patsy boy is like Clarence Wilbur in work, and a natural comedian.
Also he is a harpist, and a good one. Introducing the harp into
the centre of the turn, he scored an unusually large success, de-
servedly so, too, besides giving a classy touch to the whole. The
"Cissy" is a baritone, although using a falsetto while speaking. He
brings good fun, helped on by a passable Hebrew. The teacher
does well as a "Dutchman," and makes quite something out of "Sch-
nitzelbaum," as worked by him. The girls do not figure largely,
excepting to help out in talk and the choruses, although one leads
"Schoolmates" for the finale. This is nicely worked up by the Patsy
boy, but a new song should be inserted here. There is little rough
stuff in this "school act," and it will be liked on almost any bill,
playing differently from the usual run. It is the best "school act"
seen since the Edwards turn had Herman Timberg in it.

--Sime Silverman in Variety, February 24, 1912, page 17.

• OWEN McGIVENEY

   Recalling all the fuss and stir that one's wedding caused, changing from bridal togs into traveling ones, remembering the ring, the
minister's fee, kissing mother-in-law and things equally pleasant and
disagreeable, will give you a slight insight into the tempest which
Owen McGiveney, quick change artist and actor, experiences. Mr.
McGiveney plays the characters involved in the murder of Nancy
Sykes in Oliver Twist. Nary another actor turns a hair in this pretty
little example of the law's wrath. Among the different characters
he is Fagin, the master thief; Nancy, the murdered, and Bill Sykes,
the murderer. The exits and entrances are so interlaced that the
characters fairly pass each other before the footlights. To watch
Mr. McGiveney behind scenes is as bewildering as the mother who
made for her son a pair of breeches, both sides alike. She never
knew whether he was coming or going, nor which side to spank.

   However, the critics have no occasion for such a decision when
Mr. McGiveney's creations come into orchestra view. Crediting him
with finely etched portrayals, it is his diving out of the wigs, safety
pins and corsets of one character into the complexities of another
and beating the second hand's record, too, while doing it, that
gives him the greatest rank of entertainer. He could fill the position of switchman, generalissimo, in the heart of a railroad yard and
not even get mixed the smoke of north, south, west or east trains.
But we would rather have him on the stage.

--Frederick James Smith in Dramatic Mirror, March 15, 1919,
page 381.

• McINTYRE AND HEATH

To describe [James] McIntyre and [Thomas] Heath in Hayti*
would be like diagraming Lew Fields' dialect. The in Hayti portion
of the title is quite beside the question. The management would be
doing both public and author full justice if it dubbed the musical
play simply "McIntyre and Heath."

To be sure, up at the Circle, where these burnt cork artists
are appearing, there are a stage full of girls, an all-night libretto,
hot and cold lyrics, a running score, open plot and other musical
comedy modern improvements, but they count for nothing. The play
distinctly is not the thing. McIntyre and Heath are the entire dramatic "joy ride."

When McIntyre (never mind the character) explains how Heath
(Same directions) assaulted him with a "sickly tomatus," it is eminently
proper for persons in the audience to double up with merriment.
When, in the succeeding act, Heath puts McIntyre through a mock
drill, the onlooker is to be excused if he rolls out of his seat in a
paroxysm of laughter. And when McIntyre finally is made President
of Hayti and begins to wreak his vengeance on Heath, hysteria is
quite permissible under the code.

There isn't a New Theatre idea in the entertainment. Prof.
Brander Matthews never would forgive himself for looking in upon
it, and Literary Director John Corbin would blush forevermore should
he find himself so much as reading the Circle's electric sign. Yet,
to the ordinary human being who is not ashamed to laugh without
permission McIntyre and Heath in Hayti is recommended. The piece
wouldn't uplift a waterbug, it will not advance civilization a single
peg, yet it's worth seven dozen of The Master Builder.

                              --Channing Pollock in The Green
                                Book Album, November 1909,
                                page 1016.

• RAQUEL MELLER

The big question among American theatregoers concerning
Raquel Meller does not seem to be "Is she worth hearing?" but "Is
she worth ten dollars a seat?" To those who phrase their query in
this form we would unhesitatingly reply: "No, not to you."

You yourself are the best judge of whether or not you have
ten dollars to spare. (And incidentally, why all this to-do about

_____
*Opened at the Circle Theatre, New York, on August 30, 1909, and
ran for 50 performances.

a frank box-office price of ten dollars from people who go night
after night to agencies and beg, on their bended knees, to be tapped
for twelve and fifteen dollars a seat for a revue?) Once you have
decided that you have ten dollars to invest in an evening's entertainment, for Heaven's sake forget it and shut up. You'll get your
evening's entertainment, all right—and more.

You cannot check up your ten dollars spent on Señorita Meller
by any of the conventional standards of the theatre. You will see
flashes of fine acting, but you can see as good in any one of five
plays in town. You will hear several charming songs delightfully
sung, but not your blessed ten dollars' worth. You will see a variety
of subtle characterizations, but for two dollars and seventy-five cents
you can attend Ruth Draper's recital and find five characterizations
to Meller's one, all of them more difficult, more varied, more subtle.
(There is, of course, no basis for comparison between Ruth Draper
and Meller. One appeals to the intelligence, the other to the pit of
the stomach.) And, furthermore, for the first five minutes of Meller's
appearance, you would be willing to swear that you could find a
dozen more beautiful women within a ten-dollar goldpiece's throw.

And then something begins to happen. Spring comes! The
old arteries begin to assume a gala activity. You suddenly become
convinced that here is one of the world's beautiful women. Then
you realize that she is one of the world's sad women. Then one of
the world's gay women. The stage is eliminated as an agent. It is
a direct producer-to-consumer appeal. You are conscious of the fact
that there is a Personality being projected from in front of those
black curtains and that you are directly in its path. It is an experience which you probably never will forget. Whether or not it
would be worth ten dollars to you, we cannot say.

> --Robert Benchley in Life, May 6,
> 1926, page 27.*

• FLORENCE MILLS

Merely to watch her walk out upon the stage with her long
free stride and her superb shameless swing is an esthetic pleasure;
she is a school and exemplar of carriage and deportment; two other
actors I have seen so take a stage; Cohan by stage instinct, Marie
Tempest by a cultivated genius. Florence Mills is ... "une force
qui va."

---

*Benchley was so amused by the translations from the Spanish of the songs
in Raquel Meller's repertoire that he published his own versions, reprinted
in The Benchley Roundup, edited by Nathaniel Benchley (Harper & Brothers,
1954).

--Gilbert Seldes quoted in Theatre
Arts, Vol. 26, No. 8, August
1942, page 499.

• BORRAH MINEVITCH

Coincident with what seems to be a growing fad for mouth
organs comes this youthful harmonica soloist, who seemingly floored
the house with his appearance and then went on to render four selections to much approval.

Minevitch, as to the front he presents dressed in a dinner
jacket, begins where most of the dance orchestra boys proverbially
end. For that reason he's a cinch with the feminine patrons before
starting. His playing sounds intricate and smacks of expert technique during the minifold variations of the theme melody, whatever
it may be. The repertoire is away from "blues," and mainly confines
itself to popular dance selections of the semi-classical type. Minevitch
seemingly depends upon his manipulation for effects to get the numbers across.

Not without showmanship, this boy had sufficient presence
of mind to pass up an encore which he could justly have taken without being charged with larceny, and, plus his clean-cut appearance,
should be well able to kill time with a route.

However, the understanding is that he sails for London early
in June, where he should find it an easy existence.

--"Skig" [Sid Silverman] in Variety,
May 13, 1925, page 10.

• VICTOR MOORE

The only poor thing about Victor Moore's turn it's too short.
Some vaudevillians don't believe in brevity. They glue themselves
before the footlights for a longer time than some awful child elocutionist. One vaudeville secret is to know when to stop. Moore
did it too soon. He could have filled another five minutes with nary
a let up in the laughs. He comes on like a genial man about town.
His jovial personality catches the audience at once. One of his first
lines, "I am one of a race that is slowly dying out, for I am bar-
tender," started the roaring. He makes few gestures with his hands,
nor do they hang down his sides as if tied with weights. He is one
of the easiest poised monologists on the stage. Experience shows in
his voice, too. It's full of inflection, but under perfect control.
Never once does he gasped for breath which so many of them do in
monologue work. His material was all based on comical anti-prohibition,
and his first exit had a big ovation. His second exit was made on a

splendid line. "When the world gets like heaven won't it be h--l,"
which, of course, places him in "g" with the audience, and they
wanted "more of Moore," even if the rest of the material might have
not been so rich, they desire further entertainment by his personality.

--"Higgins" in Dramatic Mirror,
May 6, 1919, page 672.

* POLLY MORAN

Yes, this is the same Polly Moran, the one who could put over
more funny stuff off the stage than Tommy Gray and Felix Adler
together. Those were the days! Then Polly got married and told
about it. It was either her marriage or open time that sent her from
vaudeville to pictures. Polly was in pictures for four years, and yet
they say Mack Sennett is a tough guy. And all those stage comics
who wanted to be funny before the screen, what they said about
Mack Sennett! But they never said they weren't funny and, as Sennett said nothing, who knows what happened on the Coast. Anyway,
they came back, and Polly Moran remained out there, to become known
as "Sheriff Nell" of the screen. Polly, your jovial little Polly, who
always beat you to the laugh after she had caused it, made audiences
laugh by pantomiming in pictures. She did other things, rode a
horse like a wild Indian, gave Hart a run for gunplay, ran mining
towns right off the reels, and otherwise cut up before the camera
man. The Fifth Avenue, the last half, where Miss Moran was reappearing in vaudeville, showed one of her "Sheriff Nell" film comedies at the opening of the show, the screen also mentioning the original Nell would later appear in person. Polly herself showed next
to closing, all dressed up, with a velvet slouch hat of the tammy
style and a wig. It was a blonde one. When Polly grew tired of it,
she took it off. Then she was a brunet. Meanwhile she sang parodies, mostly set to familiar and popular melodies. She also kidded
her pictures, after chasing the spot around the stage. In a parody
on "The Rosary," Polly brought out some knitting, and, holding it
up, sang to "My Hosiery." Her last number was a straight song,
probably called "The Folks That Won the War." It's an exellently
written lyric and misses no one in the mention. The song gave Polly
a big getaway. Polly's long restful (?) engagements before the
photographer have improved her voice, if she's improved it in no
other way. It's good enough now for Polly to juggle high notes with
it. Polly might use a short run of a "Nell" film in her turn and
talk about it. If Polly told the truth about all she thought of pictures and perhaps herself in them, what could be funnier? But
without that, Polly Moran, in her semi-nut impromptu way, makes a
good single, with or without her celluloid rep. She can get across
on the big time, and when she finally resumes her former friend-
liness with the stage, those other comedians in "one" who buy their

impromptu material and call it "kidding," had better look out for
Poll, for she's a bear with that stuff.

                                        --Sime Silverman in Variety, No-
                                        vember 22, 1918, page 16.

• MORAN AND MACK

    We are a little sorry to hear that the team of Moran and Mack
is no more and that Mr. Mack has a new partner. Mr. Wells may be
very good (we haven't seen him yet), but it always seemed to us
that of all semi-straight-men Mr. Moran possessed the most individuality and skill. In our enthusiasm for the lethargic Mr. Mack we
were apt to neglect Mr. Moran's contribution to the philosophical
discussion. He was always so cross and scowling and so thoroughly
impatient with his companion's phlegmatic search after Truth that he
built up quite a character of his own, which was no small task in
the face of the overpowering presence of Mr. Mack. We hope that
he will go into business for himself now.

                                        --Robert Benchley in Life, Decem-
                                        ber 16, 1926, page 19.

                        *   *   *

    Phonograph records of the Two Black Crows doing their "Early
Bird" number were sold in such enormous quantities that it is safe
to presume that almost everyone in the country has heard the extremely witty dialogue that made George Moran and Charles Mack
famous. Their fame rests entirely on exploitation given them by
this canned process. They were not headliners until their records
achieved such amazing popularity and earned for them their box-
office value. They enter talking pictures and do for this latest method
of canning only what they had done for the phonograph. Why Bring
That Up? is a Paramount picture directed by George Abbott, starr-
ing Moran and Mack whose contributions to it as black-face entertainers consist of the "Early Bird" and the prison turns which they
have been doing practically entirely throughout their theatrical careers
as a team. The two stars are surrounded by an elaborate and highly
entertaining production and their acts are woven into a coherent,
interesting and human story, making the whole thing rather a satisfactory screen offering. During the "Early Bird" number, which was
done in the picture precisely as it was done on the stage and on the
phonograph records, I ceased grinning only when I laughed outright,
for its dialogue has a high content of pure and delicious humor. I
laughed in the same way during the prison-rock-breaking number,
but at the same time I was disappointed. I had seen and heard Moran
and Mack so many times in their old acts that I expected something
new and original in the picture. Surely it is possible to get some
more brilliant nonsense like the tragedy of the early bird and the

worm. If their first picture had presented the team in something new, they would have had an opportunity to repeat, but as Why Bring That Up? merely shows Moran and Mack doing stuff that all the world is familiar with, the public will shy away from their next picture upon the theory that it is but another repetition. However, that is something that the future will take care of. Paramount is to be congratulated upon the elaborateness and the attractiveness of the production with which the Two Black Crows are surrounded. The story is set entirely in a backstage atmosphere, and as it is something that George Abbott knows more about than he does about anything else, it is not to be wondered at that he presented this mysterious region with more realism and conviction than we formerly have seen on the screen. Rehearsals of choruses and players were interwoven into the story in a manner that did not lessen their suggestion of being merely rehearsals, but which at the same time made them highly entertaining. A clever method of covering a time lapse was a dissolve from the chorus rehearsing on a bare stage to the same chorus on the same stage on the opening night of the show. There are several little things about the picture that might have been improved. In a hospital scene we have a nurse crying over a patient. Nothing is more impossible than that. Bert Swor hits Charlie Mack over the head with a bottle and nearly kills him, yet the police apparently showed no interest whatever in the action. George Moran plays himself in the picture, his own name being used, yet he is characterized as a silly ass who fell for the blandishments of Evelyn Brent. Are we to assume that George Moran does foolish things like that, or that he merely was playing an actor who does such things? Evelyn Brent gives another of her very splendid performances, and Harry Green and Bert Swor are entirely adequate. I have been seeing Swor in pictures for a long time, and I was impressed particularly with his work in this one and with his fine talking voice.

> --Welford Beaton in The Film Spec-
> tator, August 24, 1929, pages
> 7-8.

• HELEN MORGAN

Helen Morgan ... James Montgomery Flagg says she is a composite of all the ruined women in the world. Robert Garland would rather hear her sing "Bill" sitting on a piano than hear Jeritza sing "Tosca" standing on her head. Gilbert Seldes finds it difficult to disassociate her entirely from the quality of genius; Percy Hammond describes her as a raffish nightingale, and Edna Ferber sees her as an orchid slightly decayed.

She was born Helen Emma Riggin in Danville, Illinois, twenty-seven years ago. As a child she sat on Uncle Joe Cannon's lap, listening to his stories. Her mother taught Sunday school, and Helen sang in the choir of the First Church of Christ Scientist in Danville.

Her father died, and she and her mother were left to fight for
a living. Today she is a great star. Asked to explain her success
she answers with one word, "HUNGER." It was hunger that made
her pack crackers for the National Biscuit Company, it was hunger
that forced her to wait on tables, manicure nails, operate a compto-
meter model, work as ribbon clerk in Marshall Field's, sing in cabarets,
and dance in the back line of the chorus of "Sally." It was never
Helen Morgan's ambition to become a star. That position was brought
about by hunger. She took to the stage because it offered bread
and butter, and promised cakes and ale.

Winning the title of Miss Mount Royal in a Canadian beauty
contest in 1923 started her on her stage career. She opened a vaudeville tour in Hagerstown, Maryland, after coming to New York to be
greeted by Mayor Hylan. Upon completion of her vaudeville engagement she returned to New York to study for light opera at the Metropolitan Opera School under Edouardo Petri. But her funds gave out,
and she was forced to look for work. She tried out for a job in
the chorus of The Follies but was rejected. Finally she was chosen
for the back row of Sally on its last trip out. After that, night
life in Chicago, cabarets where she worked with Ruth Etting and
Tamaris, the dancer, for sixty dollars a week.

Her first recognition came from Amy Leslie, the Chicago critic.
Miss Leslie wrote several pieces about her and took her to New York
to meet Ziegfeld. He gave her a job in the chorus of Louis the
Fourteenth. Helen waited until Miss Leslie returned to Chicago so
as not to hurt her feelings, and then quit. Lean days followed.
She lived at the Community Church Club on 48th Street where the
room was five dollars a week. Then she got shelter free with a girl
whose sweetie occupied the extra bed all night, and left for work
early in the morning. As Helen worked all night at stags and in
the clubs, it was a highly satisfactory arrangement. She used to go
to Gertner's and order spaghetti--very filling--and wait for song
publishers and pluggers to buy her coffee.

Then Billy Rose hired her for the Backstage Club, an up-
holstered garage on 56th Street. Here she first sat on a piano.
The club was so crowded that it was the only place from which she
could be seen. She used it as a stage. Ring Lardner who is always
assisting young musical students claims he helped Helen Morgan to
the top of her first piano. But at any rate, the girl on the piano
at the Backstage Club soon became an attraction. The club was
packed every night with celebrities and producers. She hadn't been
there five days before George White signed her for the Scandals of
1925. Then came Americana, a thousand and one nights in the night
clubs, an engagement with the Grand Guignol Players in which she
appeared in Louis Parker's dramatic sketch, "Minuet" under the name
Neleh Nagrom, which is her own name reversed, and then Show Boat.
It is interesting to note that when Ziegfeld signed her for Show Boat
she was abroad, and he did not remember her as the ugly duckling
who danced in the rear line of Sally.

Show Boat with "Old Man River," "Bill," and "Can't Help Lovin'
Dat Man o' Mine" made theatrical history and Helen Morgan. The
first time she stepped on the stage of the Ziegfeld Theatre in the
small role of Julie in Edna Ferber's classic, she became a star. Sweet
Adeline and the motion picture Applause clinched her place in the
theatrical firmament.

The most striking feature of Helen Morgan's character is her
sincerity. She refuses to say anything she does not believe. She
refuses to sing anything she doesn't feel. When she sings lachrymose
songs she cries because she actually feels the emotion she is utter-
ing. That is why she has sung only some thirty different selections
in the past five years.

She is extravagant and over-generous. The year before last
she earned $117,000 and spent every cent of it. How it went, she
does not know. It took her mother and the government to discover
that most of it went to charity. She once adopted an infant only to
have its mother take it back after Helen had gone to great expense
to have doctors cure it of an ear ailment.

She thinks nothing of spending $600 for a simple dress and
ordering a half dozen at a time. She likes perfume, loathes stockings
that have been washed and for that matter, stockings that haven't
been washed, affects berets, thinks it's good luck to put a garment
on backwards, often goes out of her house or the theatre for a drive
in her roadster, attired only in a fur coat with not a strip on underneath, and she doesn't wear jewelry because she doesn't want to
make other girls envious.

Her tousled, black hair which falls in short silky ringlets has
become a trademark, but she is letting it grow long. Her legs are
unusually frail and entirely out of proportion to the rest of her body.
Her eyes change in color, and her hands which are lovely, are long,
slim, and white, with tapering fingers rouged at the nails. She
wears sandals, and when she goes for a beauty treatment she has
her toe nails rouged also, bringing along her own jar of polish.

She has a love for fostering artistic talents. She is continually goading on and encouraging young artists, writers, and musicians. She herself can write and draw a bit. She plans some day
to write her own biography. Her nickname is "Mousie." All her
stationery has a picture of a mouse on it, and even her cable address
is "Mousie, N.Y." She's nervous and temperamental, but at the same
time she's reliable. Usually she's before time in keeping appoint-
ments, and she's seldom missed a performance.

She's been engaged countless times, and is constantly in love
with a few men. Old sweethearts are always dropping into her club,
and she usually has a devilish time remembering their names.

She attended schools all over the country, but most of her
education was gotten from books and conversation with people. To-
day she is a well informed, highly intelligent and cultured woman.
Her latest hobby is collecting first editions, and SHE READS THEM.
Her favorite writers are James Joyce, James Stephens, Saki, Ernest
Hemingway, and D. H. Lawrence.

Her ambition is to some day push back her piano, toss away
her songs, and appear in dramatic roles. What will she play? Anything. So long as it permits her to be sincere. Many critics have
suggested that she would be an ideal "Camille." Perhaps some day
she will. Or perhaps Miss Ferber will take the character of Julie
to tell what happened to her after she disembarked, in a sequel to
Show Boat. But until then, she will go on singing her sad songs
with tragic, heavy lidded eyes, with tears coursing down to the tips
of her beautifully torn mouth, little realizing that the piano's her
world, and she's on top.

> --Irving Hoffman in Life, February
> 1932, pages 34-35 and 53.

• KEN MURRAY AND CHARLOTTE

Ken Murray, a young man, is one of those swift talking nut
comics who run from one gag into another with lightning-like rapidity.
The Charlotte is a girl who sings at odd times, but aside from that,
means nothing to the turn.

Murray is a promising monologist. If he throws out some of
his old gags, he'll step right along. His working outfit consists of
a business suit plus an opera hat, a clarinet coming into action later
in the turn.

Some of his jokes are in questionable taste, especially when
anyone considers the million and one proclamations from the Head of
the House concerning cleanliness in vaudeville. And one or two that
aren't in bad taste are so old that to use them around New York,
not to speak of the well known stone's throw of Times Square, is
silly. But most of the time Murray clicked and clicked heavily, his
delivery being confident but not fresh. He has a good sense of
pacing the act and when he comes to the end, he gives a climax and
gets off--commendable.

New material he needs more than anything else. Right now he
has the natural ability of a first rate single turn.

> --"Sisk" [Bob Sisk] in Variety,
> April 14, 1926, page 12.

● MAE MURRAY AND CLIFTON WEBB

In presenting a series of dances of the kind that New York's best social centers are paying homage to at present Mae Murray is ably assisted by slenderly built Clifton Webb. Five colored musicians on the stage to play the accompaniments, with a grandstand drummer. Miss Murray is graceful, light and airy and she trips in a manner calculated to draw the plaudits from those who are crazy about it. In a becoming pink charmeuse outfit over chiffon Miss Murray's pretty arms, hands and feet seemed set to music. That Palace audience Monday night went plumb daffy over her dancing. In praising her splendid dancing Webb should not be overlooked. They open with a fairly fast waltz entitled "D'Arlequin Waltz," followed by the "Brazilian Maxixe" and the "Barcarole Waltz," (claimed as a creation of Miss Murray's), it making a fine impression. For the finish they danced the "Cinquante Cinquante," mixture of tango-trotting steps done in lively fashion. The drummer did a Texas Tommy with the traps that for a moment diverted attention from the dancers.

--"Mark" [Mark Vance] in Variety,
March 20, 1914, page 18.

● KARYL NORMAN

It was pleasant to see Karyl Norman's name placed prominently with the title of his act, "The Creole Fashion Plate," for he deserves credit for the striking beauty, memorable charm he has created. His act is no commonplace one; on the contrary, the beauty of his ballad singing might well take an enviable place on the concert stage where such artists as Cecil Fanning win applause. His knowledge of costuming and staging is no less amazing than his knowledge of music and feminine graces. His hanging draperies are lavish and handsome; his costumes, especially the black vampire gown and the evening cloak are marvels of style and brilliance. But these things are merely secondary to the value of the act itself, because that is preeminently a fine thing. Mr. Norman is distinctive among female impersonators, for he is quite free from unpleasant mannerisms. He appears to be wholesome and virile, almost two complete personalities. The one is a robust straightforward manly youth, the other a skilled student of human nature, who can characterize remarkably through the medium of woman's attire. It is interesting to add that though Mr. Norman was playing his second week at the Riverside, he had about five encores and was compelled to give a curtain speech.

--Bernard Sobel in Dramatic Mirror,
October 9, 1920, page 638.

*   *   *

Norman opened on Monday afternoon at the Palace [New York] showing his new routine fully completed, with the result that in

opening after intermission, he ran off with the hit honors of the
bill, and to the bargain, with a late show in progress had the audience wanting more, so badly, that he had to beg off with a speech
after rendering several encores. Norman is now working in two,
using a drop in one of solid black, and a beautiful silver cyclorama
for his set in two.

His costumes are more gorgeous than ever, all of them being
different than those used last year, not only in style, but in the
type of materials used. Each one shown is more resplendent than
the other shown before, and that's saying some. Norman is in great
voice, and even despite the amount of times he has been seen in
New York, he left them gasping with surprise on Monday afternoon
when he took off the wig.

His work is artistic. His showmanship perfect. Among the
published numbers he is using are "I Want My Manny," "Cherie,"
"Weep No More," and "Daisy Days." Eddie Weber, who was seen with
Eva Tanguay some time ago, conducts the orchestra for Norman,
and does so in a manner which leaves no fault to find.

> --"Hoffman" in Dramatic Mirror,
> October 22, 1921, page 598.

• TALBOT O'FARRELL

Talbot O'Farrell is making his "big time" New York vaudeville
debut at the Palace this week, with the returns for the big Irish
tenor all in his favor Monday afternoon. O'Farrell during his turn
begged allowance for any shortcomings inasmuch as he no sooner hit
these shores than he bumped up against the "Flu" and was prevented
from opening according to his stage schedule. O'Farrell reminds one
of the robust tenor stars of former American minstrelsy--Richard J.
Jose for instance, in the way he works up his songs, in fact his
singing is similar in more ways than one. His voice isn't the greatest in the world but it is musically sweet and the big fellow--reminds
us also of Walter C. Kelly in some respects--and he has a range that
is high and expressive. On his low register O'Farrell doesn't range
so voluminously but his top notes are reached with fervor and effect.
In "one," O'Farrell devoted 15 minutes to his act, O'Farrell relying
on several ballads for his opening. The first was "The Kingdom
Within Your Eyes," the second "An Old-Fashioned Lady," the third
"If I Could Paint A Picture," with a little prayer song, "Send Back
My Boy To Me" that was used for an encore. There is something
likable about O'Farrell that will make him popular in vaudeville. He
has personality, bigness, voice and an easy, natural way of singing--
shows no inclination to mug his words or try for the classics--and a
routine that does not include any done-to-death American ballads.
That "Old-Fashioned Lady" number is a pure gem.

--"Mark" in Dramatic Mirror, February 14, 1920, page 268.

• TONY PASTOR

For an artist who appears at irregular intervals, and who sang
songs, as he admitted from the rostrum, which were over forty years
old, Tony Pastor last Monday evening received an extraordinary reception. When the card with his name was posted, the audience
applauded long and loudly, refusing to allow the singer to proceed.
Mr. Pastor quieted the house down, and announced his first selection
would be "Sarah's Young Man." For the second selection, Mr. Paster
gave "Down in a Coal Mine," and for the Chorus invited the audience
to join in, very much as the stage "song pluggers" of to-day do.
Mr. Pastor used no "sheet" to inform those in front the words of
the chorus, nor did he have to drill it into them. Everyone in the
house was or seemed to be familiar with the lyric, of which the chorus
is:

>"Down in a coal mine,
>Underneath the ground,
>Where no ray of sunshine
>Ever can be found;
>Digging dusky diamonds
>All the season 'round;
>Down in a coal mine
>Underneath the ground."

The song made a hit. It just tore 'em all to pieces. It was,
in fact, a "riot." "Down in a Coal Mine" knocked them off their
seats; it held up the show, and the audience went clean bug. Mr.
Pastor sings as he did years ago, top hat, gestures and all. He is
just the same Tony Pastor; a nice young fellow, understands his
business; not a day older, and the everlasting hit of vaudeville.

--Sime Silverman in Variety, March
28, 1908, page 14.

• MISS PATRICOLA

Opening in a spot is rather a superficial business for Patricola
for she possesses enough natural personality not to have to emphasize
what many artists haven't when they enter the stage door. Immediately, she clinched the audience with her first number "Sweet Adeline," and the orchestra became so enthusiastic that they chirped
into the chorus. Next, "Johnny in Town" in full light went even
better. Her rendering "Does Anybody Know Casey" with a few
Oriental twists broke several gloves. Her violin playing showed skill,

too. Patricola is such a personable young woman that she could
entertain almost any audience.

--"Gray" in Dramatic Mirror, March
1, 1919, page 312.

• MADAME OLGA PETROVA

Madame Olga Petrova has returned to vaudeville. Few actresses
have caused editorial pens so much perplexity as to the proper clas-
sifying of her particular style of work. Some of the scribes have
got real mad about the difficulty and others have used excessive
flattery as the easiest way to untie the knot. Such a state of editorial indecision makes her a distinct novelty. This status could
not but make her better vaudeville property, for novelty when held
up with certain standards has a Bradstreet's rating in the booking
offices. She still gives her parrot song and an excerpt from The
Shulamite. Her "Don't Cry, Little Girl," makes a splendid opening
number. Using her own set of wine-colored draperies is an effective
background. These part to give local color by revealing a South
African scene when she renders the dramatic reading. Doubtless
the six weeks allotted to her will be extended indefinitely.

--"Higgins" in Dramatic Mirror,
March 1, 1919, page 312.

• EDITH PIAF

The "continental" revue currently being presented to the New
York public at the Playhouse Theatre is unquestionably continental.
It would, in fact, be difficult to conceive of a more completely French
entertainment than the series of divertissements which build up to
and include the songs of Mlle. Edith Piaf. The latter is "starred"
in the uncompromisingly grand manner on the program and on the
marquee. Her singing occupies the second half of a two act menu
of amusement. She has been heralded as the "sensation" of Paris.
And she might well become the sensation of New York. Her material,
all of it original, is provocative and poignant and her voice and delivery have the undefinable quality which for lack of a better word
is usually called "soul." The orchestral and choral accompaniments
which make the background for her austere appearances are so good
that they almost drown the star's artistry at times. Whether, however, she and her curtain-raising supporting acts really constitute
a whole evening's entertainment is open to question. Edith Piaf and
her company, excellent as they are, still have the impact of a series
of individual performances such as New York is accustomed to see
at the Ruban Bleu, the Blue Angel, the various Cafes Society and
elsewhere in the night clubs.

Stemming from the school of European street singers that has
given us in the past such personalities as Raquel Meller, Mlle. Piaf
plays the trappings down.   She appears without any glamorizing im-
pedimenta in a rusty black dress against grey velvet curtains.

La Piaf's number one boys, of whom there are nine, are called
"Les Compagnons de la Chanson." They are, without question, the
rich man's Marx Brothers. Their subtle nonsense is a pure delight
and hardly requires a working knowledge of the French language.
The other subsidiary vaudeville performances are far above the usual
five-acts-five standard. But little Piaf interspersed with a dash of
"Compagnons" would have created more of a French-without-tears
impression.

--Thomas Brailsford Felder in Cue,
Vol. 16, No. 45, November 8,
1947, page 17.

• POLAIRE

Sometimes advertising makes the reputation of actors and actresses. The enterprising managers, like a much bill-boarded patent
medicine, seem sometimes to "work while you sleep." When one goes
to bed at night, there is some little nobody appearing in an incon-
spicuous part in a bad play in an unheard of city. Next morning
one finds in the newspapers that Nobody has become Somebody.
While the type was not small enough for her name on the program
the night before, the electricians are busy on the sign in front of
the theatre this morning. To-night her name will be flashed to the
world. She has arrived. And sometimes, it seems that advertising
does it.

Systematic publicity campaigns often make stars; or at least,
few American actors or actresses reach stardom on the American
stage without systematic publicity campaigns. Thousands of dollars
have been spent to let the public know that Mrs. Leslie Carter is
a wonderful delineator of scarlet women, and she has red hair (although she is said to leave it in the dressing-room when she leaves
the theatre) and thousands of dollars have been spent to let the
public know that a cute little girl with the cute little name of Billie
Burke is so dainty and sweet that she couldn't represent a scarlet
woman on the stage. More thousands have been spent to tell the
public that Marie Dressler makes them laugh, that Mrs. Fiske is so
intellectual that she narrowly escapes having a constant headache,
and that Ellen Beach Yaw has an unusually high top note in her
voice.

But the fact remains that Miss Yaw has a high top note, that
Mrs. Carter characterizes scarlet women, that Billie Burke's cuteness

and sweetness constitute her principal dramatic equipment and that
Mrs. Fiske's reputation for "brains" pretty cleverly dovetails with
the plays in which she appears. Each lady--or her manager does
it for her--sees to it that all "booming" in the public prints bears
at least a remote relation to the quantity or quality of what she has
to sell to the public.

Read Richard Bennett's "interviews" about how he loves the
world, how he wishes that he could "save one mother from one day's
suffering, or save the life of one little child" and one has only to
turn to the advertising columns to find that Richard Bennett is appearing in Brieux's play of "social prophylaxis," Damaged Goods.

Read Olga Nethersole's attacks upon the hypocritical rich, particularly the rich who own tenement houses and permit the lives of
little children to be endangered by firetraps, and one recalls that
the little child burned to death in a trap of this kind forms the big
third act climax to The Writing on the Wall.

Read how Alla Nazimova despises most of the people in the world,
how they bore her with their little lives and little cares, how she
would like to go away off somewhere to some Sahara and there com-
mune with herself and find her soul--and on the next page of the
paper is the advertisement for Nazimova in Bella Donna or one of
the Hedda-women or Nora-women of a north of Europe dramatist.

They all seem wise, all are following the advice of Andrew Carnegie, which he borrowed from an ancient source; "they carry their
eggs in one basket, and they keep their eyes on the basket,"--all
of them excepting one little creature who doesn't know as much as
she should know about the American's ways and manners. She came
from Paris, and to Paris she returns, as quickly as her American
tours end and she can make an out-going boat.

I speak of Polaire, the rather eccentric little Frenchwoman who
is so busy with her acting and her troubles that she doesn't have
much time to attend to such matters as publicity campaigns of the
American variety. Of course most of her troubles are imaginary, as
are most of the troubles of all prima donne of the lyric and dramatic
stages; but to her they are real. She suffers and she likes to suffer. She would not be happy and calm and quiet for anything.
Rather would she end it all with a sharp blade or a dose of rough on
rats.

Polaire likes to be unhappy. She told me so. She is nervous
and she would not have it otherwise; she frets, storm about, works
herself into a rage, fairly gloats over her perspiring passion; and
even when she is exhausted and ready to drop from sheer fatigue,
she declines to sit down, but insists upon standing, because she is
more unhappy so, and Polaire is happiest when she is most unhappy.

Yet how is this little artist known to American readers? To be sure,
she is a wild thing, an untamed and untamable girl whose genius in
what are known as "big moments" of plays cannot be doubted. She
is the possessor of an ugly face, an exceedingly small waist, and
fluffy hair that she permits to stand out from her head for ten or
twelve inches, giving her something of the appearance one might expect from a young witch in an African swamp; her feet are large;
so is her mouth; she makes pets of young pigs, around the necks
of which she has beautiful collars studded with jewels; she permitted
herself to be photographed with a ring in her nose, as a protest
against what the world calls culture and refinement; she has a blind
dog, that is lame in one leg; when drawing a salary of fifteen hundred
dollars a week, she lived at a nine-dollar-a-week boarding house.
These and many more "eccentricities."

      Polaire is out of joint with the times. She would rather carry
a spear and run through a jungle after a hyena than be a pampered
and petted little person of the drawing room. She loathes refinement.
She protests that she will be a barbarian, although the rest of the
world becomes civilized.

      And the result might be anticipated. Small waist, blind dog,
pet pig, nose ring and ugly face attract so much attention that none
is left for an estimate of Polaire, the actress, the very great artist
who is more than "emotional," more barbaric than tragic, and yet
more artistic than sensational.

      Polaire hasn't cared very much by what means people were
brought into the theatre to see her. She wanted the people--that
was the principal thing, and not alone because the actress who can
bring people into the theatre may demand an enormous salary. She
now receives three thousand dollars a week and travels in a private
car through America; but she could live nicely on thirty dollars a
week; and while she is a veritable miser, putting aside nearly every
dollar that she earns, it isn't the money that concerns her most.
She knows that she's an actress, that she is much different from the
others who call themselves actresses.

      "They" say that the day of emotional acting has passed, that
it ended with Sarah Bernhardt. Polaire says that it hasn't fairly
begun, and she does things on the stage that Sarah Bernhardt would
not have dared to do, along the same lines of what is called artificial emotionalism, because she knows that it isn't artificial. It's true.
She acts and feels it, so she is in a position to contradict.

      Yet in all the pages that have been printed about Polaire,
heralding her coming to America, in the columns of comment that
greet her along the way, there is comparatively little about the real
Polaire, there is little legitimate or conservative criticism of her acting. She is rarely allowed to express herself intelligently and clearly,

because she is too spectacular as an individual, and to the world
at large, her art suffers by the attention that is paid to her whims,
fads and prattlings.

The fact remains, however, although one wouldn't suspect it
from the sensational manner in which she is circused across the land,
that in many quarters Polaire is thought to be one of the most promising actresses in the world at the present time. Like so many others
of her admirers, I suppose, after seeing her act, I felt that it was
a pity for such a consummate artist to be so utterly misunderstood
by the great majority that is unable to see her. I recalled, after all,
that Madam Sarah passed through this storm of sensational advertising in America years ago and that she has lived to derive great pecuniary profit from it. They said that Sarah had pet pythons and
tigers, that she slept in a coffin, that she did this and that, all
quite impossible things to the minds of the people who knew Sarah
Bernhardt. Perhaps Polaire would outlive such crudities as pet pigs,
nose rings and blind dogs.

So, full of these thoughts, I sought out Polaire for an interview. I, for one, wanted to write a safe and sane story about this
artist, something that would tell who she was, what she was trying
to do and what were her aspirations in life. The invitation came
and I called upon her at the hour she had named, which it happened
was just after she had come off the stage. My intentions towards
the lady were not only honorable, but even commendable. In my
choicest and most diplomatic language, I wanted to tell her that I
regretted that she had become a circus freak in America, instead of
a legitimate artist, which none knew, better than she, was the real
fact of the case.

But sadly I admit that one who wants to think of Polaire only
as an artist should never meet her in real life. He should never
see her beyond the stage of make-believe. Or at least, one should
try to meet her when she is happy--which very rarely happens.
After two minutes in her dressing room, I realized why it is that
she is an extraordinary critter to people who have written about her
for the public; almost instantly, I perceived that one who may chance
to find her in a tantrum, as I found her, has never seen acting on a
stage of the theatre that compares to what may take place in the
dressing room.

As I approached her door, I could hear her raging, spitting,
hissing, and howling like a mad woman. Perhaps she was rehearsing
and this was my "moment," so I tapped at the door. She flung it
open and greeted me cordially. "Kindly seat yourself over there and
excuse me," she snapped, as she pointed to a chair. Instantly she
began again and I saw that a little musical director of the orchestra
was cowering before her. He had ruined her big scene, or at least
she told him that he had done so. When she gave him the cue for
loud music, he had stood there like a ninny, or a worse than ninny,

his baton limply in hand as if he were asleep. He had failed to realize
that he was directing the music for Polaire. He had forgotten that
she was a Frenchwoman and an artist, that she was on trial before
the American people, that she had a new art, a great art. She had
been insulted before an audience. Her art had suffered. She called
on all the furies to prove what she said was true.

Musical director opened his mouth to speak, but she didn't
care for explanations. If he had called to "explain," she'd do that
for him. She literally raved, bounded about the room like a caged
tigress, snatched up a trick knife and standing on a trunk waved
it furiously over her head. She pointed it at him as she yelled.
She jumped down, grabbed up a big bath towel, squeezed it into a
knot, picked up rouge jars and quickly had them all tossing through
the air like a trained juggler.

Then, in the midst of the proceedings, she would remember,
and bowing quite politely, would come in front of me and beg to be
"excused." She had been insulted; her art had suffered.

Then she caught hold of the knife and screaming words at the
musician, waved the thing frantically over his head. In reality, she
was showing him how to wave the baton; I thought that I was to be
the only witness of a murder, and I shamefully admit that I rather
looked forward to the spectacle. All my life I had wanted to see a
woman act--I had spent many years trudging down the theatre aisles
with that promise held out before me. I was seeing real acting, and
I was satisfied.

Finally, the musical director faded through the door. He had
been taught a lesson. What Polaire said, she meant. Woe to him,
if he ever again failed to give his trumpeters the cue when she was
ready.

"Sit down," I entreated after we were left alone, for she was
still pacing around nervously, tossing the knife to the ceiling and
catching it dexterously by the handle when it came within reach.
She had given me a chair and it seemed only proper that she should
be seated for our interview. But alas, I soon realized that her answers to my questions would be a torrent of words, which not even
a skilled shorthand reporter could have understood.

"Sit?" she screeched back at me. "Why monsieur, perhaps I
shall not be able to sit again this night."

"Then stand up," I thought, but tactfully did not put my
thoughts into words.

"My art has suffered, ah, I am insulted before the American
people. Go ahead, ask me what you will and I will endeavor to
answer."

"I see they have billed you as 'Madam Polaire,'" I suggested.
"Permit me to congratulate you. I never heard that you had a husband."

"Idiots!" she yelled. "Why do they do such things. 'Madam
Polaire!' The very thought of it makes me sick. I have a husband?
I be a wife? It is not for artists of the stage to become the wives
of men. We give what we have to give to the people in the audience,
if we are true artists; we care not for husbands!"

Moving about before me was the ugliest face I had ever seen;
therefore, the next question: "Is beauty an asset to the actress?"

Polaire paused. "What has beauty of face got to do with the
dramatic art? It is ridiculous. Art is something more than a smiling, simpering face; in fact, art is something deeper than beauty;
it is something that has a soul, something that is warm or something
that thrills. Bah for a pretty face! I'm glad that I have my face,
which has been compared to everything from the Sphynx to a hyena.
But I am an artist. See the people in the audience to-night; were
they looking for merely a pretty face? I spoke a foreign language,
but they understood me--that's the thing: to convey a message to
the people who come to see you. You can see pretty faces on the
street, at church--anywhere."

Perhaps it would have been the same, if I had asked her something that suited her caprice. She might have stormed just the same.
As it was, it seemed that I was torturing her. My questions seemed
to give her pain, for she writhed and groaned as she answered them.

"What is your name?" was next.

"Why Polaire, of course."

"But it's Something-or-Other Polaire, or Polaire Something--
what is it?"

"Why is that necessary? They know me as Polaire in Paris,
as Polaire the artist, if you please. Polaire is enough."

"What did your mother call you?"

She laughed like a young fiend with a red-hot poker and threw
the knife to the ceiling again. Perhaps her mother had called her
things that made her smile when she recalled them.

"Well, it's Emilie," she said finally. "Emelie Polaire--but I
hate Emilie and I have never used it; Polaire is enough."

"Are we too refined, too cultured?"

Polaire grabbed up the bath towel again and waved it above
her head as she emitted a sound like a screech-owl. She wrung it
into a knot and threw it at the window as she jabbered. She talked
and talked and what she meant to convey was that we have all become
a lot of silly monkeys, puffed up with our own slim knowledge of
things, weaklings who catch cold when a gust of wind strikes us,
sickly creatures who think a lot more about microbes and bacteria
than we do about having a good time. She would have us big fellows, muscular and brawny, with beards on our faces and clubs in
our hands to knock over the wolves in the forest, if there were wolves;
and she believes that women should also be wild creatures with strings
of beads on their necks and the inevitable nosering to indicate their
inferiority, a symbol of barbarism.

That Polaire speaks only French is a disadvantage, because
she means much more to people who can understand her words, people
who can hear her bite and snarl at phrases in much the manner of
Bernhardt. But it's all a pretty good test of real art--big art. English audiences understand Polaire because she speaks in a language
more universal than French or English. It seems, sometimes, to be
the world-language, because she makes her meaning plain to the un-
cultured and uneducated, while she provided an equal thrill to the
refined and effete. And stragely enough, audiences love her. There
is the first minute of surprise, when she goes on the stage. They
look at her big mouth and big feet--perhaps they think of the pet
pig--but quickly Polaire takes hold of them, and it is wonderful what
she is able to do with audiences.

And little actresses tell us that the day of emotional acting is
over--that it passed with Madam Bernhardt, in whom it found its
greatest exponent! Not so long as there is a woman on the stage
as Madamoiselle Emilie!

Her critics are divided in the opinion of her future. She has
been eternally, it seems, appearing in one-act plays. Polaire one
minute and trained dogs or monkeys the next, with acrobats preceed-
ing her. Real lovers of dramatic art would like to see Polaire in a
full sized play. They would like to see her in shade as well as in
the light. Perhaps there will be some difficulty in finding the play-
wright who will give her a drama that she deserves.

At the present time, she seems to require something that en-
ables her to engage in wild outbursts that are just a little more
fierce than would be expected of any except the most extraordinary
human beings. Le Visiteur, in which she is appearing this season
before American audiences, is such a play.

An actress has returned to her boudoir for the night, after
a meeting with her lover. She tells her maid that he has "dared"
her to be brave under all circumstances. She swears that she could

be and would be, and she concludes that he will put her to the
test; so when she hears a noise in the garden beside the window of
her room, she suspects that it is her lover, or at least some one
engaged by him. She will not appear to be frightened, so she dis-
misses her maid, after telling her of her suspicion, lights a cigarette
and sits down to read a magazine.

A burglar appears at the window and enters the room. She
greets him rather kindly and invites him to enter. He does and
immediately demands her jewelry. She hesitates, but gives him a
ring and then thinking that she may dissuade him from his purpose,
she sings. He laughs. In reality, he is an "Apache" of the worst
sort. Then she dances, but that disgusts him. He takes a seat in
the middle of the room and tells her to take off all her jewelry. She
attempts to play with him, but finally realizing that her situation
may be desperate, she takes off her jewels.

"Go to the window and look in the garden," says the burglar;
"perhaps that will show you what sort of man I am." She does and
in the moonlight sees the dead face of her lover. The burglar had
caught him there and had stabbed him in the back. Now fully aroused
to her frightful condition, she sees that her only hope is to battle
hand to hand with the intruder. She dances around his chair and
reaches for the knife at his side, but he is too quick for her. Then
she throws her arms about him and kisses him wildly and passionately.
He is dizzy from the effect. She dances, sings and kisses him again,
finally succeeding in getting the knife, which she plunges deep into
his neck, while she still dances, sings and yells in an almost unbelievable frenzy born of fright.

The maid enters. "A nice time of night to be amusing your-
selves," she says, believing it all to be the trick of which she had
heard the suspicion. "I'm going to bed."--Curtain.

Polaire gives a powerful characterization of the actress--perhaps
performs the part as nobody but Polaire could do it. And I believe,
for one, that if she can do this as she does, she is also capable of
other work in a vastly different key--that in her we have a great
actress, worthy of the name.

--Archie Bell in The Green Book
Magazine, June 1914, pages 833-
840.

• ADA REEVE

Ada Reeve is an internationally known name of fame in vaudeville circles around the world. It is 13 years since Miss Reeve last
appeared in New York in 1912. That's quite a while. Meantime she
has traveled professionally to many climes, scoring in each as she

has on her English homeland and as she did in America when previously here.

Two of the songs Miss Reeve is singing at the Palace are from
her former New York repertoire; "Good Old Days," the stronger of
the two, and "Beware Young Ladies," now opening her act as it did
in 1912. The new songs here are "Because I'm a Lady," comic;
"Sweet Maytime and You," "Silly Questions," comic; and "Ain't It
Nice?" comic, to conclude.

There's a dignity to Ada Reeve, also class. It's immensely
to her vogue and reputation that she can return to American vaudeville after a lapse of 13 years to find that though time and customs
over here on that stage have passed along to many changes, her impressionable singing can still stand out.

Before an English audience Monday evening who greeted Miss
Reeve in the same cordial manner they did Bransby Williams on the
same bill, the English singer had an easy time. Her return seems
opportune for a full trip, for you don't see an Ada Reeve every day,
whether 13 years ago or now.

> --Sime Silverman in Variety, No-
> vember 11, 1925, page 14.

• HARRY RICHMAN

Richman has stepped some since he appeared as a piano accompanist for the Dollys and Mae West, and since he tried out as a vaudeville single. Having made a rep and established two followings, on
the radio and in the night-club field, he has taken on unction,
weight and confidence.

Richman now struts himself without a blush, and takes on all
the mannerisms of a star. And it must be acknowledged that the audience helps him get away with it without a dissenting voice. His
reception was immense, and his own numbers went like wildfire. Combining some of the technique of Ted Lewis with an emotional similarity
to Al Jolson, Richman, adding his own impressive appearance and
insolently, though not offensive familiar manner, has the audience
problem in either hand.

The scene is a replica of his club, with the [Eddie] Elkins
band assembled and five waiters (practical) in view, two of them
captains. After two musical numbers, Richman enters in tux, and
actually hoofs. He pants a little, but makes a serio-comic announcement with some wise wheezes, introducing the saccharine dancing
and singing Muriel De Forest, who scores; Yvette Rugel sings an opera
aria for a wow. Bee Jackson knocks 'em dead with a Charleston. The
band does not get much chance for recognition.

Richman does several numbers single and with Miss De Forest, seeming at times to be "plugging," but selling his songs with a vigor that is surefire.

It was obvious that he was drawing, and two sorts, the radio fans upstairs and the cake-eater crowd in the boxes and below. It must be a costly turn, even though Richman could afford to work it for nothing in view of the latitude allowed him in boosting his cafe, which he does incessantly.

His finish seemed abrupt but the curtain calls gave him and his whole troupe (even the waiters) several legitimate calls.

In New York this outfit is a cinch at least within the radio radius of local air-service. And as entertainment it will get by anywhere.

--"Lait" [Jack Lait] in Variety,
February 4, 1925, page 8.

• BLANCHE RING

The return of Miss Blanche Ring to vaudeville at the Colonial Theater this week is in the nature of a theatrical event.

Miss Ring has a good voice and good looks, but even these might not count if she were not possessed of a personality that fairly breathes good nature and that something which is called magnetism because we don't quite know what it is.

Miss Ring may well believe with the inventor of sayings that she cares not who writes her country's songs, so long as she can sing them. Have you ever thought of the really remarkable number of very important songs that have become intimately associated with Miss Ring's name? Well, there is The Good Old Summer Time," one of the cyclonic hits of six years ago; and "The Belle of Avenue A," and "Bedalia," and "My Irish Molly, O," and "Waltz Me Around Again, Willie." But wait, there's still a new one to be added to this already impressive list, and it wears the unusual title of "Yip-I-Ady-I-Ay."

Miss Ring sings several songs at the Colonial this week, some of them better than others, but all seemingly of sufficient worth, as she sings them, at least, to get the entire audience in humming sympathy with her. She coaxes her audience with "Bonnie, My Highland Lassie," teases them with "Kiss Me Right," leads them on with "The Billiken Man," and sets them fairly crooning with delight with her "Yip-I-Ady-I-Ay."

There isn't another singer on the American stage to-day who

has Miss Ring's odd little knack of making the orchestra move its combined head, the balcony hum and the gallery shout out loud with her.

Miss Ring does something more than merely make you wish to join in her songs. She has the splendid faculty of taking songs of flippant and altogether light-waisted measures and singing them so they sink deep down into the receptacle commonly called the heart of the public.

Miss Ring is a mighty big card at the Colonial this week, and is worth all the big type and the undoubtedly big salary that Percy G. Williams is paying her to entertain his patrons.

--New York Star, Vol. I, No. 19,
February 6, 1909, page 5.

*   *   *

Blanche Ring never has much difficulty in finding song hits, and it is a lucky songwriter who can get the magnetic Blanche to put his song in her collection. She seems to be able to make a hit out of a song that other performers would not even sing if they were on a salary to sing anything handed to them. Just as soon as she begins to warble the chorus and to reach out her arms as though to draw all their fear away from them, the audience--not only in the gallery, either--becomes courageous and begins to whistle or hum, and even break into song, and the song is made.

--The Standard & Vanity Fair,
Vol. XLV, No. 1075, March 19,
1910, page 19.

- THE RITZ BROTHERS

Al, Jimmy and Harry Ritz have been around but not together, this [15-minute act at the Albee Theatre, Brooklyn] being their initial try in trio. It's a clever combination, the three being dapper young men. Their opening is a novelty in exaggerated red bow ties, plus fours, wide breeches and red sox for the "collegiate" atmosphere and song.

Their stepping is okay if somewhat familiar in some conceptions.

A uke specialty with a "hot" caliope-yodel accompaniment of the Cliff Edwards' school also clicked.

The turn is corking vaudeville for any grade and will build up as it goes along.

--Abel Green in <u>Variety</u>, September
30, 1925, page 14.

● BILL ROBINSON

Bill Robinson, colored, is the same who a few years ago was
of Cooper and Robinson. Later Robinson appeared as a single turn,
migrated to Chicago, where he established himself as an entertainer
at a cabaret, Marigold Gardens, remaining quite some time. He again
became a single, playing the middle-west and is now re-bowing to
the east.

In the turn as shown Tuesday night at the 5th Ave., Robinson
went through extremely mild for the position he occupied, next to
closing, until he reached his tap dancing finish, that might be called
a drill dance, as he went through in part drill maneuvers while stepping and tapping. To end this bit Robinson danced up and down
the steps leading from the stage to the orchestra aisle, adding a
little business to it and repeating the up and down several times.
This cinched him with the audience and it is by far the best thing
for the turn. It is good enough to hold him on the big time in an
earlier spot but can carry him through next to closing elsewhere.

Opening with a short song and dance, Robinson did a kidding
bit of "thunder and lightning," thunder by the bass drum and lightning by mugging, then into talk, principally about a bullet and Germans in France, after which he did a vocal humming of a trombone
playing a ballad.

Robinson was neatly dressed, clung closely to his stage work
but displayed nothing for real attention until reaching the drill dance.
That seemed to be enough, and while it is holding him in for a return
eastern visit, he had better fix-up the preceding portion of the act.
for it can stand fixing. He might throw out all the talk. There's
no need and probably no use of Robinson trying to be a monologist.

--Sime Silverman in <u>Variety</u>, August
5, 1921, page 15.

● WILL ROGERS

Will Rogers explains the reason for his new act to the audience
in few words. He says "I've been getting away with this junk for
so long that I thought you would get wise to me sooner or later so
I went out and dug up a little new stuff with which to bunk you for
a few more years." Rogers is doing an act quite different from his
former offering, even though the rope is still the main feature. It
is Rogers though who is liked. His personality, careless manner and
broad grin are worth more than the most intricate tricks that could

be figured out. Some of the lariat throwing has been dropped to
allow Rogers to give an imitation of Fred Stone in his lariat dance.
Rogers is a surprise when he starts dancing, and gets away with it
big. To make it more difficult, he shows how George Cohan would
do the dance were he to start throwing the rope. This brought a
storm of applause. With the dancing goes talk in which Rogers "kids"
his imitations. There are many laughs folded in the few remarks.
As a finish Rogers introduces a young girl about whom he tells won-
derous tales as regards broncho riding. A broncho is lead out and
with the aid of two men the young woman is placed in the saddle,
holding her position easily, while the horse jumps and dives all over
the stage. It makes a bully good finish to an all around entertaining specialty that is an improvement over Rogers' former act, which
was good enough.

> --"Dash" in Variety, January 14,
> 1911, page 17.

*   *   *

Even though he stated that there was never a Christian ever
made good at the Winter Garden, minus this remark Rogers would
have made more than good. After several months in pictures, Rogers
has returned to vaudeville with a better act than before.

Every morsel of his material is bright, snappy, and up-to-the-
minute. Most of his monologue is political and it certainly was well
put over by him. Although his rope stunts added greatly to his
turn, he could have omitted these for a few moments and just talked,
for his dry rural way of delivery had the house roaring after every
story he delivered. His best story is that of Shubert, Jolson and
the town Barns being turned into theatres. Whoever originated this
story should be given a medal for it certainly fits Rogers to a T.
On his entrance a tremendous reception was accorded him, and on
his exit Rogers should never forget the ovation. He has come back
stronger than ever, with one of the best talking singles in vaudeville to-day.

> --"Rose" in Dramatic Mirror, No-
> vember 19, 1921, page 743.

*   *   *

Had he and Wiley Post not been killed in a plane crash in
Alaska in 1935, Will Rogers would have celebrated his 100th birthday
today. As it is, he has been dead for 44 years and two generations
have grown up to whom his name and, more important, his place in
American history mean little. His gentle, unvindictive humor is perhaps out of step with the harsh wit of many of today's comedians,
but his political jibes are most certainly as relevant as ever. His
criticism of politicians and government bureaucracy is no less fresh.

To understand Will Rogers' special place in the hearts of Americans in the '20s and '30s one need only consider the impact of his passing, the newspaper headlines, the stunned faces of his millions of radio and movie fans, the huge memorial service at the Hollywood Bowl and the two-minute silence in his honor observed by audiences in 12,000 cinemas across America.

Or President Roosevelt's simple yet direct statement that "He loved and was loved by the American people."

Will Rogers was a trick rope artist, a vaudeville performer, a Ziegfeld Follies star, a lecturer and a newspaper reporter. In short he was America's foremost entertainer and its premier philosopher. He acted as the nation's conscience as well as humorist laureate. Yet, if his memory survives, it's chiefly because of the more than 60 motion pictures in which he starred, from Laughing Bill Hyde in 1918 through In Old Kentucky in 1935, films which have captured his personality and his homely message of faith and tolerance.

By the time of his death, Rogers was earning $250,000 a feature and, with Shirley Temple, was the most popular screen star at the box office. This for a series of unpretentious features, with more ad-libbing than reliance on the prepared script. Rogers improvised because he disliked learning lines. His leading lady in David Harum (1934) and The County Chairman (1935), Evelyn Venable, recalls that his way was better than the script, and that, because he would not give the actor playing opposite him in the scene the right cues, that actor had to listen and adapt his or her answer to fit what was being said. Thus there was a live, unprepared aspect of Will Rogers' films, a naturalness and a feeling that the performers were really thinking and living their parts.

Perhaps Will Rogers' general ad-libbing and easygoing attitude towards his films had something to do with his general disdain for movies--he would never have called them films--as anything more than entertainment. As early as 1924, in Big Moments From Little Pictures and Uncensored Movies, he was poking fun at the cinema's superstars, Douglas Fairbanks and Rudolph Valentino, and, via the titles, making deflating, if not disparaging, remarks about the movies. When told that film was an art form, he responded, "Everything that makes money and gives pleasure is not art. If it was, bootlegging would have been the highest form of artistic endeavor."

At the 1934 Academy Awards banquet, he made a speech in which he commented, "If the movies are an art, I kinda think it'll leak out somehow without bein' told, and if they're a science--then it's a miracle." In Doubling for Romeo (1921), he dubbed California "the land of movies, real estate agents, cafeterias, and climate."

Yet for all his relaxed attitude toward the cinema, his longtime leading lady, Irene Rich, is quick to point out that he had "a very

sane and sensible approach" to his work. The movies offered Will
Rogers a unique opportunity to get his thoughts across to the American people, perhaps even more so than his newspaper columns.

In so many of his films he was the smalltown, unpretentious do-
gooder; he was rightly dubbed the Mark Twain of the movies. In
his first talkie, They Had to See Paris, released in 1929, Will Rogers
expressed his opinion of Coca-Cola: "That's the Champagne of America," and of caviar, "It's a good job those things are fashionable,
'cause they ain't nothing else." Of Americans' fixation with foreign
travel, he said, "I bet there's thousands of Americans over here
that never did see their own state's capital."

A devout Democrat ("It takes nerve to be a Democrat here,
but it takes money to be a Republican"), Will Rogers found ample
opportunity in his films to give his views on politics and politicians.
They were easy prey for his wit, because as he noted "My little jokes
don't hurt nobody, but when Congress makes a joke, it's a law.
When they make a law, it's a joke."

In Ambassador Bill (1931), he has great fun in comparing the
Republicans fighting for the freedom of the mythical kingdom of
Sylvania with the U.S. Republican Party, and when a visiting senator
proudly announces that America does not meddle in the internal affairs of other countries, Rogers responds, "Tell that to the marines!"

In films such as The County Chairman and Judge Priest, Rogers
played the quintessential small-town politician, not above a spot of
chicanery, but only when it would help the basically honest candidate,
be it himself or another, to win. In, of all films, A Connecticut
Yankee (1931), he makes the classic statement, "I'm kinda like Mus-
solini. I don't want any titles, I just want to be the boss." And
thenceforth, at King Arthur's Court, that is what he becomes, Sir
Boss. Nor is there anything dated about Will Rogers' political quips.
In The Country Chairman, he hails his choice for state prosecutor,
"That's just the kind of men we want in politics in this country--
men who are not candidates."

It is the films that Will Rogers made with John Ford--Doctor
Bull (1933), Judge Priest (1934) and Steamboat Round the Bend
(1935)--that are the best known and the most shown today, but it is
the other, lesser known productions, such as The County Chairman,
beautifully conceived and directed by John Blystone, or Henry King's
State Fair (1933) and Lightnin (1930) which offer us finely drawn
portraits of Rogers the man.

However, Frank Borzage's They Had to See Paris may well be
considered to have offered the actor his best role, transplanting
Rogers from his home town of Claremore, Okla., to Paris and allowing him to speak out for youth's being permitted its fling. The film
also provides a classic example of what Will Rogers meant to his

audience. He had never kissed a woman before on the screen until this film, and the producers and Rogers decided to allow it here only because the woman in question was Irene Rich, his leading lady in almost all of his silent features.

(A year later, Louise Dresser was to try to have Will Rogers, her husband in the film, kiss her at the final fadeout of Lightnin', but Rogers told her, "I'd rather wait till I get home. I'd be ashamed.") Audiences had grown to accept Miss Rich as Will's screen wife.

Even so, the kissing sequence produces the most kittenish performance by a leading man in any film. He gives Irene Rich a dainty peck, wipes his mouth quickly with his handkerchief, is told by his screen daughter Marguerite Churchill that he is blushing, and admits that he feels he has been unfaithful. All this on camera.

It typified Rogers' wholesomeness and his belief in upholding a firm, yet tolerant, moral stance. Movies were after all only movies, but they had a profound effect on their audiences, and Rogers believed they should reflect his beliefs and his philosophies of his life, be they comic or serious. And there is much seriousness in his comedy ad-libs. In his quiet way, Will Rogers was a committed film maker. One can pay him no greater compliment.

                                   --Anthony Slide in Los Angeles
                                   Times, Calendar, November 4,
                                   1979, page 29.

• PAT ROONEY

     Pat Rooney became his own best critic Monday evening at the Royal, when, in a speech at the conclusion of the new turn Rooney and Bent are presenting, Mr. Rooney mentioned it was only the eighth time they had played it; that before long they expected to have it shaped up for laughing purposes like any of the other former Rooney and Bent acts. It was almost miraculous a new act admitting faults in a big time house, but Pat was right. And his own acknowledgement softened the blow, besides installing confidence into those of the audience that a chap with sense enough to admit shortcomings had sense enough to remedy them. The new Rooney and Bent act carried no author's name on the program. It is placed via a special drop before an apartment house, somewhere uptown in any town. Marion Bent is the daughter of a physician. His sign, Dr. Bent, is in a window on the ground floor. Marion and Pat arrive from opposite directions, but reach the door simultaneously, each with a grip. There the plot seems to end and it is as much of a mystery where it commenced, or why it happened at all. The principals address each other by their given names, have some inconsequential dialog (it could be said pointless dialog), and the best line in the turn (about dresses being cut shorter or sidewalks lowered), has been retained from the

couple's last act. When the turn was over there remained only Pat's
dancing, a couple of songs and Marion's dresses to be remembered.
One of the songs sung by Pat, on "Exemption" is in a comedy vein,
dwelling upon the reasons for exemption claims. It started off like
a world beater in a novel scheme for a war comic, but the second
verse killed the number as though it had been bombarded. That
second verse was in bad taste these days, and Pat should have it
rewritten altogether. The other number was "I've Got an Idea," written
especially since "Little Pat and Mabel" were mentioned, with Pat answering in the lyric that they had Little Pat but where was Mabel?
In the act is a nut chorus song on "The Queen of the May" that Pat
started to "plug" for funmaking but the affair wasn't worth the effort
and the audience declined to become interested, even after the sheet
with the chorus was let down. A bit with a couple of stage hands
or "company" had a laugh or so and this can also be worked up.
It was Pat's dancing that pulled the turn over and Pat had some
dancing to do, following by a few minutes only the Bennett and Rich-
ards turn which holds one of the best eccentric dancers on the stage.
But Pat got away with it and he will get away with this act, for Pop
Rooney is a thorough vaudeville showman. He and his wife are among
the most popular of the big time favs. Marion always looked well,
danced with much spirit and took capable care of her share, but the
act won't be there until it is made.

> --Sime Silverman in Variety, No-
> vember 2, 1917, page 23.

• ADELE ROWLAND

    The Palace program terms Miss Rowland, fresh from musical
comedy, a diseuse. In her new act Miss Rowland tries to get away
from the conventional series of songs. Wearing a not especially becoming costume of gold and green, and aided by Will Donaldson at
the piano, she opens with "Come Back to Georgia." Then she gives
an imitation of a woman in the audience watching her act. After that
she parodies "Smiles" into "Styles," does "The Tale the Church Bells
Told" and several Irish songs. Indeed, Miss Rowland shows a decided leaning toward the Irish melody. After that she repeats her
"Nurse," which is still the best thing she does. After that comes
"My Irish-American Rose" and the jazz number "Rockin' the Baby
Around." Miss Rowland received a huge bouquet of roses on Monday
afternoon at the Palace and went quite well, although, on next to
closing, a few people left during her act. Miss Rowland should stick
to story songs like "Nurse." She does these differently, whereas
dozens of others can do the conventional Irish songs as well or better than Miss Rowland.

> --Frederick James Smith in Dra-
> matic Mirror, January 25, 1919,
> page 166.

• BENNY RUBIN

Benny Rubin, back as a $1,500 single with a film rep, hasn't changed much. Out there he learned to talk about his pictures, in a gagging way, but still talking about them. But he didn't forget how to do a vaude act. At the Palace Rubin walloped them with a "nut" song opening, goaled them with three Hebe dialect stories in succession, whammed them with some snappy talk, also in dialect, then knocked them cold with a tap dance finish.

On both sides of his own turn Rubin m.c.'d for the other acts on the bills, also participating in an after piece with Dora Maughan and Harry Richman. He didn't waste a moment, getting a laugh every time he tried to, and he tried often.

Rubin has jumped to the top flight of stage comics, with dancing and gag writing ability added to his comedy delivery. He's welcome anywhere vaude can play him.

--"Bige" [Joe Bigelow] in Variety,
July 30, 1930, page 79.

• LILLIAN RUSSELL

What matters how she sings or why she sings, she's Lillian Russell, and there's only one. Headlining for a second week at the Palace, Miss Russell looks even better than she did last week. It may be the new dress, a peacock green diagonally draped, with a couple of peacock feathers for a headdress, and the Lillian Russell, as she stood on the Palace stage, in her "getting on" years, is still showing up the Broadway beauties, whoever they are.

With numerous counter attractions in almost the middle of the season, it was a chance to hold over Miss Russell at the big house that demands so much in the way of a program, but likely the management decided upon Lillian for the second week, owing to her unexpected driving strength last week, or through the absence of an attraction equal in her importance presenting itself in time. Whatever the cause, the retention did the unexpected, for the Monday night attendance was very light--for the Palace.

And the show around the headliner was wobbly. It got a poor start during the first part, and didn't grow much better in the second half. It may have been the house though. The emptiness in the rear left it hollow and the audience wouldn't enthuse. If any act touched the hit classification besides Miss Russell, it must have been the Chip-Marble sketch or the Whiting-Burt team.

Miss Russell had to make a speech, her twice daily one. It was why she had returned to the stage--because some A.K. accused

her of "getting on," also remarking it was probably time for her to
quit. That was enough, said Lillian. She came back just to show
'em and she may stick 10 years more, remarked Lillian, who added
the applause made her feel just as she did when 16—and Lillian Russell on the stage now doesn't have to fess up to much more than
that on her look.

--Variety, November 12, 1915,
page 16.

• CHIC SALE

There seems little need to introduce Chic Sale. It is Urbana,
Illinois, that attracts immediate attention. For Urbana (vaudeville-
ized) constitutes Chic Sale's stage offering.

He was born and raised near there. Some seven years ago he
got into the habit of dropping over to a near-by college town where
some of his friends had quarters in a fraternity house, and making
visits. All of them could do parlor tricks but Sale: he could not
play the piano, sing, dance or act. Finally in desperation, he tried
some imitations of Urbanans. In the language of the fraternity house,
they were a "shriek."

So was the stage-germ born. Father resisted. Master Chic
gathered some old clothes about him and sewed a wardrobe. He
bought women's "rats" and turned them into wigs and whiskers.
With this equipment and a repertory of six or eight Urbana characterizations, he essayed vaudeville in "The Country School."

And "The Country School" has made thousands chuckle and
giggle and gurgle for six years. Whenever Chic Sale feels that he
needs a new character, he hies himself to Urbana and attends a few
Friday night meetings at the little outskirts schoolhouse. They are
still there.

The original of his old "cornetikist" lives with his father and
mother. "Why," said Chic Sale recently, "I couldn't fail to do just
exactly as he does. Every one of his rheumatic movements, every
squeak of his voice, his tobacco spitting—I simply can't help doing
them when I am playing his part.... And my worst trouble is with
my little introductory speech. That frightens me at every performance. When I am 'in character,' I am at ease.

"I don't work for applause; I work only for laughter, the
bubbling sort that keeps rippling back and forth and then breaks
into a gust. That is worth more than money to a performer."

--The Green Book Magazine, Vol.
15, No. 3, March 1916, page 517.

● RAE SAMUELS

Miss Samuels could have secured credit for "stopping the show"
if she had wished to jockey with the applause. Instead the girl
made a speech after her fifth song. None of the applause came from
"pluggers." It could be seen and heard all over the house. Ray
[sic] Samuels, with her regular way, a performer's way that is her
own, of putting over a song made some of these mushroom 'hits' at
the Palace this summer look foolish by comparison. The girl is singing but one published number, using it as her second, and getting
good laughs out of the lyric. Her "rube" song was a homer. There's
no girl who sings a rube number as well as she does. An Italian
song about an aviator was very well done, and "I Should Worry"
was the finish, it going much bigger than could have been expected
once again in New York. The opening song, a levee rag, has little
merit and is only held up by Miss Samuels' handling of it. She has
a pianist at a concert grand. As a single, Ray Samuels looks pretty
good. She's a thousand per cent, better today than when first opening in New York. Her position on the bill [opening intermission at
the Palace Theatre] was not the best.

--Variety, August 7, 1914, page
15.

● JIMMY SAVO

Except for his eyes, which are as expressive as those of an
inebriated fawn, Jimmy Savo in repose resembles a sack of mail before
shipping. The baggy suit that is almost his trade-mark is carefully
misfitted for him by a fashionable Park Avenue tailor.

In action, Jimmy's pantomime is as wistful as that of a tot who
discovers the face of a truant officer behind a Santa Claus beard.
He can provoke more hilarity by rolling his eyes than other comedians
do with their jokes. And he's hard to pin down on paper because
his wit is not only in words but in his entire personality.

Although born on New York's East Side over papa Savo's cobbler
shop, Jimmy owns a 13th Century castle in Umbria, Italy. "It came
with my wife, Nina," he explains. Until recently liberated by the
Yanks, his castle was equipped with hot-and-cold running Nazis, says
Jimmy, and he's saving up to have the place thoroughly fumigated.

At six, Jimmy learned to juggle with rocks. At seven he made
amateur nights his preoccupation. At 12 he was a seasoned vaudevillian, billed as "The Child Wonder Juggler," to which he added
sidelines of ropewalking, dancing, singing, pantomime and wistful
comedy. Since then his progress has been a tornado of howls.

Off stage, Jimmy Savo is still the juggler, to the consternation of antique dealers. Recently he walked into a snobbish auction gallery, and after browsing around a bit, picked up an expensive Chinese plate. He examined it with a rapt expression that turned to stern disapproval.

As anxious attendants watched him, he apparently came to a drastic decision, tossed the plate high in the air and started walking away. A split second before the expected crash, of course, he wheeled and adroitly caught the plate. The attendants were later revived.

Typical Savoisms: "Lady Godiva was the world's greatest woman gambler. She put everything she had on a horse."

"When I asked her for something that would warm my heart and remind me of her she presented me with a hot-water bottle."

"I don't mind a man going around telling lies about me, but he'll hear from me if he dares to tell the truth."

Jimmy likes to tell the one about the small boy who caught up to a man on the avenue.

"Have you lost a dollar, sir?" the little boy asks breathlessly.

"That I have," says the other. "Did you find it?"

"No," answers the little boy, "I just wanted to find out how many dollars were lost this morning. Yours makes the sixty-fourth."

> --Matt Weld in Pageant, January
> 1945, page 15.

• SAVOY AND BRENNAN

My God! He's coming in!" I heard cried in a hoarse contralto as John Garrity shot me into the dressing room.

We were back stage at the Garrick, where The Greenwich Village Follies was the tenant, and for an awful instant I fancied we had broken into the chamber of a prima donna without any clothes on. A long naked back and dodging from view behind the ample skirts of a ladies' maid, and my heart was jiggling with embarrassment when my eye caught the welcome sight of a pair of pants. Checkered they were, and belonged to Mr. Jay Brennan, who sat in them at the back of the room.

"Welcome!" he said softly, lowering his blued eyelids and fluttering their lashes as is his wont. "It's Mr. Stevens, Bert."

Mr. Savoy came up from behind his ladies' maid partially reclad;

which is to say that his dresseress had buckled him into a pink cor-
set. Thus attired, he greeted me man to man with, "Sit down, Mr.
Stevens--at your own risk!" And after the retreating manager he
called, as he adjusted his red bobbed wig, "If you hear anybody
getting killed in here, Mr. Garrity, pay no attention!"

Five minutes and we were as peaceful as a disarmament conference. Time was, they told me, when Savoy and Brennan looked
on the likes of me as on an old school Russian with a knout. Oh,
but I had been a bad boy to the artists of female impersonation,
invariably spoiling their newspaper and breakfast for them the day
following a Chicago opening. But this time, here on a chair by the
door, while Mr. Savoy painted his smile, I was almost human. They
went so far as to wish I'd been at last night's party.

"Really, Stevens," said Mr. Savoy--and his words seemed to
come from the heart--"you should have been with us."

"That's Bert's new line for next year--'You should have been
with us.' How do you like it?" inquired Mr. Brennan.

"I think it will become immortal along with 'You must come
over' and 'I'm glad you asked me.'" said I, quoting with mixed emotions.

"It was the other one that really put us on the map as de-
stroyers of the English language," said Mr. Savoy.

And this reminded his panted partner of a telegram sent by
Charles Dillingham to Morris Gest on the occasion of Mr. Gest's securing the lease of the Century Theater and Roof without, perhaps,
full realization of all the obligations entailed. "Dillingham," said
Mr. Brennan, "wired Gest, 'You don't know the half of it, dearie';
and the newspapers picked up the telegram and Bert's line became
famous over night."

"Much as I like to talk about myself," beamed Mr. Savoy, "I
feel that I must change the subject long enough to introduce you to
Mrs. Jones."

So their big motherly dresseress and I shook hands, and I
said something about a woman doubtless being more sympathetic for
an act like theirs than a man.

"You're right, Stevens," said Mr. Savoy. "They tell me Mary
Garden's got a valet, but as for me, I contend it takes a woman to
understand a woman's clothes."

"Mr. Eltinge had a Jap for years, but now that he's tried a
woman he wouldn't have any other sex in his dressing room," Mrs.
Jones herself attested.

"Besides," Mr. Brennan contributed, "you can't depend on a man in a show like this, with so many girls in it. Just when you want him to lace you up he's out in the wings with the women."

"And why put temptation in the poor devil's way?" cried Mr. Savoy to all Randolph street; and for me, he added, "Anyhow, Steve, I always feel safer in a woman's hands."

That was Bert Savoy's character, and he was going to stick to it!

"Believe me, Ashton," Mr. Savoy was saying, and saying passionately, as Mrs. Jones helped him with a change, "it's the women that lead me on to say the awful things I say on the stage. Out in front they lead me on with their knowing laughter, and from home they write or telephone me little feminine things which they have heard and which they think will betray womankind in our act. One of the chorus girls was telling me to-day that she'd asked a new chorus girl if she'd ever seen Grant's tomb, and she answered she didn't know he had one."

"But there's nothing bold in that one," Mr. Brennan objected. "Tell him about the girl that took the man out to dinner where the lights were dim and the music soft and the wine cold, and he said, 'I've never been in a place like this before,' and she said, 'My God! I'm out with an amateur!'"

So Mr. Savoy told me; and, not getting it quite right, they both told me, and I think I added a line or a word or something until it was a noble specimen of the third-rate gag.

"But I'll never tell another on the stage like that one I told just now," said Mr. Savoy. "Ashton, I'm glad you weren't out in front."

"What was it?" I asked in the interests of censorship.

"Well, Jay was saying that the house detective said a man jumped out of a tenth-story window at three o'clock this morning, and I said the man must have been listening at our keyhole. You should have heard the women in the audience laugh! They screamed. It was terrible; it was too much; it jarred. I wouldn't pull that joke again, not even with Charles Dillingham in the house--and he always eggs us on, and's going to star us next year, maybe, in You Must Come Over, written by Avery Hopwood. So far as I'm concerned, that joke is out. Once was too much."

"Tell Mr. Stevens about the Spanish beauty who tried to kill herself when we first worked for Dillingham," said Mr. Brennan by way of compromise.

"Her name," said Mr. Savoy, "was Tortalita Valencia--Jay can spell it--Jay's the speller of the firm--and she was with us in Miss 1917 and had a poison ring, guaranteed to kill with one bite. She flopped the first night and came by our dressing room door sucking that big pearl ring with the death in it. 'She's murdering herself,' I yelled, and went at her to relieve her stomach. I was rough, but sincere. There was a fight all over the stage, before the others knew what I was trying to do, and it was some fight, Ashton; you should have been with us. Dillingham would have died of rage if he hadn't laughed so much."

"He said his wife heard about it and was going to sue for a divorce and name Savoy and Brennan.--Quick, Bert, there's your cue."

Mr. Savoy ran for it, Mr. Brennan following him with shorter steps; and it occurred to me that of the two Mr. Brennan would make the more ladylike impersonator, if that were the idea, which, of course, it isn't.

Mrs. Jones was talking to me like a woman well paid and placed. "They're wonderful," she said. "They're more modest than the girls," she said. "They're just like my own boys," she said, "and when one of 'em gets to grumbling at the other, I say, 'Maybe he's nervous to-night, so don't pay any attention,' and smooth it over."

"A girl was just telling me," said Mr. Brennan when the couple came back, "that she and another girl passed a book store next door to a picture house where Douglas Fairbanks was being shown in The Three Musketeers, and the book store window was full of the Dumas romance. 'Ain't the printing press wonderful?' said the other girl-- 'they've got the book out already.' Not so good, eh? You tell him, Bert, about the time you made Edison laugh."

"It was at a banquet to the great inventor, and I did my darned-est, Ashton. And when I got back to the show I told one of the girls I didn't gave a damn--the very word I used--what the audience did for me to-night, because I'd just told one or two that made Thomas Edison laugh. 'Did you know,' she asked me, 'that Edison's deaf?'-- I don't think so much of that, either. Purity is all right, but don't overdo it. Not this season. Because this season, Ashton, is a very blase season for actor folk, and requires lots of pepper. If ever there was a season, Ashton, when I felt like letting down my hair and being the woman I oughtn't to be, this is the season.

"But my type, the type of woman I represent," Mr. Savoy proceeded, "won't permit me to be too abandoned. You know the type, Ashton, the type of woman that knows everything and knows nothing; that wants to make you believe how bad she is and never gives herself a chance to be bad--laughs herself out of it. I'm that way myself; I never have what you would call a perfect good time-- I always talk myself out of it.

"But as I say," he went on, enlarging the character, "this is a blasé season and there's such a thing as being too conservative. This is no season for poise and particularity (you spell it, Jay), and the thing for a poor girl is to have her room rent paid in advance."

Mr. Savoy's wig was off, exposing a highish, baldish forehead. From a bedizened and unlovely woman of the night he had been momentarily transformed into a good-looking man who might have been author of a book or president of a rubber company or proprietor of a hotel.

"Do you ever appear on the stage with your own bald brow?" I asked Mr. Savoy.

"I wouldn't resort to such a thing!" he flared, I've never in my life got out of my character for an audience--I have too much respect for their intelligence. Nothing could induce me to walk mannish for them, or say a basso 'Hello, Bill!' or pull a wig. I'd never pull a wig on an audience."

"Do you think female impersonators ought to get married?"

"Yes, Ash, I do," answered Mr. Savoy, who is single.

"And then," Mr. Brennan completed, as he fluttered his blue lids, "when they felt the act flopping, they could pull the wife instead of the wig."

> --Ashton Stevens in Actorviews,
> Chicago: Covici-McGee, 1923,
> pages 113-118.

●   FRITZI SCHEFF

Comic opera is so often sung without voices musically trained that the falling of a grand opera star to its stage is an event so noteworthy that it has attracted considerable attention. Fritzi Scheff was not in the first ranks of the more dignified school, but she possessed a good voice excellently trained and a sense of humor which seemed wasted in grand opera taken seriously. She is admirably adapted to just such a piece [Barbette, which opened at the Broadway Theatre, New York on November 16, 1903, and ran for 59 performances] as that provided by Messrs. [Victor] Herbert and [Harry B.] Smith, although the librettist has not given her material with which she can show to advantage her very considerable acting ability. Mr. Herbert has given her musical opportunities, and she makes them tell. She is well supported, among others in the cast being Richie Ling and the always agreeable Eugene Cowles. Mr. Louis Harrison is the comedian. Mr. Smith's humor and Mr. Harrison's interpretation of it are of the same vintage.

We have had comic opera prima donnas who could act but couldn't sing; others who could sing but couldn't act; some who could do neither. Fritzi Scheff can do both.

--James Metcalfe in Life, December
3, 1903, page 528.

*   *   *

Early in the autumn season, as the musical shows were just getting under way, a new electric sign suddenly blazed out above an uptown theatre. It was a sign which bore with it an overwhelming sense of the past--a sign designed to make any local Rip Van Winkle rub his eyes and decide that his sleep was not yet over. With blissful disregard for the intervening years, it flamed forth the legend: "FRITZI SCHEFF IN MLLE. MODISTE." Except for the fact that the bulbs were larger (and probably brighter), they spelled out the same letters that once dominated a half-forgotten season. It was on Christmas night, 1905, that they first appeared above the old Knickerbocker. For one startled moment, the present Broadway wanderer found some difficulty in remembering that this theatre was Jolson's, that the year was 1929, and that the sign marked a belated renaissance, twenty-four years after.

Once inside the theatre, you were still pursued by the haunting sense of triumphs long since passed. The house was packed to the doors with as responsive an audience as ever crowded the Knickerbocker in the days of the earlier run, but the echoes of that long-muted applause had in them a new quality. It was a pensive and teary audience that greeted the return of Mlle. Modiste--an audience which Broadway knows as the crying-into-beer variety, assuming (erroneously) that there is any decent beer left to cry into. There was more or less surreptitious eye-mopping on the part of frozen-faced first-nighters and audible sniffs coming from the most unexpected sources. Part of this was due to the music itself, which is moving as only pure melody can be. And, added to this, was the irresistible effect of a scene of spontaneous gaiety, reconstructed in the shadows of the years that have come in between. An old tragedy may still be tragic but an old comedy can be utterly heart-rending. The rediscovered charm of Mlle. Modiste lies partially in this; its melodies are so fresh and light-hearted and irresponsibly lovely, and the gay, dim world it celebrates has passed so irrevocably with the passing of its gallant composer.

All the Herbert revivals have this quality, but Mlle. Modiste more than any of them. And this was because, with the entrance cue for Fifi, the Beautiful Hatshop Heroine, there whisks out of the wings a trim, impudent little figure with the face of an engaging and faintly malicious kitten. It was the reëntrance of the only possible Mlle. Modiste in the person of Mlle. Scheff, who took up the role after almost a quarter of a century as if she had left it for an

incidental weekend. "As we were saying when we were interrupted,"
her impertinent nonchalance implied, and she coolly disposed of the
intervening years by the simple process of ignoring them. She sang
the memory-haunted "Kiss Me Again" with the air of a young prima
donna discovering a new and surprising melody. And the rattle of
her drum in "The Mascot of the Troop" seemed to beat out a gay
tattoo of defiance aimed straight in the faces of the surrounding
spectres of age and death and time.

With the principal figure in this most dramatic of revivals thus
snapping her fingers at the years, it is difficult to consider them
as actually existing. As one who had never seen her before this
return, we found the distance in time it spans unbelievable. Yet
the records stretch back to a far-away musical season in Vienna when
the young daughter of Dr. Gottfried Scheff and Anna Jaeger, a well-
known and beloved concert-singer, was starting a precarious career
in such bits as fall to the lot of the aspiring music student. One
of these bits in a Munich performance arrested the attention of the
lynx-eyed Maurice Grau in his yearly exploration of the Continent;
he departed from that city with young Fritzi's contract firmly held
in his masterly grasp. A little later, Fritzi herself arrived at the
Metropolitan Opera House, where professionally she became known as
the most vivacious Musetta in that season's production of La Bohême.
Personally, the excitement she added to that operatic jungle of assorted temperaments brought her the half-awed if affectionate title
of "Le Petit Diable." At about this time, Charles B. Dillingham apparently decided that a "Petit Diable" was just what his company
needed and, after a few hours of his persuasive arguments, Mlle.
Scheff said farewell to the homely, friendly Opera House in Thirty-
ninth Street to study the operettas of an American composer whose
work even then had far passed the stage known as "promising."
His name was Victor Herbert, and it is everlastingly to the credit of
the Scheff musical judgment that she recognized his melodies as
worthy to meet the challenge of most of the airs she had been warbling in the type of opera somewhat oppressively called "grand."

As far as we can gather, the first of these brought no particular fame to their leading singer. There may have been minor triumphs
which are lost in time, but her first spectacular spotlight came with
that Christmas night when the erstwhile Musetta stood between the
modestly retiring figures of Victor Herbert and Henry Blossom and
bowed her acknowledgment to an audience gone hysterical with delight. The mauve-decade custom of unharnessing horses and jolting
a prima donna in the carriage up Broadway (an uncomfortably athletic
tribute, we have always thought) was no longer in vogue--but it was
that kind of an evening. There were flowers and serenades and
suppers at Delmonico's--and a limitless flow of rapturous adjectives
from the gentlemen of the press. And the young visitor from Vienna
found herself identified overnight with one role and one operetta--
an identification which, to her somewhat irritated bewilderment, has
marked her as Mlle. Modiste to this day.

Her inescapable connection with this production has been still
further accented by her association with one song. The memories
of that languorous, provocative melody floating out to the refrain
of "Kiss Me Again" are as irrevocably linked with Fritzi Scheff as
Carmen's "Habañera" ever was with Calvé. And, life's little ironies
being what they are, it is not surprising to learn that Mlle. Scheff
fought to her utmost (which is no mild degree) to get the song out
of the score.

"I said, 'But it is impossible,'" she now confides. "I told Herbert, I told Blossom--it cannot be sung. Look at the range, look at
the intervals, I begged them. Can anyone sing it? Can I? Am I
a 'cello?"

Obviously Messrs. Herbert and Blossom had no comeback to
this last baffling inquiry. But such was the persuasive power of
their entreaties that she was finally induced to restore the song when
the piece opened in New York. (It was actually out of the score on
the road tryouts.) And with the first swooning intimations of the
"Sweet summer breeze" and the soft insinuating repetitions of the
refrain (she made it something like "Ki-uss me, ki-uss me again")
the house went mad with delight again and the singer realized that
the song was hers for all time. Even now, after all these years,
she seems to feel some slight resentment against it. But the audience
had made it hers alone, and even a "Petit Diable" doesn't dispute
the gallery gods.

Mlle. Modiste ran for three years, a fabulous run for days
that had never known either Abie or his Rose. After two more Herbert productions, only mildly successful, she left Dillingham for the
Shuberts, and a season of Gilbert and Sullivan which included The
Mikado, with a sprightly young newcomer known as Alice Brady.
There were successes and near-successes under this changed régime,
but nothing remotely touching the triumph of Mlle. Modiste. In fact,
the years soon began that diminuendo of fortune which so often follows a sensational hit, and we get inklings of weary, drab seasons
which found her singing in picture houses, in vaudeville, and playing in road companies in a repertoire which included, amazingly, the
role of Aggie Lynch in Within the Law. How gray these years were,
what heartaches they involved can only be imagined--you will never
learn it from the brisk, assured little autocrat now restored to her
spotlight as the unconquerable Fifi. "When Milton Aborn asked me
if I could bring it back I said, 'But of course,'" she announced
calmly. "Some of the others were afraid of a flop but I laughed to
myself," she added. "A thing like Mlle. Modiste doesn't flop, it gets
better."

And to this theory the audiences of Jolson's and the Casino
have been noisily committed.

The career of Mlle. Scheff is surrounded by the usual fantastic

legends--of temperamental fireworks, of an incredible entourage of
servants, companions, and trunks whenever she travelled, of milk-
baths and straw-covered streets. However exaggerated these legends
may be, her life, actually, has had an infinite variety of color and
dramatic incident--including three marriages. The first was Lieutenant von Bardeleben of Vienna, who, in addition to his military activities, seems to have had some courtly connections with a valentine
shop. He faded amiably out of the picture soon after the success
of Mlle. Modiste. The second was John Fox, Jr., whom she met at
a supper in her honor at Delmonico's. This romance (which was
started by a spirited combat over the lateness of his arrival) lasted
almost up to the time of his death. The third was the actor-manager
George Anderson, who still emerges from time to time in her life for
casual friendly greeting. Although all three were divorced, the en-
tente between them and their former wife seems to have been miraculously preserved. "There is nothing in marriage--or in divorce,
for that matter--that is worth getting bitter about," Mlle. Scheff observed sagely. It is a commentary on the Holy State which Count
Keyserling himself would hardly venture to dispute.

Now that she has regained her place in the spotlight, Fritzi
Scheff hasn't the slightest intention of relinquishing it. There will
be a road tour of Mlle. Modiste and, after that, the possibility of
a new production. These projects are subject to the usual chances
of accident and delay, but personally we have complete faith in the
"future" whch she discusses so confidently. After what we saw on
that opening night, we are assured that the Mascot of the Troop can
continue indefinitely to rattle her drum in the face of Time.

--Alison Smith in The New Yorker,
November 16, 1929, pages 30-32.

• MALCOLM SCOTT

One of the funniest and most delightful laughing surprises of
the Summer vaudeville season was introduced to us last week by William Morris at the American Music Hall in the person of Malcolm Scott,
the English comedian. Mr. Scott turns out to be a plump person,
nearly middle aged, with a round, good humored face, a speaking
voice which lends itself easily to the burlesque kind of fun, which
forms the body of his work, and a dancing ability very superior to
the vaudeville average. His first appearance is made as Catherine
Parr, the last wife of Henry VIII, and in the curious costume of that
lady's period the comedian delivers a monologue touching upon topics
very old and very new. It might be that this monologue feature of
Mr. Scott's turn will be far less valued by American audiences than
the later portion of his act. Some of the monologue is not very bright,
to American ears, but this shortcoming will no doubt be quickly reme-
died since Mr. Scott, from several remarks he drops, is rapidly learning the difference between the kind of pun which is a riot in a London

music hall and a deadly bore in an American vaudeville theatre.   It
is at the conclusion of this monologue that the funniest part of Mr.
Scott's turn comes.   This is the burlesque of Maude Allan's Salome.
Costumed flimsily in the approved Salome get-up, numerous beads
and bangles, a crown-like headdress, and a transparent skirt of
some thin black material through which the dancer's limbs are always
to be seen, the comedian writhes, heaves, wriggles, poses, twirls
and skips about with delicious satire and burlesque of the numerous
ladies who have attained prominence as the Wilde heroine.   The excruciating moment in Mr. Scott's Salome comes when the dancer,
whirling wildly about, approaches that which is the object of his
adoration, a quart bottle of whiskey.   Creeping upon it as stealthily
as the usual Salome approaches the head of John the Baptist, Scott
makes sure of its identity and then breaks forth into a mad, whirling dance of joy, throwing himself upon the object of his affection
and hopping ecstatically about.   Nothing funnier than this moment
has been seen in a New York vaudeville theatre.   The burlesque is
pure artistry, subtle and screamingly funny.   After the Salome effort Mr. Scott essays to explain the power of pantomime as exempli-
fied in the dancing of the corps de ballet.   He explains that in the
movements of the ballet one is supposed to be easily able to follow
the plot of the story the dancers are attempting to portray.   He attempts to illustrate his meaning by dancing gracefully about in regulation ballet fashion, on tiptoe and with much exaggerated gesture.
Then, breathless, he explains: "That means her brother-in-law has
returned from Australia with money!"   Mr. Scott's pantomime in this
instance is at least as true to the mark as that of Miss La Rue, on
another part of the American's bill.   Malcolm Scott is a warm weather
joy, and if Miss Hoffman and her countless Salome associates want
to see just how silly they look they could do no better than to drop
into the American some day and watch this English caricaturist.   May
the Scott's stay in the land be long and to Mr. Morris, for our ach-
ing sides, many, many thanks.

                                    --The New York Dramatic Mirror,
                                    August 14, 1909, page 19.

• BLOSSOM SEELEY

     Blossom Seeley did remarkably well Monday night [at the Brigh-
ton Theatre, New York], considering that she was suffering from a
severe cold that not only interfered with her singing, but affected
her dancing as well.   To anyone who had seen Miss Seeley put over
the "Todolo" in The Henpecks, it was apparent in a moment that she
was not herself.   Miss Seeley sang but three songs, repeating the
"Todolo" dance for an encore.   Under ordinary circumstances, she
could easily do five songs.   Miss Seeley has nothing to worry about
just at present.   There is a wild craze on in New York for the "rag"
style of singing and dancing, at which no one has yet shown who
can handle this better than she.   When right, Blossom Seeley will

make the music-publisher-made-rag-singer appear to be standing still.   When Blossom starts those hands agoing, and begins to toddle, you just have to hold tight for fear of getting up and toddling right along with her.

--"Dash" in Variety, July 1, 1911, page 16.

*   *   *

Blossom Seeley is herself again.   She came back at Hammerstein's Monday, in the right sense, with three new songs, each one getting over, although one of her best numbers, "On Circus Day" was employed to open the turn, making "Trolley Car Swing" (the second song) seem tame by comparison.   Miss Seeley can sing rags; there's none better at it.   She sings them all over, but this jumping in and out of productions, to vaudeville and back again, will never help a "single" who depends upon origination to help "make" a number.   It seems to destroy the vaudeville stride, or at least confuse it.   Likewise the absences heap up the difficulties of securing songs for vaudeville that have not been previously used.   However, Miss Seeley broke it right Monday, and can keep right on.   Besides the two mentioned, she has a good number in "Robert E. Lee."   Although it was 11:15 when this, her third song was finished, the applause obliged her to respond with "Todolo."   That got over too.   Miss Seeley followed all the singing at Hammerstein's, and realizing her position, worked so quickly she gave the four numbers in ten minutes.   No one walked out, and that they patiently waited after Master Gabriel and eleven o'clock attested strongly to the "Blossom Seeley" name on the program and her popularity.   Miss Seeley was prettily dressed and did not change costume, not having the time if the dresses were there.   With "Trolley Ride" first and "Circus Day" second, the act will be A No. 1.

--Sime Silverman in Variety, May 25, 1912, page 16.

• ELLA SHIELDS

Ella Shields, who comes to the States as the latest of foreign entertainers to bid for popularity and favor in American vaudeville houses, is at the Palace this week.   Miss Shields should thank her lucky stars that she had not been heavily billed and expected to accomplish the impossible as to wrecking such a beautiful house like the beauty-shop Palace as imported comics have been expected to of late with their landsliding comedy.   Miss Shields to most of that Palace crowd Monday was an "unknown"--a complete stranger--yet before she was half through the audience sat up and took notice of everything she did.   It couldn't help it; Miss Shields was giving the folks an act worthy of their attention and appreciation.   True, she

reminded us of the days of Vesta Tilley when she sauntered on in
male attire, but her style, voice, unaffected way of working and
gracefulness when tripping a few steps a la light fantastic were such
that she was accepted as an artist worth while. Miss Shields first
donned English walking attire and sang a number with a tag line,
"Just Another One" that was of quiet construction but having a
musical accompaniment that was pleasing. Then she switched to a
natty suit of navy blue--the clothes of the regulation His Majesty's
Navy and offered "In The King's Navy," a number that had a typical
English twist and accompaniment, with Miss Shields dancing a few
steps interestingly. Her classic and the gem of her stage contributions was the "I'm Burlington Bertie" number. Miss Shields dresses
as the poverty stricken English chappie, who despite being a "down-
and outer," chucked off from royalty's realm and even the middle
classes, can't refrain from wearing his rags like a nobleman and pro-
menading where the folks of caste and high society "prom." The
lyrics are amusing, entertaining, and runs a gamut of comparisons
with the persons of high rank and prominence in wealth and society
that is productive. Miss Shields handles the song like the artist she
is, and the Palace was so appreciative that it called her back enthusiastically and she responded with a topical ballad. The Palace
audience voted Miss Shields a bully good entertainer.

--"Mark" in Dramatic Mirror, January 15, 1920, page 63.

• NOBLE SISSLE AND EUBIE BLAKE

      Sissle and Blake are colored entertainers, but wholly different
in style from acts of its class. Although of straight appearance they
might be expected to unload a section of jazz, but instead the men
offered a routine of special songs which might be termed as being of
high class order, not, however, anything of the classical. The pair
have been writing songs for some time. Recently they returned from
overseas and were members of the widely known Jim Europe's band.
Sissle, who possesses a good voice and to whom most of the singing
is allotted, held a commission as lieutenant. The turn opens with
Blake at the piano, he using a lusty touch. Singing from the wings
Sissle enters with "Good Bye Angeline," which drew attention. There
followed the only bit of rag, it being "Doggone Baltimore Blues,"
with Blake duetting at times. "Affectionate Dan" by Sissle went but
fairly, but his rendition of "Mammy's Little Chocolate Colored Child,"
a corking melody, sent the going upwards again, with nifty returns.
Blake had a session with a specialty using one of the melodies with
an Asiatic label. The orchestra joined for the finish, going full blast,
but Blake's playing could be plainly distinguished above all. For a
closer the men gave "No Gal as Sweet as Mirandy," and exited in
"high yallow" fashion. But they reappeared for a demand encore.
Sissle explained it was a number they wrote while in France (the only
mention of overseas service) and was to their mind descriptive of

action in going over the top.   The number is probably called "Patrol
in No Man's Land."   Sissle acted the number, getting down on all
fours for the most time.   The house got real excited over it and the
heaviest returns of the show were registered.   The finale number is
going to be of aid for it is well worked up.   The turn should land
in big time for the men are able entertainers and their work is a
contrast from others.

> --"Ibee" [Jack Pulaski] in Variety,
> June 27, 1919, page 19.

• AILEEN STANLEY

    There's a graciousness and charm about Aileen Stanley that is
hard to put into words, and it fits perfectly with the sort of heart-
throb songs she sings.   "Just Like Jimmy and Me," "Just Some Pigs,
a Hen and a Cow" and "Walkin' My Baby Back Home," sung in just
the right tempo to make them effective, earned Miss Stanley heavy
applause [at the New Palace Theatre, Chicago].

> --Nat Green in The Billboard,
> February 28, 1931, page 18.

• JOHN STEEL

    Patrons of the last few years' editions of the Ziegfeld Follies
need no introduction to John Steel.   His voice has been a feature
of the production whenever he has been one of the participants in
the Ziegfeld festivities.   Now the habitues of the vaudeville theatres
are to have their opportunity to enjoy Mr. Steel's singing.   His debut
at the Riverside [Theatre, New York] last week proved beyond the
shadow of a doubt that he will be a big success in the two-a-day
field.   His program consists largely of ballads and song numbers
that he had popularized in the Follies.   Among them are "Tulip Time,"
"Only a Kiss," "Girl of My Dreams," "Tell Me Little Gypsy," "Rose
of My Heart," the ever popular "Eli, Eli," and a song written by
Dorothy Jordan, entitled "The World Can't Go 'Round without You."
The audience at the Riverside could not get enough of Mr. Steel's
work and recalled him again and again.   He was assisted at the piano
by Jerry Jarnigan, one of the best accompanists in the vaudeville
world.

> --"Ross" in Dramatic Mirror, June
> 18, 1921, page 1041.

• FRED STONE

    We always feel like a depraved old rounder for not laughing

at Fred Stone. He is a splendid fellow, with a genial and ingratiating presence, obviously a comedian to make honest folk laugh, and
we sit there, like Scrooge at a Christmas party, with never so much
as a smile crossing our hard features. We wish him all the luck in
the world, and get a certain sanitary satisfaction out of watching him,
but, for us, there is such a thing as clean fun reaching a point of
cleanliness where it is practically sterile. This is unquestionably
a reflection of our personal character and we feel it cleanly.

> --Robert Benchley in Life, Novem-
> ber 29, 1923, page 18.

● VALESKA SURATT

Some people have a genius for playing up their own personalities, for making their own names so attractive that no one can resist their spell. Valeska Suratt has such a power no matter what
she may play and no matter how badly or well she may play it, people
will always go to see her, drawn by the spell that she has created.
In "Jade," her new act, Miss Suratt gives to the public her most
pretentious act, a "psychological bit of mysticism" for which she has
furnished the motive and which Chester Du Vonde has fitted into
play form. It is, furthermore, a complete play with a real plot which
concerns the vain attempts of an Oriental prince to outwit an American
heiress. Shanghai is the locale and the characters concerned are
Sing Duck a Chinese servant; Elinore Catlin (Miss Suratt), an American heiress; Prince Lu Chu (Howard Sinclair); Tom Catlin (Ernest
E. Pollock) and Patrick Fitzpatrick, a part especially well done by
John Allman.

Throughout three scenes of real beauty, Miss Suratt, assisted
by her capable company, gives a performance that vibrates with life
and the Valeska Suratt personality. Praise is due the rich beauty
of the settings, for this is an act that is lavish, unusual and well
worth seeing.

> --"Davis" in Dramatic Mirror, Aug-
> ust 13, 1921, page 233.

● EVA TANGUAY

Eva Tanguay made her vaudeville debut last week. Miss Tanguay's chief claim to recognition is a superabundance of energetic
vitality that finds vent in a series of movements in which every muscle
in her body is brought into full play. She began her performance
by singing a song called "To Please the Boys," and followed it with
a coster ditty. In singing these she wore a very clumsy dress,
which was merely a covering for the dazzling costume reserved for
her final song. Both of the first songs caused no enthusiasm, as

they were very poor. The band gave her a good start for her third
song, which was in march time. The words and music did not matter
much, as Miss Tanguay put so much business and ginger into her
work that the audience did not get a chance to find out what the
song was about. A wise man once said that action is the key to
success on the stage, and if this be so, then Miss Tanguay was the
biggest kind of a hit. She has some very odd little dance steps,
and she worked up her finish so smartly that she was recalled again
and again [at Hammerstein's Victoria Theatre].

> --The New York Dramatic Mirror,
> March 19, 1904, page 18.

                    *   *   *

The Palace audiences moved forward with expectancy, the
trombone sounded above the blare of the orchestra--and Eva Tanguay
was back again on Broadway.

As electrical, as restless, as impudently gleeful as ever, "the
evangelist of joy," brought along some new melodies. One sputters
with this lyric spark:

> "There's a method in my madness,
> There's a meaning for my style;
> The more they raise my salary,
> The crazier I'll be."

Then, too, Miss Tanguay sang, "What's in a Name," spelling
out her own name letter by letter--"t" for temperament, "a" for
action, etc.--as proof. "Good-by, Everybody," concluded her seven
songs, but she was called back to do, "I Don't Care," once more.

All the numbers are Tanguayesque--that is, distinctly, thun-
derously personal. She even commented upon the white-gloved Johnny
Ford leading the orchestra. Somehow, we feel that Miss Tanguay
would achieve far more if she sang a song or two of some depth.
But audiences probably love her best as an invigorating exponent
of hurry and joy.

We're sure the real Tanguay has unsounded depths.

> --Frederick James Smith in The
> New York Dramatic Mirror, May
> 26, 1915, page 17.

                    *   *   *

Eva Tanguay represents the resourcefulness of the American.
It has been reported to the reviewer in her beginnings, she was not
a great success as a provincial touring actress. But did that faze

her? Did it faze John Rockefeller in Cleveland, O., when the beginnings of the great institution which was later to become the Standard
Oil were not successful. He thought and planned some new angle
of promotion--something which other financiers before him had not
tried. At last he succeeded. So with Eva Tanguay. The reviewer,
even after she had a small measure of success, saw her at the Lyceum
theater, Cleveland, Ohio, in a musical show. Even then in this second class little theater tucked away almost behind a church, the critics did not believe she had the talent which some day was to become
the greatest influence that vaudeville box offices have felt. She,
like the Standard Oil Co., has worked herself up into a flourishing
institution. Why? Because she thought out something different.
Who ever heard an actress knock herself on the stage? She had
been knocked by a great many critics so she said good bye to the
legitimate and framed up a vaudeville act and beat the knocking critics at their own game. She has made out of herself the biggest
theatrical novelty the theatre has ever known in the world. Had she
elected to play Juliets for all her life, she would now be in the smallest of small bedrooms eating hash. But no, she had nerve, she had
initiative, she had pluck. She thought up something new and sold
it as no salesman ever tried to sell. She has won. What's more to
say?

--"Higgins" in Dramatic Mirror,
April 29, 1919, page 636.

● HARRY TATE

"Fishing" is funnier than "Motoring." Both sketches belong
to Harry Tate and are satires on popular pastimes. In "Fishing"
the humor is broader and there are English colloquialisms scattered
throughout which might be translated into the American vernacular
with benefit. The humor of a man going fishing with nine bottles
of whiskey and a shotgun cannot be mistaken. The setting is pretty
and realistic. No more may the English be accused of a density in
quick appreciation of humor. To follow Mr. Tate and his company
in "Fishing" requires an alertness of mind, for the subtle points
are passed over rapidly. There is continual laughter during the
twenty minutes occupied in showing the audience how an "amateur"
can catch a solitary fish by stealing it from another's hook. Mr.
Tate gave an excellent performance of the typical Englishman and a
bibulous angler. The company includes five persons, each earning
distinction in his respective role. Harry Kennedy as the "lone fisher-
man" pressed the principal closely. Thomas Tweedlang, the "village
idiot," caused plenty of mirth in a laughable part. There is no question as to the success of the piece. If Mr. Tate's other farces even
approach the two he has shown us so far they should be hurried
right over.

--Sime Silverman in Variety, October 13, 1906, page 8.

● FAY TEMPLETON

        Once an artist--always; nevertheless it is once more emphasized
that even artists must have material. To the accompaniment of a
tremendous reception Fay Templeton appeared upon the stage of the
Victoria Monday night shortly after 10 o'clock and in her famous
widow's gown from Weber and Fields old music hall, sang "Fishing."
In a brief monolog, consisting mainly of the phrase in both French
and German "Isn't She Large?" she leads up to the song "Though
I'm Stouter Than I Have Been, Still I'm Thinner Than I Was," finishing it with comedy trills and high notes, a contrast to her rich contralto tones, which she made use of immediately afterward with one
verse of "Poor Little Buttercup." Here a change of costume is re-
sorted to for "So Long Mary" from 45 Minutes from Broadway, in
which she employs five boys and five girls to go through the same
"business" as was done in the show. There were persistent demands
for an encore and her most famous ditty from Weber and Fields--
"Rosey Posey"--came in for a single verse. Somehow or other, the
whole thing simmered at the finish. Miss Templeton was not accorded
the full homage due so great an old-time favorite--and artist.

                            --"Jolo" [Joshua Lowe] in Variety,
                               February 28, 1913, page 18.

● THE THREE KEATONS see BUSTER KEATON

● VESTA TILLEY

        Even at the ten dollars a minute, supposed to be paid Miss
Tilley by Percy Williams, she will doubtless prove a profitable investment, for there was no question Monday night as to the genuine welcome accorded her by the pay patrons, even though some few of
her personal friends did make fools of themselves at her entrances
and exits. There were two in row C who applauded only after the
others had stopped and then until the others commenced again. In
this way they gained for the singer a tag of applause that she probably valued no more than did those for whose benefit the demonstration was probably intended. At no time does Miss Tilley need a
claque; she is too firmly established in the favor of the playgoers.
She occupied thirty-seven minutes in the afternoon and forty-one in
the evening, singing five songs at each performance. She offered
to stop at the fourth, but the audience would not be satisfied in
the evening until she had given "Algy." The others were "Down
Lover's Lane," "The Royal Artillery," "The Seaside Sultan," and
"Following in Father's Footsteps," which last showed Miss Tilley at
her best as the rollicking Eton boy who is only too glad to follow
the parental example when that parent happens to be a sower of wild
oats. The military song might be cut out, it lacks the swing of her
other offerings and is a little out of the color. Miss Tilley has

advanced markedly in artistic impulse since she first made herself
known to us, and she is something more than a singer for she brings
to her work expression, feeling and that indefinable something termed
personality. Moreover she is the one male impersonator on the stage
to-day who really looks like a boy; her costumes are exact and she
wears a wig that might well be her own hair, so exactly does it fit.
She shows some stunning styles and that these too were of interest
was evidenced by the fashion in which the occupants of the front
rows rose in their seats to see what sort of shoes she was wearing,
the footlight shield making it impossible to see the stage floor without rising. But Miss Tilley is something more than a clothes horse.
She is a leader of style and every detail of dress is merely the com-
plement to her detail of rendition. She is an artist throughout and
in the engagement she will probably break all records.

> --"Chicot" [Epes W. Sargent] in
> Variety, May 5, 1906, page 6.

*   *   *

After an absence of three years Vesta Tilley returned last
week and proved beyond a vestige of doubt that she is as popular
as she ever was, if not more so. That she is as artistic in her
methods and as captivatingly exuberant in her personality it is almost
needless to say, and the packed houses at the Colonial Theatre all
of the week demonstrated her drawing powers far better than any
eulogism could possibly do. In costuming Miss Tilley is as dapper
as ever, and her English tailors have garbed her in attire of the
latest modes. Although it was not required, as far as the entertaining powers of Miss Tilley are concerned, it would seem that the management might have given her a stage setting more in keeping with
the artist's high standing and her own perfection of detail in her
art. The set used seemed all too barren for the occasion. As an
opening song "When the Right Girl Comes Along" proved effective,
and the audience on Thursday afternoon warmed up to the singer
after the first few bars had been rendered. For this song Miss Tilley wore evening clothes of the very latest cut, with a single breasted
black top coat and a silk hat. "Jolly Good Luck to the Girls" was
even more entertaining and was enjoyed to the full. This is a sort
of military number and a red subaltern's coat and dark soldier trousers were worn, the usual accompanying English short stick being in
evidence. "The Seaside Smile" recalled Miss Tilley's last appearances
in America, and the familiar song was loudly applauded. For this
offering the singer appeared in a double breasted coat of swagger
cut, white or cream colored flannel trousers, low canvas shoes of
a white and a Panama hat of rakish shape, while a monocle completed
the picture of the English chappy. As a closing song, "I'm Following
in Father's Footsteps" was most acceptable, and the opening strains
by the orchestra were received with vociferous applause, proving how
popular the song is and how well it has been remembered. The same
Eton suit and tall chapeau was worn as previously. Miss Tilley finally

was called before the lights for a brief expression of her gratitude
for the applause received and the half hour of her appearance all
too short.

                                    --The New York Dramatic Mirror,
                                    April 17, 1909, page 9.

• SOPHIE TUCKER

From the small time to the big time is a long jump and many
there are who have slipped or stumbled in the attempting of it.
Sophie Tucker is another recruit from the lower rungs of the vaudeville and amusement ladder, who is about to find her own. She certainly deserves it! Seldom is such a vivacious, intense and entertaining personality found in one body. Miss Tucker fairly lifts a
person out of his seat. She has a very powerful voice of the "coon
shouting" calibre, but which she uses to such good advantage that
the harshness of it is forgotten and her higher and lower notes are
quite pleasing. But it isn't her voice--it's her ability to act. Musical comedy will undoubtedly soon take her away from the variety
stage and we will then no longer hear her sing "The Cubanola Glide,"
"My Southern Rose," "Carrie and Harry," and "The Wild Cherry
Rag." On Thursday afternoon she received five bows and was then
forced to give an encore. But her gown! Whoever designed it must
have thought the main idea is to get everything in the trimming line
on one gown. 'Nuff said!

                                    --The New York Dramatic Mirror,
                                    September 11, 1909, page 15.

                            *   *   *

To Sophie Tucker at the Colonial this week the wide open arms
of vaudeville are extended after a long absence, Miss Tucker for
weeks and weeks being a big happy feature at Reisenweber's and
later going out with the McIntyre and Heath show, Hello Alexander.
The Colonial gave Miss Tucker a greeting that unquestionably warmed
the cockles of her heart and Miss Tucker in return sang as only Miss
Tucker can sing and had her syncopation boys reel off the line of
jazz that is extremely popular at this age. The applause was so
long and enthusiastic that Miss Tucker had to make a little speech
of thanks, saying that she was mighty glad to get back to vaudeville and that she would probably stay in it for some time to come.
We have always enjoyed Miss Tucker's singing and that she has kept
abreast of the times is plainly evident in the new act she is doing so
nicely and satisfactorily at the Colonial this week. Miss Tucker acts
as a sort of stage hostess, even having her jazz experts as her
guests. They have made so much money Miss Tucker announces that
they can afford to be her guests. Miss Tucker asks them to play.
Nothing doing. They are lounging around a prettily decorated room

that suggests all the comforts of club and home. Miss Tucker then
appeals to the house leader and he declines. Then she starts a jaz-
zedy song by her lonely. The boys cannot resist the impulse to play
and one by one they connect with the instruments and join in. Then
comes some happy minutes with Miss Tucker singing "Vamp a Little
Lady," "Won't You Bless Everybody That's Worth Blessing In My
Suwanee Home?" "I Never Knew I Had a Wonderful Wife," "We Are
Simply Full of Jazz," "Nobody Knows," "The Wonderful Kid from
Madrid," and "When Fan Tan Takes Her Jazz Band to Tokio." They
are all good but three stuck us as being brand new and whales for
vaudeville, namely, the Suwanee, Madrid Kid and Tokio numbers.
They were sent over with telling effect and worked up unusually
well by Miss Tucker and band. And she puts over the [Irving]
Berlin ballad in better shape than anybody yet we have heard sing
it and that takes in the composer himself. Miss Tucker has a butler
and a maid and everything to make her new act stand out differently
from anything she has yet attempted. In fact it is an act that can
stand playing consecutively and repeat at any old time. It's a great
act of its kind. Here's hoping vaudeville doesn't let her get away
again.

> --"Mark" in Dramatic Mirror, De-
> cember 25, 1919, page 1993.

*   *   *

A hand fell heavily on my arm, and for an instant--I know not
why--I thought it was the hand of my competitor and my friend,
Percy Hammond of the Chicago Tribune. But the blow was followed
by a laugh of equal weight, and even ere I turned in the crowd I
recognized the friendly thump and laugh as Sophie Tucker's.

"What have I ever done to you that I should come to this town
and play twelve weeks and never see you, or hear from you, or not
even get a 'Hello, Sophie!' in the paper?" Sophie wanted to know.

"Nothing, Sophie; you've done nothing," I tried to explain--
"only, things are--hem!--different. I wear shell rims now and don't
go to vaudeville any more. My editor won't let me."

"That must worry you a lot!" laughed Sophie Tucker. "I've
been trying to get hold of you for weeks, to take you out to Edelweiss on a Wednesday Bohemian night and show you all the actors
and--and my new stuff. You know, I've reformed."

"No!"

"Honest to God! I don't shout any more. I'm all class now.
You wouldn't believe it's me, the subtle way I put a song over."

"Sophie," says I, "this is terrible. When can we get together
and talk it over--for the paper?"

"Right now," says Sophie, kidnaping me, hooking her magnificent right in mine, cramming me into the crowded elevator and shooting me up seven flights to her hospitable pair of rooms in the Sherman.

There were birds, fruits, flowers, music, a piano, bottles, photographs and a bed in Sophie's frontmost room—everything you could imagine but a book. Sophie took the big chair and I took the bed. She rocked in the rocker while she talked, and sometimes I rocked on the springs.

"No, sir," she said—for emphasis more than for respect— "there's no more rough stuff for me. I've canned it. It's out— forever. I'm so damned refined now you wouldn't know me."

"This is terrible!" I repeated inadequately.

"Oh, I know you used to laugh your head off in the days when I shouted. You used to say you liked me best when I taught the trombone its place and made the electric lights flicker. But I've got something better for you now. I've got Art. I've got—

"Hel-lo darling. Come right in. There—that's for you."

And Sophie gave her own padded chair and a kiss to a rival dramatic critic, who had entered unannounced.

"I'm just telling him," said Sophie to my rival, "that he wouldn't know my act any more."

"He wouldn't know your 'Floradora' number," said this other critic, who knows everything. "I'll have to show you the business of that song, Sophie, especially the business with the hat."

"I'll be glad to get it," said Sophie. "I study all the time I ain't working. He wouldn't believe the time I put in on a song to get it just right.—Ashton, it's a fact, by the time I put on a song it's a classic. My whole act is classic, a series of classics—because I change my act all the time. That's the reason I can play eleven weeks big time solid in Chicago at the Majestic and Palace and State-Lake—because I give 'em new stuff all the time. But, oh God! the hours of study it takes. Sometimes my brains just itch.

"But it's worth it, to get what you want and do it like an artist," Sophie vowed with lighted face. "I've just picked," she went on, "and remade a new one with marvelous story and lyrics. It's called 'The Soda Water Blues,' and if it doesn't give you the grandest, gloomiest laugh you ever had I'll buy you a new car. All my five boys dress up for it as bartenders, and I get stewed on vanilla and chocolate. That's something I've never done before!"

"I tell Sophie," said my rival, rocking easily where Sophie had rocked, "that she's the ballad-monger of the streetwalker and the drab. No lady of the underworld could hear Sophie sing a heart song without shedding tears."

In the laughter which this evoked, the distinguished dramatic critic for a great newspaper (for two cents) disappeared into Sophie's other chamber, ostensibly to telephone, but really, I fancied, to give me a chance alone with Sophie.

"I wish you wouldn't go, darling," said Sophie; then to me (she didn't darling me): "Ashton, do you know I'm making more money than any woman in this business today?"

"No! How much?"

"I wouldn't give you the figures on account of the income tax. But for God's sake don't put that in! They'll be on my tail."

"I'll say you said it laughingly."

"'Said Miss Tucker laughingly!' All right," laughed Sophie. "They read those darn fool things you write. You wouldn't believe it, the way folks read some of your things. Remember that interview you wrote with me as a singing waitress? They used it in my last divorce. But where am I? Oh, yes, money. They wouldn't give me all this money if I didn't deliver; if I didn't have the class, the finish, the subtlety. I'd never got it if I'd stuck to the rough stuff; I'd never got anywhere or anything."

"Sophie, are those pearls real?"

She unclasped the necklace and placed it in my hand.

"Heft 'em!" answered Sophie.

They weighed true. Sophie's other gauds spoke for themselves. Her bracelet was of diamonds, likewise her watch, and her rings held single gleaming stones whose surfaces were smaller than a quarter but greater than a dime, and there was a wicked winking one as big as a policeman's button which heaved at her breast.

"You ought to build a theater," I said, by way of relieving the strain.

"I'm going to," said Sophie. "That's what I'm going to do with some of my money. I'm going to build right here in Chicago the Sophie Tucker Theater and the Sophie Tucker Hotel and the Sophie Tucker Restaurant. Why not? I'm an institution here now. My name is the best kind of a draw. There aren't three greater money-getters in the world than a theater, a hotel and a restaurant, and I'll be there with all three. And believe me, boy, I'll get the first-class trade."

"Society?"

"Sure, Society. I don't meet nothing else, hardly, out at
Edelweiss Gardens, where I'm hostess and everything. And it isn't
any 'Good evening, Miss Tucker,' either--it's 'Hello, Sophie, old
dear.' And I don't mind telling an old friend like you that it isn't
everybody could hold that job out there. It requires a lot of brains
and a lot of common sense and--don't forget this--tact."

"Do you dance with 'em, Sophie?"

"I should say!"

"How do the Society johns dance?"

"Marvelously. They're the kind! They make me forget my
married life and divorces. They treated me like--like the Queen of
Sheba. You never saw such popularity. And proposals! I never
knew there were so many proposals."

"Of marriage?"

"Whatdoyoumean 'of marriage'? Of course they're of marriage.
You know what they call me now in this town?"

"Theda Bara?"

"Hell, no! They call me The Blizzard--I've swept the town
so."

"But you couldn't dance a little bit in the old days," I was
reminding Sophie when my kissed competitor joined us.

"You weighed a ton," said this rival critic without malice.

"I know; I couldn't lift a leg when I was at the La Salle in
Louisiana Lou. But you ought to see me now, Ashton. I can dance
anything that's danced in two shoes. I frame some of my own steps."

"Write your own songs?"

"Well--I reconstruct everything I touch. I get wonderful ideas,
and reconstruct to fit myself. It was hard at first. It took brains.
But it's natural with me now. It's going to tickle you to death to
see how classical and how personal I've made my work."

"Whatdoyoumean personal?"

"Me--myself--Sophie Tucker. I put myself into the words, into
the story, of every song I sing. I dramatize myself. I'm my own
heroine."

"Life is incomplete till you've heard Sophie sing 'I Used to
Love You.'" observed the rival drama critic.

"Everybody that hears me sing it thinks it's my own divorce
I'm singing about," said Sophie--"I make it that personal. Listen"
(and she slowly hymned, lifting a nourished shoulder to the rhythm):

> "I used to love you, but it's all over now,
> You've got it all over town
> That you threw me down--
> But you shouldn't let that kind of story go roun'."

A pair of critics employed their unaccustomed hands to applaud.
One of them told Sophie she was a marvel. Another that she ought
to be in the movies.

"I may try that, too," said the undaunted Sophie. "I've had
a letter from Fox, asking me to make a test picture."

"With lions?" I asked.

"Whatdoyoumean with lions!" exploded Sophie. "But"--she
seemed to reflect--"why not? What's a lion or two to a woman who's
had my husbands--eh, old darling?" And again Sophie Tucker be-
stowed a kiss upon my rival--the incomparable Amy Leslie of The
Chicago Daily News.

> --Ashton Stevens in Actorviews,
> Chicago: Covici-McGee, 1923,
> pages 141-146.

•   RUDY VALLEE

Rudy Vallee and his Connecticut Yankees, nee Yale Collegians,
a billing they dropped presumably because of confliction with another
Yale Collegians band, proves anew the magic of radio as a star maker.
Vallee with his singing instrumentalists has been on the air prolific-
ally the last few months, as often as three times a week from one
station (WOR) and as many as four different stations in the same
week (WOR, WJZ, where he had a commercial; WMCA and WABC, on
behalf of another commercial, Herbert Diamond's Entertainers), sup-
plemented by his Heigh-Ho nite club, Hotel Lombardy, and latterly
the New Venice dance programs.

Etherizing thus extensively and intensely, Vallee risked over-
doing himself, but somehow sidestepped that and, instead, cinched
himself with the dial fans. All this has culminated in the Victor-
Radio-Keith-Orpheum alliance annexing Vallee for itself exclusively
for Victor records, National Broadcasting (WEAF), exclusive broad-
casts and Keith bookings, doubling from the Lombardy hotel and New
Venice.

Vallee opened cold at the 81st St. the second half and was
held over for the first four days of this week, an unusual departure
for this house. The neighbors on upper Broadway went strong for
the personable octet whose quiet, subdued rhythmic syncopation is
as much the appeal as their unique lyric interpretations.

With silly little props such as an assortment of carnival hats,
and simple hokum pantomimic business to further stress the lyric
significance of their ditties, theirs proved a pleasantly unique style
of popular entertainment. The chief appeal is the quiet simplicity
of their music. There is no fanfare, no heavy arrangements, no
hullaballoo. They rely strongly on their vocal interludes, with some
comedy derived from a couple of saucy lyrics. The keynote of their
instrumentation is a charming softness, with plenty of rhythm from
piano and traps.

The personnel comprises two violins, two saxes, piano, string
bass, drums and Vallee standing in the center of the group, but
never forward, alternating between sax and clarinet. There is no
brass. It all runs to strings and reeds, making for smooth, soft
syncopation.

Vallee plays his tunes in short medleys, as on the radio, including some of the familiar favorites, several of them original numbers, including "Deep Night," "Sweetheart of All My Dreams," "Sweet
Lorraine" and that Brazilian tango which was the second encore.

Vallee can come into the Palace any time.

--Abel Green in Variety, February
13, 1929, page 45.

• VAN AND SCHENCK

Van and Schenck need never worry about anything as long
as they stick together and their voices stick with them. These boys
are there, from personality to ability, and they bottled up one smash-
ing hit at the Brighton house [New York], notwithstanding they were
next to closing and appeared around eleven bells. The heavier chap
has versatility and puts over three dialect numbers in great shape.
The piano man has a distinct style of manipulating the ivory accompaniments and his tenor voice is good and strong. Van and Schenck
have some good songs, but they get more out of "That's Your Pass-
port to the Heavenly Land" than any of the rest. It's some song,
the way they put it over. Van and Schenck form one of the best
teams of its kind in vaudeville. They should get over anywhere.

--"Mark" [Mark Vance] in Variety,
August 30, 1912, page 19.

● VESTA VICTORIA

It is about eight years since Vesta Victoria last appeared over
here, and at that time she did not sing in character. At the Colonial
last Monday upon the occasion of her first appearance in ten years
Miss Victoria changed her costume for each selection. Suffering from
a cold, probably acquired on the trip across the pond, and with
the drawback of an orchestra which could not grasp the possibilities
of the music on short notice, the Englishwoman was obliged to respond
with two added numbers to the repertoire which she had prepared.
The songs, in the order of singing, were "Turkish Girl," "Waiting
at the Church," "The Artist's Model," "I Never Had a Mother or a
Father" and "The Next Horse I ride On." Of these, "Waiting at the
Church" was the success, made more especially so by the bridal
dress worn by Miss Victoria while singing it. "The Artist's Model"
has been heard before, from Edna Aug, under the title, it is believed,
of "In the Summer Time" (not "Good Old Sumertime"). "Turkish Girl"
and "Mother or Father" have no merit in melody, lyrics or otherwise.
"The Next Horse I Ride On" has a breadth which Miss Victoria will
bring out when she gets her "land legs." She does a dance after
one song, approaching the "loose" style known over here. It is
equally liked with her songs. Miss Victoria "made good" easily. She
is the truly blown-in-the-bottle music hall artist of the first grade.

--Sime Silverman in Variety, February 24, 1906, page 6.

*   *   *

With the reappearance of Vesta Victoria in this country at the
Colonial Theatre this week comes a successor to her former famous
and popular song "Waiting at the Church." It is "Poor John." This
is one of three new numbers Miss Victoria sang on Monday evening.
Of the others, "All about Him" is a sequel to the big song hit of last
season, and the first selection. "Never Trust a Policeman," while
comic, will never be a large success here. "It Ain't All Honey" and
"The Artist's Model" were recollections of the past, and, of course,
the English comedienne had to sing her trademark for the final encore. The audience insisted upon it through two minutes of applause,
but the edge was taken off by the sequel which is melodious and
humorous. "Poor John," however, is Miss Victoria's star piece. The
chorus of it was sung by the audience at the second verse. Miss
Victoria more than duplicated her former success. "Thirty-six minutes" is ample proof of that. Monday afternoon forty-two minutes
were required. Miss Vesta has not lost any of her charm; she still
remains the magnetic, pretty, buxom character songstress, the idol
of the New York public, unexcelled and impossible of imitation. Many
try, but all fail.

--Sime Silverman in Variety, January 19, 1907, page 8.

● NELLIE WALLACE

Nellie Wallace began her second American engagement at the
American Music Hall last week and scored the biggest individual hit
on the bill, and her eccentric comedy singing act was one of the funniest seen upon the vaudeville stage this season. Miss Wallace is a
distinct artist in her own field and for broad, low comedy entertainment few can equal her. She wore three costumes--the first consisting of a brownish cloak, single breasted, with a little flat hat, while
she carried an umbrella; the second was a combination of a black
plush tight fitting jacket and a gray checked skirt with a small poke
bonnet, and a little brown muff; the third started with a red Bertha,
then came a brown striped skirt which ended in a long black train,
with a wide sheaf cut out on the left side. A little eccentric hat
with one lone feather stopped the head, and she carried a staff with
a single hose attached. Her songs included "By the Side of the
Silvery Moon," "I Was Born on a Friday" (Frank Daniel's song in
Sergeant Brue). "Three Times a Day," that old time comic ballad,
and a sheaf gown song. All of her added business was decidedly
funny and of a distinct individual character which few could imitate,
and needless to say she was one great big hit. Miss Wallace should
become as big a favorite this trip as Vesta Victoria used to be.

--The New York Dramatic Mirror,
November 27, 1909, page 17.

● FLORENCE WALTON

There is only one Florence Walton. She shares the headline
prominence at the Palace this week with Willard Mack. She is assisted in her dancing presentation by Allan Fagan who did splendidly
with her with one exception. However Miss Walton's work was superb
and she wore a costly array of new clothes that comes from one of
Paris' smartest shops and showed the class that has established Miss
Walton as an international favorite. Miss Walton and Mr. Fagan have
evolved an uptodate fancy dancing routine that runs mainly to the
waltz and one step. Miss Walton does a solo that shows the artist
to have exceptional ability. Miss Walton carries two musicians, a
violinist and a pianist. During breathing spells two violin solos are
offered. American vaudeville thrice welcomes Miss Walton back upon
its stages. She certainly spells dance class.

--"Mark" in Dramatic Mirror, October 16, 1920, page 686.

● FANNY WARD

Fanny Ward is back on the stage after an absence of 12 years,
according to her own announcement. The means of bringing about

her return is an Edgar Allan Woolf sketch, especially written. Where
the picture boys write a scenario around a title, Woolf has revised
the idea a bit by apparently building an act around a punch line.
And that tag sentence squares a lot.

At that "The Miracle Woman" as read by a playing cast of four
comes over the lights in a more workmanlike manner than many another playlet turned out for a similar purpose. It probably serves
Miss Ward two ways; for herself and her beauty shop, although she
refrains from mentioning the address.

The script goes right after the comedy angle by having an
elderly man (Ben Taggart) and a youth (Dwight George) appear in
kid costumes, the result of a baby party. This allows for Miss Ward
to entrance via ribbons and one of the childish hats a Miss Loos referred to. Miss Ward makes two more costume changes, a negligee
and then to evening gown and wrap.

Meanwhile the old codger and the youth are apparently in love
with her, the older offering marriage. A middle-aged woman, armored
in masculine attire, announces herself as Miss Ward's daughter and
informs her kittenish mother than a certain gentleman threatens the
family financial status through a business rivalry. It's the same
middle-aged individual who's pursuing the ever youthful Fanny. Of
course she saves the day or situation. But not before turning over
his gift of a string of pearls to the boy.

He of the greying hairs, overhears the transferring of his
present and the explanation as to what relation the youngster is to
Miss Ward comprises the wallop. Funny, too, and offsetting a couple
of sagging moments in the reading matter.

Miss Ward was seemingly unruffled Monday night and played
easily. No denying her appearance from the shoulders up is remarkable but someone should question the advisability of short skirts,
even if they're the best in the world for her--and they're not. However, Miss Ward preaches preservation of youth for women throughout the act and the visiting femmes evidently like it.

The remaining cast members foil adequately considering. At
this particular performance Miss Ward delivered herself of a speech
after more flowers than the Palace generally views in a season went
over the foots.

A pre-act announcement stated that Miss Ward made her stage
debut in 1880, and the kid's still trouping either at the Palace or in
her physical factory.

Not too heavy applause for Miss Ward but a neat quota swelled
by a small gathering of friends in full evening clothes who referred
to Willie Solar by saying, "Did you see the funny man?" They looked

as if they hadn't been in a vaudeville house for years, and probably won't be again with or without Miss Ward, for--the Governor's Lady and Judy O'Grady--!

> --"Skig" [Sid Silverman] in Variety, December 8, 1926, page 23.

• CLIFTON WEBB see MAE MURRAY AND CLIFTON WEBB

• WEBER AND FIELDS

["Mike and Meyer's Trip Abroad" at the Auditorium, Chicago] borders on the old travesties these two comedians made famous. Has plot and is full of life and ginger, and the chief members of the company take part. The plot concerns the fortunes of Michael Dillpickle (Joe Weber) and Meyer Bockheister (Lew Fields) who are doing Europe on a letter of credit. Mrs. Wallingford Grafter (Nora Bayes), Pierre Poisson (George Beban), and Josh Kidder (Harry Clark). [sic] Poisson is about to lose his hotel and is in despair. Mrs. Grafter comes to him with the notion he sell some of his works of art and thus recoup his fortune. He decides to sell his famous statue of "The Dying Gladiator" for $10,000, even if it does go to a man in Englewood (localism). The tourists get the idea that they may get rid of their letter of credit by purchasing a half interest in the Poisson hotel in order that they may get free food for a couple of days before the proprietor learns of its worthlessness. Later it is discovered the statue has been broken and there is much despair until Mike and Meyer offer to pose as the statue and deceive Mrs. Grafter. This is where the most ludicrous part of the entertainment comes in. The two in grotesque style, and all in white, pose, and are subjected to all sorts of annoyance. One of the big laughs is where Meyer, who is prone on the pedestal, says plaintively: "Meyer, I am laying on a nail." The comedy is fast and furious. Some of it is new and some old. The scene is embellished with a large chorus. Tango dancers flit in and out adding variety. Harry Clark has a number with the chorus in which he does some active dancing; Miss Bayes wears green hair, and there are numerous other novelties. It is an act such as suits the people in it, but demands just such people to put it over.

> --"Reed" in Variety, February 27, 1914, page 16.

*   *   *

From the lowly precincts of the music halls has arisen a new pair of pragmatists. The names that appear on the bills are Weber and Fields, but the hands are the hands of William James. And so and so and so and so.

The method of these zanies is eclectic. From Zeno the Stoic
they have taken the doctrine of "six-times-six-is-thirty-six." From
Anaxagoras the theory that the Whole is less than any of its parts.
From Francis Bacon the denial of Truth as a substantive. From L.
G. B. three dozen woolen stockings and a crate of oranges.

Take for example the scene where Mike and Meyer are discussing occupations (in itself pure dialectics):

> MEYER: Vot are you doing?
> MIKE: Voiking in a nut factory.
> MEYER: Doing vot?
> MIKE: Nutting.
> MEYER: Sure--but vot are you doing?
> MIKE: Nutting.
> MEYER: I know, but vot voik are you doing?
> MIKE: Nutting, I tole you.
> MEYER (poking his finger in Mike's eye): Ou-u-u-u, how I
> lofe you!

Here we have the new philosophy of the subconscious, the
stirrings of a new American humor which derives from the modern
German school of Merkwürdigkeit, or Es-giebt-also-es-ist. In the
American mind is being born, through the medium of the music hall,
a consciousness of national social satire which bids fair to revolution-
ize thought on this side of the Atlantic. Could a better example be
found than the following dialogue between these two superclowns in
their latest show:

> MIKE (referring to off-stage noises): A soldier has been shot.
> MEYER: Vere vos he shot?
> MIKE: In de eggcitement!

Here, in these words, lies America. The America of to-day,
with its flaring gas lights, its thundering cable cars, the clatter of
its hansoms, and the deafening whistle of its peanut stands. The
young, vibrant spirit of America, locked in the message of two clowns!
And, with the coming of jazz, twenty years from now, we shall see
the full expression of the young nation's strivings toward the Greater
Smooch.

And how are you?

> --Robert Benchley in Life, October
> 7, 1926, page 9.*

---

*This review was deliberately written as if it had been dated in the
1890's.

● MAE WEST

Mae West is a "single" now. She has been about everything
else, from a chorus girl in the Folies Bergere and head of a "three-
act" to principal in a Ziegfeld show. That she escaped from the
latter evidences some strength of character and this becomes apparent
in a way during the act at Hammerstein's. The girl is of the eccentric type. She sings rag melodies and dresses oddly, but still lacks
that touch of class that is becoming requisite nowadays in the first
class houses. Opening with "Parisienne," which did rather well,
the second song, "Personality," let the turn down so far it was difficult to overcome it, although "Dancing-Prancing" her third number
is a first rate one, and was followed by "Rap, Rap, Rap," Miss West
"ragging" this while seated upon a chair, closing the turn without
a wait with a "loose" dance. There's enough to the act just now for
it to pass, if Miss West can be taught how to "get" an audience.
She's one of the many freak persons on the vaudeville stage, where
freakishness often carries more weight than talent, but Miss West
should be coached to derive the full value from her personality.

--Sime Silverman in Variety, May
25, 1912, page 16.

● FRANCES WHITE

Frances White is taking a dip into vaudeville, this being her
first effort at the two a day, and from the way she went over Monday evening [at the Winter Garden, New York] it certainly was not
much of a success for Miss White. Her repertoire consisted of over
half a dozen songs, most of them very poor ones. Assisted by a
piano accompanist, Miss White's first number "Personality" received
fair applause. In making her change after the first selection an em-
barrassing stage wait was responsible for the house becoming restless. "Poor Little Orphan Annie," her second number fared better
than the first. Her Chinese offering was neatly put over, but there
was no "punch" to the song. "Monkey in the Zoo" and "Mississippi"
were Miss White's best efforts, and even those numbers did not seem
to put her over in the "hit" class. A piano selection rendered by
her accompanist fared well. "You Must Have Been a Beautiful Baby,"
followed with a few amateurish dancing steps, were her final efforts.
Miss White exited to very little applause.

--"Rose" in Dramatic Mirror, December 10, 1921, page 851.

● BERT WILLIAMS

With a routine of talk and songs entirely new, Bert Williams
has again demonstrated his unique ability of making pure delight out

of materials that in other hands would be commonplace. He has two
stories that are veritable gems, as well as two characteristic "coon"
songs guaranteed to win a hearty laugh from the most blase. He
opens with a comic "I'll Lend You Anything," which should have a
place of honor near the finish in company with the ditty "Believe Me,"
which is used at the close. The yarn about the "African Dodger"
is a capital bit of humor, but the yarn about a colored circuit preacher
is probably a more intimate bit of southern negro story. Both are
altogether delightful as told by Williams. It is not likely that anyone
else could get them over. A "Chantecler" song won applause and
laughter, and several numbers with which Williams has become identified filled in the rest of his act. At Hammerstein's Williams was an
immense success. The net result of his Monday night appearance
was encore after encore until he had exhausted his repertoire and
a speech of thanks at the end.

> --"Rush" [Alfred Greason] in
> Variety, April 23, 1910, page
> 12.

*   *   *

Placed on a bill where he was preceded with laugh-evoking
acts that ordinarily would have left an audience exhausted, Bert
Williams nevertheless loomed a Goliath of giggles in a next-to-closing
position on his Palace premiere after many years in production. Williams is a natural story teller, and his deliberation in narrating a
yarn makes its point instantly apparent to every listener. He sang
his famous "In the Evenin'," and climaxed his act with his poker
pantomime, which is familiar to all theatergoers yet holds fresh interest with every resurrection. His return to vaudeville is for a limited
period, and dissemination of this fact is having the effect of packing
the ample capacity of the Palace at every performance.

> --Dramatic Mirror, December 14,
> 1918, page 869.

*   *   *

Some night my old friend Bert Williams, the very fine comedian,
is going to give me a shock. Some night when I ease into his dressing room for a reflective pipe he will be cheerful and he will be
talkative--and I will curl up in a swoon.

I've known him more years than some comedians or critics are
old; and he is still the mournfulest of all the men I know. He is
even more mournful than Ring Lardner, who used to inhabit a corner
of Bert Williams' dressing room and match long gloomy silences with
him.

I missed Ring Lardner when I went back stage at the Studebaker

to see Bert Williams. Mr. Chappy said he missed Ring Lardner, too,
said it was never so quiet and restful in the dressing room as when
Mr. Lardner and Cap (as he calls his employer) got to saying nothing
to each other for twenty minutes at a stretch. Mr. Chappy has been
Bert Williams' valet for twenty-two years, and ought to be a good
judge of muted gloom.

"I don't know which of those gentlemen," said Mr. Chappy,
while Bert Williams was working his first shift in Broadway Brevities,
"is the silenter, and I ain't saying you couldn't get a person out of
a deef and dumb asylum that would beat either one of 'em. But I'll
contend with my last dollar that they ain't a dumb man in the world
could beat 'em both."

Bert Williams came back to listen to trouble, which seems to
gravitate to him as naturally as a penny to a slot. Somebody had
been doing wrong again to Broadway Brevities, poor thing! and as
ever Bert Williams was shouldering the black man's burden. A couple
of minor comedians had "jumped the show," as the phrase is, taking
with them the orchestra parts of the number that opened the second
act. The leader, the stage manager, everybody was in a fume. They
described the dirty trick with language in kind but inadequate--but
I didn't know it was inadequate till Bert Williams summed the atrocity
in a single word, deep from his diapason:

"Sabotage!"

He sat loose while Mr. Chappy rerobed him for his next ap-
pearance--in the ancient dress-suit and white cotton gloves and too
small silk hat.

I think he stood up to change his pants; but I am not sure.
I know he sat there, loose, jointless, wordless, while Mr. Chappy
handed him his kinky wig and some prepared work with which to
blacken a light lemon-colored line on his forehead that showed below
the wig.

The coat of this disreputable dress-suit is green from age.
The pants are black only where they have been patched; the chassis
of them is in hue a stale heliotrope. When I first saw those heliotrope pants--and they were veterans then--we had not been at war
with Spain.

"Same pants, Brother Williams," said I, in whom the habit of
conversation is incurable.

"Same," he assented, and, marvelously enough went on: "Same
pants in which I appeared before the crowned heads of Europe."

It sounded very funny. Perhaps that was because it was so
very true. There was a time in Europe, you know, when you weren't
much of a king if you hadn't seen Bert Williams.

"I'm glad you've got a good song--at last."

"I'm glad, too, Brother Stevens."

"How'd you find this 'Moon Shine on the Moonshine'?"

"Didn't; it found me. Sang it for the record, picking out the notes and words as I went along." He illuminated by holding up an imaginary score. "Hit. Thought I might as well learn it for the show. So I worked it up. Pretty slow. Four months.--Drink?"

"No; still no. But where do you find it these days?"

"Don't; it finds me. Get a reputation as a regular seven-days-a-week consumer and you'll never suffer; there's a bootlegger waiting for you in every port."

"Well, I don't mean to flatter, but, Brother Williams, you certainly had the reputation of holding more--"

"Unearned."

"You didn't--!"

"Didn't hold it. I drank it, but I didn't keep it. I was like the old Romans. Every now and then I'd drink four or five big glasses of plain water and--liquor would leave me. Then I was ready for another set of drinks. It was a system."

"But why? You weren't selling the stuff."

"Why? Because, Brother Stevens, the saloon was the only club in which a man of my color could meet a man of your color. And I like my friends; like to be with them; like to be seen with them. I could do that in the saloon--some saloons. Other saloons, a few, weren't particularly cordial. You know." I knew.

"'Heavy' saloons, I used to call them. I'd pop my head in the door of one of these 'heavy' saloons, and not seeing anybody I knew right well, I'd say, in my best London accent: 'Sorry! I thought Mr. Stevens was here. He promised to meet me here at five-thirty.' You see, I knew your time for this place, knew Brother Lardner's time for that place--I had everybody's schedule, and it required a lot of drinking on my part when you were all on time at your favorite drinking places."

"And when we weren't there?"

"A trifle harder on the feet, that's all. A little more standing around, diffidently ... waiting ... waiting for Mr. Lardner, or Mr. Houseman, or yourself. I always said I was waiting for somebody

... even when I was only waiting for anybody ... anybody who'd breeze in and say, 'Hello, Bert! what you doing here?' and give me a chance to chum and make myself at home. Funny what a man'll do for human companionship!"

"I hear Al Woods will make a star of you next season."

"A star? I asked him to bill it 'The Pink Slip <u>with</u>.'"

"Good play?"

"I think so. I'm a porter in the hotel at Catalina Island; an awful liar; but a character. And I've got a song coming along that ought to have character in it, too. I sing it with a dog; with a gangling-legged outcast dog. A lady has given me a dollar to take this dog out and feed him, and her husband has given me five dollars to take the dog out and drown him. There ought to be some character in that song, not to say problem. I'm working it out--slow-- way I do everything, Brother Stevens. But I think I ought to be able to understand the way that old black porter feels. "Yes," he added, in that mellow, melancholy bass, "and I think I ought to be able to understand how the dog feels, too."

--Ashton Stevens in <u>Actorviews</u>,
Chicago: Covici-McGee, 1923,
pages 227-231.

● WILSON, KEPPLE AND BETTY

Quite some time ago Wilson and Kepple, male team, were paired in a comedy and dance act, which showed promise, according to a <u>Billboard</u> reviewer. Now, with the assist of the very charming Betty, they are doing an all-dancing affair that fulfills the prediction. The beauty of the act is in its production. It has been effectively staged and routined. The dance numbers are presented in a clever and distinctive way. Act is handsomely dressed, too. The legwork of the trio is not to be overlooked, for they are good steppers, with clogging their forte.

Act gets away to a novel start with an automatic miniature bus, looking like the Fifth avenue kind, making its entrance. Betty is perched in a chair on the top deck, while one of the boys is in the driver's seat. The other fellow comes out to replace Betty on the bus. He sits in the chair and taps to the concertina accompaniment of the driver. Their other punch bit is a stair dance, tho not typical of Bill Robinson. All three clog on the stairs, either together or singly. Betty is also spotted for a solo, and Wilson and Kepple pair off in a neat eccentric number. Were in the howdy spot here, and got a hearty sendoff. A good bet for better houses.

--"S.H." in <u>The Billboard</u>,
March 8, 1930, page 14.

● ED WYNN

    There is no sense in trying to review Ed Wynn's <u>Grab Bag</u>.*
All there is to say is that it is mostly Ed Wynn. And if you are a
real Ed Wynn fan it will be necessary only to cite one moment of
the show, when Mr. Wynn brings on a large bass-viol ostensibly to
favor with a selection. As he stands absorbed in preliminary explanation, the instrument, which is made of rubber and inflated,
slowly collapses until, by the time the artist is ready to play, he
discovers nothing in his hand but a deflated wreck. You may have
to pay a lot for a seat, but wouldn't that be worth it?

--Robert Benchley in <u>Life</u>, October
30, 1924, page 18.

---

*<u>The Grab Bag</u> opened at the Globe Theatre, New York, on October
6, 1924.

PART II: GENERAL COMMENTARY

● THE VAUDEVILLE THEATRE

by Edwin Milton Royle

    The Vaudeville Theatre is an American invention. There is
nothing like it anywhere else in the world. It is neither the Cafè
Chantant, the English music hall, nor the German garden. What has
been called by a variety of names, but has remained always and everywhere pretty much the same--reeky with smoke, damp with libations,
gay with the informalities of the half-world--is now doing business
with us under the patronage of the royal American family.

    Having expurgated and rehabilitated the tawdry thing, the
American invites in the family and neighbors, hands over to them
beautiful theatres, lavishly decorated and appointed, nails up everywhere church and army regulations, and in the exuberance of his
gaiety passes around ice water. He hasn't painted out the French
name, but that is because he has been, as usual, in a hurry. Fourteen years ago this may have been a dream in a Yankee's brain; now
it is a part of us. The strictly professional world has been looking
for the balloon to come down, for the fad to die out, for the impossible thing to stop, but year by year these theatres increase and
multiply, till now they flourish the country over.

    Sometimes the vaudeville theatre is an individual and independ-
ent enterprise; more often it belongs to a circuit. The patronage,
expenses, and receipts are enormous. One circuit will speak for all.
It has a theatre in New York, one in Philadelphia, one in Boston, and
one in Providence, and they give no Sunday performances; and yet
these four theatres entertain over 5,000,000 people every year, give
employment to 350 attachés and to 3,500 actors. Four thousand people

pass in and out of each one of these theatres daily. Ten thousand dollars are distributed each week in salaries to the actors and $3,500 to the attachés. Take one theatre for example, the house in Boston. It is open the year round and it costs $7,000 a week to keep it open, while its patrons will average 25,000 every week. On a holiday it will play to from ten to twelve thousand people. How is it possible?

A holiday to an American is a serious affair, so the doors of the theatre are open and the performance begins when most people are eating breakfast; 9:30 a.m. is not too soon for the man who pursues pleasure with the same intensity he puts into business. There are no reserved seats, so one must come first to be first served. One may go in at 9:30 a.m. and stay until 10:30 at night.

Not over 2 percent of an audience remains longer than to see the performance through once, but there are persons who secrete campaign rations about them, and camp there from 9:30 a.m. to 10:30 p.m., thereby surviving all of the acts twice and most of them four or five times. The management calculate to sell out the house two and a half times on ordinary days and four times on holidays, and it is this system that makes such enormous receipts possible. Of course I have taken the circuit which is representative of the vaudeville idea at its best, but it is not alone in its standards or success, and what I have said about the houses in New York, Boston, and Philadelphia applies more or less to all the principal cities of the country, and in a less degree of course to the houses in the smaller cities.

Some of these theatres are never closed the year round. Some are content with three matinees a week in addition to their night performances. Others open their doors about noon and close them at 10:30 at night. These are called "continuous" houses. It is manifest, I think, that the vaudeville theatre is playing an important part in the amusement world and in our national life. Perhaps we should be grateful. At present it would seem that the moral tone of a theatre is in the inverse ratio of the price of admission. The higher the price, the lower the tone. It is certain that plays are tolerated and even acclaimed on the New York stage today which would have been removed with tongs half a dozen years ago.

So far as the vaudeville theatres are concerned, one might as well ask for a censorship of a "family magazine." It would be a work of supererogation. The local manager of every vaudeville house is its censor, and he lives up to his position laboriously, and, I may say, religiously. The bill changes usually from week to week. It is the solemn duty of this austere personage to sit through the first performance of every week and to let no guilty word or look escape. But this is precautionary only.

"You are to distinctly understand," say the first words of the contracts of a certain circuit, "that the management conducts this house upon a high plane of respectability and moral cleanliness," etc.

But long before the performer has entered the dressing rooms, he has been made acquainted with the following legend which every-where adorns the walls:

NOTICE TO PERFORMERS.

You are hereby warned that your act must be free from all vulgarity and suggestiveness in words, action, and cos-tume, while playing in any of Mr.--'s houses, and all vulgar, double-meaning and profane words and songs must be cut out of your act before the first performance. If you are in doubt as to what is right or wrong, submit it to the resident manager at rehearsal.

Such words as Liar, Slob, Son-of-A-Gun, Devil, Sucker, Damn, and all other words unfit for the ears of ladies and children, also any reference to questionable streets, resorts, localities, and barrooms, are prohibited under fine of instant discharge.

GENERAL MANAGER.

And this is not merely a literary effort on the part of the man-agement, it is obligatory and final. When we have about accepted as conclusive the time-honored theory that "You must give the public what it wants," and that it wants bilge water in champagne glasses, we are confronted with the vaudeville theatre, no longer an experi-ment, but a comprehensive fact.

The funniest farce ever written could not be done at these houses if it had any of the earmarks of the thing in vogue at many of our first-class theatres. Said a lady to me: "They (the vaudeville theatres) are the only theatres in New York where I should feel ab-solutely safe in taking a young girl without making preliminary in-quiries. Though they may offend the taste, they never offend one's sense of decency." The vaudeville theatres may be said to have established the commercial value of decency. This is their corner-stone. They were conceived with the object of catering to ladies and children, and, strange to say, a large, if not the larger, part of their audiences is always men.

What I have said does not describe all theatres which may have "fashionable vaudeville" over their doors. Godliness has proved so profitable that there be here, as elsewhere, wolves masquerading in woollens, but the houses I have described are well known. Nor have the stringent regulations of these theatres exiled the "song and dance man" who was wont to rely on risqué songs and suggestive jokes-- they have only forced him to happier and saner efforts, and the re-sult is not Calvinistic, on the contrary, nowhere are audiences jollier, quicker, and more intelligent, and the world of fashion even is not absent from these theatres primarily designed for the wholesome middle classes.

I never for a moment suspected that these admirable regulations could be meant for me, or that indeed I was in need of rules
and regulations, but my self-righteousness, as was meet, met with
discipline. I had a line in my little farce to this effect: "I'll have
the devil's own time explaining," etc. I had become so familiar with
the devil that I was not even aware of his presence, but the management unmasked me and I received a polite request (which was a command) to cast out the devil. I finally got used to substituting the
word "dickens." Later on, the local manager, a big, handsome man,
faultlessly attired, in person begged me "to soften the asperities."
Need I add that this occurred in Boston? When I travel again, I
shall leave my asperities at home.

A friend of mine was leaving a spacious vaudeville theatre,
along with the audience, and was passing through the beautiful cor-
ridor, when one of the multitude of uniformed attachés handed him
this printed notice:

> Gentlemen will kindly avoid carrying cigars or cigarettes in
> their mouths while in the building, and greatly oblige.
>   THE MANAGEMENT

My friend was guilty of carrying in his hand an unlighted cigar.

How careful of the conduct of their patrons the management is
may be seen from the following printed requests with which the em-
ployees are armed:

> Gentlemen will kindly avoid the stamping of feet and pound-
> ing of canes on the floor, and greatly oblige the Management.
> All applause is best shown by clapping of hands.

> Please don't talk during acts, as it annoys those about you,
> and prevents a perfect hearing of the entertainment.
>   THE MANAGEMENT

When we were playing in Philadelphia a young woman was singing with what is known as the "song-sheet," at the same theatre
with us. Her costume consisted of silk stockings, knee breeches,
and a velvet coat--the regulation page's dress, decorous enough to
the unsanctified eye; but one day the proprietor himself happened
in unexpectedly (as is his wont) and the order quick and stern went
forth that the young woman was not to appear again except in skirts
--her street clothes, if she had nothing else, and street clothes it
came about.

These are the chronicles of what is known among the vaudeville fraternity as "The Sunday-school Circuit," and the proprietor
of the "The Sunday-school Circuit" is the inventor of vaudeville as
we know it. This which makes for righteousness, as is usual, makes
also for great and abiding cleanliness--physical as well as moral. I

almost lost things in my Philadelphia dressing room--it was cleaned
so constantly. Paternal, austere perhaps, but clean, gloriously
clean!

     The character of the entertainment is always the same. There
is sameness even about its infinite variety. No act or "turn" con-
sumes much over thirty minutes. Everyone's taste is consulted, and
if one objects to the perilous feats of the acrobats or jugglers he can
read his program or shut his eyes for a few moments and he will be
compensated by some sweet bell-ringing or a sentimental or comic
song, graceful or grotesque dancing, a one-act farce, trained animals,
legerdemain, impersonations, clay modelling, or the stories of the
comic monologist. The most serious thing about the program is that
seriousness is barred, with some melancholy results. From the artist
who balances a set of parlor furniture on his nose to the academic
baboon, there is one concentrated, strenuous struggle for a laugh.
No artist can afford to do without it. It hangs like a solemn and
awful obligation over everything. Once in a while an artist who
juggles tubs on his feet is a comedian, but not always. It would
seem as if a serious person would be a relief now and then. But
so far the effort to introduce a serious note, even by dramatic artists,
has been discouraged. I suspect the serious sketches have not been
of superlative merit. Though this premium is put upon a laugh,
everyone is aware of the difference between the man who rings a
bell at forty paces with a rifle, and the man who smashes it with a
club, and the loudest laugh is sometimes yoked with a timid salary.
The man who said: "Let me get out of here or I'll lose my self-
respect--I actually laughed," goes to the vaudeville theatres, too,
and must be reckoned with.

     So far as the character of the entertainment goes, vaudeville
has the "open door." Whatever or whoever can interest an audience
for thirty minutes or less, and has passed quarantine, is welcome.
The conditions in the regular theatres are not encouraging to progress. To produce a play or launch a star requires capital of from
$10,000 upward. There is no welcome and no encouragement. The
door is shut and locked. And even with capital, the conditions are
all unfavorable to proof. But if you can sing or dance or amuse
people in any way, if you think you can write a one-act play, the
vaudeville theatre will give you a chance to prove it. One day of
every week is devoted to these trials. If at this trial you interest
a man who is looking for good material, he will put you in the bill
for one performance, and give you a chance at an audience, which
is much better. The result of this open-door attitude is a very interesting innovation in vaudeville which is more or less recent, but
seems destined to last--the incursion of the dramatic artist into vaudeville.

     The managers of the vaudeville theatres are not emotional per-
sons, and there were some strictly business reasons back of the
actor's entrance into vaudeville. We do not live by bread alone, but

by the saving graces of the art of advertising. It was quite impossible to accentuate sixteen or eighteen features of a bill. Some one
name was needed to give it character and meaning at a glance. A
name that had already become familiar was preferred. The actor's
name served to head the bill and expand the type and catch the eye,
and hence arose the vaudeville term--"Head-Liner."

This word is not used in contracts, but it is established and
understood, and carries with it well-recognized rights and privileges,
such as being featured in the advertisements, use of the star dressing room, and the favorite place on the bill; for it is not conducive
to one's happiness or success to appear during the hours favored by
the public for coming in or going out. The manager was not the
loser, for many people who had never been inside a vaudeville theatre
were attracted thither by the name of some well-known and favorite
actor, and became permanent patrons of these houses.

At first the actor, who is sentimental rather than practical, was
inclined to the belief that it was beneath his dignity to appear on
the stage with "a lot of freaks," but he was tempted by salaries no
one else could afford to pay (sometimes as high as $500 to $1,000
per week) and by the amount of attention afforded to the innovation
by the newspapers. He was told that if he stepped from the sacred
precincts of art, the door of the temple would be forever barred
against him. The dignity of an artist is a serious thing, but the
dignity of the dollar is also a serious thing. None of the dire sup-
positions happened. The door of the temple proved to be a swinging
door, opening easily both ways, and the actor goes back and forth
as there is demand for him and as the dollar dictates. Indeed, the
advertising secured by association with "a lot of freaks" oiled the
door for the actor's return to the legitimate drama at an increased
salary.

Manifestly, it has been a boon to the "legitimate" artists. To
the actor who has starred; who has had the care of a large company,
with its certain expenses and its uncertain receipts; who has, in
addition, responsibility for his own performance and for the work of
the individual members of his company and for the work of the company as a whole, vaudeville offers inducements not altogether mea-
sured in dollars and cents. He is rid not only of financial obligation, but of a thousand cares and details that twist and strain a
nervous temperament. He hands over to the amiable manager the
death of the widely mourned Mr. Smith, and prevalent social func-
tions, Lent and the circus, private and public calamities, floods and
railroad accidents, the blizzard of winter and the heat of summer,
desolating drought and murderous rains, the crops, strikes and panics,
wars and pestilences and opera. It is quite a bunch of thorns that
he hands over!

Time and terms are usually arranged by agents, who get five
percent of the actor's salary for their services. Time and terms

arranged, the rest is easy. The actor provides himself and assistants and his play or vehicle. His income and outcome are fixed, and he knows at the start whether he is to be a capitalist at the end of the year; for he runs almost no risk of not getting his salary in the well-known circuits.

It is then incumbent on him to forward property and scene-plots, photographs and cast to the theatre two weeks before he opens, and on arrival, he plays twenty or thirty minutes in the afternoon and the same night. There his responsibility ends. It involves the trifling annoyance of dressing and making up twice a day. In and about New York the actor pays the railroad fares of himself and company, but when he goes West or South, the railroad fares (not including sleepers) are provided by the management.

The great circuit which covers the territory west of Chicago keeps an agent in New York and one in Chicago to facilitate the handling of their big interests. These gentlemen purchase tickets, arrange for sleepers, take care of baggage, and lubricate the wheels of progress from New York to San Francisco and back again. The actor's only duty is to live up to the schedule made and provided.

The main disadvantage of the Western trip is the loss of a week going and one coming, as there is no vaudeville theatre between Omaha and San Francisco. To avoid the loss of a week on my return I contracted for two nights at the Salt Lake Theatre. My company consisted of four people all told, and my ammunition, suited to that calibre, was three one-act plays. To give the entire evening's entertainment at a first-class theatre, at the usual prices, with four people was a novel undertaking.

I finally determined to add to my mammoth aggregation a distinctly vaudeville feature, and while in San Francisco I engaged a young woman who was to fill in the intermissions with her song-and-dance specialty. Scorning painful effort to escape the conventional I billed her as "The Queen of Vaudeville," whatever that may mean. We were caught in a tunnel fire at Summit and delayed thirty-six hours. I threatened the railroad officials with various and awful consequences, but the best I could do was to get them to drag my theatre trunks around the tunnel by hand over a mile and a half of mountain trail, newly made, and get me into Salt Lake just in time to miss my opening night, with a big advance sale and the heartrending incident to money refunded. We were on time to play the second night, but my Queen, starting from 'Frisco on a later train, had shown no signs of appearing when the curtain rose. I made the usual apologies. The evening's entertainment was half over when a carriage came tearing up to the theatre and my Queen burst into the theatre without music, trunks, costumes, makeup, supper.

She borrowed a gown from my ingenue, which was much too small for her; a pair of slippers from my wife, which were much too

big for her, makeup from both ladies, and went on. She leaned
over, whispered the key to the leader of the orchestra and began
to sing. The orchestra evolved a chord now and then, jiggled and
wiggled, stalled, flew the track, crawled apologetically back, did
its amiable best individually, but its amiable worst collectively. No
mere man could have lived through it. But the young woman justi-
fied my billing. She ruled, she reigned, she triumphed. Pluck and
good humor always win, and so did the Queen of Vaudeville.

When high-class musical artists and dramatic sketches were
first introduced into vaudeville, I understand policemen had to be
stationed in the galleries to compel respectful attention, but now these
acts are the principal features of every bill, and if they have real
merit the gallery-gods are the first to appreciate it. So it would
seem that vaudeville has torpedoed the ancient superstition that the
manager is always forced to give the public just what it wants. At
first his efforts were not taken seriously either by the actor himself
or the public, and many well-known artists failed to "make good,"
as the expression is, largely because they used "canned" or embalmed
plays, that is, hastily and crudely condensed versions of well-known
plays; but many succeeded, and the result has been a large increase
in the number of good one-act farces and comedies, and a distinct
elevation in the performance and the patronage of the vaudeville
theatres. This has been a gain to everybody concerned.

It cannot be denied that the vaudeville "turn" is an experience
for the actor. The intense activity everywhere, orderly and systematic though it is, is confusing. The proximity to the "educated
donkey," and some not so educated; the variegated and motley sam-
ples of all strange things in man and beast; the fact that the curtain
never falls, and the huge machine never stops to take breath until
10:30 at night; the being associated after the style of criminals with
a number, having your name or number shot into a slot in the proscenium arch to introduce you to your audience; the shortness of your
reign, and the consequent necessity of capturing your audience on
sight--all this, and some other things, make the first plunge unique
in the actor's experience.

One comedian walks on and says, "Hello, audience!" and no
further introduction is needed; for the audience is trained to the
quick and sharp exigencies of the occasion, and neither slumbers
nor sleeps.

One of the first things to surprise the actor in the "continuous"
house is the absence of an orchestra. The orchestra's place is filled
by pianists who labor industriously five hours a day each. As they
practically live at the piano, their knowledge of current music and
their adaptability and skill are often surprising, but they are the
most universally abused men I ever met. Everyone who comes off
the stage Monday afternoon says of the pianist that he ruins their
songs; he spoils their acts; he has sinister designs on their popu-

larity, and he wishes to wreck their future. The pianist, on the
other hand, says he doesn't mind his work--the five thumping,
tyrannous hours--it is the excruciating agony of being compelled to
sit through the efforts of the imbecile beings on the stage. It is
the point of view!

The Monday-afternoon bill is a tentative one, but thereafter
one's position on the bill and the time of one's performance are fixed
and mathematical for the remainder of the week. The principal artists
appear only twice a day, once in the afternoon and once in the evening, but there is an undivided middle, composed of artists not so
independent as some others, which "does three turns" a day (more
on holidays), and forms what is picturesquely known as the "supper
bill." The "supper bill" explains itself. It lasts from five o'clock,
say, till eight or eight-thirty. Who the singular people are who do
not eat, or who would rather see the undivided middle than eat, will
always be a mystery to me. But if they were not in esse, and in
the audience, the management would certainly never retain the "supper bill."

The man who arranges the program has to have some of the
qualities of a general. To fix eighteen or nineteen different acts
into the exact time allotted, and so to arrange them that the performance shall never lapse or flag; to see that the "turns" which
require only a front scene can be utilized to set the stage for the
"turns" which require a full stage, requires judgment and training;
but there is very little confusion even at the first performance, and
none thereafter.

Many of our best comedians, men and women, have come from
the variety stage, and it is rather remarkable that some of our best
actors have of late turned their attention to it. This interchange
of courtesies has brought out some amusing contrasts. A clever
comedian of a comic opera organization was explaining to me his early
experience in the "old days," when he was a song-and-dance man.
"The tough manager," he said, "used to stand in the wings with a
whistle, and if he didn't like your act he blew it and a couple of
stagehands ran in and shut you out from your audience with two
flats upon which were painted in huge letters 'N.G.,' and that was
the end of your engagement." Then he proceeded to tell with honest
pride of his struggles, and his rise in the world of art. "And now,"
said he to me, "I can say 'cawn't' as well as you can."

Our first day in vaudeville was rich in experience for us, and
particularly for one of the members of my little company. He was
already busy at the dressing table making up, when the two other
occupants of his room entered--middle-aged, bald-headed, bandy-
legged little men, who quickly divested themselves of their street
clothes, and then mysteriously disappeared from sight. Suddenly
a deep-drawn sigh welled up from the floor, and turning to see what
had become of his companions, the actor saw a goodhumored face

peering up out of a green-striped bundle of assorted legs and arms.
He was face to face with the human lizard, and his partner in the
Batrachian business, the Human Frog.

"Good Lord! what are you doing?" exclaimed Mr. Roberts.

"Loosenin' up!"--laconically.

"But do you always do that?"

"Yes, Now!"

"Why now?"

"Well, I'm a little older than I was when I began this business,
and yer legs git stiff, ye know. I remember when I could tie a knot
in either leg without cracking a joint, but now I am four-flushing
until I can get enough to retire."

"Four-flushing?"

"Yes, doin' my turn one card shy. You understand."

And the striped bundle folded in and out on itself and tied
itself in bows, ascots, and four-in-hands until every joint in the
actor's body was cracking in sympathy.

Meanwhile his partner was standing apart with one foot touching
the low ceiling, and his hands, clutching two of the clothes hooks,
striving for the fifth card to redeem his four-flush.

"Number fourteen!" shouts the callboy through the door.

"That's us!"

And the four-flushers unwound and, gathering their heads
and tails under their arms, glided away for the stage.

Presently they were back panting and perspiring, with the information that there was a man in one of the boxes who never turned
his head to look at their act; that there was a pretty girl in another
box fascinated by it; that the audience had relatives in the ice business and were incapable of a proper appreciation of the double split
and the great brother double tie and slide--whatever that may be;
and the two athletes passed the alcohol bottle, and slipped gracefully
back into their clothes and private life.

This unique and original world has its conventions, too, quite
as hard and fast as elsewhere. The vaudeville dude always bears
an enormous cane with a spike in the end of it, even though the
style in canes may be a bamboo switch. The comedian will black his

face, though he never makes the slightest pretense to negro characterization. The vaudeville "artist" and his partner will "slang"
each other and indulge in brutal personalities under the theory that
they are guilty of repartee; and with a few brilliant exceptions, they
all steal from each other jokes and gags and songs and "business,"
absolutely without conscience. So that if a comedian has originated
a funny story that makes a hit in New York, by the time he reaches
Philadelphia, he finds that another comedian has filched it and told
it in Philadelphia, and the originator finds himself a dealer in second-
hand goods.

It is manifest, I think, that vaudeville is very American. It
touches us and our lives at many places. It appeals to the business-
man, tired and worn, who drops in for half an hour on his way
home, to the person who has an hour or two before a train goes,
or before a business appointment, to the woman who is wearied of
shopping; to the children who love animals and acrobats; to the man
with his sweetheart or sister, to the individual who wants to be diverted but doesn't want to think or feel; to the American of all
grades and kinds who wants a great deal for his money. The vaudeville theatre belongs to the era of the department store and the short
story. It may be a kind of lunch-counter art, but then art is so
vague and lunch is so real.

And I think I may add that if anyone has anything exceptional
in the way of art, the vaudeville door is not shut to that.

--Scribner's Magazine, October
1899, pages 485-495.

• WHAT I DON'T KNOW ABOUT VAUDEVILLE

by Acton Davies

"Vaudeville--a place where a great many bad actors go before
they die." I don't know that this definition of this word has found
its way into any of the dictionaries as yet, but it certainly ought
to. In the first place, I should never have been asked to write
about vaudeville, because, for one thing, I know very little about it
nowadays, and, for another, I have got a grudge against it. Vaudeville has robbed me of too many happy hours in the variety theatres
to ever expect a boom from me. I feel quite sure that I am not the
only dramatic critic who is free to confess that there was once a time
a good variety show was the spice of his life. And why not? What
could be more restful and soothing to a man tired out by reviewing
a long series of "new and original American plays," from more or
less foreign sources, than to find a quiet afternoon's intellectual fun
in watching the performance of first-class acrobats, erudite dogs, or
listening to the dialect strains of a first-class serio-comic. Nowadays

if a dramatic critic goes to a vaudeville performance he finds the
greater part of the headlines are made up of dramatic extinct vol-
canoes, names which in many instances have outlived their useful-
ness and cleverness on the legitimate boards and now distended out
of all proportion to their worth are starred at the head of the performance. Some of them have been fortunate enough to secure these
short plays; in that case they may be pardoned, but even then it's
altogether too much like work for a critic to sit down and enjoy their
performance. I don't think I exaggerate the case at all when I say
that there are hundreds of true lovers of variety shows who are kept
away from the performances by the number of plays which are now
infected into the bill.

Again, it takes a highly clever actor to adapt himself to the
new environment of a vaudeville. Between him and the legitimate
variety performers there is a wide gulf fixed--one of those gulfs
which no suspension bridge can ever span. The actor, in nearly
every instance, regards his dip into vaudeville as a vast condescension on his part, and looks down on the legitimate variety actor as
a being belonging to an essentially lower orbit, a being of a distinctly
cruder grade. The variety man meanwhile detests the interloping
actor with all his soul. The fact that the star of the moment draws
just about three times as big a salary as he does is enough to mad-
den him, but there are usually abundant other reasons as well.

I have yet to meet an actor even among those few who have
really scored big hits in vaudeville who have a good word to say for
it. Of course, they nearly always preface their denunciations with
a request that they must not be quoted--probably because they
might want to return to vaudeville some day--but that doesn't lessen
the force of their roasts in the least. Even so high salaried a vaudeville star as Miss Lillian Russell looked as elated as a child just out
of school when I met her in the foyer of one of the Broadway play-
houses on Monday night. I was astonished to see her there, as I
thought she was still drawing in three thousand dollars a week for
singing four songs twice a day, so when I asked her "What does
this mean. Are you no longer a Proctoress?" she replied, "Thank
heavens, no. Little Lillian has packed her little dinner pail away
in lavender and is going to be a lady again until next March." From
which remark I gathered that even in Miss Russell's exceptional case
all that vaudevilles is not Valenciennes.

The whole method of the variety stage is so different to that
of the regular boards that I cannot see why the average actor should
ever expect that he could score in it. Tabloid drama or comedy may
be all very well in its way for those who like it, but it needs an
exceptionally strong and magnetic actor to hold a variety audience
for eighteen or twenty minutes, the length of the average "turn."
In a legitimate play this same actor would have secured important
scenes strung through three or four acts. In vaudeville if he doesn't
hit out straight from the shoulder at once he is lost. The variety

performer has been brought to this line of work and scores accordingly: it is his business to do and to do quickly almost everything which an actor on the regular stage is taught and schooled to avoid. To my mind there is infinitely more charms and originality displayed among the variety actresses to-day than there is among the actors. I could name at least a score of variety performers who have gone into legitimate musical work in the last few years, but if you asked me at a moment's notice to name the actors and acresses who have established themselves as permanent successes in vaudeville I am sure that I could count them off easily on the fingers of one hand. And here's another thing against vaudeville from my point of view. Variety actors may transfer to the regular stage and then return to vaudeville and prove just as clever as ever, but I have yet to see a single actor who having played in vaudeville for any length of time returns to his stage as good an artist as when he left it. Almost invariably the vaudeville rapid-fire methods of accentuation and playing for points tells against him when he reappears in a legitimate drama.

That actors and actresses by their wholesome rushing into vaudeville have hurt their financial standing with the theatrical managers is undoubtedly true. One of the biggest managers in this country, who usually had from one hundred and fifty to two hundred actors on his salary list, whether they are playing or not, said to me: "The actors are simply cutting their own throats by rushing into this vaudeville business. It's true that they draw a very large salary for a few weeks, but how long does it last? And then thrown down and out in most cases. Take my own experience, for instance. This year outside of the few really important artists, I have no actors under contract. I merely engage them for the run of the play, and thereby save myself a great deal of money. If the actors don't stand by the managers why should I stand by them? They don't hesitate to rush into vaudeville for a few extra hundred dollars and cheapen their market value to me, but if they have any following at all they draw their clientale along with them, leaving a yawning space in my balcony or gallery, as the case may be. And once having seen an actor for fifty cents it is against human nature to expect that anyone is going to cheerfully pay $1.50 or $2.00 to see him again. It would be foolish for me not to admit that vaudeville has hit many of the regular theatres hard during the past two or three years, because it has. Its cheap prices and the big attractions it frequently offers have seriously affected our receipts, particularly in the upper portions of the house, so for the future I am going to make it a rule not to employ actors who have figured in vaudeville unless I discover that I cannot possibly get along without them."

Talk with any of the theatrical managers and you will find that their views of the subject are very much along these lines.

A good variety show is one of the finest tonics in the world, but vaudeville when for the most part it consists of fallen stars in

mediocre wishy washy one-act plays is one of the finest producers
of mental dyspepsia that I know of.

--Variety, No. 1, December 16,
1905, page 2.

• IS "VODEVEAL" NECESSARY?

by Louis Reeves Harrison

Don't you think we have had enough of the cheapest and poor-
est form of entertainment ever slung over the apron of the stage into
the face of a self-respecting and unoffending audience?

There is a picture theater near my house which is so airy and
comfortable that I would like to go there every day. The reason I
do not is because I cannot stomach more than one unsavory dish of
"vodeveal" a week. The mere thought of enduring a second dose
of the nauseating acts presented in that house drives me away to
some more congenial place of entertainment. I do not know how much
the manager of that place pays the Dutch comedian who plays wretch-
edly on several excruciating instruments, but if this unmusical performer's salary was added to that of the ghastly soubrette who re-
cites a threadbare song in a cigarette voice and the total applied to
raising the quality of the miniature orchestra, I would go, my friends
would go, and we would send others. There is no advertisement
superior to a satisfied customer. I do go once in a while, being of
a hopeful disposition, but regularly I walk several blocks further
down the street, even on cold nights, and deposit my contribution
at a less pretentious place. So do others. There is nearly always
a waiting line at the modest place. They only give four pictures
there, but these pictures are well projected on a superior screen,
and the girl at the piano is a Jim-Dandy.

I did not notice that girl at first, possibly because she was
not rubber-necking or smiling at the hatchet-face in the front row,
but I gradually became conscious that the most ordinary pictures
shown seemed to have taken on a new guise, all the merit that was
in them came out and was fully appreciated because that quiet little
girl at the piano knew her business and attended to it instead of
neglecting it to give an impression that she was superior to her job.
I became interested even in one of those decadent survivals of primi-
tive photoplays in which white men with whiskers on their legs chase
red men with feathers on their heads because the music was so spirited
that I found myself excusing the dime-novel drama. I looked around
me and saw a nice class of people enjoying themselves, mostly men
with their wives and children and I asked the man next to me if the
place was always so well patronized. He told me that it was to be
enlarged in a few weeks because it was impossible to accommodate all
who came during busy hours of the evening.

"As far as I am concerned," he added, "I come here as much to hear that girl play as to see the pictures."

I paid more attention to the girl. She was not enough of a natural musician to improvise, but she had a large assortment of sheet music on the rack from which she made intelligent selections. She had evidently done some thinking ahead, possibly she had read a summary of the plays in advance, anyway she was on time at every change of scene with something suited to the sentiment. There was nothing particularly brilliant about her performance, but it was in good taste and satisfactory to those who came to be entertained.

I went back to the more pretentious theater, and, noticing that it was only about half full, I asked the proprietor why he handed out such indigestible stuff as "vodeveal."

"I don't like it," he said, "but the people want it and I have to give it to 'em."

That is what _he_ thinks. It is quite possible that a number of people are really drawn into his place by the variety entertainment, but I doubt if they equal the number driven away by it. Those driven away are the most desirable patrons; they are the steadies who have acquired the habit; in this case they have acquired the habit of going elsewhere.

"Vodeveal" had nothing to do with bringing these theaters into existence; to the contrary it put many of them on the fritz. Most of these theaters were impossible before the advent of moving pictures and they would be just as impossible now if the pictures were withdrawn, yet every conceivable slight is put upon that essential portion of the entertainment which brought most of these theaters into existence and is keeping them alive today. Of course intelligent managers do not slight any portion of the business, but a good many of them do not realize how annoying it is to sensible people in the audience when the jackass at the drum keeps up a running fire of conversation with the pianist or the latter lapses in his performance to play with one hand or practise an accompaniment for some forthcoming song. These things may seem trivial to the jackasses in the orchestra, but they distract attention from the pictures in a way that is irritating to a large percentage of the patrons, especially to those in the front row. On the stage, behind the screen, those who are about to come on with an unmusical act, tune their instruments while there's a picture play in progress and all along the line there are evidences of hostility shown to the picture production wherever it is given in combination with "vodeveal." Whether this hostility is due to ignorance or prejudice makes very little difference; it so seriously injures the photoplay presentation that theaters devoted to pictures alone in combination with superior instrumental music as an harmonious accessory are drawing the biggest crowds.

Given a well-ventilated theater with comfortable seats and
polite attendants the best possible plan to fill it is to present new
pictures with fine projection to appropriate music. Thousands are
able to go every day to such exhibitions where hundreds would patronize cheap "vodeveal" once a week. The man who first presents
a highclass picture on up-to-date principles will find money falling
into the box office drawer like the food which sustained the children
of Israel in the wilderness.

> --The Moving Picture World, Vol.
> 8, No. 14, April 8, 1911, pages
> 758-760.

• PUTTING IT OVER

by Will M. Cressy

If Noah Webster had been as well posted on things theatrical as he
was on most every other subject, you probably would find this definition in his dictionary:

> PUTTING IT OVER: To speak a line, to sing a line, to
> do a piece of action in such a way as to cause an audience
> to see, understand, comprehend and appreciate the intention
> and meaning.

While this ability to "put it over" is an important help on the
legitimate stage, it is an absolute necessity in vaudeville. In a play
where there are a dozen other performers, a man or woman may be
devoid of this talent and still succeed in a measure. While the lines
spoken by this player may not make any appeal to the listener, they
may be spoken clearly enough and with the proper enunciation so
that the story is carried along. And the other players will "put it
over."

But on the other hand, if a player _does_ possess this strange
power of "putting it over," the worst lines in the world or, in fact,
the absence of lines, cannot hold him back. The first part that
Richard Mansfield played consisted of six speeches, all alike. Six
different times in the course of one scene he had to say:

"What!"

But so strongly was stage talent inherent in him that he was
able to put such feeling and expression, such different moods, mean-
ings and emotions, into this one simple word that his wonderful ability was made apparent.

Several years ago I saw John L. Sullivan's production of--

Honest Hearts, I think it was. There was just one player in the
cast that I can recall. And he had only one scene and no lines at
all. His directions were evidently to "come on, hand the leading
lady a letter and exit."

The average player would have slipped on a linen duster and
a slouch hat, have entered, handed the letter to the leading lady,
and departed. This chap was not an average player. He must have
spent an hour on his makeup, and weeks collecting his wardrobe.
He made the part a deaf-and-dumb man. His efforts to convey to
the leading lady, all in pantomime, how he came by the note, who
sent it, and why, and the various troubles he went through in getting
there, were so artistically done that for several minutes the audience
sat convulsed with laughter. At his exit he had to come back and
bow his acknowledgments of the applause that followed. I do not
know who he was, where he came from, or where he went. But I
would wager that if he is on the stage to-day he is a successful
actor.

As I have said, a player may possibly go on year after year
earning a living on the legitimate stage without this talent of "putting
it over," but he can never do that on the vaudeville stage. In vaudeville every artist from the opening act to the closing act must "put
it over." If he does not possess this quality, the probabilities are
that he will never get into vaudeville. And if he does, he will get
out much quicker than he got in.

This putting-it-over quality is not the result of education,
practice, teaching or Lutherburbanking. If you do not have it when
you are born, you will never have it. And when Providence is distributing this particular faculty, it picks out no particular class or
condition of people. Our vaudeville entertainers of to-day come from
every class. I believe there is not a nationality in the world that is
not represented. And our own American artists are recruited from
every class and every trade and profession. Among my own personal
acquaintances I can recall performers who were painters, artists,
waiters, dressmakers, society women, street-car conductors, sailors,
college graduates, osteopaths, cowboys, scene-painters, stock-brokers,
lawyers, telegraph operators, miners, doctors, ministers, bartenders,
trap-drummers, bank clerks, theater ushers, blacksmiths, milliners,
jewelers, medicine-show fakirs and those from dozens of other occupations which by no stretch of imagination could be construed into
schools for actors.

And while this ability of "putting it over" is universal among
vaudeville artists, no two use precisely the same method of accom-
plishing the same result. One can talk it over; another can sing it
over; a third will act it over. But always there will be some little
peculiar faculty, some queer, quaint mannerism, that distinguishes
each particular player.

Quite a few years ago (not too many) there was an awkward, redhaired little tike of a girl on the bill with us. I should say that she was sixteen or seventeen years old. She had two almost-notes and half a dozen imitation ones in her voice. But after watching her during two or three shows I went to her and told her that she had one talent that in the years to come would bring her recognition and success. For she could sing a song better with her <u>hands</u> than most people could with their voices. To-day there is no <u>woman</u> on the stage more loved and idolized than this same little red-haired girl with the eloquent hands. Her name is Irene Franklin.

A few years ago there came to our shores a little French chorus-girl. She had almost no voice at all and was not uncommonly beautiful; but she had a pair of big eyes that could make every married woman in an audience certain that she (the actress) was after her own personal husband. And those eyes have made Anna Held one of our best known stars.

If Vesta Tilley, the English music-hall idol, could not sing a note nor speak a word, she could <u>walk</u> her songs successfully. There has never been a player who could paint a character more clearly by word or note than she can by her walk.

Our own Elizabeth Murray is another "walker." During her singing of a negro melody you seem to see a continuous stream of darkies parading across the stage before you, as she strides, glides, slides and shuffles back and forth.

Have you ever heard Eddie Foy accused of possessing a voice? Why he'd feel insulted if you charged him with such a thing. He does not <u>need</u> a voice or words or notes. All he has to do is to walk on the stage and <u>howl</u>. His personality will "put it over."

And to show that this power may be entirely outside of any personal charm, take our "Dick" José. He is fat, awkward, with a shock of gray hair, a big, round baby face, and--he stutters. But once let him open his mouth and pour forth his golden notes in some simple, touching ballad, and--well, reach for your handkerchief, for you are going to cry.

I knew one comedian (I knew him well, for I wrote his sketches for him, and it was the hardest work I ever did in my life) whose hips formed the dividing line between success and failure. From his hips down he was great; he had the funniest legs I ever saw. But from the hips up he was awful. He could not get a laugh with the best speech that was ever written.

Speaking of legs, many a player has won success with his legs as his principal asset. (Particular attention is called to the gender of the pronoun in that sentence.) Fifty years from now, white-haired old ladies will still be talking about Henry "Adonis" Dixey's legs. (And their husbands will still be seeing visions of Frankie Bailey's--talents.)

Can you picture what kind of an act Charlie Semon, "the Narrer Feller," would do without his spaghetti-shaped legs?

But on the other hand, to show that legs are not necessary to success, there is Ernie, who bills himself as a "monopede," who not only does all sorts of acrobatic feats with his one leg but, with the aid of his crutch, is a graceful dancer.

And two of our oldest and most successful vaudeville entertainers are Conway & Leland, who muster but two legs between them.

Arms may be considered rather necessary to stage entertaining. But Unthan, born without arms, gives twenty minutes of most interesting entertainment. He plays cards, shuffles and deals, plays the cornet and the violin, does a little sharp shooting, dresses and undresses himself and shaves himself. He does it all with his feet.

E. M. Holland lived in a land of eternal silence: he never heard the speeches of the other players; he never heard the bursts of laughter nor the applause of an audience; he was deaf. And yet through a system of counting which he had perfected, he would play the most complicated scenes, picking up his cues exactly on time.

One of the best cases to-day of this power of "putting it over" in the face of handicaps is Charles Chaplin. Without the aid of voice, words or sounds he can by his actions alone, "put over" comedy scenes as few can with these aids.

We have now seen how certain people "put over" actions and comedy without words; now let us take up that class of our entertainers who talk their points over. And we will find just as much difference in methods here as we have found among the others.

One man cannot get a laugh out of the best line ever written; the next man can get laughs out of the multiplication table.

A few years ago Nat Wills and Ezra Kendall were our leading monologuists; one entire season they played in the same show. Both were monologuists; both walked out "in one" and told their stories and sang their songs. But there all similarity ceased. Nat forces a line over. His comedy is like a shot out of a cannon; it goes out over the audience and explodes like a bursting shell; and like the bursting shell, it strikes everybody. Mr. Kendall, on the other hand, would wander around among a sea of words and quaint ideas; he always had an air of surprise that anyone should laugh at them.

For another striking contrast in methods, take Frank Fogarty and Charlie Case. Fogarty snaps his points at you--quick, sharp,

snappy squibs and remarks, like shots from a gatling-gun. Case
gently and softly lifts his points up to the top of that wall that
stands between the artist and the audience, and giving them a gentle
push, lets them fall over.

Ray L. Royce Smiles a point over.

The Farber Girls laugh it over.

Lew Hawkins smokes his over.

Kate Elinore blows them over.

Only Heaven, and Dave Fitsgibbons, know how he "puts it
over." He has neither appearance, style, beauty, voice nor anything else; there is neither rhyme, rhythm nor reason in anything
that he does; and he does it all badly at that. But there is not a
man on the stage to-day who can keep an audience screaming with
laughter as can this same David boy.

Another wonderful case of personality is Bert Melrose. Here
is a chap who wanders out on the stage in a Scotch-clown make-up,
stays there fifteen minutes, does one single acrobatic trick, taking
fourteen and a half minutes to get ready for it--and is funny enough
to make a wooden cigarstore Indian laugh.

The moral is--be yourself.

First find out if there is not some one thing that you can do
better than anything else. If there is not, then don't start in vaudeville. If there is, go to it! Do not waste your time watching somebody else to see how they are doing it. Do not try to copy or imitate anyone else; if you do, you will be either a failure or at best
a mediocre success. Do it your own way. Let the other fellows
imitate you.

And no matter what this one peculiar faculty is, if there is
anything in the world you can do better than anyone else, there is
a place for you on the vaudeville stage. We have men on the stage
to-day drawing large salaries for chopping wood, spinning tops,
rolling hoops, skating, dancing, playing billiards, painting pictures,
clay-modeling, lariat-throwing and a dozen other things that a few
years ago were never heard of on the stage. And these men did
not spend their time studying music, stage technique or how other
artists did things. They simply took this one talent which they possessed and worked and studied and practiced on it until they were
the best in the world in that one particular line.... So--be yourself.
Put it over and come on in. The (vaudeville) water is fine.

                                    --The Green Book Magazine, March
                                    1916, pages 547-552.

- THE GREAT AMERICAN ART

by Mary Cass Canfield

If one were indulging in an orgy of aesthetic pigeon-holing,
one might, casting an appraising eye on the world, conceivably
label architecture and painting as the particular triumphs of the
French, words as the medium of the English, music as the instinc-
tive expression of Germany. Tying tags in this broad but effective
fashion, it is interesting to ask what, if any, is the great American
art?

Toward the solution of this question a visiting English actor-
manager once threw a helpful hint; but an evening last summer at
Mr. Ziegfeld's Follies provided the final answer. The acute foreigner
remarked: "As far as I can see, the only real American art is ragtime." This observation slowly bore fruit through several seasons of
musical comedies, cabaret shows and vaudeville performances; and
the great revelation occurred that hot night at the New Amsterdam
Theatre. For the Follies seemed finally to proclaim that vitality,
originality and capacity for perfection, hallmarks of the artist, find
full elbow room and immediate appreciation in the happy-go-lucky
eccentricity of our vaudeville world. Every good musical comedy is
now sheer vaudeville; all pretence of a plot has disappeared, thus
leaving the musical show a far more homogeneous art. Part of one's
attention is not diverted to the following of a creakingly impossible
scenario. Instead one can wholly enjoy an honest variety show.
Variety is the contemporary and national cry. We do not say exactly: "In nothing too much"; rather do we say: "In everything as
much as possible, but not for too long." One of the results is the
kaleidoscopic drama of what England would call our "halls," a drama
whose voice, whose message, whose reason for being, is ragtime.

"Say it with music." So far America, the hoi polloi, if you will
(but the hoi polloi is the nation), has not said anything except with
music. National restlessness lives in the conflicting rhythm of jazz.
In the precise insouciance of ragtime, leap out America's own effi-
ciency and lack of reflection, its good nature, its self-conscious
smartness, its childish and oddly pathetic craving for gaiety.

Ragtime is the noise that fills a too empty room, it is the
drunkenness of prohibitionists, the longing for movement and color
of those who sit on packing cases and look in vain for beauty and
rhythm up and down Main Street. It is barbarically fierce in its
effort to conquer vacuum and the horn of the talking machine is its
loud mouthed interpreter, generously underscoring the violent cheer-
fulness of its staccato. Barbaric it is and yet subtle, a medley of
strange minor gradations running through the major implication of
its tone, like the disquiets, the doubts, the melancholy, distressing
the American's determined attitude of optimism.

Ragtime is our folk song. It would seem that we have not
developed sufficiently to have evolved anything authentic beyond folk
song, any distinctive art of our own in the plastic or literary field.
Stray geniuses, Whitman and Emerson, have only served to show up
the careful orthodoxy of their fellows. Literature, particularly poetry,
shows signs of pulling out of the rut of foreign imitation. Robinson
and Frost, Masters and Sandburg are building up an art which mir-
rors America and expresses the national temperament. They are
thus founding an American poetry. But their voices, heard by the
few, are but thrush chirps in a wilderness; and the great American
art, the art of the people, for the people, by the people, remains
ragtime.

Perfection is the aim and the sign of great art. Mr. Ziegfeld's
Follies, or the Winter Garden, or an afternoon of vaudeville at the
Palace are perfect of their kind. It is, therefore, with sincere enthusiasm and without a trace of irony that one recommends these
phases of the American drama as the highest example of a national
art. Vaudeville is happy; therefore it is both good and beautiful.
Laughter preaches fellowship better than sermons; enjoyment throws
magic loveliness, a golden glow, over a bare stage where a comedian
in a check suit gregariously leans against a backdrop lamp post.
What is more, ragtime haunted vaudeville, unlike the paintings of
Mr. Alden Weir, the novels of Mr. Winston Churchill or the criticisms
of Professor Brander Matthews, delights us with the unexpected.
Irony cannot exist in the face of such vanquishing vitality, such
ingenuity of setting and entertainment, such speed, effectiveness,
grace and lightness of touch. No song or dance or comic skit is
too long; brevity, queen of qualities, smiles triumphantly out at us
between the quick rises and falls of innumerable, fantastically colored
curtains. Vaudeville leads us breathless but interested, from acrobats to sentimental songs, from pony ballets to well played one-act
tragedy. Every musician in the orchestra is mentally on his toes,
every pulley is supergreased. To concentrate on the stage management of the Follies is like watching a thoroughbred take a series of
fences. The revolving stage has a soul, it bounds forward to its
task with a swagger, it prides itself on never making a mistake. It
is American. One's brain reels at the thought of how many rehearsals have brought this Protean miracle into existence. Elaborate sets
succeed each other, great masses of people parade across the stage
and are gone, the orchestra melts from one tune to another, all with
the bewildering ease of mastery. The pulchritude of the performers,
the quality of the dancing, of the humor, of the costumes and scenic
effects, cause our vaudeville to tower above the vaudeville of any
other country, as the Woolworth Building would tower above the In-
valides. English "two a day" is heavy in comparison, Parisian "café
concerts" are meagre and tawdry. In the Follies there were ballets
full of imagination in conception and mounted with splendor and
taste; the dancing of them by artists of only medium quality was the
only factor which prevented them from scoring a triumph. Done by
the Russians, they would have been irresistible. But, at least, they

showed that American vaudeville is willing, although a bit amateurishly, to concern itself with pure beauty.

Closer attuned to the general audience is the humor of such shows. Humor is as much a necessity to us as sweets; and perhaps for the same climatic reason. Nerves strung to top pitch demand both food and relaxation. Nowhere is the strength of our demand for humor better gauged than by the response it found in cabaret and vaudeville dancing. Shimmying, shuffling, eccentric and awkward movements are only answers to the national love of the grotesque. About the grotesque, which is a tragic thing, a negation of beauty, an expression of inhibited or disappointed search for the ideal, one could, had one the space, philosophize at length. The theory that our really characteristic art is a reaction from sensuous starvation and like all reactions, a violent thing, is certainly borne out by such manifestations as Mark Twain's bitter chuckle or the calculated extravagance of our dancing; our dancers are experts in rhythmic dislocation, in accurately timed physical buffonery. All art is exaggeration. But in the American exaggeration there is always a self-criticism, an undertone of humor, which is an attempt at fire extinguishing that does not reduce but curiously discolors the flame.

Grotesque or not, vaudeville represents a throwing away of self-consciousness, of Plymouth Rock caution, devoutly to be wished for. Here we countenance the extreme, we encourage idiosyncracy. The dancer or comedian is, sometimes literally, egged on to develop originality; he is adored, never crucified for difference. Miss Fannie Brice and Sir Harry Lauder are examples of vaudeville performers who have been hailed, joyfully and rightfully, as vessels containing the sacred fire, and who have been encouraged into self-emphasis by their audiences; they are now, as a result of this appreciative stimulus, rare and interesting artists in their field.

Vaudeville, as our most vital art centre, is a treasure house of individuality. In the Ziegfeld Follies, Will Rogers, a superman of coordination, swinging his lasso, complicated whirls and emitting dry patter at the expense of cabbages and kings, was quite justly the idol of his public. In the same spectacle, Gallagher and Shean sang a whimsically ridiculous ditty, which was Gallic in its next lightness and yet American in its easy familiarity. A vaudeville comedian in America is as close to the audience as Harlequin and Puncinello were to the Italian publics of the eighteenth century. He is, like them, an apparent, if not always an actual improviser. He jokes with the orchestra leader, he tells his hearers fabricated, confidential tales about management, the other actors, the whole entrancing world behind the scenes; he addresses planted confederates in the third row, or the gallery and proceeds to make fools of them to the joy of all present. He beseeches his genial, gum-chewing listeners to join in the chorus of his song; they obey with a zestful roar. The audience becomes a part of the show and enjoys it. And there is community

art for you. Until the cows come home, Mr. Percy Mackaye can
write pageants, celebrating civic virtue and so amply supplied with
parts that they can only be acted by an entire township; he will
never achieve the unforced and happy communion which reigns within
the fifty-cent walls of the local Keith's and Proctor's.

The capacity for peaceful penetration of any art is surely a
sign of its vitality. We read contemporary English novelist's and
poets. If we can, we wear French dresses; some of us buy French
pictures. Walt Whitman was discovered in England and there is a
beautiful French translation of his complete works. Emerson is not
unknown in Europe; Baudelaire long years ago translated the gifted
and sombre Poe into icily chiseled and admirably appropriate French.
Oceans are crucibles, smelting machines for art. Only the best survives their perilous passage. And now for the last decade, Europe
has adopted our dance tunes. The Parisian intelligence, cold and
sharp as a steel needle, yet always prepared sensitively to oscillate
in the direction of the aesthetically significant, has for some time
pointed due west at this true American music. Young poets celebrate
it in their verse, young composers, Darius Milhaud, Georges Auric
and the others, write ballets and symphonies in which may be heard
the irresponsible "cancan" of ragtime. John Alden Carpenter, perhaps the most vivid talent among our own composers, will occasionally shift from coolly subtle disharmonies, illustrating poetic or lyric
subjects, to write a Krazy Kat Ballet, clever and, shall one say,
whole legged, glorification of jazz.

> Come on and hear, come on and hear,
> Alexander's Ragtime Band.

One likes to think of the straight, hard, young rows of our
soldiers marching through gray French towns to the devil-may-care
lilt of their native noise. To weary hearts, made old by anxiety,
such sound may have seemed vaguely shocking, the laughter of a
child in a house of mourning. But at least, it brought a message
of confidence; it embodied a resilient vitality ready to fly right at
difficulty, a defiant sense of the ridiculous, inclined to turn death
itself into a dance.

The joie de vivre of jazz is perhaps, as has been hinted, a
trifle hectic, it represents a young and superficial straining away
from barrenness; but at any rate, it is sincere, it is spontaneous,
it is communistic. We can allow the Metropolitan Opera Company laboriously to put on Red Indian Operas by undeniably American composers; Mr. John Sargent can paint pseudo-classic and wholly insig-
nificant figures on the walls of the Boston Museum; Mr. Daniel Chester French can make as many bronzes of Lincoln as he likes. But
the only American art, the escape of everyman, discouraged by
bleakness, worn by rush and machinery, into the blue of enchantment and rhythm and laughter, the art with Dionysian frenzy in it,
the valid, the great American art, so far, is to be found on a blazing

stage, full of shapes acrobatically dancing to the exact beat of drums
and the seductively insincere moan of saxophones.

> --The New Republic, November
> 22, 1922, pages 334-335.

• THE VAUDEVILLE PHILOSOPHER

by Marshall D. Beuick

A vaudeville philosophy of life is influencing the mental attitude and the actions of many Americans in their everyday activities.
The race must play or be entertained, of course, if it is to be a
happy and efficient one, but it need not be directed in its habits
in a manner that occurs daily on the vaudeville stage. The influence
is poor, not speaking from a moral standpoint, and, despite what
Mr. Gilbert Seldes may say of one of the lively arts, it has not the
breadth and variety common to many dramatic productions and discovered occasionally in the motion picture scenario.

On the stage and on the screen, actors are interpreters of
plays created by persons living in various environments. For vaudeville, however, the sketches and skits are usually written by actors
themselves or by those who have served an apprenticeship on the
"boards." The result is that a reflection of a common, limited, and
not too optimistic view of life, is presented in the variety theatre.

There are certain standard subjects that are used almost every
night on the vaudeville stages throughout the country. An audience,
composed of many persons mentally fatigued after a day's work, learns
a philosophy that embraces such precepts as: marriage is an unfortunate institution to which the majority of us resign ourselves; women
are fashion-crazy, spend money heedlessly and believe that their
husbands are fools; politics is all bunk, prohibition should be prohibited; mothers are the finest persons in the world ... next to grand-
mothers; fathers are unfortunate persons upon whom fall most of life's
woes; marital infidelity is widespread; clandestine affairs of most
any sort between at least one married person and another of the opposite sex are comical; and finally "nothing in life really matters.
The main thing to do is to get all the money you can and keep your
mother-in-law as far off as possible."

In these "concepts" there are many obvious ideas, and they
seem to satisfy a vaudeville audience; but such "precepts" embrace
few fundamentals of life.

Of course, in vaudeville the ice man and the traveling salesman are responsible for much marital unhappiness. They are, in
fact, the root of infidelity and divorce, according to the sociology

of vaudeville. Unfortunately, the majority of these dialogues and
monologues, served to the public for as much as one dollar and ten
cents, are the products of minds which have been formed back-stage
and on the road for many seasons. In consequence, such typical
humor, as is suggested in these three jokes, echoes from the vaudeville stage:

> "Love makes the world go 'round."
> "So does a punch in the jaw."
>
> "Marriage is an institution."
> "So is a lunatic asylum."

"I married my wife's sister because I didn't want to break in
a new mother-in-law."

There is, besides, another brand of humor that depends for
its effect largely upon the ridiculous. In a dance and song act, a
laugh can be easily raised by announcing the next song in the following manner:

> "When It's Night-time in Japan, It's Wednesday over Here."

This kind of laugh provoker is not frequent, but a few of
them are sprinkled through a skit to give it a guise of "originality."

William James found that Americans were unusually susceptible
to the pattern-setters. In what he called the "Gospel of Relaxation,"
he examined idioms and local peculiarities which he believed came
about "through an accidental example set by some one, which struck
the ears of others," and were quoted and "copied till at last every
one in the locality chimed in."

James might have been thinking of the vaudeville stage when
he expanded these observations further by saying that "we here in
America through following a succession of pattern-setters whom it is
now impossible to trace, and through influencing each other in a bad
direction, have at last settled down collectively into what, for better
or worse, is our characteristic national type--a type with the production of which, so far as these habits go, the climate and conditions have had practically nothing at all to do."

There are no data and plotted curves to show that climate and
conditions have had nothing to do with the creation of these attitudes
of mind and expression of manners. It is therefore impossible to
check up James, just as it would be to verify the statement that the
conditions of vaudeville or back-stage life tend toward the creation
of a peculiar philosophy which, through its appeal to human psychological phases of sympathy, suggestion and like-mindedness, is
passed on to an audience.

William James bemoaned the prevailing traditions, saying that he thought it was "high time for legends and traditional opinion to be changed." Many of us feel the same way when we consider the proposition slightly. But, what hope is there while there are so many newspapers with their numerous vaudeville cartoons, trashy magazines and vaudeville philosophers. We are told that the public deserves the newspapers and magazines it gets, for it creates the demand for them. The same may be said as readily of vaudeville. But, do many vaudeville theatre managers try to discover what the public deserves?

Some vaudeville organizations appear to have been courageous because their managers have discovered that, when high-browisms are slipped into programs accompanied by modified jazz, they "go." Consequently we are beginning to find better humorists on variety "boards," aesthetic dancers with excellent training and gratifying interpretative ability, singers who demonstrate quality and power, a reflection of proper training, and musicians, who, in talent, are not far below the artists numbered among the symphony orchestras. The public enjoys these better bills and augments its spontaneous applause with a desire, perhaps, to show its appreciation for what it believes is highbrow artistry. Nevertheless, the comedian, with his well established vaudeville philosophy, is still on the bill and he is sometimes a headliner.

Balieff's Bat Theatre, no doubt, demonstrated to vaudeville managers more things which the public could enjoy besides the dancers, musicians and higher types of one-act sketches enacted by, at least, second-rate dramatic artists, and as a result there have been sketches or acts, presented in imitation of Balieff's Chauve Souris. But, these and other similar innovations have not surplanted the vaudeville Socrates.

Despite the conveyance of a back-stage philosophy of life to the audiences, there are not many examples of political propaganda creeping into dialogues or acts as might perhaps be expected. There naturally always arises the fear of offending the political sentiments of groups in the vaudeville audience. This is the automatic censor of most political allusions on the stage. The soldier's bonus was supported, prohibition is laughed at in the vaudeville houses of the large cities, and in Eastern cities references to the Ku Klux Klan invariably raise a laugh in the vaudeville theatre.

Managers permit these things in the belief that their audiences' attitudes toward this "propaganda" is the same as that of the actors present. The producers and actors have little desire to be propagandists for such performance might not be good business. If business and boosting converge, the manager need have no fear of allowing propaganda for its own sake to be written into the skits.

Just before the United States entered the war, songs were

sung in vaudeville that appeared to be peace propaganda, but which were probably nothing more than shrewd interpretation of public sentiment. In those days "I Didn't Raise My Boy to Be a Soldier" and "The Land of My Best Girl" were popular. But, when the war fever arose in us, there was heard the strains of "Over There" at almost every vaudeville performance.

In France it has been charged against music hall proprietors that they purposely kept alive La Revanche through songs and dialogue. This circumstance was probably no different from the war fever in our own theatres. It was a case of what the public wanted or what it expected.

The majority of vaudeville entertainers occupy the role of opinion circulators and supporters of established opinion, besides being transmitters of their personal reactions to life. They are not propagandists, and there is no sinister plot among them to glorify established opinion. Most of them may be indifferent to conventional political institutions and conventional modes of living, but they know that a vaudeville audience delights in proving its respectability by applauding witticisms that bolster up those conventions which are under serious critical observation.

It is an easy undertaking to influence the minds of persons seeking relief from mental activity. They are in a state that finds them too mentally lax to resist what sifts into their thoughts while they are being entertained.

"The least degree of suggestibility," Professor McDougall tells us, "is that of a wide-awake, self-reliant man of settled convictions, possessing a large store of systematically organized knowledge which he habitually brings to bear in criticism of all statements made to him." Other degrees of suggestibility, he believes, are due to deficiency of knowledge or convictions relating to the topic suggested; the impressive character of the source from which the idea is communicated; peculiarities of the character of persons; and abnormal states of brain like hysteria, hypnosis and fatigue.

The number of self-reliant men "of settled convictions and so forth" in a vaudeville audience is probably as great as the number of Christ's disciples. But persons most desired for exploitation by the managers and actors are those with deficient knowledge of those who are impressed by the character of the source from which some suggestions are communicated. They are numerous. Playing in vaudeville theatres upon these fatigued persons who have deficient knowledge and are easily impressed, it is a simple undertaking for the actor to present a joke and cap it with the authoritative statement, "remember what Kipling said about a woman and a good cigar!" And, these things are done.

Survey an audience in a theatre of the variety species, and

you will see it almost instinctively act in concert. Vaudeville philosophers never heard the term "concerted volition" that is used by
sociologists and psychologists, but they know in other terms they
have seldom if ever been called upon to express, that the basis of
all sympathetic like-mindedness, as Professor Franklin H. Giddings
says, is found in a predominance of prompt response to stimulus,
emotionalism, imaginativeness, suggestibility and the habit of reason-
ing from analogy. This explanation is the gist of the theory of concerted volition. And, how satisfactorily the vaudeville laboratory
furnishes the demonstrable proof!

What can be done to offset the expansion of this vaudeville
philosophy? The vaudeville theatre cannot be obliterated like the
saloon. It is an important amusement institution to several million
Americans. And, like any institution it evolves. But, will the evolution bring something healthy and valuable?

Better sketches are already beginning to appear in vaudeville
written by others than those from back-stage, and higher grade
musicians and comedians and dancers look to the variety stage more
now than formerly for appreciative audiences. The public will continue to go to vaudeville shows as long as people respond to like-
mindedness in crowds, while humanity must play or be diverted and
as long as men respond to suggestibility. Regardless then of how
vaudeville may evolve there will always be presented some form of
vaudeville philosophy of life to credulous theatre-goers.

Any suggestion that play and art have an indispensible moral
function which should receive attention that is now denied, calls out
vehement protest, Professor John Dewey tells us. He did not have
in mind the professional moralist, "to whom art, fun and sport are
habitually under suspicion."

Those who are interested in art as producers or artists at once
imagine that some kind of organized supervision if not "censorship
of play, drama or fiction is contemplated which will convert them
into means of moral edification." This is a natural fear, as Professor
Dewey points out, of surrendering art to reformers.

"But, something quite other than this is meant. Relief from
continuous moral activity--in the conventional sense of moral--is itself a moral necessity."

Perhaps, it is not even enough to say that it is "a moral necessity." It is a psychological necessity that will, under the most
repressed conditions, find an outlet comparable with the one that
Gorky tells about in the description of men in Russian villages, who,
after work, tied the tails of two rats together to enjoy the observ-
ance of the unique struggle that resulted.

The improvement of vaudeville rests very largely in the hands

of the dramatic profession itself. The highest types of actors and
actresses are invariably welcomed to the vaudeville stage. The managers are glad to receive them with most anything they wish to present. But, a feeling lingers among artists that they are descending
from their high artistic plane. This has deterred many a fine dramatic artist from stepping onto the variety boards. At the same time
the better actors frown upon the condition in vaudeville which they
could easily inculcate with better concepts of vaudeville philosophy.

Those artists who have a social purposefulness in their work
and who may feel that they are not widely enough appreciated, might
do as the militant reformer, Carrie A. Nation, did. She stopped at
nothing to talk temperance and to sell miniature hatchets. She appeared in vaudeville on the Bowery in New York with a Bible in her
hand to tell the underworld her story, and she played the leading
role of the mother in Ten Nights in a Bar room.

I do not suggest in saying this that the dramatic artist should
become a propagandist and uplifter. But, those of the highbrows
in drama who have stooped to conquer the vaudeville audience have
thrilled to the applause. This is the most effective method of in-
culcating better and more truthful concepts in vaudeville philosophy
and at the same time of giving the public what it deserves.

> --The Drama, Vol. 16, No. 3, De-
> cember 1925, pages 92-93 and
> 116.

• VAUDEVILLE MUST BE SAVED

by Alexander Bakshy

The past season in particular was filled with plaints about the
unprecedented number of failures on Broadway resulting in dozens
of dark houses and a whole army of unemployed actors. Yet in spite
of the keen public interest in the fortunes of the theater the fact
that there is only one straight vaudeville house on Broadway today--
Keith's Palace Theater--does not seem to attract much attention. It
is only on special occasions--such as the recent sale of the Hippodrome and the proposal to demolish this legend-wrapped playhouse,
or the centennial celebration of vaudeville, held in 1926--that vaudeville is recalled in the press and in public discussion. A visitor
from other lands, if he suddenly found himself in Times Square, would
hardly suspect the existence in this country of that unique and ancient art.

The decline of vaudeville in New York revealed itself earlier
in the closing down of such Broadway houses as Tony Pastor's, Ham-

merstein's, and the Colonial. Now comes the downfall of that greatest house of spectacles--the Hippodrome. The same tendency is at
work in the capitals of Europe. In London, for instance, such famous
houses as the Empire, the London Pavilion, the Tivoli, and the Ox-
ford have become movie palaces (or at least have ceased to house
vaudeville) within the last ten years. There are still several straight
vaudeville houses left in the theatrical district--the Palladium, the
Holborn Empire, the Alhambra, the Coliseum, the Hippodrome, and
the Palace--not to mention the numerous neighborhood music halls,
but just as in New York their number, particularly in the central
section of town, does not increase.

The paradox is that in spite of its practical disappearance from
the Times Square amusement district and in spite also of the critical
condition in which this district finds itself today, vaudeville not only
exists but apparently even prospers. Here are a few pertinent
figures. The largest nation-wide vaudeville enterprise--the Radio-
Keith-Orpheum Circuit--operates about 700 theaters served by 25,000
artists and having an average weekly attendance of some 12,000,000
people. In Greater New York the same interests control forty-eight
theaters with an average weekly attendance of 560,000 or nearly a
quarter of the 2,500,000 who patronize the theater--whether it be
devoted to drama, vaudeville, or movies--within that territory.

It must be admitted that only five out of the 700 theaters,
namely one each in New York, Pittsburgh, Chicago, Los Angeles,
and San Francisco, serve their public with "straight" vaudeville.
All the others divide their program between vaudeville and movies.
But though originally the concession of half the program to the
movies was undoubtedly a tribute to a rival power which was rapidly
becoming more formidable, today it signifies no more than the desire
to provide an entertainment of real variety. In fact until the appearance of the talking picture the gains were entirely on the side of
vaudeville, which even invaded the movie houses and drove the pictures to a position of acknowledged inferiority.

Why does vaudeville, to all appearances, prosper in the provincial and often very backward localities, while in the cities, which
are the centers presumably of theatrical culture in every country,
it fails to hold its own and is slowly but surely dying out? Why
has vaudeville lost favor with the most exacting section of the metropolitan audience? Is it because, as a form of theatrical art, vaudeville is too crude? Or has it deteriorated from its once proud perfection? Or have metropolitan audiences acquired new and different
tastes in theatrical entertainment?

The first suggestion is the most likely answer--and the most
indefensible. "Vaudeville is essentially one of the lower forms of
theatrical art which inevitably takes the back seat when faced with
the competition of such superior forms as drama and musical comedy."
What preposterous trash passes here for an aesthetic theory! The

popular notion of art is that it is something very serious and very
solemn, while entertainment means trivial and light-hearted distrac-
tion. It is true that what is known as music-hall, cabaret, variety,
and vaudeville entertainment (the name vaudeville was introduced in
this country by B. F. Keith some forty years ago in order that the
"clean entertainment" supplied by his respectable houses might be
distinguished from the popular but less respectable "variety") has
one fundamental characteristic which differentiates it from all other
forms of modern theater. It is frankly an entertainment. The stage
is simply a platform, i.e., a raised place which serves no other purpose to enable the performers to display their gifts before an audience. The modern drama tries to be on the side of the angels
by preserving religiously the big and therefore "serious" form of
a long play. But vaudeville needs no such devices to provide art
that is vital and earnest, even if it is not always "serious." In its
basic tradition it is much more the legitimate successor to the theater
which was the superb ornament of ancient Greece, Renaissance Spain,
Elizabethan England, India, and Japan than the so-called "legitimate"
drama of this and the past century can ever claim to be.

    That present-day vaudeville is not what it was cannot be denied.
Because it has practically disappeared from the centers of culture,
it is ruled by standards which are established not by the most sensitive and lively sections of the public, but rather by the less exacting standards of the provinces. It is possible that B. F. Keith and
E. F. Albee deserve a certain amount of blame for the condition of
vaudeville in America. Much as they, as well as other theater owners,
have encouraged talent in vaudeville, their policy of "mass production,"
the very size of the organization they have developed, and the fact
that they must cater to the interest and tastes of a large provincial
audience could not fail to have the same demoralizing effect upon
vaudeville as mass production has had in another field of popular
entertainment--the movies.

    There are still incomparable artists on the vaudeville stage,
such as Sophie Tucker, Belle Baker, Bill Robinson, Owen McGiveney,
Toto, Brothers Arnault, and a few others. But many of the best
performers in vaudeville have gone to the musical-comedy stage--
George Cohan, Fred Stone, Al Jolson, Eddie Cantor, Fannie Brice,
Joe Cook, Will Rogers, W. C. Fields, Fred and Adele Astaire, to
mention a few. As a result, the average program even in the better
class of vaudeville houses is often excruciatingly dull and talentless.

    It is within the power of those who control vaudeville bookings
to keep up its standards. The whole system must be reorganized
on a basis which will enable its stars to remain in vaudeville, whatever may be the temptations of musical comedy, for compared with
the youthful sprightliness, concentration, and marvelous precision
of perfect vaudeville, musical comedy is like a lady far past her prime,
inordinately made up, and garrulous to an extreme.

It scarcely needs proving in this country of high-powered sales-
manship that public taste is subject to outside influences. But even
without resort to artificial means the American public can be educated
to appreciate vaudeville. In fact it already does. There were this
winter two companies in New York which proved not only how glorious vaudeville can be but also how great a hold it can have on the
public. I refer, of course to the Chauve Souris and the Ruth Draper
Company. There are few things more colorful than Balieff's human
dolls, and no magic can achieve more than is achieved by Ruth Draper--
noble, cattish, passionate, pathetic Ruth Draper.

Why not more companies like them? There are several dark
theaters on Broadway. Good vaudeville can be made as successful
there as any play or revue. But it must be good. It must be unity
and coherence in the performance as a whole. The scope here for
original ideas and for a healthy creative rivalry is unlimited.

--The Nation, Vol. 129, No. 3342,
July 24, 1929, pages 98 and 100.

• VAUDEVILLE'S PRESTIGE

by Alexander Bakshy

It is an acknowledged axiom that there are fashions in art--
fashions which make one particular form of expression popular today
and unpopular tomorrow. Less familiar, it seems, is the fact that
there are arts in fashion, as well as arts not in fashion. Lithography,
for instance, since its discovery by Senefelder one hundred and thirty
years ago, has passed through alternating periods of popularity and
neglect on the part both of the public and of the artists. Etching
and water color have also had a rather checkered career. But the
most remarkable instance of the influence of fashion we find in the
recent history of the ballet. In the first decade of this century the
stage ballet was regarded as a routine-ruled form of art, compounded
mostly of acrobatics and entirely deficient in the creative spirit. The
romantic revolution in the dance started by Isadora Duncan, Ruth
Dennis, and a few others voiced the resentment of the cultured sections of the public with this state of the classical ballet, but the latter
remained unaffected and continued to hols its position somewhere
on the fringe of the aesthetic consciousness of the period. Then, in
1909, Serge Diaghileff, whose lamented death has just been recorded,
opened his first season of Russian ballet in Paris, and the startled
world suddenly realized that ballet, even classical Italian ballet, was
not at all dead but merely slumbering, and that higher artistic standards and inspired leadership were enough to awaken it to a new life.

One recalls these facts in speaking of vaudeville, since today

vaudeville is not in fashion. It is blighted by artistic decay to a
degree that threatens its popularity even with its not very exacting
patrons of today. In spite of the fifty thousand vaudeville artists
in this country, the programs even in the leading American theaters
seldom contain more than one or two really satisfying numbers. The
rest are the veriest junk which only the utter degradation of vaudeville standards has permitted to be performed. The criticism will
doubtless seem harsh to those who regard the situation from the point
of view of the immediate interests of the profession. The trouble is
that vaudeville has lost "class" as an art form, and this is only one
step removed from ultimately losing itself.

The situation in which vaudeville is found today is not devoid
of irony. Here is, by the standards it maintains, the lowliest form
of stage entertainment, and yet fundamentally it is the highest of
them all--a form of theatrical art richly fragrant with the glorious
aroma of the theater, and, moreover, the only one that is capable
of withstanding the onslaught of the talking picture. The rivalry
between the stage and the screen may bring about certain commercial
developments favoring the former or the latter, probably within the
next few years. The artistic rivalry, however, the competition of
quality, of merit, is certain to take a much longer time to reach the
critical phase; and then the choice will lie not between the actor in
the flesh and the actor in the shadow, but between the art of direct
and personal appeal to the audience and the art of indirect and non-
personal appeal. It will be realized that the modern dramatic stage,
dominated largely by the desire to create a picture of life on the
stage boards which carries the imagination into a world beyond the
theater, will find in the improved talking picture (perfect speech,
stereoscopic and color effects, and so on) an antagonist endowed
with incomparably greater technical resources for creating that very
illusion of a life existing outside the theater. There will be one
weapon, however, which will never be found in the armory of the
talking picture--the power of direct and personal appeal to the audience which today distinguishes the art of vaudeville more than any
other form of stage entertainment. It will be, therefore, as the
protagonist of this personal dramatic art, as against the impersonal
art of the legitimate stage, that vaudeville is destined to play the decisive part in the final struggle between the stage and the screen.

There is still then, the possibility of a great future for vaudeville, provided it can raise its standards to a level commonly accepted
in other arts. Will it do so? The powers that be in the vaudeville
world may well ponder over the fact that the policy of playing down
to the uncultivated tastes of the audience is bound to defeat its own
ends, for with a little more backsliding there will be finally no vaudeville left. On the other hand, they must overcome their fear of the
so-called highbrow art. Surely, the devil is not as black as he is
painted. One recalls again the Diaghileff ballet. It would be difficult to imagine anything more highbrow from the standpoint of democratic vaudeville than this old art of kings and princes decked out

in the ultra modernistic trimmings of Montparnasse. And yet, just
so embellished, the Diaghileff ballet drew the high and the low to
the London Coliseum, as one of the acts of a vaudeville program, for
two months every season during a period of several years.

So incredibly backward, so inert and self-complaisant has vaudeville been all these years that it was never for a moment disturbed
by the stirring events in all the other arts which, since the beginning of this century, have revolutionized our very concept of beauty.
The vaudeville stage platform today is the survival of the early
nineteenth-century theater. Even more than the stage of the modern
legitimate theater it betrays no effort to provide a physical founda-
tion, a pedestal, a rostrum for a frank display of the performer's
talents. Vaudeville's attempts at pictorial effects are usually of the
good old late-Victorian type, and if modern, shriek with the vulgarity
of the cheap magazine covers. In music it still clings to jazz and
sentimental songs. The whole atmosphere of the American vaudeville
today is compounded of routine effort and second-rate talent. It is
time that vaudeville woke up. Otherwise it will share the fate of
many another pastime that has been outlived and no longer satisfies.

--The Nation, Vol. 129, No. 3348,
September 4, 1929, page 258.

• SMART-CRACKERS AND CHEESE

by Rob Wagner

If We Were King

Last week we wrote a most devastating editorial practically
eliminating the modern circus as a form of entertainment. This week
we are going after vaudeville with the same purpose in mind. Not
that we are a devastater by nature, for our Attilatic efforts are addressed only to weeds of Art, thereby permitting the flowers a chance
to come back, or clearing the soil for newer and more beautiful growths.
Notwithstanding the staggering influence of our editorials throughout
the nation they are, after all, merely academic opinions, but some
day when we get to be king our opinions will become imperial ukases
of utter finality. So while waiting for our countrymen to place us in
the position of enlightened despotism, we will have to be content in
merely preparing the public for those changes they are too dull and
stupid to make for themselves.

"Now, When I Was a Boy--"

All art progresses or decays. We feel that vaudeville is in a

decided period of decadence, and to prove our point it is necessary
to compare presentday vaudeville with its past glories. The danger
in such comparisons lies in the tendency to include "happy memories"
which inevitably color one's critical judgment. Our own father, for
instance, insisted to his dying day that he'd never had a decent
cup of coffee since he was mustered out of the Army of the Cumber-
land in 1866. We do not doubt that a youthful and vigorous appetite
colored his opinion. Nor do we share the popular belief of people
reaching a contemplative period of life who think that everything
was better when they were young. We know that foods are cleaner,
more wholesome and of better quality than ever before; that the
schools of 40 years ago were jokes compared with those of today;
and even in the catagory of entertainment, stage plays are very much
finer than those of the preceding century. But that circuses have
lost their beauty and vaudeville its color and punch ought to be
obvious to anybody who can detach himself from memories.

Who Really Knows the Public Taste?

These deplorably negative thoughts came to us after a rare
visit to the Orpheum two weeks ago to see our old friend, Julius
Tannen, with whom we had a long visit at the Writer's Club the next
day. Julius agreed that vaudeville had changed, but he doubted of
present-day audiences would enjoy the vaudeville of the past. Maybe
so; maybe not. But it is evident that they don't particularly enjoy
present-day programs. Every week or so we read of famous vaudeville houses that have closed or have gone movie, and on the evening we went down to see Julius there were empty seats on all sides
of us, despite the fact that the Orpheum is considered the best vaudeville house in a city of a million and a half people. Obviously there
is something wrong with entertainment that doesn't do better than
that. Nor can the cause of such a slump be passed along to the
change in public taste, for this same public is seeking in other fields
exactly the form of entertainment that vaudeville used to provide.

Variety Shows Once Had Variety

It is our opinion that much of vaudeville's decadence lies in
its loss of carnival and color. Early vaudeville was largely eye and
ear entertainment, leaving mind entertainment to the dramatic stage.
Nowadays about the only eye entertainment they give us in a vaudeville theatre is a movie or two, while the rest of the program is largely
devoted to gags, smart-cracking and dialog. In other words, the
vaudeville of yesteryear was sensual; the present vaudeville intellectual (!) Let us take the program we witnessed the night we went
down to hear Julius. The first act was a comic movie that could be
seen in a hundred other places for a quarter. The next was a news-
weekly that was similarly ravished from the cinema temple. The third
was a couple of socalled comics that had no optical beauty and very

little wit. The fourth, Cora Greene, "Internationally-Noted Creole
Songstress," a mulatto girl with no beauty, a harsh voice, and who,
judging by her reception would have to omit America from her international admirers. Next, Ray West and his band--High-school boys
jazzing popular tunes and painfully trying to introduce a note of
carnival by holding frozen smiles. Every cabaret and hotel has such
an art. Then--Julius Tannen.

Cabaret Singers and Chamber Music

Julius was, without doubt, the best modern entertainer on the
program. After his first appearance he came out between each act
and furnished a sort of narcotic for the remainder of a sagging program. But even Julius' part of the show was neither optical or sen-
sual--(Julius is a nice looking chap, but not a Rudy Valentino!)
It was addressed entirely to the mind by a rapid fire of jokes whose
appreciation was exclusively mental. Came Carter de Haven in an
"artistic offering" with his son and daughter, in which he sang a
very tame topical song and the three of them did a little dance, the
whole act depending upon a "domestic happiness" note rather than
color. Next, a rather amusing but physically offensive little chap
with a large female sidekick who furnished a butt for the fellow's
idiocies. When they finished you realized they had not sung one
good song or done or said anything worth remembering. At last
came the headliner, Miss Helen Kane, and I fully expected to be
left gaping. Thirty-five hundred a week surely ought to bring forth
something notable. What we saw and heard was a rather comely young
lady who sang several fairly bright songs with a baby voice, an old
stunt excelled in by numberless amateurs.

Trained Seals and Acrobats

As a rule everybody walks out after the "spot" so that the
trained animals and jugglers go through their "closing" acts to a
half-filled house. In this case Julius Tannen managed to hold the
crowd by his very enthusiastic boost for a chap named Felovis, "Sensational European Juggler." Felovis' reception should prove to the
Orpheum managers that it is their own showmanship that is at fault
rather than public taste, for, if I am any judge of the "feel" of an
audience, Felovis was by far the most entertaining person on the
bill. In the first place he ravished the eye by appearing in a rich
and beautiful set and then the sheer artistry of the man held our
eyes spell-bound to the very end. With the simplest props in the
world, a twelve-inch stick and a large rubber ball, he performed
amazingly difficult and beautiful stunts. Only after years and years
of patient effort could he have arrived at such agility and physical
perfection. When at the finish he compelled the ball to circumnavi-
gate his graceful body in all directions and then spin like a top on
the insecure edge of the stick held in his mouth, the audience broke

into cheers--the only cheers of the evening. Yet he occupied the
ignominious position of "closing the show."

When Vaude Was In Its Glory

Felovis was the only one on the program that echoed the time
when vaudeville was really wonderful entertainment. In those "old-
fashioned" days we had such great presidigitators as Hermann, Houdini and Keller, whose "slight-of-hand" and "illusions" are puzzling
to this very day. We'll never forget seeing Hermann brush a hat
full of silver dollars right off the top of a bald-headed man sitting
beside us in the audience, and as for Keller's and Houdini's cabinet
tricks and mediumistic exposures, you can't say they are less entertaining than a young lady singing baby songs by a baby-grand piano.
Then there were the Japanese jugglers and equilibrists in their handsome robes performing feats of skill and grace with the most exquisite props in the world. Even in tights the Great Shafer Family of
acrobats were beautiful to look at, and you can imagine how classic-
ally gorgeous they'd be today when they would be permitted to perform their prodigious feats practically naked.

Artists and Smutsters

One might go on and recall the Hanlon Brothers with their
phantasmic acrobatics, the plastic sculptor who in an instant's manipulation of putty produced wonderful likenesses of famous men and
women. There were tight-rope and slack-wire artists and superlative
clowns. Even the individual entertainers like Bert Williams, Albert
Chevalier and Harry Lauder were not merely mouthing other people's
gags and singing other people's songs; they were great creative
artists. In other words, the old-time performers were men and women
who had spent years and years in perfecting their acts and had
achieved technic as superlative as that possessed by Willie Hoppe,
Bobby Jones and Helen Wills. "But the present public does not care
for acts of skill," say the impresarios. Then how about the gallery
that follows Bobby Jones around the links just to see him hit a ball
with uncanny precision? His technical skill is exactly that of Felovis.
"But Bobby's skill is in competitive sport," they answer. Not neces-
sarily. You can get just as big a crowd out to see an exhibition
match. "Well, anyway it's sport, not showmanship." We'll answer
that by quoting from last week's Variety:

"Closing were Momo Arabs, a troupe of nine whirlwind
acrobats who held them in to the stroke of five, and what
more could be expected?"

That's just what Felovis did.

Thespis Walks in Manure

Now let us examine this so-called "refined vaudeville" that is
addressed to the whole family. What do we find?--color, carnival
and ravishing music? No, the entertainment has become simply a
gray, colorless procession of smart-cracking gagsters, dance teams
and little one-act sketches with an occasional head-liner singing refined (!) songs in a baby voice. Instead of the great foreign and
native artists of yesteryear, a couple of Jewish boys will come out
and "kill ten minutes" with cheap banter and cheaper songs. An
Irish lad with a native wit but no artistry will walk in off the street
in an ill-fitting suit and kill another ten minutes with a few wise
cracks of doubtful taste. In fact, not until vaudeville became "refined" did we ever see the "nance" either in person or in imitation
on the public stage. That sort of perverted humor was left to the
smoking room of the lodge. One would not accuse Variety of squeam-
ishness, but this is the way it reports a recent act at the Orpheum:

"Richman's opening shot was : 'You don't have to go to
Europe to marry a broad.' And the Orpheum paid him $4,000
a week for that stuff. After the vacuum and his departure,
the box-office may recover....

"The nearest to a clean gag was when the girl asked him
if he wore knickers playing golf, he replied: "No, I play
with white people.' He might have thought of that when he
was entertaining, too."

In panning another vulgar comedian on the same program,
Variety says:

"His master stroke was: 'I knew him when he didn't have
a pot to cook in.' Great for two-a-day vaude! Then he
cracked about having to lay off for eight weeks and only
filling in here by saying: 'Always keep the act clean and
you lay off longer.'"

The Nance--Why Not the Lesbian?

In other words, keep the act smutty and you'll work longer?
Doubtless there are a lot of vulgarians and sex-sick people who
enjoy nasty jokes in public and even cherish the sickening gestures
of the pervert, jauntily referred to as a "nance." But we are convinced from the diminishing popularity of vaudeville and the growing popularity of pictures and Follies shows that the great majority
of those whose lives are gray love color, skill and sheer beauty in
preference to sophisticated smart-cracking and the jaded thrills of
sex-perversion jokes. Yes, they even love the despised acrobats
of vaudeville who are now finding expression in Follies shows with
their "adagio" acts. Combining acrobatics with classical dancing

almost in the nude, we are at last seeing and enjoying the sheer
beauty of the human body when not edited by "modesty." Our dramatic critic last week referred to Ye Ed as a hopeless Puritan, but
when the hard-boiled, rough-neck critics of Variety are shocked at
the very stuff they are supposed to celebrate, perhaps there is a
touch of Puritanical decency in the worst of us.

We See the Doughnut at Last

But, as we said before, the purpose of our devastating dia-
tribes is not to kill vaudeville, but only to sprinkle lime upon the
weeds so that the flowers may grow. If in the first enthusiasm of
their new toy the movies should go smart-crack and nance, as there
is already a tendency (note the Lemaire comedies), vaudeville will
have a grand chance to soft-pedal the gray, tiresome sameness of
their smartalecs and stage a renaissance of real colorful entertainment. We'll bet a year's subscription to The Script against a broken
slate pencil that if the Orpheum had "headlined" their performance
with Felovis and "closed" with the creole singer or one of their ugly
pairs of vul-crackers, they'd have been surprised how hungrily
their patrons would have eaten up the show.

If this editorial doesn't bring them to their senses, your only
hope is in making us king!

--Rob Wagner's Script, Vol. 2,
No. 5, September 14, 1929, pages
1-2 and 32.

• VAUDEVILLE FIGHTS THE DEATH SENTENCE

by Philip Sterling

American theatre audiences, long accustomed to taking what is
handed to them have apparently paid scant attention to the rapid
disappearance of vaudeville from the popular stage during the past
six years. This may have been due to the fact that during this
period there was a decided trend away from the box-office queues
toward the breadlines.

In any event, the causes of variety's fall to its current sad
estate are close at hand. They may be traced from Longacre Square
directly down Broadway and up Pine Street to the Chase National
Bank and a few other institutions whose financial control of the movie
industry have given the money-men powers of life and death over
America's entertainment. With the advent of the talkies, radio and
the depression, the money-men decreed death for vaudeville.

The simple retrenchment policies of all business enterprises
during the depth of the depression is not enough to explain the
forcible ejection of vaudeville from the theatre, because in the theatre business the retrenchment policy wasn't simple. It entailed a
complete rebuilding of the financial foundations and the administra-
tive and distributive superstructure of the movie world. And as
the movie world went, so went vaudeville for the cross country network of theatres which makes it feasible and profitable for actors
to work continuously by traveling short distances was largely in the
hands of the financiers who by 1931 had taken complete control of
the movie industry.

In the process of rationalizing movie production itself, there
developed a now perfected plan of making full-length "program" pictures which had no particular merit but which helped fill out an entertainment bill from which vaudeville had been eliminated. This was
so because the monopoly theatre chains, RKO, Loew's, etc., having
fired the body of vaudeville actors virtually en masse found it necessary to provide an acceptable substitute attraction at once, particularly in years when it was hard to lure a single dime from the pockets
of Americans for any non-essential. Following the old show-world
dictum, the producers immediately decided to give the suckers more
for their money without worrying too much about quality. This move
stepped up production, too, at a time when the movie industry was
on its wobbliest legs in history. The question of whether independent
theatre managers or the customers would like it, wasn't a consideration. The deadly block-booking system makes exhibitors, like their
patrons, take what they get. Thus grew up the somewhat tedious
institution known as the double feature bill which generally gives
the theatre audiences two lousy movies for the price of one half-
decent one.

The double feature, and radio, which offers everything in
vaudeville except personal contact, are still two of vaudeville's chief
bugaboos.

Now, after six years in the death-house, vaudeville is beginning to put up a fight. There is a chance that the fight may be a
winning one because it is being conducted by an economic organization of the vaudeville artists themselves. There are about 43,000
members in the American Federation of Actors. Like the members
of the American Newspaper Guild, they have begun to put behind
them the false traditions of their profession's glamour which in former
years isolated them from other wage-earners.

They are members of the American Federation of Labor, proud
of it, and damn sorry they didn't think of it before. The reason
for that, however, lies in the history of company unionism as embodied in the National Variety Artists. But that's part of another story.

The pertinent thing is that the American Federation of Actors

has for more than a year been conducting an energetic "Save Vaudeville" campaign. Logically, this raises the questions: Is vaudeville
worth saving and how can it be saved?

Many unthinking though well-meaning patrons of the dramatic
arts may immediately reply:

"Vaudeville is a cheap, out-moded stage form that is dying not
only because of external economic and social influences but because
it has always been essentially banal, innocuous, and boring." In
this reply there may be a half-grain of truth. Speaking strictly for
himself, however, the writer believes that vaudeville is worth saving
and that it has not always had those essential faults named above.
Vaudeville is a valuable theatre form, valuable, as is the rest of the
theatre, not simply as a highly effective social instrument but as an
excellent means for revitalizing the folk-flavor of the stage.

Its main faults are not inherent ones. They lie in the current
content of vaudeville which has been gradually squeezed dry of all
vitality by the deadly hand of monopoly control in the same manner
that the cinema, the legitimate stage and radio have been devitalized
by the same agencies.

The encyclopedias credit one Olivier Basselin, a fuller of Norm-
andy as being the father of vaudeville. The word itself is supposedly
a corruption of les Vaux de Vire, the valleys of Vire, where Basselin
worked and wrote his barbed satirical drinking songs directed at the
landholding clergy, the French feudal court, the aristocrats and the
landlords. But whether the encyclopedic information is accurate or
not, vaudeville, since those fifteenth century days, has devoted its
lilting songs, its light-footed, light-hearted dancing, its glib tongue
and its nimble hands to comment, criticism and burlesque of the life
of the common people.

Until the twentieth century, the formal drama, the legitimate
stage, were even further beyond the reach of the people and removed
from their interests than is the case today. Vaudeville, in one form
or another with its pithy turns, its intimate contact between audience
and performers, has, as a result, existed in every modern country.

The evolution of vaudeville in the United States, however, was
different. Like the rest of American life, its various stages of de-
velopment were rapidly and violently telescoped. When vaudeville
began to make its first consistent appearances in this country some
seventy-five years ago, it was quickly seized upon for exploitation
by the Barnums and other "great" showmen of the period.

In other countries vaudeville had developed as a folk-expression
which drew its material to an extent at least, from the problems and
the every-day lives of the people, of its audiences. In this country
it evolved from the raucous, obscene side-show exhibitions which were

held out by the showmen as come-ons for the stuffed whales, the two-headed calves, and the wax work figures on the inside of the tent.

When Barnum and his ilk had cleaned up in the hinterland, they headed east again and opened up pretentious theatres. Their attractions were modified and refined until Jenny Lind replaced Jo-Jo, the dog-faced boy, because presentation of Jenny Lind could command higher prices. Here was the beginning of the entertainment and show business monopoly that came to full bloom with the perfection of the movies. And once the monopoly got under way, the chances for an American vaudeville stage with a genuine folk vitality went permanently aglimmering.

It should be pointed out, however, that even despite the petty censorships imposed on vaudeville from within and from without the most popular and successful acts have been those with some slight amount of social content. The examples of Clark and McCullough and Gallagher and Shean are typical but it would be difficult to multiply them in the history of the vaudeville stage. Another indication of vaudeville's inherent vitality--denied the right to make fun of social and political happenings, it has never ceased to make fun of itself. There is no type of act in vaudeville that has not been burlesqued by some other act.

Up to this point the record of American vaudeville is not particularly bright. Why, then, is it worth saving?

The answer is this: Bad vaudeville is not worth saving but there has been and can be such a thing as good vaudeville. Good vaudeville combines individual virtuosity in anything from juggling to doing bits of Shakespeare and the live folk-spirit and dash which makes for creative entertainment. The flexibility and mobility of vaudeville make it an appealing form for social comment, and there is no contradiction between this and entertainment. The more vital the social content the more entertaining vaudeville will be.

The theory is that people seek entertainment to relax, to forget their troubles. But such relaxation and forgetfulness are emotionally and almost physically unsatisfactory unless they evoke a response or an emotion of which the individuals in the audience are aware after they leave the theatre.

Nobody remembers the infinite variations of "Who was that lady I saw you with last night?" But when you hear the story about the man who stormed into an office and demanded a job, you have subject matter for humor which lies close to the heart of virtually any audience. The man in this case was rebuked by the prospective employer. The rest of the story goes like this:

Employer: That's no way to ask for a job. You've got to be polite. Come back in an hour and try it again.

Applicant: (Returning an hour later with meek countenance and hat in hand) I beg your pardon, sir. But you recall that you were kind enough to tell me I could return here and make application for employment. Is that privilege still open to me?

Employer: Yes. And this certainly is an improvement on your first appearance.

Applicant: Well, you can go to hell. I've got a job.

The audience to which the writer heard this yarn told was justly enthusiastic in its response. How much more deeply this moved them than a stale pun with a sexy innuendo was obvious.

The simple conclusion of all this, and one with which important vaudeville figures agree, is that if vaudeville is to be revived and preserved it must have new material and new theatres free from the paralyzing grip of commercial monopoly.

How new theatres and new material are to be acquired is, of course, no simple problem. A discussion of the subject with Ralph Whitehead, executive secretary of the American Federation of Actors, convinces this writer that the fate of vaudeville lies in the hands of the members of the profession. Organization on an adequate scale and close collaboration with the rest of the labor movement offer a real possibility of rescuing and raising vaudeville to higher levels than it has ever known.

It is possible to envision the enlargement of the union's booking office, the establishment of a string of vaudeville theatres from coast to coast closely allied to the union or even owned outright by the actors themselves and thus free from monopoly censorship. Even better, he pictures solid coast to coast year-round bookings for vaudeville shows under the sponsorship of trade unions and other labor groups. After all, here is where vaudeville's real strength lies. It doesn't need a theatre. It can spring to life and do its stuff in any hall or out of doors.

Another possibility is that hundreds of dark theatres could be opened by the use of Federal subsidies and that official stiff-necked censorship could be avoided by actor and audience control of the theatres. Such a program, with its admitted difficulties, could be achieved by effective organization and the combined mass pressure of the actors and the rest of the labor movement.

Mr. Whitehead, who may be regarded as an official spokesman for the vaudeville artists, agrees that the medium needs new material, but just how new and how sharply changed, he isn't sure. He believes that a process of audience-education would be necessary. There is no doubt, however, that a process of actor-education would be an even more pressing need.

Vaudeville actors who have grown up in the stultified atmosphere of mother-in-law jokes, mammy songs and sexy double entendre will have to begin, as did Gallagher and Shean, Will Rogers, Dr. Rockwell, Ed Wynn and Eddie Cantor, to look to the newspapers and to current events for the substance of their acts, only they will have to look deeper into the headlines than their predecessors. They will also have to look into the headlines with greater sympathy for the interests and needs of the wage-earners and lower middle class who constitute the bulk of their audiences.

At least one vaudevillian has already shown himself to be aware of this need--one Steve Evans whose fascinating and intelligently conceived impersonations this writer saw in a typical New York neighborhood theatre. It may be accident that Mr. Evans' portrayal of John D. Rockefeller playing golf on his ninety-sixth birthday is so devastatingly satirical but the enthusiasm of the audience's response should tell him and other variety artists that here is a track worth pursuing. Most moving of all his bits is his characterization of a Polish steel worker getting drunk on pay-day. Those who are redder than the rose may say that the bit is a libel on the working class. Evans acting skill in portraying a drunkard, his oral deftness in portraying the vagaries of a Slavic tongue wrestling with an unfamiliar tongue, are not the point, however. What makes his Polish bit vital vaudeville art is the manner in which he conveys the motivations of the character he portrays. You feel that here is a guy who's got a right to get drunk. Your sympathies are entirely with him. You want to climb over the footlights, make the big, shambling good-natured fool put his money back in his pocket and take him home to his wife. But when he suddenly discovers that he hasn't the "pflent-yeh moonyeh" of which he has been boasting, you realize that he has been robbed not merely by a pickpocket who preys on drunks, but by the life he lives. When he goes staggering off stage with a crying-jag about his wife and the six kids waiting for him at home, you are moved.

--New Theatre, Vol. 3, No. 2,
February 1936, pages 17-18 and
30.

• CRITICS ANALYZE VAUDEVILLE'S CHANCES: A SYMPOSIUM OF NEW YORK AND CHICAGO NEWSPAPER MEN

For the past 10 to 15 years the favorite subject of show people seems to have been the decline, corruption, anaemia, strange illness and death of vaudeville. To this day few people agree as to whether vaudeville is dead or not, whether vaudeville is coming back or not, or whether vaudeville is wanted by the public or not.

Everybody seems to have a pet idea that would bring back vaudeville. Everybody seems to feel he knows why vaudeville declines. The Billboard, naturally, has a few violent ideas on the subject, too. But we feel that perhaps all of us in show business are too close to vaudeville to really understand it. We carry with us prejudices acquired because of our personal experiences in the trade. For that reason The Billboard asked several New York and Chicago newspaper men who had been writing about and reviewing vaudeville shows to tell the trade, thru these columns, what was "wrong with vaudeville" and, more important, what could be done about it.

"Vaudeville ... Is Dead"

Brooks Atkinson (The New York Times)--As part of a symposium on "What's wrong with vaudeville?" The Billboard asks for a few complaints. On the whole, there is nothing wrong with vaudeville except that it is dead. Apparently enough crackling acts can be assembled for one or two business-like shows, but probably you have already encountered most of them somewhere in the neighborhood within the last six months, and the backlog of experienced acts is a frail one. The experienced half of the vaudeville show put on at the Majestic two months ago was uproarious, but the inexperienced half was woeful and business was catastrophic. These comments are written prior to the opening of Frank Fay's new show at the 44th Street Theater with a bill that looks promising on paper. But the fabulous success of Hellzapoppin and the success Billy Rose had with vaudeville at the Casa Manana as long as the supply of acts held out suggest that the public still likes the vaudeville style of entertainment. No one who likes vaudeville has ever been reconciled to the realistic business fact that it failed.

Vaudeville, however, is a specialized technique that cannot be trifled with. Far from being an inferior form of entertainment, as some people snobbishly assume, it is a distinctive style with laws of its own. Fundamentally, it requires performers magnetic enough to dominate an inclosed area on a stage. They must be so exuberant or skillful that they can capture an audience's attention instantly and hold it until the act is over. Vaudeville is a form of free, bold, crisp and dynamic showmanship. Since vaudeville dies, one devilish mechanical device has crept into show business that is completely anti-vaudeville in effect. The microphone freezes everyone who stands behind it. Distortion of the voice is bad enough; the cheap microphones used in some of the frowzy joints give the human voice an unbearable metallic ugliness. But bad as that it, it is less fatal to enjoyment than the power the microphone has to kill the personality behind it. It reduces everyone to physical apathy. If the performers have to hide behind a microphone an audience might as well be home--in fact, would be better off at home.

"Young Performers Tone Deaf"

This is the most common weakness of the young performers who
have grown up in an age of radio and night club singing. They
are tone deaf. The brass-tongued clangor of voice amplification does
not annoy them. But if we are ever to have vaudeville again it is
more significant to observe that, paralyzed by the microphone, they
have never learned how to dash on the stage with the authority of
an honest performer and how to use the whole stage and keep it warm
and glowing. Huddling behind the microphone, they regard it as
a talisman that will protect them from the sea of faces on the other
side of the footlights. They have no way of discovering that the
first job of a vaudeville performer is to break down the resistance of
the house by direct force of personality. No one can hope to be a
vaudeville performer who lacks the vitality to sing a song directly
into the ears of an audience or to keep the patter running merrily
from all parts of the stage. If a performer cannot make his voice
carry in a vaudeville theater without benefit of Edison he had better
do his etiolating in a night club, for he is no vaudeville performer
but a robot and only the simulacrum of a free man.

"Spontaneity So Important"

In show business there is no substitute for the spontaneity
of a human being. Altho vaudeville and the musical stage are not
the same thing, they are cousins, and it might clarify the subject
if we consider two musical stars who have the vaudeville gift to an
extraordinary degree. Take Ethel Merman and Jimmy Durante in the
current Stars in Your Eyes. What a pair of public entertainers--
energetic and flamboyant, breezy and broad! They throw nothing
away. Whatever song or antic the show puts at their disposal they
give to the audience with something to spare in the way of good humor
and frankness.

Jimmy began in the night clubs many years ago with Clayton
and Jackson in a rowdy-dowdy piece of horseplay--shouting gags,
committing mayhem on the piano, throwing hats helter-skelter across
the stage. There was not much sense in it in either the night clubs
or the old Palace, but it was enormously friendly and exhilarating.
Since then our Broadway Cyrano has had a considerable career in
New York and Hollywood. But he has not let it improve his culture.
His voice is still hoarse, his style is still fresh from the sidewalks
and his gleam of good nature is abundantly sincere. In the current
circus they have given him a braggart song called "Self-Made Man,"
and it suits him, for that is what he is--a street corner clown who
has pulled himself up by his nose straps into a widely relished stage
buffoon. He radiates energy; he can take hold of an audience by
merely walking on the stage.

"That Electric Personality"

     Altho Ethel Merman came into show business at the time when
vaudeville was virtually finished, she also has the electric personality that takes charge of the stage immediately. She attends strictly
to the business of singing songs and speaking lines with clarity,
swing and vigor. It is always astonishing to observe how much tone
and meaning she shakes out of a song. She ranks with Sophie Tucker
in command of the calliope medium. In Stars in Your Eyes she also
emerges as a comedian with as much swagger as Mae West and a great
deal more comic integrity. A realistic thinker, she is not plagued
with pretensions. She does not try to be ravishing, glamorous,
coquettish or smart. She tries only to make the most of her talent
as head woman in a musical show. Hers is an enormous talent, for
her voice is resonant, her sense of rhythm is infectious, her mind
is alert and her personality frank and wholesome. Altho the Majestic
stage is large, she does not waste any part of it, even when she
has it all to herself, and altho the house is large, she can fill it
with hospitality.

     If vaudeville is ever revived it will be by people as magnetic
and courageous as Jimmy Durante and Ethel Merman. It is no medium
for fuzzy-minded acts, tepid personalities or microphone mechanics.
Only a few experienced and professional acts are available in this
country now, and the beginners have no place to go to learn vaudeville technique. Joe Cook could teach them. But after his melancholy experience with Off to Buffalo! he has retired again to Sleepless Hollow, where his audience consists of the hired man.

"Vaudeville Too Old Fashioned"

     Bob Sylvester (The Daily News)--I think the only thing wrong
with vaudeville today is that it's still vaudeville. Unfortunately,
that's more than enough. While every other theatrical formula has
undergone change, revision and a new set of glands, dear old variety
goes right along as usual.

     It's the same show every time--only the bodies are different.
The dumb act opens, the singer sings, the flash act flashes, the
funny fellow is funny and then everybody moves to the next town,
thus making way for the new bill which opens with the dumb act,
and then the singer, and then the flash act and then ... etc.

     There's never been a theatrical formula which lasted forever,
but vaude insists on trying to, and I think that it's becoming obvious
to us all that this stubborness on the part of everybody connected
with vaudeville emanates from fat heads rather than sentiment.

     As far as Broadway is concerned, it seems as tho anybody
can put together one good variety show. The next one ain't quite

as good, and after the third one somebody runs off with the money bag. The old excuse about "no talent available" is doubtless true concerning vaude, but for some reason there seems to be enough talent for radio, films, musicals, etc.

No, I think we've seen the last of it. Frank Fay's bill which opened March 2 represented the best that could be put together, but I think all of us sat there and chafed at the sloppiness, slowness, lack of rhythm and ragged routine which are attendant upon every vaudeville bill. Perhaps they were always attendant--maybe we are just noticing them now. The other forms of show business have caught up with vaude and passed it right by, but vaude won't believe it. Jake Shubert wouldn't dare produce the Passing Show of 1922 today, but vaudeville and its dear children still believe that the acme of entertainment was the dear, dead old Palace of the vanished era.

"Vaudeville Is an Art"

Ashton Stevens (The Chicago American)--"Is there any hope for vaudeville? What can be done to make it more attractive to the public?"

The questioner is The Billboard, which says, "Trade papers are too close to vaudeville to see it clearly."

Certainly there is hope. I have buried vaudeville as often as Whitford Kane, the world's champion First Gravedigger, has buried Ophelia. But vaudeville unfailingly has refused to stay dead.

Just now too many of its practitioners, of both the very small time and very big time variety, are living on the numerous and neglected night clubs: and not always living in the manner to which their art should be accustomed. It takes more than magnetism and a microphone to get a hearing in a nitery. Drink is the curse of the listening classes.

Stage vaudeville, such as is beheld at the big movie houses, would be more attractive if its bookers weren't so silly and snobbish about what they call "big names." The Palace recently booked radio's Fibber Magee. He was a "big name" at a big salary and a big disappointment even when he removed his pants for what was certainly not a big laugh. One of my clients, Jack Read, wrote indignantly, asking how I reconciled my disesteem for Mr. Magee's stage act with Variety's good report. I can only answer that that report bears out The Billboard's surmise that trade papers may be too close to see the subject clearly.

Vaudeville, as you care to call it, is an art, a profession, a craft. Ask W. C. Fields, Eddie Cantor, Ed Wynn, G. M. Cohan,

Burns and Allen. Tough, devoted, unclimbing years in the patrician
two-a-day of yesterday made them what they are today in broader
but not better fields.

Anybody can be a radio actor, almost anybody can be a movie
actor, one in a hundred can be a play actor, but hardly one in a
thousand has the immediacy and spell to be a vaudeville actor. It's
the hard way, but the great way, and I can prove it by Walter Huston.

"There Is a Place"

Edith Werner (The New York Mirror)--Yes, I do believe that
there is a place for vaudeville in the current entertainment scheme.
But a new streamlined vaudeville. Let's forget the triumphs (and
slow extermination) of the past and start afresh.

I, for one, would like to see fewer tap dancers, jugglers, un-
funny boy and girl "comedy" teams and circus routines. I welcome
personal appearances of screen stars, but only if they have something
definite to offer (many think their mere presence is sufficient). A
good master of ceremonies perks up performers and audience and is
a decided asset on any bill.

Given a well-balanced variety presentation, with new faces as
well as old favorites, the public, satiated with lengthy screen fare,
will take it to heart.

"Doesn't Like Microphone"

Claudia Cassidy (The Chicago Journal of Commerce)--I am no
help at all on the vaudeville question because I care very little for
vaudeville and invariably time my picture house trips to miss the
stage show. In the old Palace days it was different, but this back-
of-the-microphone movement is too much for me.

--The Billboard, Vol. 51, No. 14,
April 8, 1939, page 32.

• VAUDEVILLE REBORN

It's 12:10 on Thursday afternoon, May 19th 1949 ... the first
vaudeville bill at the Palace in fourteen years won't start for twenty
minutes, but the crowd has already filled the seats ... in the rear
of the orchestra they're standing five deep ... the last scenes of
a technicolor Western, Canadian Pacific, are unfolding on the screen
... in the press section, the writers are ignoring the film ... they're

scanning the audience for familiar "show business faces" ... they
spot Bert Wheeler, Dave Apollon, Joe Laurie, Jr. ... the movie
finishes with a clinch ... the newsreel comes on ... and after that,
a film announcement heralding the return of vaudeville ... as the
words roll up to the top of the screen, the pit orchestra softly plays,
"There's No Business Like Show Business," and you can feel the expectancy of the crowd ... then, as the curtains are drawn together
across the screen, the orchestra plays another chorus, this time
"fortissimo" ... the audience lets go with a deafening cheer ... the
kind of salvo you hear when "the next President of the United States"
is introduced at a political convention ... the applause continues
unabated, and just when you think it can't get any louder, it does,
for the first act is "on" ... the annunciators (those familiar cards
on the sides of the stage) tell you the two dancers are Mage and
Karr ... but the reception couldn't be more rousing if they were
Astaire & Rogers ... other acts follow ... it's not a "name" bill, but
today no one on the stage can do any wrong ... a couple of guys,
without the use of instruments, imitate a dozen different orchestras
... they're wonderful ... a British comedian does a monologue in a
dentist's office ... he's wonderful ... a knockout dance duo tears
up and down the stage ... they're wonderful ... eight acts in all
... an hour and fifteen minutes long ... and when it's over, no one
gets up, for in the semi-darkness of the theatre, a tall, husky figure
is sprinting down a side aisle to the stage ... the lights suddenly
go on again ... and standing front and center is Milton Berle! ...
it's a treat no one in the house expected ... he is without make-up
and also without his customary poise ... the audience senses his
nervousness and understands it ... he talks about the "old" Palace
... he helps his mother onto the stage, and they swap two or three
gags ... he brings Pat Rooney out from the wings, and together they
soft-shoe it to the tune of "Daughter of Rosie O'Grady" ... Berle
and the entire cast of the day's show pose for pictures on stage ...
flash bulbs are popping back stage, in the aisles and in the balconies ... when the picture-taking is over, Berle blows a kiss to
the crowd, and when the theatre lights go on, dozens of customers
can be seen hurriedly putting away their handkerchiefs before getting
up ... vaudeville has come home again.

--Cue, May 28, 1949, page 34.

- "MY VAUDEVILLE YEARS"

by Grace La Rue

PART ONE

"It's wonderful you remember all those things," said Mother. "You were only four years old when we went to the wedding. It's true the bride wore a bright blue dress, made princess style with white china buttons down the front." We both laughed. "They were farmers, nice people," she added.

Mother and I were sitting on the veranda of our suite at the Hotel Arlington in Santa Barbara; we had come down from San Francisco for a two-weeks' holiday. It seemed good to be stretched out in an easy chair in the warm California sunshine after a long, hard season in Chicago. Utterly relaxed, my thoughts kept wandering back to my childhood, perhaps because I was with my mother again after months of separation. As a child, and even after I was grown, my mother had been my ideal of a beautiful woman.

Mother's father, John Buffalo Christian, was a rich man as wealth went in those days. He owned and operated the largest cotton-ginning mill in his part of the country--California (!), Missouri. He also owned a large plantation with many slaves. The latter he had inherited. Most of them took the name of Christian, and were proud of it.

Some years later, Jasper, the oldest boy of Old Ev, Grandfather's housekeeper, was head porter at the Baltimore Hotel in Kansas City. The first time I played there, he came to the stage door to see me. He was gray then and getting on in years. I've heard that he often cautioned his children, "You be careful how you act and what you do; remember, you-all's name is Christian."

On the Fourth of July, within a month of my mother's fifteenth birthday, she rode with her father, two brothers, and four sisters to the county fair, all on horseback. At the fair mother met William Newton Parsons, whose family had lately moved to Missouri. A week before, he had danced with her at a party where she had gone with her older sisters. At the fair, Billy never left her side, and, late in the afternoon, he persuaded her to ride his sister Molly's horse,

254

find a minister, and marry him. My grandfather was so enraged
over this elopement, he never really recovered from the shock. Of
this marriage there were two girls and a boy. I was the oldest.

Mother said my father was very handsome, had an uneasy
easiness about him. He knew no restraint; had a frightful temper.
He was considered the best judge of horses in several states. He
owned race horses and made frequent trips to Kentucky for the purpose of buying and trading horses; was often gone for several weeks
at a time; seldom wrote to mother, and she never knew where he was
or when to expect him home.

When I was about six years old father went away and mother
never saw him again. It seems he had been in a horse-trading deal
with two brothers, Gypsies, near Kansas City. Father had made
love to their young sister who fell madly in love with him. Her family
thought he wanted to marry her. Each time he came to us and returned to them, they questioned him about his absence. He only
said: "It's none of your damn business!" It was a joke to him.
He was making money with them--as for love-making, he made love
to every woman he met.

But once the brothers followed him and learned that he was
married and had a family. There was a terrible quarrel and they
threatened to kill him.

After some days of drinking, he came home for the last time.
Several years later, while sitting in a saloon in Little Rock, Arkan-
sas, the Gypsy brothers, whom he had not seen during this time,
came through the swinging doors. My father instinctively put his
hand on his revolver, but before he could draw, they shot him
straight through the heart. Thus, at the age of thirty-one, came
the untimely death of my tempestuous father.

At the age of twenty-one, my mother was left with three children to support. Mother's sister, Mary, took my sister, Ida May,
to live with her; and a dear friend, Maggie Lyons, who lived on a
farm near Chanute, Kansas, took my brother, Roy, leaving only me.
I had always been a delicate child. At last, in desperation, mother
placed me on a farm with a family named Gates, near Maggie Lyons'
place, hoping the outdoor life and plenty of milk would help me to
grow strong.

The day I went to the Gates Farm stands out in my memory
above any other day of my childhood.

We had been visiting with mother's sister, Kate. Nothing had
been said to me about being separated from mother. I know now
why, the night before, she had held me in her arms and cried. The
next day, Uncle Charlie drove mother and me to the Gateses twelve
miles away, arriving about four o'clock. A cold winter day.

Vividly I recall the Gates Farm as it looked that afternoon--
the trees bare, the sky gray, the wind sharp. A white picket fence,
a narrow walk leading to the white two-story frame house.

Mr. and Mrs. Gates met us. Mrs. Gates, extremely thin,
medium-blond hair and faded blue eyes; about forty, and a typical
old maid. She married Mr. Gates, a year before, and
considered herself lucky to get him. Mr. Gates was a big man, with
a bushy beard; looked like pictures I have seen of Oom Paul Kruger,
the Boer president. He had a son by a former marriage. Tom,
eight days older than I. They wanted a girl to grow up and help
with the work.

We were taken into the front room, so cold we sat with our
coats buttoned up. I did not grasp the veiled conversation about
my remaining at the farm. I remember the sun was shining slant-
wise through a parted curtain. Mother held my hand in the sunlight
to show how delicate I was. It looked transparent and pink inside.

Soon mother kissed and hugged me and told me to go with Tom
to see the baby chickens. When I returned it was dark, and she
had gone. That day I passed from the only childhood I was ever
to know. My grief was indescribable.

My first supper at the Gates Farm was a strange affair. A
large bowl of bean soup was put on the table. Mr. Gates, with
bowed head, said "grace." I sat staring. I had never heard any
one say grace before. He helped each one to a bowl of soup, which,
with bread and butter and a glass of milk, composed the meal.

After supper Mrs. Gates took me upstairs to a room with a
slanting roof and told me to undress for bed. Mother had brought
a bag of clothing, although I had not noticed it. I was wide-eyed
and silent. I had never slept by myself in a room before. That
night I cried myself to sleep, and many nights thereafter.

The beginning of my life with the Gates family is like a dream
to me now. I felt I had been given away by my mother. The Gateses
never spoke of her.

Tom and I walked two miles to school, most of the time through
heavy snows. There was so much work to be done before school,
we were always late and ran most of the way. Tom helped his father
feed the cows and pigs while I helped Ma in the house, made my bed,
washed the dishes, and fed the chickens.

After about six months, I milked nine cows morning and night
in addition to my other chores. The same round of work to be done
after school, then supper and lessons to study.

I was taught to do everything the right way--churning butter, skimming milk, pealing potatoes and apples with as little waste as possible. Mrs. Gates watched closely. She would say, "There is a place for everything; learn to keep everything in its place."

I rode horseback without saddle and seldom used a bridle. I looped the halter around the horse's nose and led him to the fence to get on his back.

In summer Tom and I would ride to bring the cattle home. This we always enjoyed. Many times when a storm came up suddenly, it became dark as night, and we would stand still and wait for a flash of lightning to see the cattle. Then we would hug our horses' necks with our arms and ride swiftly toward them.

I was intensely afraid of lightning. With it playing around us, Pa Gates would hold my hand and say, "There is nothing to be afraid of." But in my heart I was still afraid.

One evening Mrs. Gates sent me to the spring for water. A storm was coming up. I stood in the kitchen door, hesitating. "Go on," she said. There was a blinding flash, and that is all I remember. Pa Gates found me unconscious. They revived me and put me to bed. Nothing was ever again said about lightning.

Every spring there were acres of corn, wheat, and vegetables to be planted, and certain days for hog-killing. We had a large smokehouse where dozens of hams and sides of bacon hung from the ceiling.

There was always great excitement and preparation at harvesting time. Pa Gates hired a thrashing-machine crew. Although this caused extra cooking and work, it was as thrilling to me as a circus.

The first day of spring, Tom and I were turned barefoot for the summer, and only wore our shoes on Sunday. My long blonde hair, parted in the middle and braided during the week, was allowed to hang loose on Sunday.

Many scattered recollections of those years at the farm came back to me. One sultry summer day, Ma was baking pies. When done, she placed them on the window sill to cool. Suddenly we noticed it was getting dark. From the kitchen door we saw a funnel-shaped cloud, very black, Ma grabbed my hand and pulled the door shut behind us. We ran for the cyclone cellar. Breathless, we dashed into the cave and forced the door shut against the terrific wind.

Inside it was pitch dark. The butter and milk were kept in this cellar. I thought of the pies on the window sill. After a few minutes, we peeped out. The sun was shining. The cyclone had passed us by. The pies were untouched where we left them.

The lightning-rod man interested me keenly. He breathed with great difficulty. Ma said he had asthma. I followed him about with childish curiosity watching him unload the rods and wires. After dinner I took him to see the watermelons, piled high. Tom and I showed him how we ate a melon. Picking a big one, we held it high and dropped it. It burst open, and we dug our hands in and took out the heart. I have eaten watermelon in many parts of the world, but none ever tasted so good as those Kansas melons.

Although Pa Gates read the Bible every evening, he was a man who believed in whipping children. He whipped Tom often, but hesitated to touch me. But one night after dark, Ma sent me to the spring. Barefooted, I was afraid of snakes in the dark, and asked Ma to leave the kitchen door open so I could see my way. Pa said, "What's the matter with her?" "She's afraid," said Ma. Pa reached for the whip hanging by the door. My heart stood still. I remembered Tom's screams when Pa whipped him. Pa took me into the yard saying, "I'll teach you to be afraid!" I could see the angry, resentful expression on Tom's face when Pa struck me. The next day I was very ill.

I had been at the Gates Farm almost three years, and I hadn't received a letter from mother for over a year. I often wondered why she had stopped writing to me. One day, Pa Gates found me crying. I told him it was because I had not heard from mother. He said in an offhand way, "Oh, I guess she's forgotten about you; besides, she adopted you to us."

I was eleven years old and beginning to think for myself. So the next time Pa and Ma went to town and I was alone, I determined to find out what was in that top wardrobe-drawer, where the horehound candy and other things were kept that we children were not supposed to see. I pushed the dining-room table up against the wardrobe, placed a chair on top of the table and climbed up. I found several letters from my mother which had never been given to me. She asked why I had not written to her. I was surprised, for I had written several letters during the past year. She said she had heard they whipped me, and if there was any more of it she would take me away; that I had not been legally adopted by them.

I was very much excited at this discovery, and from that moment, I determined somehow to get away from the Gates Farm. On the afternoon of the day I found the letters, I was working alone in the cornfield near the main highway. A man driving in a buggy stopped as he drew near. There was a sewing machine in the back of the buggy. He asked the road to Humboldt. I told him, and he thanked me, then added, "What's a little girl like you doing working in this hot sun?"

I explained I had to plant corn in the places where it hadn't come up. "What a big help you must be to your father and mother," he said. "Pa and Ma are not my father and mother," I replied. "My mother lives in Kansas City."

"That's where I live."

I ran and climbed on the fence. "Oh! could you find my mother for me?"

"Why, yes; if I know where she is." I told him mother's name and where I sent my letters. He set it down in a little book. I begged him to make her understand and to tell her to come and get me or I would surely die. He said, "Don't fear, little girl; I will find her as soon as I get to Kansas City."

Within a few days, Pa Gates received a telegram. Telegrams were unusual in the country. He left his work and went to a nearby country store where he sometimes traded. He did not get back until after I had gone to bed. I could hear him and Ma walking about and talking more than usual.

About four-thirty next morning Ma called me. It was still very dark. Ma said Pa wanted to get off early to town, and we must hurry.

After breakfast I started to wash the dishes when Ma came into the kitchen. "You are going to town with Pa. He is sending you on the train to Kansas City."

Even now I can feel the joy I felt that morning. I wanted to scream, but I was afraid even to speak. The sewing-machine man had found my mother!

The only thing I regretted about leaving the farm was parting with Tom. I never saw or heard of him again.

The short time I lived in Kansas City was a period of unforgettable experiences. I felt the urge of life ahead of me as though I were being pushed along by an unseen force.

> --Rob Wagner's Script, Vol. 18,
> No. 428, September 11, 1937,
> pages 4-7.

PART TWO

[Stella Parsons was twelve years old when she escaped from the Gates farm to the protecting arms of her mother in Kansas City. The little girl from the country was fascinated by the bright lights and the city clothes of her sister, Ida May--"She looked like a beautiful doll."

But it was not long before Stella realized that her mother
was having hard sledding to support her little family by
dress-making. So....]

Mother said I was too young to work. However, unknown to
her, I searched the want ads in the Kansas City Star. Finally I
found this one:

Young girl for amusement work; no experience required. Apply
at the Midland Hotel to Mr. X. between eight and nine in the morning.

The following morning, I surprised Evelyn, our colored maid,
by appearing for a very early breakfast. I evaded her questions
and hurried off.

Mr. X seemed surprised to see so young a girl. With a broad
smile, he asked, "Will there be any family objections to your going
on the stage?" My heart bounded at the word 'stage'; but I said,
"no." "Come with me," he said. "I can show you in a few minutes
what you are to do."

We got on a street car and rode to the far outskirts of the
city, where there were tents and banners flying--a regular county
fair. He led me into one of the tents and turned me over to a motherly-
looking woman who took me into a room and put me in a pair of light
blue tights. They were much too long and wrinkled at the knees,
but she said there was no time to do anything about it. Over the
tights she put a spangled tunic; she then curled my hair and rouged
and powdered my face. After surveying me with satisfaction, she
led me into the main tent.

There, in the center of the tent, was a large wagon with two
horses hitched to it. Extending down the middle of the wagon-bed
was a long board. I was told to lie face down on it with arms stretched
above my head. A wooden bar was placed against my feet, another
for my hands to push against. When the horses were shipped up,
I was to push with all my might against the bars with my hands and
feet, to give the impression that I was strong enough to keep the
horses from moving the wagon. It was a trick, of course--which I
never quite got into myself. In fact, I was interested only in the
four dollars I was to earn for the day.

After we had rehearsed for a while, Mr. X took me outside the
tent and helped me up on a platform beside a barker who began shouting to the passing crowd, "Come inside, folks! See the strongest
girl in the world pull against a team of horses!".... I stood up there
before the crowd--not quite thirteen years old--clad in badly fitting
blue tights, and feeling very self-conscious.

Every half hour and far into the night, we repeated the act.

The tent was always crowded. By the time the last show was over,
my legs hurt so that I could hardly keep from crying. But in my
pocket I had that four dollars! I caught the last car to town, reached
home, and slipped through the summer kitchen without waking anyone.

Mother cried when I handed her the four dollars, but made me
promise....

Yet, within a week, I was off again, in answer to an advertisement for small girls to act as pages in the show at the Grand Opera
House, where Julia Marlowe was playing a week of Shakesperean repertoire. To my great delight, I was one of two girls chosen. They
dressed us in page suits of black velvet with lace collars and cuffs--
delightfully becoming. In several scenes, we stood quite near Miss
Marlowe.

> [The opening of school interrupted Stella's stage career,
> but not her ambitions. She and Ida May practiced danc-
> ing, and Stella decided upon a stage name that couldn't
> be nicknamed, like "Stell." After a search through the
> family Bible, she chose for her surname her grandmother's
> middle name, La Rue, and for her given name, her own
> middle name Gray. She became "Gray La Rue!"]

The Smell of Sawdust

Ida May and I often walked home from school with the two
adopted daughters of Mr. Lemon of the Lemon Brothers' Circus.
One day, they invited us to come to the winter quarters of the circus in Argentine, a suburb of Kansas City, Kansas. They were
being trained to ride bareback and practiced every day after school.

I shall never forget the first time Ida May and I sat on the
ring-bank, made of dirt, and watched the younger girl practice.
She was not more than nine years old, and small for her age. She
wore pink tights, and a very wide leather belt around her waist;
the belt was the biggest thing about her. A rope was attached to
a swivel at the back of the belt, then through another swivel at top
of the center pole, by means of which the trainer controlled her
entirely. When she missed a trick, instead of falling, she was pulled
into the air and then let down gently to the ground.

By running for it, the girl was tring to learn to jump on the
horse in a standing position. Each time she jumped, the trainer
pulled the rope to help her alight on the horse's back. Her pale
little face, with her hair pulled back, looked so tiny, and her small
legs were so thin, I wondered why they did not break when she
landed on them. She was afraid, and after an hour or so of practice, was always in tears. After the practice she was given an

alcohol rub, then dinner; and her tears were forgotten until the
next day, when she had to go through the same routine over and
over again.

Mr. Lemon became so accustomed to seeing Ida May and me
around the winter quarters that, when school closed, he asked us if
we would like to go with the circus to sing and dance in the concert.
He assured Mother we would receive the same good care as his girls,
and if we became homesick, he would send us home. It would be a
nice vacation for us; and, besides, he would pay us a small salary.
Mother give her consent, and we were delighted.

Each day, Ida May and I rode horseback in the parade and in
the entrée quadrilles, and did a song and dance specialty in the
concert. When the afternoon performance was over, and the main
tent cleared, we practiced all kinds of circus stunts--the rings, the
ladders, and the bars. There was a trio of acrobats, the Prevosts,
in the show. One of them afterward formed a partnership with Rice,
and they became internationally famous in vaudeville as Rice and Pre-
vost.

My greatest thrill that summer was when, in answer to my constant pleadings, Mr. Lemon let me drive a four-horse chariot in hippodrome races at the end of the show. He also let me ride in the cow-
girl races.

After about two months, Mr. Lemon one day tried to discipline
Ida May for breaking some slight rule. After dinner, she called me
from the dressing-tent and led me to the railway station to find out
if there was a train for Kansas City that night. She was raging with
anger. We found we could get a train at eight o'clock. Running
back to the sleeping-car on the sidetrack, we packed our suitcases
and slipped out without being seen. When we walked into our home
next morning, Mother was just reading a telegram from Mr. Lemon
telling of our disappearance.

And so ended another episode in my changing life; two months
spent with the dearest people in the world--for circus folk are known
for loyalty to one another and protection of their own. I have never
been sorry that I learned the meaning of the "smell of the sawdust."

Young Sing-and-Dance Team

Peabody's Museum, where the best of the vaudeville played
then, was run by a nice man, well liked. Soon after we returned
from the circus, we went to see him and showed him our act. I
sang, and we did the "Sailor's Hornpipe," the "Highland Fling,"
and the "Skirt Dance," with splits and cart-wheels. He engaged
us at a salary of eight dollars a week.

I made our costumes in the woodshed, which we used as a playroom. For the Highland Fling I made pleated plaid skirts and black velvet jackets; for the Skirt Dance yellow cheesecloth skirts, very full.

Our first day at the Museum, we told Evelyn--who had the care of us while Mother was in the hospital--that we were going to Aunt Molly's. On opening day, we did six performances; by ten o'clock that night, I had nearly lost my voice singing: "Won't You Walk into My Parlor Said the Spider to the Poor Little Fly,"--and we limped so that we could hardly get home.

Evelyn was waiting for us; she had kept our suppers warm. We told her with great pride that we were Actresses now. We begged her not to tell Mother, as it would only worry her. Evelyn didn't like it, but she guessed it would be better if Miss Lucy (meaning Mother) didn't know. So, each night, Evelyn met us at the Museum after the show and brought us safely home. How we ever got through that week, I don't know. After it was over, we slept for days.

When Mother heard about our working at the Museum, she was more angry than she had ever been about my theatrical ventures. The next few days, I felt instinctively there was something in the air concerning me. One morning, I overheard Mother saying to Evelyn, "Evelyn, I can't keep you any longer. I'm going to put Stella in a convent. I know it will cost more than I can afford, but I have got to do it."

That same day, I was taken out to the convent, a short distance from town. I was in tears when we left, and all the way out there on the street car, I never spoke.

I learned many things in the convent. For one thing, I was enabled to develop my natural takent for sewing and was taught how to cut and make dresses correctly by patterns. I also received my first music lessons there. And when a little play was presented by the girls, I was given the leading part!

It seemed that every way I turned led me somehow to the theater. After my success in this little play, I dreamed by the hour of going on the stage--the very thing that Mother had sent me to the convent to forget! There had never been any theatrical folk in our family, so I received no encouragement whatever; but I began to feel quite certain about what I would do with my life, if I got the chance.

After I had been at the convent about three months, Mother came to see me. In the midst of my questions about Ida May and home, I suddenly burst into tears and begged to be taken home; and she finally agreed. She said she had not realized how much she had missed me and promised never to send me away again.

--Rob Wagner's Script, Vol. 18,
No. 429, September 18, 1937,
pages 10-11.

PART THREE

The week that Sister and I played at the Peabody Museum in
Kansas City a girl, Sadie Hart, did a song-and-dance act. I went
to see her one day after school.

Sadie was glad to see me again and wanted to know if I was
working. I told her my mother would not hear of my going on the
stage, though I would rather do it than anything else in the world.
She asked if I would do a sister act with her. "When I get to Chicago week after next, I will arrange for us to work together and will
send you money to join me there. I can also fix you up with costumes and you can pay me back later."

For the next two weeks, I simply lived in the clouds. We had
arranged for Sadie to write me in care of the Peabody Museum, and
I went there almost daily. One day, when I had about given up
hope, the door man waved a letter as I approached. When I opened
it, a railroad ticket and a five-dollar bill fell out. Sadie told me to
come to Chicago at once and to telegraph her when to meet the train.

We had been living since the beginning of the winter on the
fourth floor of an apartment building; Mother had two rooms on one
side of the hallway; the dining-room, kitchen, and bedroom which
Ida May and I shared were on the opposite side. Mother always
read in bed at night--it would be impossible to move until she was
asleep.

Luck seemed to play into my hands that evening. Ida May
had a splinter in her foot, and Mother had to call the doctor to get
it out. When he left, Ida May was lying on Mother's bed asleep, so
Mother said, "We'll just let her sleep with me tonight." This left
me alone in our room. I put my nightgown on over my clothes, got
into bed, and pulled the covers up to my neck. When Mother came
in to kiss me good night, I pretended to be almost asleep. She put
out the light and went softly out--and then, to my astonishment,
I heard her lock the door from the outside. She had thought I was
too near asleep to remember to get up and lock it.

My heart sank. I lay still, thinking, and watching the light
in Mother's room as it shone through the transom. Suddenly I got
out of bed and quietly moved a table over by the door and put a
chair on top of it; then I got out the bundle of things I had hid
under my bed earlier in the day. Then I waited. It seemed an
interminable time before Mother's light went out; and afterwards I
had to wait until I was certain she was asleep.

Finally, I took my shoes in my hand, put on my hat, and climbed onto the chair. I put my head through the transom and listened. I could hear the regular breathing of Mother across the hall. I dropped my coat--then my bundle--then one shoe. I waited. I dropped the other shoe. All was quiet. I squeezed myself through the transom, hung on till my stockinged foot found the doorknob, and dropped softly down onto my coat.

The rest was easy. I gathered up my things and hurried along the hallway and down one flight. Then I sat down on the steps and put on my shoes and my coat, felt in my pocket for my ticket, and, in a few moments, was out in the street.

It was not quite ten o'clock when I reached the station. I sat in the waiting room till nearly midnight. Then I found a seat in the day coach of the train and slept quite well all the way to Chicago. I was sorry I could not tell Mother that I was going, but I knew if I did, she would not let me go. And it never occurred to me not to go. Long afterwards, in London, she told me what a shock it had been when she awoke next morning and found me gone. She was ill in bed for several days. She did not even know where I was until she received a letter from Chicago a week later.

Stella Gray Takes a Stage Name

Sadie met me at the train and took me to the boarding-house where she and her husband were staying; and for the next ten days, we worked day and night making costumes for our act, setting routines of dancing, and learning new songs. We used Dutch clog shoes in one number, and I had many painful hours with those wooden shoes, until finally we hit on the idea of wearing ballet pumps inside the clogs.

I confided to Sadie that I had already decided on a stage name: Gray La Rue. So in our first engagement, we were billed as Hart and La Rue. But when I saw my name on the program, it read: "Grace La Rue." I protested to the manager. He explained he had mistaken "Gray" for "Grace." My first year on the stage, I spent considerable time explaining my name. At last, I simply gave up and became resigned to being "Grace La Rue" forever after.

I do not remember the name of the Chicago theater where Sadie and I played our first week's engagement; but I do recall that it was the first continuous show ever presented in the city. It was a very long program, with many acts. I remember only one of them-- Ida Emerson and Joseph Howard. She was very beautiful; he was tall and thin--the most popular singer of ballads of the day.

Sadie and I worked together for about three months. At Pittsburgh, her husband's home town, we were laid off for two weeks.

We tried to get work there but without any success. I was living
at Sadie's home, and being idle worried me. Finally, one day I went
looking for work on my own. A stock musical show was playing in
Allegheny, doing revivals of light operas. They needed four girls
to do a quartet dancing number--high-kicking, splits, and some individual dancing--and had only three. They engaged me to complete
the quartet. I moved to a small hotel just across the street from the
Allegheny Theater, and started on my own.

The work was very hard, with a matinee every day, and a
rehearsal every morning from nine till twelve. I was in many of
the numbers. When I learned that in some of them I was supposed
to wear tights, I almost quit the show; I was old enough to be conscious of being gazed at and was even shy of undressing before
girls.

A woman stage-manager--a Miss Vivian whose last name I can't
remember--was in charge, and all the girls were afraid of her. She
yelled at everybody, and without provocation would call the girls the
most awful names. Every time I heard her I became all tight inside,
and a hot feeling of resentment swept over me. I kept well out of
her way and hoped the day would never come when she would pick
on me.

Every moment I could spare I practiced dancing, high-kicking,
all kinds of acrobatics. I learned whatever I could, from anyone who
would teach me. After three weeks of grueling routine: rising early,
rushing my breakfast, hurrying to rehearsal, bolting a luncheon and
rushing back for the matinee (which always ran late so that it was
dark when we got out for dinner, with no time to rest before the
evening show), I was dead-tired. One morning my alarm clock didn't
go off--or else I slept through it. I arrived at four minutes after
nine.

Miss Vivian was in the middle of the stage when I came in. I
was told afterward that she had been on the warpath that morning,
anyway. She caught sight of me and called me over.

"You're late!" she charged.

"I know--but only four minutes. I was so tired, I overslept."

"Why lie?" she said rudely.

I straightened up, and in a clear voice so everyone could hear,
I answered, "I am not a liar!"

She yelled back, "Yes, you are a liar!"

The words were hardly out of her mouth, when I struck her
squarely in the face with my fist, as hard as I could. I knocked

her down and started after her again, but the leading man and
several others held me back. Several of her pet girls picked Miss
Vivian up and brushed her off.

"Take her away!" she was yelling. "Take her out of here!
She's fired! She's fired!"

Within a few minutes, I found myself standing outside the stage
door--without a job. Now what was I to do? When the rehearsal
started again inside, Arthur Deming, the principal comedian, came
out to me: "You know," he said in a low tone, "Vivian does not own
this show. It belongs to Mr. Davis."

I looked up at him through my tears. "Where is Mr. Davis?"

"Across the bridge in Pittsburgh, at the Grand Theater. He
owns that theater and this one, too."

I tried to smile and thank him, and started for the Allegheny
bridge, half a block away. As I walked across the bridge, the morning sun in my face, I was so miserable and so mad, that I started
crying again.

By the time I reached the Grand Theater, I must have looked
a sight. The charming woman in the office seemed surprised when
I asked for Mr. Davis, but, after a moment, she came back and
patting me on the back said, "Go in." That pat was almost my un-
doing. I started to cry again and would have fallen into her arms,
if Mr. Davis had not called to me:

"Come in, little girl. What can I do for you?"

Tearfully, I told him my story--that I had been called a liar,
and had done a terrible thing: I had knocked Miss Vivian down!
And she had fired me! Mr. Davis laughed. He called the woman
who had shown me in, and told her, and they both laughed. Then
he wrote a note and handed it to me. "Go back to the manager of
the theater and give him this. But first dry your tears and get some
breakfast. You are not fired. After this," he added as I reached
the door, "you let Miss Vivian alone, and I'll see that she lets you
alone." He must have kept his word, because Miss Vivian never addressed me again.

Several years afterward, when I was a vaudeville headliner,
Pittsburgh was one of my best towns. The Grand Opera house was
then a Keith Circuit Theater, owned and operated by this same Mr.
Davis. His wife, a very charming woman, often came to my dressing-
room to chat (she was interested in my clothes), and once she brought
her husband with her.

"Mr. Davis," I said in the course of the conversation, "I wonder

if you will allow me at this late day to thank you for a kindness
done once to a tearful, poorly clad girl, who had lost her job?" I
recalled the incident to him, and told him I was the girl. But he
did not remember it in the least. What had been all-important to
me had been only one of the many kind and sympathetic acts in his
long, successful life.

--Rob Wagner's Script, Vol. 18,
No. 430, September 25, 1937,
pages 28-29.

PART FOUR

[Summer heat closed the show in Allegheny, and the
young singer teamed up with Josie Collins, one of the
girls in the dancing quartet. They went to St. Louis
where they got a job at twenty dollars a week at a summer garden. A manager from Butte, Montana, saw them
and engaged them at one hundred dollars a week and
billed them: "Collins and La Rue--the World's Greatest
Singing and Dancing Sister Act!"
    In spite of their success, Collins became homesick
and left for Boston at the end of a month. But her
fourteen-year-old partner was offered a pinch-hit job
with "Mazie Arline" (wife of John Burke) on the same
program with the Burke Brothers. Billing was "Arline
and La Rue."]

The theater in Helena was a sort of winter garden with an open
stage, somewhat on the concert plan, with the best orchestra we had
ever had, which helped Mazie and me to make a hit. The Burke
Brothers, the headliners, of course, simply stopped the show.

From Helena we went to Seattle. Charles Burke, the younger
and unmarried one of the brothers, a wonderful dancer, started to
teach me the Irish Jig and Lancashire Clog--two most difficult dance
tempos. Every day, too, when I went to the theater to practice,
I found a team of German acrobats practicing on the stage; they
offered to teach me some acrobatic stunts. I could do a cart-wheel,
and from them I learned a round-off flip-flap and back somersault.
I did dozens of flip-flaps a day. Because I often missed getting on
my feet and landed on my toes, they became so sore I had to wrap
them in towels in order to practice. But I went on practicing just
the same. But, oh, the pain, the backaches, and sprained ankles!

From Seattle, we were booked for four weeks in Juneau, Alaska.
Three acts were engaged: Mazie and me, the Burke Brothers, and
the Hoopers, Arthur and Lillie. Arthur was a contortionist and the
principal part of their act. Lillie did very little. They also had in
their act a clever bulldog and a Yorkshire terrier. At the end of

the act, Lillie strutted up and down the stage singing, while Arthur
did wonderful contortion tricks, and the dogs turned somersaults ...
a big hurrah finish.

The trip to Alaska was to be made on a small boat up the In-
land Passage. It was my first trip on the water. On the afternoon
we sailed, most of the folks around the theater came to see us off.

The seven days on the boat going to Juneau were like a trip
to heaven. There were not more than a dozen passengers, including
our party, and I became friends with everyone--passengers, sailors,
and captain. I spent hours in the bow with the strong wind whipping my face; afternoons, I slept on the deck, stretched out in the
sun. The scenery was magnificent; in places we went through gorges
so narrow that we could reach out and touch the cliffs. We went
ashore at several places--Indian towns, whose history was carved in
hieroglyphics on tall totem poles.

A Tough Audience

Juneau in the summer--land of the midnight sun, where it was
never dark at that time of year. The theater was new. To enter
it, one had to pass through a huge gambling-room with a long full-
length bar where several bartenders worked day and night. The
Indians came to the theater in crowds and sat in the back on benches;
wrapped in their blankets, with folded arms, their expressions saying: "Make me laugh if you can!" They watched the show in stolid
silence. They never laughed at the comedians. A bald-headed wig
and red nose and whiskers couldn't make them laugh; they saw funnier make-ups walking around the streets every day. Their blankets
and clothing were beautiful, but their faces were usually painted
with pitch tar to protect them from freezing in winter and from mo-
squitos in summer. And pitch tar cannot be washed off; there is
no way to remove it except to let it wear off. The Burke Brothers,
accustomed to hearing the audience scream with laughter at their
act, had a hard time of it in Juneau.

> [Back to Seattle, then to Chicago, Miss La Rue stopped
> for a short visit with her mother in Kansas City, who
> again urged her lively daughter to quit gallivanting and
> go to school. But the yeast was working too strongly,
> and Miss La Rue was off with the Burke Brothers. To
> New York!]

I was fifteen years old when I arrived in New York for the
first time. New York had always seemed a place unreal to me--just
a word--a sort of dream-world where everything pertaining to the
stage began, and ended. I was just beginning to learn that there
was a difference in the classes of actors, of shows, and of theaters.
Up to this time, the stage, to me, had been simply the stage.

Charles Burke, twenty-seven, had not gone to school since he
was ten; therefore, his education came chiefly from reading and observation. But he was better informed in history than the average
person, and politics was his especial interest. I knew Charles drank
quite a lot; but every man I knew drank some. He knew I could
not bear the smell of whiskey, so was careful not to let me suspect
too much.

A few weeks after we arrived in New York, John Burke told
Mazie he was considering a contract for the four of us in a show,
rehearsals to start in August. Mazie and I practiced every day,
and I designed lovely new dresses, which we made; she had learned
to sew quite well. Finally the season's contract was signed with
Lawrence Weber's Parisian Widows, a burlesque show. (Weber is
now a well-known Broadway manger.)

I did not know what a burlesque show was, or that it was
not considered even second-class--and felt very happy at the pros-
pect of working a whole season. Burlesque then was somewhat
like the revue of today--songs, with choruses and specialties interspersed. The girls wore tights, which was considered extremely
risqué; but they never appeared on the stage almost nude as they
do today. They always wore some kind of uniform or costume, and
the necks of their dresses were not cut at all low compared with
modern stage costumes.

Burlesque was, in fact, very much like circus life. The
cast was like one big family. The manager's wife was usually in
the show; Lawrence Weber's wife was leading woman. Some of our
finest and cleverest stars, both men and women, developed their
great versatility in burlesque shows. I learned buck dancing from
a young fellow in that show by the name of Bandy. Buck dancing
was about the same as rhythm dancing today.

Married!

One day Charles asked me to go with him to a priest. I said
I would be glad to. On the way, he stopped at a jewelry store and
asked to look at some diamond rings. He told me to try them on.
When we were in a cab headed uptown, he turned to me. "I bought
this diamond ring for you," he said, slipping it on my finger. I
was so surprised I couldn't speak. "Let's get married--now," he
added. "You know I've been in love with you ever since I saw you."

A sudden shy, self-conscious feeling toward him came over
me. I had never thought of Charles as a husband; in fact, I had
never thought about marriage at all. But I liked him.

I was not happy that first winter of my marriage. I spent many
hours alone and in tears. Night after night, when the show was over,

Charles would take me to the hotel and say, "I'll be back in a few
minutes...." and....

I worked hard; I was determined on a career. In addition to
my constant practice in dancing, I took my first singing lessons
from Emma Krauss, a soprano with our show. As a young woman,
Emma had married a well-known singer by the name of Broderick,
who played the leading role in many musical shows on Broadway.
She and her husband had traveled with the Emma Abbott Opera Company, he as leading-man and she as a singer of small parts. She
was a trained singer, had a beautiful voice and some unusual top
notes; she was very talented, but, for some reason, she had missed
the mark. Her daughter is Helen Broderick, the clever comedienne,
who played for Sam Harris in As Thousands Cheer at the Music
Box in New York City and is now in pictures.

Emma Krauss had several duets in the show with a contralto,
Miss Rose; but the latter was rather indifferent to her work and
was often absent from performances. One day when she sent word
she could not sing at the matinee, I heard they intended to cut the
finale of the first act, their duet. I hurried to Emma's dressing-
room and begged her to ask the manager to let me sing it with her;
I knew all the music and often sang it at the top of my voice when
at home alone. Emma closed the door and said, "Let me hear you
sing the number with me." I went through it perfectly. The manager
agreed to let me go on with her.

I had to wear a diamond headdress for the number, and an
evening dress with a long train; I remember I padded the bust out
with a towel to make me look more mature. I was very nervous,
but in a seventh heaven of delight. I went through with it successfully, and Emma hugged me as the curtain fell. Everyone in the
company gathered around to congratulate me. (I learned later that
I had sung Rosa's part some of the time and Emma's part some of
the time; Emma could sing either.) Charles was very proud of me
that night.

Theatrical Boarding-House

In June Charles and I went to St. James, Long Island, a popular summer resort for actors. We lived at Obadiah Smith's theatrical boarding-house. Obadiah was a character--an old farmer, one
of the thigh-slapping, "By heck! I swan!" type that one seldom
finds off the comedy stage. Everybody ate at one big table at Obadiah's, with him presiding.

I had to find my companionship entirely with the other guests.
Charles usually slept till noon. Then he went to the barroom of
Gould's Hotel, near the station, a favorite meeting place of actors,
where he stayed until late at night, sometimes even missing his dinner.

Jerome Sykes and Jessie, his wife, were at Obadiah's that
summer and were very kind to me. Jessie, a splendid swimmer,
taught me to swim. Jerry was a famous light-opera star and a fine
baritone.

Barton and Ashley, a vaudeville team, were that year guests
at Obadiah's, too. They were among the first American acts to tour
Europe and had made an unusual hit in England and on the Continent
--which was perhaps why Annie Ashley left so superior. She was a
thin, wiry woman, with sparkling black eyes, a notorious temper and
a sharp tongue; and she was a walking encyclopaedia on the history
of the vaudeville theater. Annie saved her money and invested it
in large diamonds which she carried in a chamois bag tied around
her waist. She loved to show her gems to her friends. Her husband
and partner, John Barton, was younger than she and completely under
her thumb; I think he was actually afraid of her. Jim Barton, the
now famous comedian and dancer on Broadway, is a nephew of John
Barton.

Many well-known actors summered at St. James. Among those
who had homes there were Tom Lewis, William Collier and his wife,
Louise Allen; Helen Collier, his sister; Clarice Vance; Charles Bigelow, the well-known singing comedian--he had a glorious tenor voice;
Bob Daly; Bert Leslie; Frank McNish; Foy and Clark; Johnnie Hyams,
and Leila MacIntyre, the parents of Leila Hyams, in the movies now.

One evening, at a clambake at Tony Farrell's there were many
well-known stars. Several sang that evening, including Mr. Sykes.
I was sitting far back by myself devouring it all, and getting such
a thrill, when Jerry suddenly called out to me: "Come here, little
partner!" Turning to the others, he added, "We sing duets sometimes." And then he asked me to sing alone.

I was awfully frightened. As a rule I had plenty of nerve,
but here I was facing a crowd of all professionals. And there was
no piano; one just had to start off. But Jerry Sykes held my hand
to encourage me. My voice sounded very far away to me on the
night air. When I finished, many came to me and said nice things.
Several asked who I was and seemed surprised when they learned
I was the wife of Charles Burke.

Not long after the clambake, there was a benefit at William
Collier's private hall or theater. I was asked to dance and to sing
a trio from one of the well-known operettas with Jerome Sykes and
Charles Bigelow. Bigelow played the organ, which was down in the
audience near the footlights, and sang his part from there, while
Jerry and I sang from the stage. We made a hit, and I felt quite
important--an unknown singing with two great stars. I walked on
air for days afterwards.

William Collier was one of the most successful stars of the day,

and his home was the most important in St. James. He usually had
several house-guests (I remember one of them was DeWolf Hopper);
and it was considered quite an honor to be invited to his place for
dinner.

At the end of that first summer, Charles and I bought a little
farmhouse near the Stanford White estate, which had belonged to an
old gardener of the White's. There were three acres of land, a cozy
house with a large barn and stable, and an oldfashioned garden behind the house with many rose bushes and several varieties of fruit
trees. We paid only $3,500 for the place, and felt that, after a sub-
stantial down payment, we would be able to pay the balance during
the coming season.

--Rob Wagner's Script, Vol. 18,
No. 431, October 2, 1937, pages
28-30.

PART FIVE

[The winter of this chapter in her life was a crucial
one for Miss La Rue. Charles Burke, her husband, went
off on tour with his brother, John, and Mazie, leaving
his wife to hustle for herself. It was the jolt she needed
to stir her spirit.]

Heretofore I had danced in flat-heeled shoes and extremely
short skirts. Now I decided on something different. I worked several days and nights making a long, yellow chiffon dancing-frock.
With it I wore yellow satin slippers with high red heels, opera-length
silk stockings, and very short, tight-fitting yellow satin pants. The
latter were seen in flashes when I kicked or whirled in dancing--
quite risqué in those days. The whole costume was most becoming.

It was about this time, that I first became really conscious--
"consciously conscious"--of the fact that I was attractive. It was
when I was on my way to the music publishers one day for some new
songs. I had on a becoming little black velvet hat and a trim wrap-
around coat, and as I passed a Broadway corner I noticed several
of the cigar-store loungers eyeing me from head to foot. I glanced
into the next show window at my reflection, and it came over me as
a perfectly new idea: "Why, I have a pretty figure; I am attractive!"

Every day, I went to the vaudeville agents looking for work--
anything, if only a Sunday night performance. Finally William Morris
booked me for a Sunday night at Koster and Bials on Thirty-fourth
Street, for twenty dollars. I made a real hit, and the theater engaged me for a full week. There were several well-known women
stars on the bill, and the first night my name was not even mentioned
on the posters; but after that my turn was put later on the program,
and my name went up outside. Photographs were asked for.

My new type of single act and my lovely costume made a hit.
Charles came on Sunday to see me, and soon I was persuaded to join
his show. I found a new song, "Hiawatha," at the Remick music
publishers in Detroit. I wanted to put it in the show, but John
Burke, as stage manager, objected as usual. I wanted to do the song
with the chorus; I was sure it would be a success. But John again
refused. Then the manager came to my rescue: "Let her try it one
performance; it will not be any expense to us." What could John
say? The musical director taught the song to the chorus girls (the
treatment of the orchestration was quite new and different). I arranged the business for them--nothing difficult but very effective.

"Hiawatha" was introduced first at a Saturday matinee. I made
a rose-colored taffeta dress for it--a real picture. The song took
eight or nine encores--an unheard-of thing in a burlesque show.
The next week we played Cleveland, and the Roger Brothers' Show
was playing there at the same time; they came to our Monday matinee.
The whole company was on its toes. My new song with the chorus,
near the end of the show, was an even greater hit there than in Detroit. After the matinee a representative of the Roger Brothers came
back stage and asked for me--with a proposition for me to go with
their show the next season as leading woman. My heart fairly leaped
to my throat with joy. They were somewhat upset when they learned
that I was married; and I myself was a little uneasy as to what Charles
would say. We went to supper with the Roger Brothers after the
show that night, and Charles did not seem unfavorable.

When the show closed in St. Paul, we returned to New York,
and Charles and I signed a joint contract with Mr. Erlanger for the
Roger Brothers' new show in the fall. I went to St. James, the little
place where we had bought a cottage on Long Island. I was a very
happy girl. But fate was against me, for I never filled that contract; Charles quit during rehearsals and that automatically broke
my contract. Mr. Erlanger said he was afraid if he kept me in the
show I would let Charles influence me when the show went on tour.
Charles returned to his brother and a burlesque show. One of the
acts in that show was "Bonita with her Pickaninnies." (She afterwards became the star of Wine, Women and Song which made such
a hit at the Circle Theatre, married Lew Hearne, the comedian, and
with him became quite a success in the London music halls.) Once,
when Bonita was taken ill, I was asked to work in her place for a
few days. My type of work was entirely different from hers, and
when she returned, we talked things over and combined my act with
hers and the pickaninnies. She was a high yellow gal and I a Broadway soubrette. The act became the hit of the show. But the show
did not last long, and soon we were back in New York, out of work.

I went to St. James for Christmas, staying at the little hotel
of Mr. and Mrs. Gould. I reveled in the big snow storm which
greeted Christmas. I put on strong shoes and walked miles in it!

St. James was practically deserted in winter save for a few families. The John Kernells were there for Christmas; and Josie, the daughter, and I were good friends, although she was much younger than I. John Kernell and his brother, Harry, had been famous Broadway stars; Harry had died some time before, leaving two small sons. His wife, Queenie Vassar, a star on Broadway in her own right, afterwards married Joseph Cawthorne, the well-known comedian. After Harry's death, John worked in the varieties doing a single turn.

John Kernell kindly spoke to Tony Pastor about me, and Mr. Pastor assured him that if I would fix up an act with the pickaninnies, he would book me in his theater.

Samuel Foster Barber, the younger of the pickaninnies, was seven years old, and Louis was nine. Samuel was very black, and Louis almost white. They were very clever. I dressed them in white, stiffly starched coats and trousers, and, for a closing number, Louis changed to a long, yellow organdie dress; he looked like a high-yellow gal. They both played stringed instruments, Sam a mandolin and Louis a guitar. Samuel developed into a great dancer, and years later had one of the best colored orchestras in Boston.

My act made a big hit at Tony Pastor's. There was no orchestra--just a piano, played, at the time, by Bert Green. (He married Irene Franklin, the clever vaudeville star.) Mr. Pastor always sat in the first entrance, and when I finished my act, he would walk into the greenroom and tell me how pleased he was with me. He was sweet and kind to everybody and always ready with encouragement. The only other manager like him in this respect was Oscar Hammerstein--that is, the only other in America; in England the managers are more likely to consider the artist and management on equal terms, and to be charming and pleasant.

Charles saw how successful my act with the two pickaninnies was; so he wrote a sketch called "The Silver Moon," in which he could work with us. The Silver Moon was a restaurant which I, as a stranded soubrette, had opened with the boys as waiters. The act showed the restaurant about to fail; I had advertised it for sale, and Charles came in as a prospective buyer. We rehearsed, and played a week at an out-of-town theater as "Burke and La Rue and the Inky Boys."

Hammerstein's Victoria Theatre, at the corner of Forty-second Street and Seventh Avenue, which during the week played musical shows, began putting on straight vaudeville on Sunday nights. Up to that time no sketch had ever been booked--only singing, dancing, and "dumb" acts. But as our sketch had both singing and dancing and also great comedy value, Mr. Hammerstein engaged us as an experiment for one Sunday evening. We made such a decided hit that we were engaged for four consecutive Sunday nights.

At the close of our act, we used to bow and bow, as we had
no encore. One day Charles said, "Why don't you sing one of those
Irish come-all-ye's you learned from my mother? The musical director
can give you a chord in whatever key you want, and I'll stand beside you while you sing--and we'll see how it goes."

It went remarkably well. These songs turned out to be one of
the hits of our act. I sang them without musical accompaniment, in
the true Irish way. This was also the beginning of my individual
use of a hat while singing. I wore a hat in the closing number of
our sketch (much later, I used a hat in many of my songs); and when
I started the Irish song, I took it off and put it under my arm.

Bantry Bay

> I was seated all alone in the gloaming;
> Sure it might have been but yesterday;
> I could see the merry fishermen ahoming
> From where the little herring fleet at anchor lay.
> And the lassies with their baskets aswinging
> Came tripping 'long the old stone quay,
> And each lassie to her sailor lad was singing
> A welcome home to Bantry Bay.

There are two more verses of this beautiful, plaintive song.
It is in my song collection which I call, "Poems I Love and Songs I
Have Sung."

A Rope-Throwing Actor

We played the vaudeville houses at the beach that summer--
Atlantic City, Rockaway, and Brighton Beach. On the Monday we
opened at Rockaway, there were two small horses, saddled, standing near the stage door. After rehearsal I went out to admire them,
and had my arms around the neck of one when the owner came up.
He told me I could ride the pony up and down the side street by
the theater if I wished. He was on the same bill--a wild-west riding
and rope-throwing act. His name was Will Rogers.

Sunday night was the big night at the Victoria. The artists
looked forward to it, especially because the theater was always crowded
with actors and actresses, managers and agents. In the front row
could be seen "Diamond Jim" Brady, with Edna MacCaulay, his sweetheart; Lillian Russell and Jessie Lewisohn; Dave Johnson, the well-
known sportsman and gambler, and his wife, Evelyn; Georgia Caine
and her husband--(dear Huddy!); George M. Cohan and Ethel Levy
his wife; Sam Harris, and many other Broadway celebrities of the
day. They made a wonderful audience. The sporting world was well
represented, too: John and George Considine, who owned and operated

the Metropole Hotel on the corner of Broadway and Forty-second
Street, cornerwise across from the Victoria Theatre, were in the
audience not only on Sunday nights, but several times a week. Oscar
Hammerstein was almost always present. His son, Willie, was the acting manager--and a more gentle, sweet, mild-mannered man it would
be hard to find.

Charles and I played "The Silver Moon" several months in the
best variety theaters as far west as Chicago. There were many well-
known stars on the various programs with us. In Washington at one
time was Robert Hilliard in his sketch, "The Littlest Girl"; at the
Union Square in New York were the Keenans--Frank, his wife, Kate,
and his daughter, Frances. Mrs. Keenan was like a mother to me.

When we played at Poli's Theatre in Hartford and New Haven,
Herbert Brenon was on the bill, in a dramatic sketch with his wife;
he became a motion picture director, with such outstanding successes
as Peter Pan, and Beau Geste. And on the same bill were Will M.
Cressy and Blanche Dayne in one of the most successful comedy
sketches in vaudeville.

"Honey Boy Evans," the great minstrel singer, was at Hyde
& Beeman's in Brooklyn the week I played there. He sang his famous
song: "I'll Be True to My Honey Boy." His songs were much like
those sung by the young singers today, but at that time he was in
a class by himself.

Then there was Bonnie Thornton, the best-known soubrette of
the day, and James Thornton, her husband--a noted monologist, composer, and lyricist.

At the Circle, in New York, Della Fox was the headliner. She
sang several of her famous songs, one of which I have never forgotten; the chorus runs like this:

> "A pretty girl,
> A summer night,
> A moon serenely mellow;
> A babbling brook,
> A shady nook,
> A kiss, and all is well-o!"
> "Again the girl,
> Another night,
> Same moon, but sad to tell-o!"
> The one who kissed
> Those ruby lips
> Was quite another fellow!"

I watched her every night. Miss Fox was nearing the end of
a successful career on the stage; she retired not long afterward.

--Rob Wagner's Script, Vol. 18, No.
432, October 9, 1937, pages 20-22.

PART SIX

[Miss La Rue was finally forced to leave her talented
but intemperate husband, Charles Burke. But she wondered if Mr. Hammerstein's advice was right, and if she
could go it alone. To her delight, she learned that her
burlesque appearances had been scouted by no less a
personage than Lee Shubert, who signed her up for a
part. Her specialty in The Tourist, a musical comedy
by Messrs. R. H. Burnside and Gustave Kerker (the
latter, author of The Belle of New York) became a sensational success. The play opened at the Majestic.]

Richard Golden and Julia Sanderson were the featured members
of the cast. She was lovely; I have never seen such magnificant
eyes! She had been engaged to marry Sammy Shubert, one of the
three Shubert Brothers, at the time he lost his life in a train wreck
a few months before this. During the run of The Tourist, she met
and married Tod Sloan, the famous American jockey.

Vera Michelena, the prima donna, made her first New York appearance in The Tourist,--though she had already toured the country
for two years as a comic opera star under the management of John
Slocum. She was only eighteen, with dark hair and eyes and pale
complexion, tall, and quite noted for her beautiful legs and figure.
Others in the cast were William Pruette, the famous baritone; Anna
Boyd, who had been a star in her own right; and Alfred Hickman,
the original Little Billee in Trilby.

I was the only new member of the cast, everyone else having
played during the run in Boston.

It was a very hot night when we opened, and the audience
fanned continuously. But the show seemed to move very well during
the first act, and my one song was well received.

My specialty came just before the final song in the last act,
"It's Nice To Have a Sweetheart," sung by Miss Sanderson. I dressed
long before time and stood in the second entrance, watching the show.
I heard remarks all around me about how things were dragging, and
I couldn't help noticing it myself. The comedy scene which I was to
follow--a scene in which the comedians played dice--was long drawn
out by Mr. Golden. Suddenly I noticed Miss Sanderson standing in
the first entrance on the opposite side of the stage, as if waiting to
go on, though her song came after my act. Just then the stage
manager came to me and said, "The show is running so late, Mr.
Shubert has sent word to cut your specialty out tonight. It will go
in tomorrow night."

My heart stood still. After all my summer's work and the money
I had spent on my costume and number! Everything would be wasted
unless I was seen the opening night!

Suddenly I heard my cue from the dice players: "Come Seven!"
It gave me such a start that, before I knew it, I had bounded onto
the stage--and Mr. Kerker, who had his baton raised to begin the
opening bars of Miss Sanderson's song, got the surprise of his life.

My costume received a big hand on sight. I looked like a girl
on a magazine cover--and I should have, for I had copied one! Meantime the orchestra members were scrambling to turn back to my music
--Mr. Kerker was impatiently tapping his baton--while I simply stood
smiling. There was only a moment's pause, but long enough for some
of the audience to begin to catch on. I don't think I ever danced
as well as I did that night. My success was unmistakable. I did at
least five encores.

When I finally got away from the audience and fell, completely
exhausted, into a chair in the entrance, I was surprised to find J. J.
and Lee Shubert standing beside me all smiles. They were deeply
grateful to me for making the surprise hit of the night--a hit which
redeemed the show and added greatly to its future success. I went
home that night tired--but, oh, so happy!

Next morning when I arrived at the theater at eleven o'clock
for rehearsal, I was rushed by the company with congratulations.
They showed me the press notices. While the critics were not unan-
imous as to the success of the show, they all hailed Grace La Rue as
"a newcomer to Broadway from vaudeville," and congratulated her on
"scoring in some capital songs and a dance that was worth the money."
I recalled Mr. Hammerstein's advice to go it alone; and with deep
gratitude to him, I resolved never to work with a partner again.

Up to this time I had experienced in The Tourist company
the resentment which was generally felt by established Broadway
players toward vaudeville artists--a resentment due chiefly to the
fact that vaudeville artists so often scored with the audience, in their
specialties, over the players in the show. (Mr. Ziegfeld, in his revues, first placed the vaudeville performer in a legitimate class and
made him a sort of super-personality in the theater, since his revues
were practically made up of specialties.) The morning after my hit,
I noticed that the frigid attitude toward me had decidedly changed;
I was taken into the fold, so to speak.

[Six months at the Majestic, then on the road. Miss
La Rue caught a severe cold, left, and returned to New
York. Shubert thought it only an excuse to get back on
Broadway, and when Miss La Rue was finally well enough
to work again, she found herself blacklisted.]

Finally an agent, M. S. Benthan, sent me to see Mr. Ziegfeld, who was then preparing to bring out his first _Follies_. He said I was just the girl he wanted for his new show, that he had engaged no one as yet, but would keep me in mind. I went to see him every week--and every week was put off.

One morning when I called at his office, they told me he was at a rehearsal of Miss Anna Held (his wife) at the Broadway Theatre. I went to the theater, I found Mr. Ziegfeld standing back of the last row, talking with a man, but as it was quite dark inside, I could not see who it was. I waited until he had finished his conversation; then went up and told him who I was. "Oh, yes," he said. "Well, I don't know about engaging you. I hear from the management you worked for last time that you are not reliable; that you wanted to quit the show when it left New York."

At last I understood why I had been unable to get work the past few months!

"That is unfair!" I exclaimed, "I was very ill!"

Just then the man with whom Mr. Ziegfeld had been talking came over and said: "I heard what you were saying to Miss La Rue. I know something about her and will vouch for her if you engage her."

I did not know the man even when I saw his face; but evidently Mr. Ziegfeld had a high regard for him, for his manner changed. "Do you know who this is?" he asked smiling. And then he introduced me to Samuel Nixon, of Nixon and Zimmerman of Philadelphia-- an all-important man in the theatrical world at that time, especially to Mr. Ziegfeld, as he owned many theaters and was a partner of Klaw and Erlanger.

A Stage Milestone

I was the first girl, I believe, engaged for the first of the famous Ziegfeld Follies--The Follies of 1907--presented at the Jardin de Paris on the New York Theatre Roof.

The weeks preceding the opening of The Follies were hectic ones for me. Having been out of work so long, I had almost no money. I could not even afford to pay for voice lessons; but my teacher, Madame Lankow, trusted me to pay her when I worked again.

Long, tiresome rehearsals were held on the roof of the New York Theatre. Although I was accustomed to hard work, I had never experienced anything like this. At first I could not understand The Follies, for revues were a new form of entertainment then. Mr. Ziegfeld's policy was girls--girls--girls! Everything was secondary to

the success of the girls. That was all right. But I expected them
to do something! To my surprise, none of them could sing or dance
particularly well. I think Florence Walton and Mae Murray, a pretty,
wind-blown blonde, were about the only real dancers in the show,
aside from Mademoiselle Dazie, a ballerina, who had created a furore
as "La Domino Rouge"--a mystery to the public. Until her engagement with The Follies, she had always appeared with a red mask.

One girl in the show of great interest to me was May MacKenzie,
who had received much publicity during the Stanford White-Harry
Thaw trial as the friend of Evelyn Nesbitt Thaw. Together with
Miss Nesbitt, she was kept in virtual confinement for months, as an
important witness for Mr. Thaw. Of course, I had read something
about the trial, and was eager to know May. We became good friends
in the theater, and she used to come to my dressing-room when she
had a little time between scenes, and tell me "inside things" about
the trial. One evening while we were in the entrance waiting to go
on, she introduced me to William Jerome, the New York district attor-
ney who figured so prominently in the Thaw case. They were very
good friends.

Mr. Jerome was only one of the many prominent men I met
back stage while I was with The Follies. It was the only show I
was ever in, except one, in which men were permitted to roam around
back stage while the performance was going on--"important" men,
that is--men with influence and money.

I have many memories of famous stars of that historic period.

                    --Rob Wagner's Script, Vol. 18,
                      No. 433, October 16, 1937, pages
                      22-23.

PART SEVEN

Mae Leslie was very witty--a real wisecracker. She had been
with the Anna Held show several seasons and was a sort of privileged
character in The Follies. She was a great favorite with Julian Mitchell, who staged the show, and was given several important-
unimportant bits which gave the impression of raising her above the
show girl. Mr. Mitchell was much given to favorites. He arranged
the songs and chorus work for the girls who worked in my numbers,
but he was not particularly interested in me, as I was a specialty
dancer.

An incident during dress rehearsal further antagonized Mr.
Mitchell. In the first scene of the show, at the rise of the curtain,
I was discovered on the stage as the Indian Girl in front of a cigar
store. Throughout the scene I stood like a statue with the characteristic bunch of cigars in one hand and a tomahawk in the other,

until Dave Lewis as John Smith brought me to life with a kiss, and
I sang "Pocahontas" (by Seymour Furth). It became one of the hit
tunes of the show.

During dress rehearsal, I had to stand on the block such a
weary time in the terrific heat that I became dizzy and had a hard
time keeping myself motionless. Things were beginning to blur and
weave about by the time the moment came for me to come to life; and
when I started to step down from the block, I stepped right on down
into blackness--and came to on the couch in my dressing-room with
somebody splashing water in my face. Mr. Mitchell was very annoyed
and became more distantly polite than ever. Some one had blamed
him, I suppose, for keeping me standing so long without moving.

In another bit I had in the show, Charlie Ross played Andrew
Carnegie, and I was Miss Ginger from Jamaica. I did a song of that
title, dancing around him. At the end of the number, I finished
with several whirls and fell back into his arms. He was supposed to
catch me, of course; but at dress rehearsal I came at him so swiftly
that he let me slip through his hands to the floor and found himself
standing with one of my ankles in his hand, gazing out at the audience with an expression which brought such a laugh that Mr. Ziegfeld decided to keep the slip in--in a modified way, of course.

Emma Carus sang the finale of the first act. She was the leading woman (though Bickel and Watson with their comedy band were
the hit of the show). This finale was one of my heartaches. When
the curtain went up on a full-stage black velvet cyclorama, the stage
was completely dark. A spotlight on the center back revealed me in
white tights, high boots, white and gold military costume, with a
small gold and white drum. Emma, at the side of the stage, sang
the song. I walked down the center to the footlights during the
chorus, while the girls, in costumes like mine only less elaborate,
came on from all sides with drums.

Strip-Teasers Will Laugh

I had never worn full tights before, and I felt degraded. I
had always thought tights were only for chorus girls; but in The
Follies everyone wore them, except Emma. She was quite fat and wore
a skirt. The fact that Mr. Ziegfeld had sent to Paris for the tights
I wore didn't improve matters but rather made them worse, for they
were extremely thin, and I falt naked. But I never mentioned my
feelings to him; he would have thought my qualms silly. I did make
up my mind, however, that if Emma ever left the company, I would
ask him to let me sing her song. I did--but long afterward.

The opening night in New York (following a week in Atlantic
City), the audience was made up of all the well-known first-nighters.
It was a historic night for Mr. Ziegfeld.

The heat was terrific all summer, and when the show was over, it required an hour to cool off and dress for home. There were always young men waiting at the stage door, with motor cars. I met several through the girls. We used to drive through Central Park or sit on the veranda of the Casino in the Park, and have refreshments. Gradually the unhappy years of my life were fading from memory. But I had learned much from experience--and when I found myself growing fond of any man, I stopped seeing him. Success was what I wanted; not heartaches.

I had applied for a divorce from Charles. On several occasions a young man, Elmer Reizensteine, came to my hotel from the law office with papers for me to sign. A few years later this same young man-- as Elmer Rice--wrote a play, On Trial, which not only made a hit but a great deal of money. Since then he has written many successful plays--including Street Scene, the Pulitzer Prize play of 1929.

In September The Follies moved from the Roof Garden to the Liberty Theatre on Forty-second Street. One morning after rehearsal I was standing at the stage door when Donald Bryan came by. The last time I had seen him, a few weeks before, he had just been engaged by George M. Cohan for an important part in Forty-five Minutes from Broadway and was simply sitting on top of the world. But this morning he seemed fathoms deep in the blues.

"Listen!" he said, taking my arm. "I've just come from George Cohan's office. Mr. Savage wants to borrow me for a part in an operetta called The Merry Widow. I'm just sick about it!" I tried to cheer him up by pointing out that the operetta might be much better for him; the music was by Lehar, and it had been a brilliant success abroad. "I know the part won't suit me," he insisted gloomily. "But I guess I'll have to do it."

The next time I saw Donald, he was the hit of New York as Danilo in The Merry Widow. I would have given half my life if I could have played the role of the Merry Widow. It would have suited me, too; but nobody thought of me.... So I went on tour with The Follies.

Nora Bayes joined the company in place of Emma Carus, and I was given the much coveted song with the drum in the finale of the first act.

In Chicago, Nora gave one of the first big theatrical supper parties I had ever attended. Nora was shockingly broad in her jokes and her manner of telling them; but she was one of the most quick-witted and brilliant persons I have ever known. Once when a new arrival came up to speak to her (she knew everyone), he remarked: "Gee, it's cold outside!"

"Well, I'm prepared for it!" laughed Nora. And pulling up her

skirt, she revealed a heavy suit of red wollen underwear! She had
hunted all over Philadelphia for that red underwear, on purpose to
shock me!

Her guest of honor that night was George Ade. He had crossed
from Europe the summer before with Nora and seemed greatly interested in her. I liked Mr. Ade. I have met him several times since
then and have always found the same charm of manner.

Nora lived to laugh. She was a great comedienne and had a
most unusual voice. She was a good friend, but a dangerous enemy--
and would stop at nothing to achieve her ends. For a time I lived
with her in Philadelphia; we had a suite together at the Walton. She
was very frail, for all her bubbling vivacity, and spent most of her
days in bed. At the end of the Philadelphia run, she had to leave
the show because of illness.

Her place was taken by Lucy Weston, a young girl of English-
Irish birth, just over from London. Her specialty in the show consisted of several risqué songs done in a demure and charming manner.
We became devoted friends, in spite of the fact that I was always
frankly making fun of her odd-looking, old-fashioned clothes.

Lucy insisted she wanted to dress like me, so I took her in
hand. First, I made her discard her funny corsets and her English
woolen underwear--and she promptly caught cold and was in bed for
a week! But after we had made a few shopping expeditions together,
she was a changed girl. I also hustled her off to the dentist to have
her teeth straightened; she was pretty before--now she was beautiful. When we returned to New York in the spring, her English
friends, hardly recognized her.

Mr. Ziegfeld re-engaged Lucy for The Follies of 1908 and selected her to represent the Statue of Liberty. We were somewhat
surprised that he did not choose an American girl, but no mention
was ever made of it. One could not wish to hear more beautiful English than Lucy's, while her delightful Irish wit kept everyone laughing and made her hosts of friends.

One matineee in Philadelphia there was great excitement back
stage just before the show started; the stage manager brought the
great Fritzi Scheff to inspect our dressing-room! Her show was to
follow The Follies at the Forrest Theatre, and it seemed that she
required a number of dressing-rooms for her personal use. Madame
Scheff came in and looked about our room, not even noticing Lucy
or me, said a few words in French to those with her, and walked
out. I felt no offense--she was the great Scheff! But Lucy was
furious.

Madame Scheff and party were in the stage box at the matinee,
and we all worked especially hard to give a good performance. The

finale of the first act, as I have said before, was a military number; I sang a song with the drum, and in the chorus the girls all came on stage with drums, marched off the stage down the runways into the aisles, and back onto the stage. The whole drum stunt was a satire on Madame Scheff's number in Victor Herbert's operetta, Mademoiselle Modiste; we even marched to the music of the chorus of her number. But, of course, there were thirty girls with drums in our show, while Madame Scheff was the only one with a drum in hers.

When the girls marched down into the audience, I remained on the stage alone. To my amazement I saw that Madame Scheff and her party were leaving the box--and the theater! I learned afterward that she was offended at the very idea that anyone should presume to play a drum as she did.

--Rob Wagner's Script, Vol. 18, No. 434, October 23, 1937, pages 28-29.

PART EIGHT

From the moment my contract was signed, I searched for new songs and ideas. In those days The Follies was made up of songs by any composer. If Mr. Ziegfeld liked a song, he arranged a scene to suit it; but once the show was set, it was next to impossible to get in anything new. During rehearsals I tried repeatedly to get a hearing for the work of a then little-known song-writer--but without success. On the opening night in Atlantic City, this writer was among the many who congregated around the stage door in the vain hope that some number might be thrown out of the show and one of theirs substituted. I have often wondered if Mr. Ziegfeld ever knew that he had refused to listen to a song by Jerome Kern! Years later he spent a fortune staging a musical show by the same writer.

The critics were very good to me:

Grace La Rue made the distinct hit of the performance. Miss La Rue appears in a bewildering succession of swagger gowns, a number of excellent musical numbers fall to her, and she begins them with a dash that carries the audience along with her and makes her an overwhelming favorite.

Of course, James Buchanan Brady, "Diamond Jim," was in the front row that first night--and for many nights thereafter during the entire season--each time with a party of friends. He gave many supper parties to which the girls from The Follies were invited. Mr. Brady himself did not drink, but there was always plenty of champagne for his guests. Often, too, there were expensive favors at the table for each girl.

If a girl's gown ever happened to be spoiled at one of Mr.
Brady's parties--as often happened in those days when trains and
ruffles were in style--she would simply pin it up and go on dancing.
And next day Mr. Brady generally sent her a new dress. At the
first of his parties which I attended, I lost a broad-band gold bracelet belonging to my sister. I did not discover the loss until I reached
home; then I telephoned the cab-starter at Rector's and asked him
to search the cab on its return, and also to ask Mr. Brady please
to look for the bracelet. The next day a messenger arrived at my
apartment with two packages, one of them containing the lost bracelet, the other a bracelet from Tiffany's, set with several small diamonds and sapphires. Accompanying them was a note from Mr.
Brady, saying he was very sorry I had been worried over my loss
and that I was to accept the new bracelet with his compliments--
then I would not need to borrow my sister's again.

That year Maurice, the dancer, came from Paris to dance at
the Café de L'Opera at Forty-second and Broadway, the smartest
restaurant in New York and the first to present entertainers. Maurice
and his wife, a French girl, did an apache dance, and he did a soft-
shoe solo. Florence Walton, who was with The Follies, went to the
café every night to see him dance.

Maurice's wife was quite ill when they arrived in America and
after a few weeks stopped dancing. She died shortly afterward.
Poor Maurice was heart-broken. He sent out a call for a girl partner,
and Florence Walton begged him to let her practice with him. She
practiced so much she could hardly keep up with her work in The
Follies. At last he danced with her at the café one night and was
so pleased with her that she became his dancing partner.

Florence was not considered pretty, nor even smart-looking.
But in her great desire and determination to win success, she made
herself over completely. After a season in Paris, one would never
have guessed that the smartly groomed girl of the famous team of
"Maurice and Walton" had ever been the plain-looking dancing girl
of the Ziegfeld Follies.

Although the new Follies was a hit, the consensus was that
the Follies of 1908 was not as good as the Follies of 1907. Many
changes were made in the show after Atlantic City, before the New
York opening. My best song was taken out. It was a Scotch comedy
song, accompanied by the Highland Fling--and was the hit number
at the opening. In fact, it was too good. Nora Bayes had an Irish
song which was completely eclipsed by mine; she claimed that my song
conflicted with hers--and as she was the star of the show, mine was
taken out.

On the other hand, I had to sing a long, tiresome lyric about
"Miss Manhattan"--a "situation song," always a thankless number for
a singer. When, night after night, it did not rate a single encore,

I told Mr. Ziegfeld I simply could not sing it any longer. But he
insisted. "You must learn to sing any song, my dear, and make it
go," he said. "I'll bet that if Miss Held had that song, she would
make it a hit."

I admitted it might be true--Miss Held was a great star. If
I had known then the tale that Charles Evans, of Evans and Hoey,
told me years later about how Miss Held happened to make her hit
in America, I would have had an answer to Mr. Ziegfeld. Mr. Evans
had brought Miss Held from Paris to sing in his company; but on her
first appearance in New York, in spite of tremendous advance publicity, she was almost a complete failure. When she finished her last
song, "Won't You Come and Play with Me," and made her final exit,
there was hardly any applause. Mr. Hoey, who was a great comedian,
followed her on the stage immediately and began burlesquing her.
The audience laughed and applauded. Miss Held, thinking the delayed applause was for her, came back on the stage and bowed. Mr.
Hoey began playing up to her; she quickly fell in with the situation;
the orchestra again picked up the chorus of her song--and failure
was turned into success! Of course, Mr. Ziegfeld must have known
all this!

As my contract did not carry the usual two weeks' notice
clause, I had to stay on to the end of the season. I begged Mr.
Ziegfeld to release me, but it was no use, I was afraid to persist,
for fear I might get into trouble, and I needed the work. But I
resolved to evolve some plan for getting out of the Follies.

[After some difficulty with Mr. Ziegfeld and Mr.
Erlanger, who owned The Follies, Miss La Rue finally
gained release from her contract to go with Sam Bernard in Nearly a Hero. But not without certain regrets.]

I was to learn during my professional life that few managers
were as considerate and kind as Florenz Ziegfeld, and for this reason
I have never been sure I did not make a mistake in leaving him; yet
I feel certain I was not the type of girl he would ever have starred.

I opened with Sam Bernard in Nearly a Hero on Labor Day at
the Majestic Theater in Boston. The role of Angeline De Vere might
have been written especially for me; Mr. Bernard was kind enough
to say he liked me in it better than either of my predecessors.

The Tuesday morning following our opening I was up bright and
early, waiting for the papers. I was amazed to read across the top
of the theatrical page in large type: SAM BERNARD AND GRACE
LA RUE IN "NEARLY A HERO." Sam Bernard was one of the important stars of the day; no one had ever shared the billing with
him, much less received equal prominence! I fairly devoured the
notices. Mr. Bernard's were splendid, and to my delight I didn't
fare much worse. The following is an excerpt from one:

Grace La Rue fairly scintillated through the piece. In
costumes galore, she sang typical songs, danced, and in many
ways gave renewed evidence of her great ability of characters
of this kind. A fine appearing woman, the personification of
grace and agility in all kinds of dancing, including a bit of
the 'Salome,' a good singer and a capable actress. There
are few artists as well equipped as she to shine in musical
comedy.

With a good part--the first I had ever had--and such a warm
welcome from the critics, I felt that for the first time in my life I
was "on my way somewhere" in the theater. I loved every moment
of my work and spent one of the most perfect and enjoyable seasons
I ever experienced.

Sam Bernard was an adorable man to work with. At rehearsal
in New York one day before we opened, I was going through my
specialty for the last act--part of which consisted of a satire on the
"Salome Dance," then very much in vogue. I asked the stage manager
to have one of the chorus boys impersonate John the Baptist for me.
The scene was an exterior; one side of the stage was a set-house
with a veranda and bushes and shrubs in front of it. As I was explaining to the chorus boy how I wanted him to thrust his head out
through the bushes at a certain moment, Sam Bernard said, "Watch
me. I'll show you!"

He put on the whiskers; and at a moment when the stage was
quite dark, the spotlight being on me as I danced, Sam popped his
whiskered head through the bushes. The way he did it was very
funny and received a big laugh from the company. He tried to re-
hearse the boy to get the same effect, but it seemed impossible. At
last Mr. Bernard said, "I'll do it myself. I make an entrance following this number, so it will be no trouble." And he did it all season!
My dance consequently went over with a big laugh, as well as applause
at the finish. How many stars would have been as generous?

Opening night the success of my dance specialty kept Sam standing on the stage while I came back for several encores. The next
day I begged him to let his valet (in the play) precede instead of
follow him on the stage, thus obviating this wait on his part; but
Sam wouldn't hear of it. "You've made a big hit," he said, "and
I'm glad to see it."

Mr. Bernard paid me a great compliment at the end of the sea-
son--one which I valued very much. "You are the only woman I
ever worked with," he said, "who does not laugh at me while playing a scene with me. I have never been able to break you up by ad
libbing. And I know why: you have been well trained by working
with a good comedian." (He meant Charles.)

Ada Lewis had a very funny role; but to our great regret,

she left the company in the middle of the season and was replaced
by Jobyna Howland. I have never in my life seen anyone as nervous
as Miss Howland on her opening night, but she was splendid in her
part and made a great hit.

Another girl, with whom I became quite good friends, was Charlotte Greenwood. She had plenty of talent and made quite a hit in
a very funny scene with Mr. Bernard and six show girls. During
the winter she asked if she might understudy my part; but as we
neared the end of the season, she had had no chance to play it--
though there had been many times when I really should have stayed
out of the show because of illness. So we planned that she should
play the part one night in Syracuse. I asked Mr. Bernard's permission to go to New York that night to visit my mother; he refused
to let me go. I wrote Lee Shubert and asked his permission, assur-
ing him that Charlotte was up in my role and could play it. He wired:
"O.K." So I went. It was not being very loyal to Sam, but I wanted
to give Charlotte a chance. Of course, I did not have the pleasure
of seeing her myself, but everyone said she did splendidly. Sam was
angry with me--but not for long.

--Rob Wagner's Script, Vol. 18,
No. 435, October 30, 1937, pages
18-19.

PART NINE

[During the next few years, Miss La Rue's professional life was entangled with a second matrimonial venture. Byron Chandler, known to the press as "The Million Dollar Kid," pursued and first-nighted the object
of his affections all over the country, finally persuading
her to marry him. Many trips to Europe, punctuated by
various theatrical engagements back in America. While
Byron was devoted and in many ways helpful, he was
essentially a playboy, so divorce became inevitable,
though indeed it was he who arranged for Miss LaRue's
engagement at the Palace in London.
    Beginning with her childhood experiences and train-
ing in Variety and the Ziegfeld Follies, she finally became a featured player, then a star in musical comedy.
The Palace in London, called the Music Hall, with only
Wednesday and Saturday matinees, was a new kind of
show for Miss LaRue. Each act was what was called in
this country a "headliner." It was the ultimate test of
the individual performer, who had to stand on his or
her own pins. Success meant "tops" in the show business. Here was Miss LaRue's big chance.]

The Palace Theatre in London was the only one of its kind in

the world at that time. Very intimate, and charming to sing in, it
had an orchestra of <u>forty</u> pieces (in America we usually had twelve),
and one of the finest conductors in England, Herman Fink, was in
charge. My first orchestra rehearsal there was a revelation to me.
Mr. Fink asked me to sit down and wait while he rehearsed the
orchestra without me. He began by having the violins play my first
song through several times. Then they rested while he took the brass
instruments through the same song. Then the wood winds ... and
so on. After all were rehearsed separately, they played together.
The result was almost perfection. Each song was handled the same
way.

        Not until he had gone through my entire group of songs did
Mr. Fink turn to me: "Now, Miss LaRue, will you sing them?" Once
through was enough for me.... I wondered what an American director
would think of such care. In America, only opera and symphony orchestras were rehearsed as carefully as this.

        During my previous engagement at the Winter Garden, I had
found a song which I thought was great, and I had begged Mr. Shubert to let me put it in the show. One night as I was waiting in my
dressing-room for Mr. Al Jolson to finish his specialty just before the
finale, I suddenly heard him singing this song. I rushed to the stage
entrance and watched him make one of the biggest hits of his life with
"You Made Me Love You." I was heartbroken over it--but what was
the use? When I went to the Palace in Chicago, I used the song, and
now I included it in my London program.

        I planned to open with four songs: Victor Herbert's "I Want
To Be a Prima Donna" (from <u>The Enchantress</u>); "You Made Me Love
You," and then, what I considered to be my two best songs.

        It would have been much too short an act in America. But Mr.
Volney, the stage-manager, was somewhat disturbed at the length of
it; he said that acts in England consisted of no more than two songs
--perhaps three, if the artist was very well-known and a great favorite. "If that's the case," I told him, "I had better not open. I have
left a big salary in America to come over here and try to make a hit,
but I can't do it unless you give me at least twelve to fifteen minutes."
Mr. Volney consulted with Claude E. Marner, the house-manager,
and at length they agreed to the four songs--since it was off-season,
and Mr. Alfred Butt was not there to decide.

        After my rehearsal I was shown to my dressing-room; it was up
one flight, but an elevator was always used. It was a lovely room
with adjoining bath, which had been installed for Ruth St. Denis when
she danced there the year before. I spent several hours unpacking
and explaining my changes to my new English maid, Rosa. Fortunately
I had all my beautiful creations by Madame Frances from the Winter
Garden, so I was not worried about costumes. Rosa's salary, I learned,
would be one pound--five dollars a week. I could hardly believe it.
I had always paid a theater maid at least fifteen or twenty.

Evening arrived at last. I was very early on the program--
No. 3. Mr. Volney explained that on Monday night it was the custom
to put the new acts on first so the critics could review them and go
home; after the first night I would have a later spot. The house was
very poor; but on my first exit, after my second song, "You Made Me
Love You," to my surprise the applause was good. My two last songs,
which I had considered my best, were not received as I had expected;
however I was given several curtain calls. No one ever took bows,
as was the custom in America.

I had hardly reached my dressing-room when several friends
came rushing in to tell me how wonderfully I had done, that everyone
out front was delighted. But I was depressed over my reception.
Rosa tried to reassure me: "You know this is Bank Holiday, the dullest day of the year in London."

Mr. Marner and Mr. Volney both came to the dressing-room to
congratulate me, and could not understand why I felt so depressed;
they thought I had done remarkably well. But I could not be con-
soled. I lay awake till dawn going over and over my performance--
if I had only done this or that little detail differently.

When I awoke, the morning sun was pouring in, and there were
the morning papers:

A PALACE STAR
   Monday at the Palace. May we say Mr. Butt has something
exceptionally good in the American way, for Grace LaRue, the
well-known musical comedy artiste, made her first appearance
at Shaftsbury Avenue House. This songbird is a bright and
brilliant comedienne, with a knowledge of how to sing a serious or frivolous song. She is just delicious in her rendering of "You Made Me Love You," and her Scotch song is given
with heather-like freshness. LaRue, who presents a ravishing picture of feminine fairness, has a wonderfully magnetic
way with her.

This was the trend of nearly every criticism in the London
papers--some even more extravagant. I dressed hurriedly and went
to the Palace. Mr. Marner greeted me with a broad smile.

One of the papers quoted more than half the words of the chorus
of "You Made Me Love You." "This melody, I am sure, is destined to
be a big hit in London," Mr. Marner pointed out, "and my advice is
to use it as your closing number."

Shifting this song to the closing spot brought me several splendid recalls. Each succeeding night I was given a better reception than
the night before.

Madame Pavlova was the star attraction at the Palace; it was

the last week of her engagement, programmed "Saison Russe." She
had a large company of dancers and gave almost the same program she
had presented in New York when I saw her the previous winter. The
great Pavlova! She was so simple and plain-looking. We talked about
dancing and the world tours she had made, and she told me she loved
America. She had been dancing at the Palace many weeks, and was
going for a holiday. She looked so tired--and no wonder. Every
morning at nine o'clock she was on the stage practicing. I usually
went early for my mail and found her standing in front of the long
mirror holding onto the brass rail which she used as a practice bar.
After a half-hour of bending and stretching exercises, she went out
on the stage and pirouetted through beautiful and difficult dance routines.

My second week at the Palace, a one-act musical comedy with
several well-known English artists headed by Marie Dainton replaced
Madame Pavlova. About Wednesday of this week, Mr. Marner asked
me to remain another two weeks at a fifty dollar raise (according to
my contract). He said Mr. Butt had learned of my success and had
requested that I be held over until he returned from his holiday!

It was Monday of my fourth week when I learned, quite by accident, that Mr. Butt was out front. The theater crowd were coming
back to town and the house was sold out that night. I had become
at ease in my surroundings and was giving a splendid performance--
at least, I pleased myself, and that was not always easy to do. On
this night I received a greater number of curtain calls than ever
before.

My act was the last before intermission. I was just getting out
of my costume and into a dressing-gown when there was a knock on
my door, and Rosa said: "Mr. Butt would like to speak to you."
I was greatly surprised to see before me a good looking, tall, blond
man--not at all what I expected. I cannot say just what I did expect
Mr. Butt to look like--but he was different. He greeted me with a
charming smile and many lovely compliments and asked me to call at
his office next morning to discuss my remaining on the bill for a time.

I felt exultantly happy. To continue to work in such a charming
and refined atmosphere, with a kindly feeling all around me--something
I had never experienced before! If it might only last forever! No
thrill is equal to the great thrill of a step forward in one's profession.
Especially to one who was always ambitious to the point of unhappiness,
as I was. One life seemed so short to accomplish all I wanted to do!

[Almost overnight Miss LaRue found herself famous
in London. She was impersonated by Cissy Loftus, and
upon one occasion she heard the great Caruso sing one
of her songs in perfect imitation of her.]

Many famous artists appeared on the bill with me during my

weeks at the Palace. First Gaby Deslys; then Harry Lauder came
for a month; and after him, George Robey, one of England's finest
comedians--and many others known only on the English stage. The
great Fragson, of Paris, was on the bill for a few weeks. (Europe
seemed to have more fine men stars at the time than women.)

From time to time my engagement at the Palace was extended
for another four weeks, always with a slight increase in salary. My
popularity seemed not to wane. I had never received any "fan mail"
in America, but in England I received letters from some of the most
interesting people in London. (I have them all bound in a very
treasured book.) This was almost my only contact with society, as
I never went out.

> --Rob Wagner's Script, Vol. 18,
> No. 436, November 6, 1937,
> pages 22-23.

PART TEN

[After her triumph at the Palace in London, Miss
LaRue was deluged with offers to tour the Continent:
But before accepting, she starred in The Girls Who
Didn't in order to put over "Tango Dream," written by
her friend, Elsa Maxwell. A brief interlude in New York
to obtain a divorce from Byron Chandler, a fill-in engagement at the New York Palace, and then return to London to accept some of those flattering Continental offers.
First to Cologne, after which she planned to go to Berlin.
But it was during her appearance in Cologne that the
war broke out.
With Europe in a mess, Miss LaRue returned to New
York, now heralded as one of the world's greatest "singles." She propitiously arrived at the time when the
great vaudeville circuits were in their glory.]

It was so good to be in New York again! The war seemed far
away. It was difficult for anyone here to realize the situation in
Europe, or that, from the first day of the war, they were preparing
for a long conflict.

The next morning in Mr. Wilton's office, I met Walter Kingsley,
head of the publicity department for the Palace Theatre, and several
of the Keith officials, but not Mr. Albee.

Among those in the office that morning was Eddie Darling, who
did all the booking for the Palace, as well as arranging the programs
for all the Keith houses each and every week. He was familiar with
the name, history, and past performances of every professional in
all branches of the theater, and knew more about arranging vaudeville

programs than anyone else I have ever known. We have been devoted friends since our meeting that morning.

A route of five or six weeks was arranged for me: the Colonial
Theatre in New York to follow Boston; the Orpheum in Brooklyn;
Keith's in Washington; then the Palace in New York--after which I
was to have a week's holiday. That was one of the things I liked
about working in vaudeville; I could arrange for a vacation almost
any time. I enjoyed the independence, too, of selecting my own
programs and changing my songs as often as I chose. I was constantly looking for new songs.

I engaged Charley Gillen, the pianist who had played for me
at the Palace in April. From my weekly salary of $1,250, I had to
pay his $125 a week, railroad fares, excess baggage charges (which
were plenty), and hotel expenses; a weekly stipend for a maid in
the theater; $25 a week in tips for the stage hands; and 10 per
cent of the total amount to my agent. What was left was mine--aside
from several hundred dollars a month for new stage gowns and hats.

I insisted upon having a clause written into my contract which
stated that at all times I was to be sole headliner of any and all
programs on which I appeared. This, I learned later, was a master
stroke.

At the opening matinee in Boston, the audience seemed cold--
not only toward my act but toward all the others. I was very dis-
satisfied with my reception; but the house-manager assured me that
the comments out front were most complimentary and that my gowns
were being enthusiastically discussed. The Monday matinee audience,
he said, was noted for its coldness and indifference. "You will see,
the audience tonight will be much more enthusiastic." And he was
right.

Lynne Overman did a sketch on the same program with a beautiful young woman, Peggy Hopkins, who came to my dressing-room on
Tuesday during the matinee and introduced herself. I liked her.
She proudly showed me a large diamond ring she had just received--
the first diamond she had ever owned, I think. Peggy Hopkins Joyce
has made a financial success since then (she has always reminded
me somewhat of Gaby Deslys in her business acumen), but she herself has never changed.

From Boston I went to the Colonial in New York. While I was
there, an agent arranged a contract with Pathé Frères to make some
records of my songs, especially of "Little Gray Home in the West"
by Herman Lohr--one of the hits I had brought from England with
me. Through misunderstanding and mismanagement, the contract
was never carried out, however, and Alma Gluck later made a neat
sum from royalties on the song I introduced.

I had brought other songs with me from England, but I did not want to introduce them while "Little Gray Home in the West" was new and popular. One, "Roses of Picardy," I introduced later at the Majestic in Chicago, and the critics unanimously hailed it as one of the most beautiful songs ever heard. And when I first sang it at the Palace upon my return to New York, how the song scouts gobbled it up! Here at the Palace they were thickest. As soon as any song of the concert type was introduced, every singer in the country grabbed it, and it was soon worn to shreds.

My success with the artistic--yet popular--type of song, new to vaudeville then, paved the way for many singers to follow with better music. There were times when I went a little too far for my vaudeville audience--and realized it. Once, for instance, when I sang "The Cry of Rachel" in costume. The costume was really the inspiration for the song. When I was in Nuremberg, Germany, I had bought a small replica of the famous Nuremberg Madonna. The drapery intrigued me so much that I had it copied in gunmetal silver cloth. Then for an appropriate song to go with it I chose the concert number, "The Cry of Rachel," by May Turner Salter. Rather heavy ... but the costume was so beautiful that no one paid much attention to the song, anyway.

Again, I had some doubt as to the vaudeville possibilities of Arthur Symons' poem, "The Gray Wolf," which had been set to music for me by H. T. Burleigh; but I received marked credit for this from those who appreciated my effort toward the dramatic type of song. I was careful always to follow a serious song with something lilting and gay.

New York was dance-mad that winter--like all the other cities I played. And I was as mad as the rest. I was simply not interested in going out with any man who was not a good dancer, and heartlessly eliminated the others, no matter how charming they were. And if I happened to want to dance with a professional at a restaurant, my escort simply had to understand and not be offended. There was no excuse, as a matter of fact, for anyone's being a poor dancer in 1915; every city had its expert dancing teachers, and all the high-salaried professional ballroom dancers taught the tango and other new dances. True, the charge was high--twenty-five dollars a lesson was considered reasonable.

I had thought when I left London that the theaters were closed indefinitely; but now came the news that they were all open and packed every night. The men home from the front on brief furloughs had to be entertained to keep up their spirits; each visit might be their last, and they lived for the moment. Had I remained in London, my career would no doubt have been really successful, according to my standards--far different from the success I have attained at home. The English people have a way, too, of remembering an artist: Americans remember one's failures; the English one's successes.

Keith's Theatre in Washington was the most delightful house of all the Keith circuit to me. I played there more often than at any other theater. At my first appearance there in October, 1914, Clifton Webb was also on the bill with Gloria Goodman in a dancing act with the Balalaika Orchestra; and Leo Carrillo followed me on the program with one of the best single acts in vaudeville. This was my first meeting with these two artists. I still remember a trip we took together to Washington's home at Mount Vernon one morning; we rode on the open street car, ate popcorn out of bags, and had a lot of fun. Anyone who knows either can imagine the laughs we had.

Another time, at Keith's in Washington, while in my dressing-room, I heard two girls singing at the first matinee. Being the headliner, I was always interested when a woman singer appeared on the program ahead of me; I slipped on a dressing-gown and went to the first entrance. It was the Ponselle Sisters, Rosa and Carmela. They stood close together, enough alike to be twins, their girlish faces dark, sparkling, colorful (I have always thought of Rosa Ponselle as a lovely red rose); and I have never heard two girls sing more beautifully together.

I did not meet either of them all week, as they appeared in the first half of the program, and I came on near the end of the show. After the first matinee, I did not even come to the theater till after they had gone home. Years later, in 1927, while on a holiday in Havana I met Rosa, who was giving a concert there.

As I watched the girls that day in Washington, I thought gratefully, "They will pave the way with the audience for me." I was always delighted to be booked on an artistic program. It was a rough turn preceding mine which hurt my act. When, for an hour, audiences are entertained by turns with risqué situations or vulgar jokes, they begin at last to think they are seeing good vaudeville. Generally, anything of an artistic character following will meet with only mild success. I have heard managers say, "We must give the public what it wants." As a matter of fact, the manager gives the public what he wants ... and the average manager has little discernment. And the poor public is a docile one in America.

Not so in London. When something is presented to an English audience which it does not like it lets the actor know at once by making some familiar remark. Eric Blore, the English comedian, once told me that on his first appearance in a music hall in London, his act seemed not to be going over very well, so he thought he would try a poem. He reached the middle of the second verse, when a loud voice from the pit demanded, "Blore, are you going to keep this up, or must I come down there and get you?"

My only first-hand experience of hearing remarks from an English audience was on the opening night of <u>The Happy Island</u> with Sir

Beerbohm Tree at His Majesty's Theatre. Mr. Tree was having quite
a time keeping the stud in his shirt bosom in place; it was continually slipping. Each time, to fix it, he would turn his back to the
audience. After several attempts, a voice from the pit called: "Give
in, Guv'nor; we know it's there!"

At Keith's, in Philadelphia, I was most delighted to find my
old friend, Will Rogers, on the bill. His act just preceded mine;
and every evening we would arrive about the same time outside the
stage door. The stage door there is down a little back street, very
poorly lighted; the sidewalk is only about two feet wide. As I came
hurrying in from the cold and the wet, I would meet him, hat pulled
down over his eyes and coat collar turned up. Holding the heavy
door open for me, he would say: "Come on in, Gracie; let's get it
over with."

Will Rogers never used any makeup. He would walk through
the short hall, take off his overcoat and hat as he went, smooth his
hair back with both hands, button up his double-breasted blue coat--
and he was ready to go on. During the twenty or twenty-five minutes he was on the stage, I made up and dressed for my act. After
me came the closing turn, and the show was over.

One day while lunching at the Ritz Hotel in Philadelphia, a
man bowed to me from a nearby table. He looked familiar, but I
could not recall his name. From the headwaiter I learned it was Mr.
Nixon of the Nixon Theatre--and instantly my mind flew back to a
darkened theater on a morning of 1907 when he had championed me
to Mr. Ziegfeld and enabled me to secure my first engagement in the
Follies. As soon as I had ordered my luncheon, I went over to his
table to thank him for his help in that time of need.

--Rob Wagner's Script, Vol. 18,
No. 437, November 13, 1937,
pages 26-28.

PART ELEVEN

Vaudeville was quite different from the Variety in which I had
worked with Charles; the salaries were far greater than any we had
known, and most of the acts, even the headliners, were unknown to
me. The clause in my contract whereby I was to be the sole headliner on the bill contributed to my peace of mind, however. Often
there were other acts on the same bill which received more salary
than I did (one of the things I was to learn about vaudeville was
that the headliner is not always the highest paid), but by being
the headliner, I was assured of the star dressing-room, of the best
position on the program, and of first consideration from the stage-
manager, house-manager, pressmen, and even from the stage hands.
All this was worth more than money to me.

To one unacquainted with the workings of vaudeville, such
matters may seem trivial and unimportant. But when one plays a
different theater every week, with an entirely new crew and orchestra, it is a consoling thought, believe me, that at least one will not
have to face any arguments over status. It is the constant struggle
and aim of every act some day to become a headliner.

There was much about vaudeville that I liked. In the first
place, I was grateful for the dignified publicity which the Keith management secured for me. Never a suggestion of the "personal life
junk" which most press agents relied on, never any sensational stories; yet I had never before had the splendid exploitation I received
with the Keith management.

The courtesy and consideration accorded me by the individual
managers of the vaudeville theaters in the various cities I played was
another thing to be thankful for. I did not fully appreciate this
until I had been badly treated by several production managers. The
vaudeville managers never interfered with my program in any way.
I could change my songs just as often during the week as I wished;
and by working out my own ideas, I became finished in my work--
which most people agreed to be individual and artistic. In no other
branch of the show business could I have developed individually as
I did here.

Of course, it was hard work. Stars of the legitimate stage
often accepted bookings in vaudeville only for the high salary, with
the idea that it was really beneath them--that any old thing was good
enough for vaudeville. They soon found out that it was one of the
hardest jobs in the show business.

The vaudeville audience was made up of people who wanted
keen entertainment. It was the forerunner of the motion-picture
audience, which demands speed and action, but merit withal. And
of the radio audience. It is with radio audiences that former vaudeville artists have found the warmest appreciation--Jack Benny, Fred
Allen, Eddie Cantor, Frank Fay, Belle Baker, John Charles Thomas,
Phil Baker, Georgie Jessel.

I was always on the lookout for songs. I was generally sure
of getting a new one from Irving Berlin every time I was in New
York; he was very nice about giving me the first chance to introduce many of his songs. And Billy Rose, who freelanced for all
the music publishers, wrote many special lyrics for me. He had a
gift for writing most telling recitations to build up a song. I remember one: "I Wonder Who's Dancing with You Tonight," for which
he built up a sort of dialogue in the repeat chorus that was one of
the most dramatic I ever heard. He writes (or used to write) many
of the very funny lyrics used by his wife, Fanny Brice.

Working in vaudeville, one leads the loneliest existence in the

world. I spent hours alone. I seldom became really acquainted with
any of the other acts on the bill, for I usually went on next to closing act, and by the time I was dressed after the show, the theater
was dark, and only the stage doorman was left to say goodnight;
even my pianist had gone. So I would go back to my hotel to a
book, or some sewing, or letters, until I grew sleepy ... and then
another day just like the one before.

I did, however, meet many interesting people and form many
treasured friendships during these years, even though my contacts
were so fleeting. At Henderson's, Coney Island, Cantor and Lee
were on the same bill with me. Eddie Cantor, a blackface comedian,
signed his first contract for a Broadway show that week, if I am not
mistaken. His partner, Lee, retired from the profession to become
manager of one of George White's Shows. Lee's wife, Lilyan Tash-
man, I saw often at the stage door with him; I met her again in the
Ziegfeld Follies of 1917, and still later in Hollywood after she had
become established in motion pictures, and the wife of Edmund Lowe.
She had a host of friends whom she left all too soon.

At the Orpheum, in Brooklyn, which I played many times during those years, some of the acts on the same bills with me included
Houdini, the great magician, with Mrs. Houdini (we became friends,
and I found him a most interesting man); and Rosie Dolly, one of the
Dolly Sisters, in a dancing act with Martin Brown. They had just
come from the Winter Garden show. Martin Brown, to everyone's
surprise, not long afterward authored the play, Cobra, which had
such a successful Broadway run.

In August, 1915, I played the Palace, New York, during one
of the hottest weeks I have ever experienced. The bill was advertised as a dancing week. Aside from myself and Nat Wills, the show
was made up entirely of some of the best dancing acts in vaudeville:
Doyle and Dixon, the Ford Family Dancing Revue (brothers and
sisters), and Bonnie Glass, assisted by Rodolpho, an Italian dancer.

Vaudeville was new for Rodolpho, and with the combination of
heat and nervousness, he suffered more than anybody; he was constantly mopping his brow, and his collars wilted instantly. He brought
to the stage a supply of fresh collars every day, to change while
the special orchestra played between dances. I noticed his misery
on Monday; and next day I called to him from my dressing-room door,
telling him to come in and change his collars before my mirror if he
wanted to. (The star dressing-room was the only one on the stage
at the Palace.)

He thanked me, admitting his nervousness. "I am too soft,"
he said. "I haven't danced enough. And besides, I must lose a
little weight."

He was an excellent dancer. He and Miss Glass used to dance

at a restaurant in town in the evenings after the Palace show, and I
often went there and danced with him. He did a wonderful tango.
But dancing was only a part of Rodolpho's aims. He was bubbling
over with ambition and worked hard every day to improve his performance. He had a fascinating personality and was most attractive
to women, while men admired his fine, athletic type.

It was not long before the world knew him as Rudolph Valentino.

During my first winter in vaudeville I played Hammerstein's
Victoria in New York--the scene of so many unhappy days with
Charles. For many weeks I had been preparing a new waltz song,
"I Love You So," and I decided to introduce it this week. On the
train up from Washington the night before, I lay awake a long time
trying to get some novel idea to make it different from just any waltz
song. Suddenly I remembered the small hat I had worn at the Palace
Theatre in London when I sang "You Made Me Love You." Just the
thing! I knew instantly, I'd wear a red hat! My dress was black
lace, and the red would liven it up. Right after breakfast I rushed
to Maison Maurice on Fifth Avenue, gave them explicit directions as
to the shape, and started them scouting in haste for the color--a
peculiar shade of pinkish red taffeta. It must be ready for that
matinee, I told them. Before I went on that afternoon I told Charley
Gillen, my pianist, to watch me closely in my new song as I hadn't
the faintest idea what I would do.

After my second song I rushed off the stage and grabbed the
red hat. As I walked back on the stage with it in my hand, singing
the verse of the song, I still had no definite idea what I was going
to do with it.

> Some are born great, some are born fair;
> But I envy none under the sun,
> For I've something better than fame or gold;
> I've somebody dear to love me,
> Somebody all my own,
> And true as the blue sky above me:
> He whispers this always in tenderest tone.

I finished the verse in which I used only a few gestures--then
into the chorus, hoping that some action would come to me:

> I love your eyes when you look at me;
> I love your voice when you speak to me.

I stopped and waited--and put the hat on, pulling it well down
to one side. Still holding the edge of the brim, I walked slowly to
the center of the stage, singing:

> And when I see you walk down the street,
> There's something about you that's more than sweet--

I took off the hat and sang:

> Oh, I love the shimmer in your hair,
> And your dear hands beyond compare--

Then in dead silence I put the hat on again, taking plenty of time to adjust it carefully--and finished:

> But most of all, when you waltz with me,
> I love you so!

The orchestra joined with the piano, playing very softly, while I waltzed, wearing the red hat.

The song was an instantaneous hit and was included in my program for many months. And the red hat! Introduced as the result of a thought in the night, it became a regular part of my vaudeville days. The twenty dollars I spent for it was the best investment I ever made!

--Rob Wagner's Script, Vol. 18,
No. 438, November 20, 1937,
pages 24-26.

MARY CASS CANFIELD
    The Great American Art (1922)

CLAUDIA CASSIDY
    Critics Analyze Vaudeville's Chances (1939)

JACK CONWAY
    Eddie Cantor
    Joe Cook

WILL M. CRESSY
    Putting It Over (1916)

ACTON DAVIES
    Marie Lloyd
    What I Don't Know About Vaudeville (1905)

BENJAMIN DE CASSERES
    Irene Franklin

THOMAS BRAILSFORD FELDER
    Edith Piaf

ALFRED GREASON
    Marie Dressler
    May Irwin
    Harry Lauder
    Bert Williams

ABEL GREEN
    George Burns and Gracie Allen
    The Ritz Brothers
    Rudy Vallee

NAT GREEN
    Aileen Stanley

FLORENCE HAYDEN
    The Duncan Sisters

AVERY HALES
    The Cherry Sisters

LOUIS REEVES HARRISON
    Is "Vodeveal" Necessary? (1911)

MARK HELLINGER
    Milton Berle

IRVING HOFFMAN
    Helen Morgan

WILLARD HOLCOMB
   Frank Crumit

IRENE CORBALLY KUHN
   Elsie Janis

JACK LAIT
   Leon Errol
   May Irwin
   Harry Richman

BAIRD LEONARD
   George M. Cohan

ANDRE LEVINSON
   Josphine Baker

JOSHUA LOWE
   Wilkie Bard
   Anna Held
   Walter C. Kelly
   Fay Templeton

DWIGHT MACDONALD
   Bob Hope

KENNETH MACGOWAN
   James Barton

JAMES METCALFE
   Fritzi Scheff

WARD MOREHOUSE
   Eddie Cantor

JOHNNY O'CONNOR
   Julian Eltinge

RALPH BROCK PEMBERTON
   Irving Berlin

S.J. PERELMAN
   Jimmy Durante

CHANNING POLLOCK
   Gaby Deslys
   McIntyre and Heath

JACK PULASKI
   Fred Allen
   Aunt Jemima
   Noble Sissle and Eubie Blake

EDWIN MILTON ROYLE
    The Vaudeville Theatre (1899)

EPES W. SARGENT
    Yvette Guilbert
    Vesta Tilley

GILBERT SELDES
    Florence Mills

CHARLES A. SIEGFERTH
    Block and Sully

SID SILVERMAN
    Borrah Minevitch
    Fanny Ward

SIME SILVERMAN
    Paul Cinquevalli
    Kathleen Clifford
    Julian Eltinge
    Fink's Mules
    Eddie Foy
    Irene Franklin
    Poodles Hanneford
    Willie and Eugene Howard
    Annette Kellermann
    Walter C. Kelly
    Marx Brothers
    Polly Moran
    Tony Pastor
    Ada Reeve
    Bill Robinson
    Pat Rooney
    Blossom Seeley
    Harry Tate
    Vesta Victoria
    Mae West

BOB SISK
    Ken Murray and Charlotte

ANTHONY SLIDE
    Milton Berle
    Will Rogers

ALISON SMITH
    Fritzi Scheff

FREDERICK JAMES SMITH
    Belle Baker

MATT WELD
    Jimmy Savo

EDITH WERNER
    Critics Analyze Vaudeville's Chances (1939)

RENNOLD WOLF
    Nora Bayes